THE POWER OF CONFIDENCE

Visit our web site at
WWW.ALBAHOUSE.ORG

the Power of Confidence

Genesis and structure of the «way of spiritual childhood» of Saint Thérèse of Lisieux

CONRAD DE MEESTER
Discalced Carmelite

Translated by Susan Conroy

ALBA · HOUSE NEW · YORK

SOCIETY OF ST. PAUL, 2187 VICTORY BLVD., STATEN ISLAND, NEW YORK 10314

Originally published in French by Les Éditions du Cerf (1st edition 1969; 2nd revised edition, 1995) under the title *Dynamique de la Confiance*.

Library of Congress Cataloging-in-Publication Data

De Meester, Conrad.
[Dynamique de la confiance. English]
The power of confidence: genesis and structure of the "way of spiritual childhood" of Saint Thérèse of Lisieux / Conrad De Meester; translated by Susan Conroy.
p. cm.
Includes bibliographical references.
ISBN 0-8189-0819-X
BX4700.T5D35513 1998
282'.092—dc21 98-3989
[b] CIP

Produced and designed in the United States of America by the Fathers and Brothers of the Society of St. Paul, 2187 Victory Boulevard, Staten Island, New York 10314, as part of their communications apostolate.

ISBN: 0-8189-0819-X

Printing Information:

Current Printing - first digit 1 2 3 4 5 6 7 8 9 10

Year of Current Printing - first year shown

1998 1999 2000 2001 2002 2003 2004 2005

Table of Contents

Fourth Part: The Structure

Preface

In September of 1995 Father Conrad De Meester, an old friend, sent me a copy of his thoroughgoing study of Saint Thérèse, *Dynamique de la Confiance*. It took me six months to read it, slowly, a little bit at a time. I have the habit of writing the date when I finish a book on the title page, with a comment recording my impression of it. On the title page of this book I wrote simply: "This is a masterpiece." I set about at once to find someone to translate it so that English-speaking readers could have the benefit of the wisdom it contains. I was fortunate to find Susan Conroy to do the translation. It has been a labor of love for her, on which she has worked for more than a year. We are much in her debt for giving us such a readable version in our language.

Father De Meester wrote the book originally twenty-seven years ago as a Doctoral thesis. In 1995 he revised it to incorporate the major features of the scholarly work done on Saint Thérèse during the past quarter century. With patient study he has traced the development of her doctrine of "spiritual childhood." It was only toward the end of her life, when she reached the summit of her mystical development, that she was able to articulate what she called "the Little Way," and hand it on to us as her singular contribution to spiritual theology. It is for this contribution that Pope John Paul II recently declared her to be the thirty-third Doctor of the Church, only the third woman to receive this title.

The Little Way is no minor teaching, and it is a great mistake to trivialize it as "doing little things for God with great fidelity." It is much more than that. It is a profound *doctrine*, a theological teaching solidly grounded in the nature of God, Whom Saint Thérèse saw to be "nothing but mercy and love." This, and only this, justifies our confidence in Him, a confidence which leads us to a love that cannot be shaken no matter how sorely it is tried.

Father William O'Connor of happy memory, who taught Dogmatic Theology in Dunwoodie Seminary years ago, often reminded us that the function of theology is not to explain mysteries (mysteries cannot be *explained*), but to *define* the mysteries, to tell us exactly what it is that we believe. Coming toward the end of a dogmatic tract he would say with great excitement: "We are closing in on the mystery. We have tracked it to its lair." This is the task which Conrad De Meester sets for himself in his splendid work, *The Power of Confidence*, and which he carries out so successfully. He takes us on the long journey through Thérèse's life, as she groped her way to a clear understanding of what God was revealing to her in the Little Way. The theology of Thérèse was a lived theology, and cannot be understood apart from her life, and from her all-consuming love for Jesus and for others.

Once we understand the Little Way of Saint Thérèse of Lisieux, we shall see that it holds the answer to the great question of life: how can I, in the banal everydayness of my seemingly ordinary life, learn to love God as He wants me to love Him? A close and careful reading of *The Power of Confidence* will lead us to the answer.

✠ Bishop Patrick Ahern
Auxiliary Bishop of New York

Translator's Note

The Power of Confidence is a translation of *Dynamique de la Confiance* (Les Editions du Cerf: 1st edition, 1969; 2nd edition, 1995). In the original text, the author repeatedly uses the pronoun "we" instead of "I" which is a typical French practice known as *"le nous de politesse."* I have preserved this format in this present work.

I am deeply grateful to those who have assisted me in this work. Special appreciation must be extended to **Bishop Patrick Ahern** who commissioned me to undertake this translation. He felt that *Dynamique de la Confiance* was a "masterpiece" and must be shared with English-speaking readers. Bishop Ahern also took the time conscientiously to critique the entire manuscript and to make excellent recommendations. All who are grateful for this treasure in English are truly indebted to Bishop Patrick Ahern for initiating the entire project.

I also owe a debt of gratitude to **Paul Lerley** for his full support and dedication to this effort. Paul provided valuable assistance in proofreading the first chapters of the draft and in answering many questions throughout the project. Sincere appreciation must also be extended to **Christine Arbour** and **Marc LePain** for their timely and thorough review of my work in the first and final sections of the manuscript. I must gratefully acknowledge my brother, **David Conroy**, for his expert advice and brilliant technical assistance throughout the course of my work. His faithful support and guidance have been an invaluable gift to me. Others to whom a sincere *thank you* must be given are my sisters, **Ruthie, Margie and Julie Conroy**, who graciously took time to review the final draft and to provide me with practical support and computer assistance. A heartfelt word of thanks to my friends and family who gave me great courage and inspiration by their powerful prayers and unwavering confidence. Finally, I would like to acknowledge with sincere gratitude the following individuals whose sponsorship has helped to make this English translation possible: **Dr. and Mrs. Eugene McCarthy, William and Tina Flaherty, Mrs. Florence D'Urso**, and **Monsignor John Gillen**.

Through the kind generosity of Bishop Ahern, I had the great pleasure of meeting the author of this book, **Father Conrad De Meester**, in Rome on the day when Our Holy Father solemnly declared Saint Thérèse of Lisieux a Doctor of the Church. To Father Conrad De Meester I extend my deepest appreciation for the joy and privilege of translating his work. This has been a labor of love on the part of all who were involved, and it has inspired each one of us to know and love Saint Thérèse even more. More importantly, it has helped us all to understand at a very deep level the profound doctrine of this "greatest saint of modern times." I pray that these pages will do the same for each person who reads them.

For references to the writings of Saint Thérèse of Lisieux, I refer the reader to the seven volumes comprising *The Complete Works*, available through ICS Publications, Washington, DC. (These are translations of the French critical edition of all the works of Saint Thérèse.) For the *Autobiographical Manuscripts*, I refer specifically to the 3rd edition of *Story of a Soul*, translated from the original French manuscripts by Father John Clarke [ICS Publications, 1997]; this 3rd edition incorporates a referencing system linking back to the French texts. Accordingly, readers will readily be able to locate texts identified throughout this book. This recent edition of *Story of a Soul* also includes a select bibliography of English works on Saint Thérèse. For those who are interested, there also exists an excellent bibliography in the French 1995 edition of *Dynamique de la Confiance*. See pages XVII-XIX for the list of Abbreviations and acronyms used.

For references to the *Autobiographical Manuscripts*, I give the Manuscript (A, B, or C), with indication of page number and recto or verso side, followed by the line number (ex.: A 3 v, 27 refers to the verso side of the 3rd page of Manuscript A, line 27). The same method is used in reference to the Letters (ex.: LT 160, 848; 161, 850; this refers to Thérèse's Letter number 160, page 848; n 161, p. 850). For references to Thérèse's last conversations published in *Derniers*

Entretiens (DE), the numbers indicate day, month, and entry; for example, DE 13.7.3 indicates the third saying on July 13. In the other references, the Roman numeral always refers to the volume, the Arabic number to the page. One will find the description of all sources in the footnotes and in the pages of the Introduction and the Foreword. The double French quotation marks (« ») indicate a literal quotation. To indicate a paraphrasing, literal in terms of the meaning and for most of the words, but otherwise constructed in the author's own manner, I use simple English quotation marks (' ').

I gratefully dedicate this book to Our Lady of Mount Carmel, to whom I entrusted each page of this translation of Father Conrad De Meester's masterpiece.

Abbreviations and acronyms used *

A — *Autobiographical Manuscript*, dedicated to Mother Agnès of Jesus (1895) *
[Refer to the 3rd edition of *Story of a Soul* by ICS Publications; this edition contains a referencing system which incorporates the pagination of the French critical edition used throughout this text.]

Act — *Act of Offering to Merciful Love* (Pri 6) *
[Page 276, 3rd edition of *Story of a Soul* by ICS Publications.]

AL — *Annales de sainte Thérèse de Lisieux*
(*Annals of Saint Thérèse of Lisieux*, magazine.)

B — Letter to Sister Marie of the Sacred Heart, Autobiographical Manuscript (1896) *
[Pagination referenced in *Story of a Soul*.]

C — Autobiographical Manuscript dedicated to Mother Marie de Gonzague (1897) *
[Pagination referenced in *Story of a Soul*.]

CG — *Correspondence Générale* *
[*General Correspondence*, Vol. I (1982) and Vol. II (1988), ICS Publications.]

CJ — «Carnet Jaune» of Mother Agnès *
[«Yellow Notebook» published as part of *St. Thérèse of Lisieux: Her Last Conversations*; see DE, below.]

CS — *Le Cantique spirituel* *
(*The Spiritual Canticle* of Saint John of the Cross)
[*The Collected Works of Saint John of the Cross*, ICS Publications.]

CSG — *Conseils et Souvenirs* *
(*Counsels and Reminiscences*, published by Sister Geneviève, 1973.)
[*A Memoir of My Sister, St. Thérèse*, authorized translation by the Carmelite Sisters of New York; P.J. Kenedy & Sons, 1959.]

* Some of these references do not appear in English translation. Any work that has already been translated is indicated by an asterisk, and cited in brackets.

DCL Documentation du Carmel de Lisieux
(Lisieux Carmel's Documentation.)

DE *Derniers Entretiens* * (*Last Conversations*)
[*St. Thérèse of Lisieux: Her Last Conversations*; ICS Publications, 1977.]

DE II Volume of appendices from *Derniers Entretiens*, republished under the title *Derniers Paroles*, NEC, 1992.

DLTH *Thérèse et Lisieux* *
[*Thérèse and Lisieux*. Album of photographs by P. Descouvemont and H.N. Loose.]

ED *Études et Documents* (supplement to the AL magazine.)

HA *Histoire d'une Âme*, followed by the year of the edition (98 for 1898; 07 for 1907, etc.) *
[*Story of a Soul*, ICS Publications; please refer to the 3rd edition.]

Im *Imitation de Jésus-Christ* *
[*Imitation of Christ*.]

LC *Lettres des corrrespondants de Thérèse* *
[Letters from Thérèse's correspondents, numbered, published in CG.]

LD *Lettres diverses des correspondants* *
[Various letters, published in CG and VT.]

LT *Lettres de Thérèse* *
[*Thérèse's Letters*, numbered in CG.]

Mss Three volumes of Father François de Sainte-Marie accompanying the facsimile edition (1956) of the *Autobiographical Manuscripts*.

NEC Nouvelle édition du Centenaire des *Oeuvres Complètes de Thérèse de Lisieux* (Ed. du Cerf-DDB, 1992) *
[The Centenary's New Edition of the *Complete Works of Thérèse of Lisieux*, in eight volumes in French (critical edition), seven volumes in English (ICS Publications).]

NV *Novissima Verba*, 1927 version of *Derniers Entretiens* *
[1927 version of the *Last Conversations*; see DE.]

OC *Oeuvres Complètes* *
[*Complete Works of Saint Thérèse*, published in 7 volumes by ICS Publications.]

OCL Office central de Lisieux.
(Central Office of Lisieux, publishing house.)

PA Procès Apostolique, 1915-1917 (Teresianum, Rome, 1976.)
(Apostolic Process.)

PN Followed by a number, the 54 Poems by Saint Thérèse *
[*The Poetry of Saint Thérèse of Lisieux*; ICS Publications.]

PO Procès de l'Ordinaire, 1910-1911 (Teresianum, Rome, 1973.)
(Diocesan Process.)

Pri Followed by a number, the 21 Prayers by Saint Thérèse*
[*The Prayers of Saint Thérèse of Lisieux*, ICS Publications.]

PS Supplementary poems by Saint Thérèse.

RP Followed by a number, the 8 *Récréations Pieuses* by Saint Thérèse.
[*The Plays of Saint Thérèse of Lisieux*: *Pious Recreations*; ICS translation forthcoming.]

VF *La Vive Flamme d'amour* *
(*The Living Flame of Love* by Saint John of the Cross.)
[*The Collected Works of Saint John of the Cross*, ICS Publications.]

VT *Vie Thérésienne.*
(*Thérésian Life*, Lisieux; quarterly magazine, since 1961.)

VTL *Visage de Thérèse de Lisieux* *
[*Face of Thérèse of Lisieux* (1961): *Photo Album of St. Thérèse de Lisieux*, translated by Peter-Thomas Rohrbach, OCD; New York: P.J. Kenedy & Sons, 1962.]

«To neglect Thérèse of Lisieux's message
is to pay no heed to the Holy Spirit»

Hans Urs von Balthasar, *Wer ist ein Christ?*
(Benzinger, 1965, p. 83)

Foreword (1994)

Twenty-five years have passed since the first edition (1969) of this work published by Les Editions du Cerf in the theological collection *Cogitatio Fidei* (n. 39). Two great friends of Thérèse were the first readers of the manuscript, Father Ambroise-Marie Carré and Father Bernard Bro, director of the publishing house that offered us the setting of a long friendship and many happy Thérésian meetings. I had the pleasure of accomplishing this work as a Doctoral thesis for the Pontifical Faculty of Theology of the Teresianum, in Rome, under the direction of Father Aimé De Sutter, a great intellectual who knew so well how to live and die as a witness of God's love and as a disciple of Thérèse.

On the occasion of the centenary of Thérèse's birth in 1973, Father Bro asked me to prepare, in a small and more accessible work, the main ideas of the book whose first edition had been out of print. It is thus that *Les Mains vides* (*With Empty Hands*) was born; this book had the good fortune of meeting with wide approval and was published in fifteen languages. But the little book continued to demand the big one, of which it was the echo, and so, at the approach of the centenary of Thérèse's death (September 30, 1897), the publisher, Les Editions du Cerf, decided to republish *Dynamique de la Confiance* (*The Power of Confidence*), and to do this at the precise request of the Carmel of Lisieux which took upon itself to reestablish Thérésian references, based on the old scattered editions, according to the present critical and integral edition of the *Oeuvres complètes* (*Complete Works*). With all my heart, I thank the Carmel of Thérèse, which, already at the time of the first writing of the book, gave me the opportunity to study unpublished works, so that I could do the necessary critical work on my own account. I also thank Mr. Jacques Lonchampt, a friend and fellow veteran of other battlefields, for kindly agreeing to supervise the recasting.

If I agreed to this new edition, it is because I am conscious of having gone, twenty-five years ago, to the end of my possibilities. I do not sense the need to make fundamental modifications in it now. The formerly described findings, in relation to the Thérésian perspective of the «little way of spiritual childhood» and the moment of its discovery (Autumn 1894), have been adopted by the critics. The chronological approach to Thérèse's great intuition are no longer up in the air: there is a precise *before* and *after*. One can better follow its maturation, with its moments of crisis and denouement. After the discovery of the «little way,» made by Thérèse at the end of 1894, and after seeing the stages in the development of her spirituality — the *Offering to Merciful Love* of June 9, 1895, the «*little doctrine*» set forth in Manuscript B and in Letter 197 of September 1896, and even Thérèse's *attitudes of confidence and abandonment* in the field of her apostolate to the novices, her prayer life and the «mysterious depths of charity» (C 18 v, 259) — we are prepared to understand better the essence of the «little way.» It is an active, total opening to the Spirit of Merciful Love, an attitude which brings Thérèse very close to Saint Paul by placing her precisely at the heart of the Good News of the Living Jesus.

The only task which is impossible for me at this time is to pursue what I formerly called «the overview of the Thérésian question.» I have done no more than introduce here, on the points that touched my personal work directly, about twenty «Notes of 1994.» They are for the most part brief, except the one on the Thérésian vision of Hans Urs von Balthasar and Adrienne von Speyr (see p. 367, Appendix IV). I have also had recourse to the revised edition of *Les Mains vides* of 1988, a book that I rewrote entirely, further clarifying certain aspects of «the psychology of Thérèse, the influence of her home environment, the development of her faith, her relationship with those near to her, and her prayer» (p. 13). One will find in it, then, matters which complement certain aspects of *The Power of Confidence*.

Were I to complete the «overview» since 1967, I would pause first of all at the major event of the past twenty-five years of Thérésian history: the critical and integral edition of all Thérèse's writings, which had as principal architects Sister Cécile, of the Lisieux Carmel, Father (now Bishop) Guy Gaucher and Mr. Jacques Lonchampt. From *Her Last Conversations* to *Prayers*, what riches have been revealed to the masses, riches which, in the future, will allow authors to emphasize a thousand little unsuspected human and historical features, a thousand spiritual harmonics of the Saint! Along the same line, since 1961 the magazine *Vie Thérésienne* has not ceased to open up, so to speak, in every quarterly number, the archives «of the family» or «of the Carmel» of Thérèse.

I shall highlight here three tendencies in the way to approach Thérèse which, during the last twenty-five years, it seems to me became more pronounced.

The first concerns *Thérèse's psychology* and the human foundation of her opening to the Spirit. «Rare are those who have ever believed so deeply — so corporally, one could say — in the Incarnation of the Son of God» (J. Lonchampt, in the general introduction to Thérèse's Poems, Cerf-DDB, 1979, p. 35). A flame of love, Thérèse was a being of flesh, fully woman, a mystical wife and «mother of souls» (B 2 v, 224). As a child, she had her psychic injuries, of which God's love healed her. Time was necessary before her personality could become fully unified and structured, before her interior strength could take over and life could be fully victorious in her. Through contact with God and by faith in His grace, Thérèse succeeded in attaining health of soul and a contagious spiritual freshness.

The second tendency, more pronounced, concerns *her pastoral value*. If Thérèse is nowadays invoked less as a «sower of roses,» still more than in the past is she greeted as a master of the spiritual life, welcomed by communities and new movements as a guide for the Christian life of every day, particularly in young churches and among young Christians. For a number of convinced and committed believers, her «little way» serves as a «superhighway.» Her example of universal charity and her progress in the absolute of faith, if need be in the depths of night, enjoys great acceptance. The precision of her theology, so near to the heart of the Gospel, and the dogmatic and central riches of her thought are apparent and men and women willingly place themselves in her school. Her simplicity, far from being fundamentalist, reminds us of what is essential. For many, Thérèse is a star of hope who guides us to the «Sun of love» (B 4 v, 229), a shepherdess who leads us to the Good Shepherd. Pope John Paul II's visit to Lisieux in 1980 and the desire, expressed many times in these last years, that she be declared a Doctor of the Church, give testimony to the pastoral value of Thérèse.

The third tendency which seems to have developed in the approach of Thérèse during the last twenty-five years, is very similar to the previous one. It is *the recognition of Thérèse as a prophet*. As Francis of Assisi still is after seven centuries, so Thérèse will remain a prophet. She who, with the same breath, said: «Jesus! I love you, I love the Church» (B 4 v, 229), had the premonition that death would only increase her radiance and that at the center of her posthumous mission would be the teaching of her «little way» toward Love: «I feel that I'm about to enter into my rest… But I feel especially that my mission is about to begin, my mission of making God loved as I love Him, of giving my little way to souls. If the good God grants my desires, my Heaven will be spent on earth until the end of the world. Yes, I want to spend my Heaven doing good on earth» (DE 17.7).

Thank you, Thérèse!

Thank you, Lord of all the Ages!

Louvain, March 19, 1994
Conrad De Meester, Carmelite

Introduction to the First Edition

Church, Holiness, Thérèse of Lisieux

The Church has a permanent need of theological reflection in order to expound upon divine revelation, analyze it, integrate it into history and the world, and explain history and the world in its light. At the same time, she has need of Christians who *live* the revealed Word in all its fullness, engaging their entire existence in the realization of God's loving plan for us. These are the saints, Christians who respond without reserve.

The role of the saints is considerable. They help Christ build His Church in grace and in time. They are through their hearts, mouths, and hands the co-redeemers of their brothers and sisters. A lasting power of attraction emanates from their example. And as for reflection, their contribution is by no means negligible. This is because saints are beacons of light. Associated more closely with Christian reality and assimilating it more intimately by the rich gifts of the Spirit, they make it visible to our eyes: it becomes more accessible, because, in them, Christ comes close to us. The simple and wise who meet them, glean a message, each according to his own receptiveness, if they are willing to listen. Thus, the saint presents himself before the theologian, asking him to translate his knowledge of God into theological science.

Among the saints, some speak of God more strikingly and possess the vocation and power to attract attention to certain areas of Christian truth, sometimes forgotten by life, sometimes too little explored by thoughtful deliberation. Their mission is to awaken. They are prophets by the grace of God, co-destined for others. They constitute a real «blood transfusion»[1] for theology. They are, in a double sense, tradition.

In the present work we shall endeavor to listen to such a messenger, one whom Pius XI explicitly called «a word of God.»[2] He only confirmed the echo which Thérèse Martin's brief existence had aroused in the universal Church, an echo so strong that it could only have been a disposition of Divine Providence. It is possible that, in this day and age, we no longer realize its intensity, but then, doubt is not reasonable. Christian judgment guarantees it. Pius XI said: «It is certain that the voice of God and the voice of His people have become divinely united in exalting the Venerable Thérèse of the Child Jesus; but it was God's voice that made itself heard first; it was not His which harmonized with that of the people; rather it was the people's voice that recognized and followed the voice of God.»[3]

The word that God addressed to the world from Lisieux resounds today with greater calm, more depth, increased purity. It is revealing that the most interesting Thérésian literature dates from more recent decades. In 1947, the remark could be made: «It is only very gradually that people began to realize the wonderful depth of Thérèse's spirituality and the singular fruitfulness of her insights which are truly invaluable for the spiritual aspirations of the Church at this time.»[4] We were commemorating the fiftieth anniversary of her death at that time. Thérésian congresses were organized in Paris, Lisieux, Saragossa, and Rome. Historical, psychological, and theological studies began to compete with one another.... What is Thérèse's image today? Let us take a walk through history.[5]

---

[1] H.U. VON BALTHASAR, *Therese von Lisieux, Geschichte einer Sendung*, Cologne, 1950, p. 30 (designated henceforth as *Therese von Lisieux*...). It is always we who translate, when the title of the quoted source is given in a foreign language.

[2] Speech of February 11, 1923. See *La Bienheureuse Thérèse de l'Enfant-Jésus. Sa béatification*, Paris, 1923, p. 42.

[3] *Ibid.*, p. 41. Thérèse of Lisieux is a "miracle of virtues and a prodigy of miracles," he also said. P. 43.

[4] D.M. DE PETTER, "Peilingen naar de kern van Theresia's leven en leer," *Tijdschrift voor Geestelijk leven*, 3 (1947), II, p. 208.

[5] (*Note of 1994.*) We should remind the reader that the general survey which follows stops at 1967 (see our Foreword).

Are we not going to get caught up in a digression if we do? Perhaps. Nevertheless, I believe it will be good to do a general survey of some aspects of the Thérésian question in this Introduction, thus opening the perspectives in which this work will be situated. Perhaps these pages will eliminate some prejudgments which might curb the reader's interest.

I. GENERAL SURVEY OF THE THÉRÉSIAN QUESTION

1. *Posthumous appreciations*

After the publication of *Histoire d'une Âme (Story of a Soul)* in 1898, the Thérésian tide rose rapidly. Soon it won over the masses. Veneration started, spread, and was at times inflated. Thérèse quickly became «the beloved child of the world.» In the twenties, Benedict XV and Pius XI granted a pledge of Christian authenticity to her person *and* her message, with an insistence rarely equaled in the history of the Church. Thérèse exercised a beneficial influence on a number of Christians. But at the same time, her true face was already partly hidden behind distortions made by pens and mouths, brushes and scissors which continue to be made. In 1931, we found that the papal declarations and the work of Father Petitot — that clear-sighted precursor! — were opportune reminders of what was essential.[6]

In spite of the old or saccharine forms[7] — attractive to many, repulsive to others — which can clothe the beautiful message, that message carries on its beneficial work in Christendom. Thérèse became «the immense temple of a humanity conquered by [her],» Cardinal Pacelli said of her in 1937. «Doctors of the law became chil-

---

[6] F. FLORAND, "La 'Petite Voie' de sainte Thérèse de L'Enfant- Jésus," *La Vie Spirituelle*, 13 (1931), t. 29, p. 162. He adds with modesty: "Perhaps, however, there is still an effort to be attempted in the direction of a more synthetic study of the little way."

[7] With respect to the embellished images, FRANÇOIS DE SAINTE-MARIE notes wisely: "Thérèse nevertheless used them in order to make herself present to men throughout the whole world, to reach all the way into the huts of the bush country, the tents of nomads, the igloos…" (VTL, *Notes et introduction*, Lisieux, 1961, p. 42). See pp. XVII-XIX at the beginning of this book for the list of abbreviations and acronyms used.

dren again in her school,» and «there are from one end of the world to the other millions of souls whose interior life has succumbed to the beneficent influence of this little book: the *Story of a Soul*.»[8] If occasionally the Saint has been surrounded by «blind devotion,» if sometimes she has been named the patron or made the object of certain superstitious practices[9] or dispositions, it is undeniable that she exercises a great influence for good in the Church: she facilitates conversions,[10] she helps to suppress the remnants of the Jansenist heresy, and especially to awaken in God's people the awareness of being called to a holiness achievable within the setting of ordinary life. She instills the conviction that God Who calls helps all to reach this ideal, if they transcend their weakness through confidence in divine mercy, which wants to be made manifest in them.

It was especially after the Second World War that a period of in-depth inquiry was inaugurated: critical examination, theological exegesis, historical research, psychological findings,[11] and original publications. Let us mention some names even with the fear of being unfair to many others: Ida F. Görres, André Combes, Stéphane Piat, Marie Michel Philipon, Hans Urs von Balthasar, François de Sainte-Marie.... Unanimously, they confer on Thérèse the title of spiritual master and they emphasize her providential timeliness.

Let us point out that the psychology of Thérèse as a child has

---

[8] Speech in Lisieux, July 11, 1937.

[9] See J. MELLOT, *La Superstition, ersatz de foi*, Paris 1959, p. 24.

[10] Examples can be found in ISMAEL DE SANTA TERESITA, "Santa Teresita en la historia de las conversiones," *Revista de Espiritualidad*, 6 (1947), pp. 365-402. W. NIGG said of HA: "This prose works as if one had fire in one's hands. This book has fulfilled a mission beyond comparison. It even reached people who hardly ever took a religious writing in their hands" (*Grosse Heiligen*, Zurich, 1946, p. 430). Compare the reaction of BRUNO DE JÉSUS-MARIE, unsettled by the reading of HA [*Story of a Soul*]: "What will I say of this work? No book, even if it were by a master, has caused such a beneficial impression on me." See *Le Pére Bruno de Jésus-Marie*, Carmelite Studies, Paris, 1964, p. 10. Missionaries have often witnessed to the role of Saint Thérèse in their apostolate.

[11] Beside fine observations, subjective analysis was not missing, nor was the lack of fairness; for example, in refusing to consider the historical environment of Thérèse, or in isolating events from their context, to then ridicule them.

greatly interested authors.[12] They have noted her hypersensitivity, which made its appearance at the age of four years and eight months —right after her mother's death; her «strange sickness» (A 28 v, 113) at the age of ten in which she thought she discerned a diabolical influence; her recovery that she attributed to the Virgin Mary who appeared to her; her crisis of scruples at the age of thirteen: these experiences became the subject of much psychological study. Some spoke of emotional immaturity, or of a neurosis culminating in her illness at age ten, of a neurotic obsession during her crisis of scruples. Leaving this domain to professionals, we have no difficulty admitting these psychological troubles so evident in Thérèse as a child, provided that two things are not called into question: the purifying work of God exercised by means of natural causes and Thérèse's reaction, which was very generous, even though psychologically insufficient. The Saint emerges even more human and nearer to us. As for the authenticity of her holiness and her mission, it is protected by the beautiful psychological balance that Thérèse recovered with her «grace of Christmas» and the months of interior blossoming which followed. Psychologists themselves agree.[13] Indeed, Thérèse kept her temperament, her feminin-

---

[12] See I.F. GÖRRES, *Das verborgene Antlitz. Neue Deutung*, Fribourg (B) 1964, 2nd edition, 558 pp.; W. STAEHLIN, "Teresa Martin, la santa de Lisieux," *Manresa*, 22 (1950), pp. 125-172; E. ROBO, *Two Portraits of Saint Teresa of Lisieux*, Westminster (Maryland), 1957, 2nd edition, 238 pp.; A. BARRIOS MONEO, "Un problema oscuro en la infancia de Teresa de Lisieux. Histeria o diablo?", *Revista de Espiritualidad*, 16 (1957), pp. 25-68; T.V. MOORE, *Heroic Sanctity and Insanity. An Introduction to the Spiritual Life and Mental Hygiene*, New York- London, 1959, x-243 pp.; Dr. GAYRAL, "Une maladie nerveuse dans l'enfance de sainte Thérèse de Lisieux," *Carmel* (France), 1959, pp. 81-96; ALBERT DU SACRÉ-COEUR, *Approches du mystère de sainte Thérèse de l'Enfant-Jésus*, Paris-Colmar, 1961, p. 335 (designated henceforth by *Approches*...). Other less important studies and surveys of the problem can be found in C. PETERS, "Theresia von Lisieux in neuester Sicht," *Carmelus*, 5 (1958) pp. 269-290 or *Carmel* (Holland), 13 (1960- 1961), pp. 169-180, and in G. HINZMANN, "Theresia von Lisieux. Wandlungen ihres Bildes un ihrer Verehrung," *Geist und Leben*, 33 (1960), pp. 142-145.

(*Note of 1994.*) We allow ourselves to return also to our study "Névrose et sainteté. À la recherche de la 'véritable' enfance de Thérèse de Lisieux," in *Ephemerides Carmeliticae* (presently *Teresianum*), 28 (1977), I, pp. 104-136, where we evaluated the work of J.F. SIX, *La véritable enfance de Thérèse de Lisieux*, Paris, 1972, 288 pp.

[13] In a detailed study, Dr. GAYRAL came to the following conclusions: after the Christmas grace, Thérèse changed "forever." It is "a strong, lucid and balanced will that took shape, whereas nothing could have predicted this favorable but very uncustomary evolution from this illness." It was a case of a "total and final" cure

ity, her sensitivity which had become normal again, her education, and her style. Moreover within these contours, there was a beautiful harmony between all her faculties. She demonstrated great energy, good judgment, and an alert intelligence; she possessed the art of nuance, and a rich and open heart. Very early she developed a personality, even one which was endowed with originality. And in God's light, she reached this spiritual maturity which has been praised so much. We must — at the very least — be able to interpret, with the necessary nuances, A.A.A. Terruwe, who calls Thérèse «the saint of the obsessive neurotics.»[14] When Thérèse suffered from her neurosis, she was still far from being holy. And when Thérèse attained holiness, she had already left her neurosis far behind!

Sometimes the emotional immaturity which Thérèse experienced until the age of fourteen has been correlated with her later style and literary taste. One could say, with François de Sainte-Marie, that perhaps she «hadn't the time to fully discover her means of expression, whereas, on the spiritual level, she already had the wisdom of an elder.»[15] Moreover, it is normal that some expressions, some images, kept the meaning they had in her early youth, since the genesis of the symbols coincides so profoundly with childhood experiences.[16]

But Thérèse's style stems above all from her cultural, social, and religious environment. She never claimed «to have produced a literary work» (C 6 r, 242), even in her Poems, which were above all expressions of charity. She wrote «without worrying about the style» (A 3 v, 73), although she composed pages that were of such a nature as to enchant Henri Bremond and others.[17] With Thérèse,

---

(p. 95). Dr. Ch.-H. NODET no longer believes that Thérèse remained thereafter psychically ill. She succeeded in dominating her psychological difficulties of childhood by «a heroic and magnificently lucid sanctity.» (See «Vie affective infantile et vie morale adulte: notions "analogues,"» *Supplément de La Vie Spirituelle*, 4, February 1948, p. 409, n. 8).

[14] "De heilige van de dwangneurotici." See *Psychopathie en neurose. Ten gerieve van zielzorgers*, Romen en Zonen, 1955, p. 151.

[15] Mss I, 54. See the entire admirable stylistic analysis, pp. 53- 56.

[16] See ALBERT DU SACRÉ-COEUR, *Approches...*, pp. 27-28.

[17] See Mss I, 54.

we sometimes encounter allegories, descriptions, effusions of feeling, reverence or tenderness, which no longer please us. But let us notice, with Pius Réginald Régamey, that «what one would readily condemn as excessive sentimentality» is in her «the clumsy but sincere expression of a very authentic life of the heart.»[18] In the mouth of Thérèse, formulas easily find their fullness of meaning. These are not wrong notes, those expressions which sometimes sound strange to our ears. It is legitimate to smile at this or that expression[19] — Thérèse will be the last to be offended. But not to know how to distinguish between form and content and, for this reason, to charge the Saint with psychological immaturity, would reveal an intellectual immaturity on our part. The reader will therefore not be disturbed to find in this work some quotations that may offend his or her aesthetic taste. It is possible, because a concern for strict fidelity to the thought of Thérèse will constantly force us to use her own formulas, both those which are beautiful and those which are less so.[20] Thérèse of Lisieux's mission is not literary, but religious. If we understand this, we shall perhaps share the impression of the saintly philosopher and Carmelite, Edith Stein. To a friend who confessed that she did not like Thérèse's style, she wrote: «I am surprised at what you have written about little Thérèse. Until now, I had not even thought that it might create a problem. I was only aware that I was faced with a unique human life completely absorbed with the love of God. I know of nothing greater and I wish, as far as it is possible, to bring that same love into my own life and into the lives of those around me.»[21] And finally, have we noticed that the style of her autobiography is more temperate in its original version?[22]

---

[18] P.-R. RÉGAMEY, *Portrait spirituel du chrétien*, Paris, 1963, p. 234.

[19] This is what G. SMIT has done. See «Teresia, minnares van Lisieux,» *Carmel* (Holland), 10 (1957-1958), pp. 199-221.

[20] Sometimes we repeat the same texts, in order to highlight their importance or to consider them from different angles.

[21] See Mss I, 56. The translation is from É. de Miribel.

[22] It still remains true that Thérèse doesn't deserve a prize for literature, C. PETERS says (cf. note 11, p. 287).

2. Thérésian Studies

One of the most widespread remarks when it comes to Thérèse claims «that an entire library has been written on the Saint of Lisieux.»

Even so, the last word has perhaps not yet been said. If one maintains with Hans Urs von Balthasar that Thérèse ranks among those «prominent Church personalities who… contribute to determining Christianity well beyond their time,»[23] one understands that it will be necessary, at every turn of history, to ask oneself what Thérésian spirituality brings to the new era. In this manner, one can hope to integrate a «word of God» into history. Today even more than before, it seems good to formulate this word well, just as the post-conciliar period opens new perspectives to Christians who are always in search of greater clarity.[24]

But what especially diminishes the value of the «entire library» comes from the fact that the great abundance of these compositions dates back to a time when Thérèse's writings were not accessible in their totality and in their original version. It was only in 1948 that her Letters had their critical edition: this meant a harvest four times more abundant than that known up to that time! But André Combes affirmed, rightfully so, that Thérèse scholars had always found themselves in less than favorable conditions.[25] In 1952, Sister Geneviève published a considerable portion of *Conseils et Souvenirs*. It was only in 1956 that the entire and origi-

---

[23] «L' Évangile comme norm et critique de toute spiritualité dans l'Église,» *Concilium*, 1 (1965), n. 9, p. 23.

[24] See K. RAHNER, «Frömmigkeit heute und morgen,» *Geist und Leben*, 39 (1966), pp. 326-342. There is moreover another reason to reflect again on Thérèse of Lisieux. This saint is still near to us. And aren't we still missing the perspective necessary to come to a definitive judgment regarding her message? In 1959, M. DROUZY even believed that this stepping back to get a better perspective in order to attempt the synthesis had always been missing *(La double Vocation de Saint Thérèse de Lisieux*, Brussels-Paris, 1959, pp. 12-13). See M.-M. PHILIPON: «It will take several centuries of perspective to measure in all its fullness the spiritual and doctrinal mission of the great saint of Lisieux. From now on she appears to us… as the creator of a new age of spirituality» *(Sainte Thérèse de Lisieux. «Une voie toute nouvelle,»* Desclée De Brouwer, 1958, 5th ed., p. 56, named henceforth *Sainte Thérèse de Lisieux…*).

[25] See *Le Problème de l'Histoire d'une Âme et des Oeuvres complètes de sainte Thérèse de Lisieux*, Paris, 1950, pp. 8-11, 34-36, 44.

nal text of Thérèse's three *Autobiographical Manuscripts* appeared, an edition so avidly desired for a long time. The event marked a real stage in Thérésiology.

Did Thérèse's image emerge renewed from this process? Let us avoid extremes. On the one hand, Marcel Moré had assured — relying beforehand upon the authentic passages published by André Combes — that the changes made to the manuscripts had distorted «the very foundations» of Thérèse's spirituality and that sometimes the editors had made her say «precisely the opposite of what she had expressed, and they had done this on essential points.»[26] On the other hand, one remains surprised about the little value that the restoration of seven thousand corrections and a quarter of the original text could have had for a psychologist like Ida F. Görres: «The mountain of critical research 'produced only a mole-hill.' Neither in the Letters nor in the original text of the *Story of a Soul* could I have discovered a single sentence that can change my understanding of the Saint in any sense.»[27]

In general, the numerous examiners were of the opinion that neither the person nor the doctrine of Thérèse were distorted by the brotherly censorship that her autobiographical writings had undergone. But it is enough to browse through the long, still incomplete list that François de Sainte-Marie drew up of the *omitted* passages[28] — not to mention the *changed* words — to realize the wealth

---

[26] «La Table des pécheurs,» *Dieu vivant*, 24 (1953), pp. 15 and 46.

[27] *Das verborgene Antlitz. Neue Deutung*, Fribourg (B), 1964, 9th ed., p. 27. On this book, see F. WULF, «Die Hagiographie an der Wende,» *Geist und Leben*, 22 (1949), pp. 383-387, which reports several judgments and also M. ARTS, «Een omstreden boek over een "omstreden" heilige,» *Carmel* (Holland), 4 (1951-1952), pp. 52-74. While recognizing the powerful contribution of Görres of pulling Thérèse out from the kitsch and restoring her to the truth, one can doubt that the author knew how to transcend the psychological level enough to discover the true face of Thérèse — that in which the supernatural inscribes itself in the natural. With respect to the ninth edition (in 1964), A. DE SUTTER writes: «One closes the book with a certain uneasiness.... Would this not rather be because we haven't yet discovered the true face of Saint Thérèse, or even because (as we had the impression), wanting to tear away all the veils that hid her face, the author went too far and wounded it to the point of disfiguring it?» And he finishes by wishing «that the author might take up the work again in a general recasting, benefiting from everything that has been produced these last twenty years.» See *Ephemerides carmeliticae*, 16 (1965), pp. 228-232.

[28] Mss I, 99-129.

of historical, psychological, and sometimes doctrinal detail[29] that had remained in the shadows. As much as we know it, it lacks an exhaustive comparative study of the two texts which prevents us from drawing precise conclusions, but the new edition is nevertheless a considerable improvement.

Another reason that prompts us to undertake further studies stems from the very nature of numerous works contained in our «Thérésian library.» At the onset, let us limit our remarks to the section dealing with the «way of spiritual childhood.» There is a reason why this section is the most vast, because this was the focus of Thérèse's mission as well as of her life. When Thérèse felt that her mission was about to begin, she described it as a reminder of the love of God and as the teaching of what she calls her «little way» toward holiness, a way that she ends up discovering herself, after a good deal of gradual groping.[30]

However, in the abundant literature on this theme of «spiritual childhood,» many writings had no other goal but to nourish piety and to contribute to spiritual progress, without any scientific claim. Other works lacked one or several qualities to give complete satisfaction: they remained in the descriptive stage, did not push the analysis far enough, failed to do reconstruction work, abstained from studying the Thérésian way under its conceptual aspect, or presented questionable interpretations and conclusions. And even good scientific studies, which most often tended to be incomplete, suffered from the fact that they could not give the subject the attention and development it needed, especially because they did not yet have access to the entire and original Thérésian writings or to the testimonies of those who had known the Saint.[31] Besides, no one was obliged to attempt such a comprehensive study, and so

[29] Already in 1954, T. KEULEMANS was going so far as to say that H.U. von Balthasar would have written his book in a different way had he read the original and complete response of Father Pichon to Thérèse. We shall return to this. See «Aan de tafel der zondaars,» *Carmel* (Holland), 6 (1953-1954), p. 237.

[30] «I feel that my mission is about to begin: my mission of making others love God as I love Him, of giving my little way to souls» (CJ 17.7). The first edition of HA (of 1898, p. 241) already relates these words. Sister Geneviève says that «many a time» Thérèse came back to this subject (PO, p. 304).

[31] May we be allowed to point out that French authors often don't seem to be sufficiently enriched with Thérésian foreign literature?

we cannot be thankful enough in seeing the distance which in fact was covered.

3. *The work of Father Piat*

But has not the systematic study that we propose to do on the «way of spiritual childhood,» the light that Thérèse of Lisieux projected on holiness, been done by Stéphane Piat[32] — under excellent conditions?

Assuredly, Stéphane Piat's book did contribute greatly to clarifying the notion of the Thérésian way of «spiritual childhood.» For its expansive biographical vision, its encyclopedic information, and the author's familiarity with Thérésian writings, history, and background, it is of considerable value and it will always hold a special place in the domain of spiritual theology. Our work would therefore not want to be a duplication or a repetition of Stéphane Piat's book. In a certain sense it seeks rather to be inserted into it, to complement it. In fact, the title already announces the author's main concern, which is historical in nature. And although Stéphane Piat proceeds from the judiciously established principle that «for the Carmelite of Lisieux… life and mission converge: literally, they become united,»[33] he especially wanted to emphasize her mission by studying the *phases* of her life. As Lucien-Marie de Saint-Joseph notes in the Preface,[34] followed later by M. Trémeau[35]: the path toward the doctrinal synthesis and the theological structure remains open. Moreover, Stéphane Piat himself foresaw the possibility of a widening of the «field of investigations.»[36]

---

[32] *Sainte Thérèse de Lisieux à la découverte de la voie d'enfance*, Paris, 1964, 408 pp. (named henceforth *À la découverte…*).

[33] *Ibid.*, p. 13.

[34] «One might also wish that this doctrine, whose least nuances are exposed in their historical setting, might be made into a more vigorous synthesis. As it is, it doesn't entirely lack synthetic pages, particularly in chapter XIV (p. 356 f.). But this synthesis leaves us guessing about the theological structures that it strengthens more than it explains. After all, would this not be a manner of inviting theologians to show all the doctrinal rigor contained in the way of spiritual childhood, as the Reverend Father Mersch said? Let us hope that these works come to light by way of the well-investigated analysis given by Father Piat» (*ibid.*, p. 9).

[35] *L'Ami du clergé*, 76 (1966), p. 511.

[36] *Ibid.*, p. 13.

Our work, then, is going to concentrate on this area: a conscientious research into the nature and the structure of the way of holiness which Thérèse of Lisieux proposes. But since it is impossible to separate her mission and life «which are one» — she teaches while living and she teaches what she lives — it will be impossible to make an abstraction of the origin of this "way." Besides, its description provides a practical means of collecting the material out of which the structure will be built. We will refer to the book of Stéphane Piat for its rich biographical setting, and be satisfied with limiting ourselves to the necessary outlines. Here again, one will note that the present work is not a repetition, because another chronological division of the genesis of the «way of childhood» — of which we would also like to emphasize again the intrinsically evolutionary element[37] — imposed itself on us. Are we right or wrong? The reader will be the judge of that.

But first we must point out something once again. Some may think that we have down-played the role of hundreds of works, pamphlets, and articles that were purely *popularizing*. No. Outside of the promotion of sentiments of doubtful authenticity and a few obviously erroneous doctrinal representations, they are well in line with one of Thérèse's desires. The Carmelite did not pretend to think scientifically. She addressed her message in the first place to little ones, to the simple, to those who are like herself. To make herself understood she called upon the most common human experiences: childhood, fatherhood, love, weakness, mercy, confidence, poverty, daily existence, etc. The fact that she knew how to meld these components into a doctrine of Christian perfection explains in part the secret of her popularity and guarantees it a certain universality. And these experiences, integrated into our relationships with God, relate rather easily to one another: Thérèse's teaching — the «little doctrine» as she called it — takes hold so well, provided one understands its fundamental inspiration, that those who follow it see themselves led *by life itself* to all its essential elements. One can indeed enter into Thérèse's synthesis by many doors. And every interpretation that points out the structure of

[37] That is to say, the passage from one phase to the other. Besides the *succession* of phases, there is preparation and sometimes provocation.

Thérésian doctrine on spiritual childhood and that opens even a single door of access, even if this one is not the main door, has produced a good work, perfectible as it may be. It is there that both the value and the limitation of so many writings on Thérèse reside. He was right, the friend who told us: «The doctrine of Thérèse is so simple and at the same time so profound that everybody understands it and theologians discover marvels in it.»

II. THEOLOGICAL VALUE AND RELEVANCE OF THÉRÈSE OF LISIEUX

Quite often, qualified theologians have stressed the theological value of the message of Lisieux. It is «a message of an astonishing spiritual penetration,» said Pius XII.[38] «As always with her,» wrote Hans Urs von Balthasar, «her life is full of seeds of doctrine that theology has only to develop to be made richly fruitful by it.»[39] This great advocate of a fecundation of theology by sanctity considers Thérèse «the very great little Thérèse of Lisieux.»[40] Before him, E. Mersch had recognized in the Thérésian way of spiritual childhood «a deep theological significance»[41] and «treasures of theology.»[42]

One can ask oneself what influence Thérèse had hitherto exercised on life in the Church, and thereby on Christian thought. Let us not venture to give a complete account. But the question has its purpose, because Thérèse is counted with good reason among the «beacons that God's Hand has lit at the threshold of an atomic century»[43] and which shine not in vain. For a long time, she has guided a large portion of the faithful in their search for God. Now, she remains, with less brilliance perhaps, but by a deeper action, one of the «leaders» of Christian spirituality. It is true that her influ-

[38] Radio message of July 11, 1954. See *Acta apostolicae sedis*, 46 (1954), p. 404.

[39] *Therese von Lisieux…*, p. 132.

[40] «Théologie et sainteté,» *Dieu vivant*, 12 (1948), p. 24. See also this study touched up in H.U. VON BALTHASAR, *Verbum Caro. Skizzen zud Theologie*, t. I, Einsiedeln, 1960, pp. 195-225.

[41] "Filii in Filio," *Nouvelle Revue théologique*, 65 (1938), p. 825.

[42] *La Théologie du Corps mystique*, Paris-Brussels, 1944, t. II, p. 161.

[43] Y. CONGAR, *Pour une église servante et pauvre*, Paris, 1963, p. 123.

ence has become a little more anonymous, because her intuitions have long been integrated into spirituality. But on the other hand, among those who take life seriously according to the Holy Spirit Who leads us to the perfect Man,[44] very numerous are those who reread Thérèse. «The authenticity of her doctrine,» wrote von Balthasar, «appears in these characteristics which indicate the presence and action of the Holy Spirit: liberty, control, clarity, fullness, and joy.»[45] One rediscovers in all simplicity these same depths that seized theologians and masters of spirituality who used these as renovating elements of their disciplines. There are some cases where Thérèse held and still maintains her role, although it is not possible to specify the exact measure of it: the return to the Gospel; the summons to what is essential in the notion of sanctity, the relativity of exterior manifestations and extraordinary means — in this sense it is not exaggerated to say that Thérèse contributed powerfully to «demythologizing» the concept of holiness of her time; the summons to the universal call to holiness, even for the «little» man; the stress placed on God's mercy; the revaluation of hope; and her ecclesiastical sense,[46] reciprocal responsibility, and interaction in the Church.

This simple diagram already demonstrates it: the word that God spoke through Thérèse to our time is centered on the notion of holiness, on the way that leads to it, on the evangelical environment in which it is achieved. Yves Congar noted very appropriately: «[Her] way of childhood appears as a translation of the evangelical ideal providentially offered to the modern world.»[47] Each saint is in a way for the present, because he or she testifies by his or her life to the pre-eminence of God in every human vocation. But, among them, there are a few who, like Thérèse, concretize their search for God in an especially appealing way for the Christian of today.

---

[44] Eph 4:13. We will always quote the *Jerusalem Bible*, except for Thérèse's biblical quotations where we respect the translation(s) she used.

[45] *Therese von Lisieux...*, p. 46.

[46] «There is, with Saint Thérèse of Lisieux, certainly not an ecclesiology, but a lived understanding of the Church, of which the theologian can only admire the splendor» (Ch. JOURNET, «L'Église telle que la pense et la vit sainte Thérèse de Lisieux», *Carmel* [France], 1957, p. 16).

[47] *Jalons pour une théologie du laïcat*, Paris, 1954, 2nd ed., p. 588.

However, let us not expect from Thérèse a complete spirituality for modern man with his reassessment of all earthly values and his duties «in the midst of the world.» The word that God addressed to us through her does not envision all these concrete perspectives. But Thérèse offers us something that will forever occupy a place in the theology of the spiritual life and will exercise on it a fruitful action, and no less for our contemporaries: Thérèse does not illuminate the entire present spiritual environment where we are to sanctify ourselves, but she does describe, in a way which is timely now more than ever, the *interior core* of our search for God. We are not speaking of forms, but this core retains all its value in our «secularized» world.

People today love the true, the *essential*, and they love it in their relationship with God: this is precisely where Thérésian spirituality is ready to help them. Thérèse is an evangelical saint, nourished by the Bible, with an ideal of perfection that aims only at the full realization of the commandment — the first and the second, both twofold and single (Mt 22:36-40) — of love. Her ideal does not stop at what is secondary. It is achieved in the daily, obligatory, banal, ordinary, anonymous, little circumstances of life. Finally, Thérèse is an eminently Christ-centered saint. All these qualities render her pleasing to our eyes and give her a certain universal character, common to our situations, and an integration — it is Yves Congar and Jean Guitton who insist upon this — into the spirituality of the laity,[48] but also into the new forms of religious life.[49]

---

[48] «It seems that this lay spirituality is still searching for itself, that it hasn't found adequate expression. It is scattered. One breathes it again in the spirit of Saint Francis de Sales, or better still in the spirit of Saint Thérèse of Lisieux» (J. GUITTON, *L'Église et les Laïcs*, Desclée De Brouwer, 1963, 2nd ed., p. 144). And again: «Thérèse was not at all secular, very much the opposite. But one can say that her spirituality was of the lay type (one could say the same thing of that of Saint Francis of Assisi in his time). The virtues that Thérèse recommends are those that don't need a cloister to be exercised. These are the natural virtues formed by love. And Thérèse was great, not as Joan of Arc, in doing heroic acts naturally, but in accomplishing natural and simple acts heroically» (*Ibid.*, p. 150). Earlier, Y. CONGAR, discussing the spirituality and the sanctification of committed laity in the world, had already written: «If one follows, from the point of view that interests us here, the history of canonizations made by the popes of the 20th century, one will note with a Protestant observer [H. HERMELINCK, *Die Katholische Kirche unter den Pius-Päpsten des 20. Jahrhunderts*, Zurich, 1949] a sort of "canonization politics" consisting in giving to

But the women and men of today are nonetheless people with *limits*. Their scientific, social, and spatial conquests are accompanied at the same time by an increasing awareness of their own limitations. The Christian of today feels no differently. The idea that the duties of brotherhood are mandatory has grown far and wide. Christians find themselves with immense needs. Every day they are faced with difficult questions which emerge quickly. They realize the strain which the new signification of the earth imposes upon them. They search for more new ways of witnessing or of Christianizing, and for the meaning of many things. They must integrate all these problems into the projection and realization of Christian holiness. Often they do not see the results of their efforts, and find themselves alone, sometimes opposed. So their task of holiness appears arduous. They more quickly experience their weakness and their own insufficiency. Discouragement awaits them.

It is this which renders even more true today the words of Gustave Thibon: in this «conflict between the desire and the capacity to live..., the spirituality of Saint Thérèse of the Child Jesus — founded on the knowledge and acceptance of weakness and interior poverty — appears providentially adapted to the needs of our time.»[50]

---

modern man models of holiness and patrons for the different situations of his vocation, of his profession, of his role: models of holiness, not so much in the area of ascetic and extraordinary acts as in the line of those in Saint Thérèse's spirit of childhood, in abandonment to God's will, the perfect achievement of the duty of one's state in life, the imitation of Jesus in his humility and his love...» (*Jalons...*, p. 589).

[49] Here are two testimonies. R. VOILLAUME wrote to the Little Brothers of Jesus: «During the retreat, someone read Saint Thérèse of the Child Jesus' *Story of a Soul*. Once more, I noticed to what degree her vocation was interiorly the same as ours. Like her, we must be absolute in the ordinary things. More than others, more than members of Secular Institutes and the laity, our life of Nazareth withdraws us from any important social or professional action: the main value of our life is therefore all interior, all contemplative. By our state of life, we are all near Saint Thérèse of the Child Jesus» (*Lettres aux Fraternités*, t. II, Paris, 1960, p. 125). The Rule of the Brothers of the Poor Virgin insists largely on Thérésian spirituality of poverty of soul, humility and confidence. «It is probably there that we find the essential message with which Saint Thérèse of the Child Jesus was commissioned for our time» (*Au coeur même de l'Église. Une recherche monastique: les Frères de la Vierge des Pauvres*, Desclée De Brouwer, 1966, p. 84. See pp. 84-86). The title of the book recalls some of Thérèse's most famous words.

[50] Art. «Caractère,» in the *Dictionnaire de spiritualité*, t. II, col. 131. Thus, on the psychological plane, Thérèse's doctrine will be for many «a cure of peace and a therapy of psychological welfare» (P. BLANCHARD, *Jacob et l'Ange*, col. «Études carméli-

Indeed, Thérèse constructs her way toward holiness from these same existential experiences of insufficiency, weakness, and littleness. But she knows how to transform these experiences into a state of hope in the Father of mercies (2 Cor 1:3), from Whom she expects the fulfillment, or better still the entire content of her love. In this hope, which envelops her in a robe of sure and loving confidence, she discovers a new dynamic. That is why, as long as people of today long for the unselfish service of God and their neighbors and will dare to recognize the weakness of their own commitment, and consequently their need relative to God's mercy, Thérèse of Lisieux will never be surpassed. She will remain, as in the past, a sign of hope and — if only for this reason alone — relevant to today.[51]

This spirituality has been given, for good reason, the name «spiritual childhood,» the «little way.» But at the moment, for several of our contemporaries, these expressions are somewhat flawed. Sometimes these expressions evoke for them the idea of a way that is incomplete, illegitimately easy and therefore unauthentic, or they make them think about immaturity, a lack of personality and commitment. These phrases have, in effect, been subjected to the burden of certain unfortunate interpretations. Moreover, sensitivity to formulas constantly shifts. Some excesses have managed to abuse the idea of spiritual childhood and to make the notion childish. We end up with a religious infantilism «which our modern psychologists have rightfully denounced and from which Saint Thérèse of the Child Jesus trembled in advance.»[52] Something of the uneasiness of our contemporaries will inevitably remain in us when clarity and method will often oblige us to use these terms. But in order that all may be reassured: we hope to show that none of these reservations find in Thérèse a justified basis. On the other hand, the realistic tone with which Christ Himself earnestly invites us to become little «like this little child» (Mt 18:4), thus *symbolizing* «a

---

taines» Desclée De Brouwer, 1957, p. 210). It is also the conclusion of the psychiatrist A.A.A. TERRUWE; she appraises Thérèse as «God's gift to our time» (cf. note 13, p. 151).

[51] On the relevance of Thérèse, see also the testimonies of E. PRZYWARA and of H. HEER in: C. PETERS, *Theresia von Lisieux in neuester Sicht…*, pp. 283-288.

[52] FRANÇOIS DE SAINTE-MARIE, *Fils du Père*, Desclée De Brouwer, 1963, p. 23.

spiritual state that identifies with the littleness and humility required throughout the Gospel,» obliges us also to reject the «minimizing interpretations and the sarcasm of "superior" intelligences, that have been formulated on the subject of true spiritual childhood.»[53]

III. OUR PURPOSE AND OUR INFORMATION

Now then, the perspectives in which the present study would simply like to be situated should be more clear. But it has no ambition to exhaust the entire theological and present reach of Thérèse's message for our time. One should not expect here the answer to *all* the demands that this theme can indirectly raise: we do not pretend to give it.

What we aim for above all is to trace the lines of the genesis[54] and especially the structure of the «way of spiritual childhood,» as *Thérèse* discovered it, prepared it, understood it, and lived it. This monograph belongs then to the domain which is classically assigned to «spiritual theology,» which reflects on growth toward Christian perfection. It will analyze and restructure the charismatic message of one of the greatest figures of Christian and contemporary spirituality. It will highlight an eminent representative of the Church's holiness. It will prepare the way for a later reflection of a more strictly dogmatic nature, while it will not be able to dispense with a test of the theological justification for Thérèse's initiative which places confidence at the *center* of the way toward holiness — not as its goal, but as its dynamic core. And it will not fail to

---

[53] *Ibid.*, pp. 18-20. «This "like" [in Jesus' words] suggests likeness and profound difference at the same time» (p. 22). Pius XII, in his letter of August 7, 1947 to the bishop of Bayeux, also insist on the evangelical character of spiritual childhood. See *Analecta ordinis carmelitarum discalceatorum*, 19 (1947), p. 168.

[54] It is not our intention to study the external influences that Thérèse underwent expressly with regard to their images and formulas, and this in spite of several remarks in this line. This would be a very interesting study, but of an infinite delicacy; it would suppose a very detailed knowledge of her environment and it would bring us too far afield.

analyze the theological foundation of faith in divine mercy, inasmuch as Thérèse herself vouched for it.[55]

This study, which could otherwise be entitled «the phenomenology of a soul in its most characteristic manifestation,» inserts itself therefore in the great contemporary theological current that reflects on Christian hope. It will describe this hope as the greatest strength of a soul, not of just any soul, but of this Saint in whom — listen again to Hans Urs von Balthasar — «this [contemporary] springtime of hope has been canonized»[56] and in whom the theology of hope was deeply inspired.[57]

Here are the main lines of this work. The preliminary chapter contains *some methodological notes* in connection with Thérésian study which has its own characteristics. It will establish, among other things, the principle of unity existing between Thérèse's life and mission, which justifies our historical consideration. In the first part, we will reflect upon her *discovery* of «spiritual childhood.» In fact, on this point Thérèse received a decisive insight one day, although only in embryonic form. What was this light? When did Thérèse receive it? The answer to these two questions will set the direction for the entire remaining research. We will then know what elements of Thérèse's spiritual life we must preferably examine and how far we must extend the preparatory period. Without dating the discovery, one risks poorly situating and interpreting its precedents and its aftermaths. The second part studies the *genesis* of

---

[55] Thérèse of Lisieux also embodies a fundamental law of the contemporary anthropology of personalized orientation: the other is the perfection of my being. Indeed, Thérèse expects the perfection of her love — and that is the center of all her existence — from the Other. As for her conception of *human* others, she underwent a very instructive evolution. The other, from the *existential* point of view, is at first rather a danger to her love for God; then it is rather a means; finally, the other and the Other become a single object of her love. (See P. DESCOUVEMENT, *Sainte Thérèse de l'Enfant-Jésus et son Prochain*, Paris, 1962, x-270 pp.).

[56] *Dieu et l'Homme d'Aujourd'hui*, Desclée De Brouwer, 1961, 2nd ed. (tran. by R. Givord), p. 275.

[57] See H.U. VON BALTHASAR, *Therese von Lisieux...*, p. 276 and especially *Verbum Caro...*, t. I, p. 291 (*Umrisse der Eschatologie*): «Péguy... Bernanos and Claudel find themselves entirely in the light of Lisieux and the hope that has exploded there. In wake of this is found all the «theology of hope» of Christian-existential orientation, as it had been developed for about ten years in France and now also in Germany.» (Note that this text was written for the collection *Fragen der Theologie heute*, published in 1957.)

the «way of childhood» in Thérèse's life, until its discovery. The third part examines the *deepening* of the discovered truths and their definitive formulation. The fourth part *structures* this way toward holiness in all the hierarchy of its components, justifies it theologically, and describes the exterior manifestations of it. It concentrates on confidence which, in our opinion, constitutes the core of the «little way.» But it is not in this last section alone that the structure is explained. All along our path we shall take care to outline it, with a brief sketch of the situation where this structure arrived during its historical genesis, or in this or that formula in which Thérèse gives it to us. A glance at the table of contents can provide more abundant data on the organization of this study.

Just a couple of words concerning our sources in 1994. In the first edition of this work (1969), we indicated the various instruments with which we had worked for the study of Thérèse's texts and words, in particular the old editions of *Histoire d'une Âme* (*Story of a Soul*), the first edition of *Letters* of Bishop Combes, and publications produced by Father François de Sainte-Marie (the *Autobiographical Manuscripts* and the three volumes accompanying the facsimile edition). Since then, the *Ouevres Complètes (Complete Works)* of Thérèse have been prepared, and it is to this that the present work refers.[58]

But the reader will note that in 1967, thanks to the kindness of the Carmel of Lisieux, we already had access to all the documents which our research needed: including all the letters *addressed to Thérèse* (and since published in CG). Furthermore, for the *Poems*, the Carmel had provided us with the unpublished original texts.

---

[58] The magnificent critical edition of the *Oeuvres Complètes* of Thérèse has been prepared in 8 volumes in the French «New Centenary Edition» and in a single volume of 1,600 pages, with reduced annotation. *Dynamique de la Confiance* referred to this single volume and its pagination. Since this single volume does not exist in English, we refer the reader to the 7 volumes comprising the *Complete Works* of Thérèse, published by ICS Publications.

It is not without interest to know the time of Thérèse's letters which we mention. In case of need, we will clarify the date; but here, in general, is the correlation between the pages and the dates of writing: pp. 110-248 (1877-October 1886); pp. 266-406 (March 1887- March 1888); pp. 421-519 (April 1888-January 1889); pp. 529-683 (January 1889-September 1890); pp. 706-765 (September 1890-December 1892); pp. 781-935 (February 1893-March 1896); pp. 950-1181 (April 1896-August 1897).

With regard to the *Last Conversations*, we were able to fully study the «Yellow Notebook» and the parallel texts of the «Green Notebooks.» Let us note that the *Novissima Verba* (Latin for "Last Words") by Mother Agnès was published again in the synopsis volume of the French Centenary Edition (DE II = DP).

There exist a number of testimonies reporting the facts and words of Thérèse. Some have already appeared in «Chapter XII» and «Conseils et Souvenirs» («Counsels and Reminiscences»), which were added to the *Story of a Soul* since its first editions. In certain editions, over more than fifty years, one notes not only differences in the number of these testimonies, but also textual variations, to which it is advisable to give a great deal of attention.[59] In 1952, Sister Geneviève collected her own *Conseils et Souvenirs (Counsels and Reminiscences*, CSG), to which we refer rather frequently, particularly in our fourth part (1973 edition).

For the Process, which undoubtedly constitutes the largest volume of testimonies on Thérèse, we had at our disposal the *Summarium*, which was not public. But now, after the publication of the *Diocesan Process* and the *Apostolic Process*, it is only reasonable that we refer to these editions.[60]

Finally, let us say that the long conversations and the correspondence which we had with the Carmelites of Lisieux were certainly a great enrichment for our work.

[59] The *Story of a Soul* has often been reprinted. In his *Chronologie et concordance thérésiennes* (Rome, 1958, p. 97), Cyrille de la Mère du Dieu indicates the heads of series as the main editions (with the same pagination as the following) those of 1898, 1899, 1907, 1914, 1923, 1941, 1946, 1949, 1950, 1953.

[60] *Procès de béatification et canonisation de sainte Thérèse de l'Enfant-Jésus et de la Sainte-Face*, 2 vol.: I. *Procès informatif ordinaire*, xxviii-730 pages, Rome, 1973 (acronym: PO): II. *Procès Apostolique*, xxx-612 pages, Rome, 1976 (acronym: PA), edition of the Pontifical Institute of the Teresianum.

A chronological reminder can be useful:

Thérèse's Birth:	January 2, 1873.
Death of her mother, Zélie Martin:	August 28, 1877.
Pauline's[61] entrance into Carmel:	October 2, 1882.
«Strange sickness» and cure:	end of March-May 1883.
First Communion:	May 8, 1884.
«Terrible sickness of scruples»:	May 1885-end of October 1886.
«Christmas grace»:	December 25, 1886.
Apostolic graces, conversations in the Belvédère (at Les Buissonnets), journey to Rome:	1887.
Thérèse's Entrance into Carmel:	April 9, 1888.
Reception of the Habit:	January 10, 1889.
Louis Martin's Sojourn in Caen:	February 12, 1889-May 10, 1892.
Profession:	September 8, 1890.
Retreat preached by Fr. Prou:	October 8-15, 1891.
Her sister Agnès is elected prioress:	February 20, 1893.
Mother Agnès asks Thérèse to help the novices:	shortly after February 20, 1893.
Death of Louis Martin:	July 29, 1894.
Entrance of her sister Céline into Carmel:	September 14, 1894.
Writing of Manuscript A:	1895.
Offering to Merciful Love:	June 9 and 11, 1895.
Marie de Gonzague is elected prioress:	March 21, 1896.
Aid to the Novice Mistress:	shortly after March 21, 1896.
Beginning of the «night of the faith»:	around April 5, 1896.
Writing of Manuscript B:	September 1896.
Beginning of the *Last Conversations*:	April 6, 1897.
Writing of Manuscript C:	June 3-July 10, 1897.
Thérèse's death:	September 30, 1897.
First edition of the *Story of a Soul*:	September 30, 1898.
Diocesan Process:	1910-1911.
Apostolic Process:	1915-1917.
Beatification:	April 29, 1923.
Canonization:	May 17, 1925.

[61] It is useful to know the religious names of Thérèse's Carmelite sisters: Pauline is called Sister (and, since 1893, Mother) Agnès of Jesus; Marie is Sister Marie of the

We can now start this study with a wish. Karl Rahner maintained «that tomorrow's spirituality [*Frömmigkeit*] must be mindful of the great heritage which has been conveyed to it and that it will not be authentic unless it is persuaded in a new way of a living connection with its past.»[62] May we, in this sense, contribute to this spirituality of tomorrow, and may we do this in the wake of Vatican II, which called all Christians to the search for holiness.[63] Thérèse of Lisieux, who estimated that the followers of her way would be a «legion» (B 5 v, 232), would have been happy to read this pressing invitation.

Sacred Heart; and Céline becomes Sister Geneviève of the Holy Face. Besides these, there is her sister Léonie, Sister Françoise-Thérèse; and her cousin Marie Guérin, Marie of the Eucharist.

[62] *Frömmigkeit heute und morgen*..., p. 330.

[63] Dogmatic Constitution *Lumen gentium*, chap. v.

INTRODUCTORY CHAPTER

METHODOLOGICAL NOTES

Introductory Chapter

Methodological Notes for This Thérésian Study

Thérèse of Lisieux is a special case for spiritual theology. Deep, she is simple. Reflective, she does not systematize. Intuitive, her style remains emotional and filled with imagery. Mystical, she narrates what cannot be described. A messenger, she involves herself in the message. This «literary genre,» capable of revealing her penetrating doctrines to the man of the street, risks leading astray those who seek deeper meaning. It seems to us that a good analysis of Thérésian doctrine doesn't require so much speculative ability as it requires delicacy, sensitivity to the structure and movements of the spirit of our Carmelite.[1] With her, a concept must be understood in light of the ways in which it was «conceived» and «received» in her, ways which are quite individual, feminine, and determined by her character and her whole existence. It is not so easy to comprehend this *receptaculum*. It supposes a long familiarity with her writings. One must know her past, her temperament, her education, her kind of lifestyle and her religious environment, her mind and her heart, her graces and her desires. And one must «participate in the original strength of her vision»[2] which permeates everything.

---

[1] In his very documented study «L'Ineffable chez sainte Thérèse de l'Enfant-Jésus,» *Carmel* (France), 1957, pp. 253-265, FRANÇOIS DE SAINTE-MARIE, emphasizing in the introverted character of Thérèse a certain «reluctance to speak about herself» and in the structure of her understanding of God's mystery an intuitive and experimental predominance more than an intellectual one — that which undoubtedly makes her resort to the «pictures of fullness, but that remain confused on the plane of thought» — concludes: «It is therefore with modesty that we need to study her message, with even more modesty that we need to attempt to interpret it.»

[2] H.U. VON BALTHASAR, *Therese von Lisieux*, p. 212.

It appears useful to us, then, to precede this study with some notes concerning Thérésian methodology.[3] We choose the most useful for the present study. These are like precautions.

I. THE PERSON AND HER WRITINGS

1. Let us repeat that, with Thérèse, there is a correlation between testimony and existence. Several factors explain this relationship: (1st) First of all, Thérèse was called to make known a way of holiness that she conceived *herself*, that she prepared, assimilated, developed, and formulated; a way with which she was the first to be favored; (2nd) When she became conscious of having a mission in the Church, the *object* of this message was already almost entirely set forth in occasional writings where the nature of intimacy constantly prompted personal confessions; (3rd) Finally, still under the impulse of this late and charismatic consciousness and in light of a genuine humility which is nothing other than truth, she understood that she truly embodied the way which it was her duty to reveal and, with a certain natural and unquestionably purified inclination to help others, she proposed herself as an *example*.

It is not possible, then, to examine the message of Thérèse of Lisieux without a continual reference to her life, without an historical perspective. «Her doctrine is not so much her writings as it is her life itself, since her writings speak of almost nothing other than her life.»[4]

2. It is obvious, therefore, that the description of this message will not be very *systematic* with Thérèse. This does not mean that her doctrine doesn't contain, as a background, a coherent system, but her writings do not make it explicit. Except for Manuscript B which contains an *ex professo* clarification of her «little doctrine» and some miniature explanations, we chiefly find a number of fragments and details, in contact, it is true, with the great underlying currents of her thought. She admits in her Manuscript A: «I will

---

[3] On the *general* methodology of the hagiography, see for example M.-M. PHILIPON, *Sainte Thérèse de Lisieux...*, pp. 9-14.

[4] H.U. VON BALTHASAR, *Therese von Lisieux...*, pp. 23-24.

talk freely and without worrying about the style or the numerous digressions I will make» (A 3 v, 73), «I don't have time to reflect before writing and I write at so many different times,» but she continues to write «with the simplicity of a little child» (A 56 v, 164). The writing of Manuscript B gives evidence of hurriedness and the author warns the recipient that the explanation is made «so poorly that it seems to me impossible that you will understand it» (B 1 v, 221). As for Manuscript C, she doubts that, at certain times, she was able to «write ten lines without being disturbed» (C 17 v, 257); as for her reflections, she gathered them as though she were «fishing with a line»; she wrote whatever came from the tip of her pen! (CJ 11.6.2), and her words appear to her to be «confused and poorly expressed» (C 6 r, 242); it is a «skein» (C 18 r, 258) which «has no continuity» (C 6 r, 242). Her other writings, still less prone to encourage a systematic exposition, fall into the same pattern. If one notices, in addition to this lack of systematization, that Thérèse's terminology is rather vague, technically unfounded, and that it undergoes a delicate but unquestionable evolution, one will readily agree that with Thérèse, the meaning of a word or the significance of an image is linked closely to the immediate context and to the time of her life in which she uses it. For Thomas Aquinas, «substance» could always have meant the same thing; for Thérèse Martin, «abandonment» or «littleness» no longer meant precisely the same thing in 1897 as it did in 1888 or 1893.

The danger of slipping some arbitrary meaning under these simple and emotional terms is therefore not imaginary, and we see by this how much we must remain in close biographical relation with Thérèse. Besides, since this common vocabulary relates to universally known experiences, it always risks concealing in part the depth of its content. Jean Guitton said very appropriately that it is «these words [and he offers the term "childhood" as an example], those that are the most seemingly clear, which are the most misleading.»[5] Simple is the opposite of complicated, but not the opposite of profound. And what is simply profound gives food for thought.

The absence of systematization, moreover, makes us aware

[5] «Le Génie de sainte Thérèse de l'Enfant-Jésus», VT, 1964, p. 105.

that Thérèse did not clarify *all* the implications of her doctrine and its evolution. One finds oneself faced with the delicate task of discerning in her writings certain lines, certain insinuations, which are these few small gems that complete the mosaic.

It still follows that the testimonies of others concerning her life and her teaching are not without importance. We shall speak of these later.

3. Except for her *Act of Offering to Merciful Love* and some poems, all of Thérèse's writings were intended for others. It goes without saying that she does not open her heart in the same way to everyone. However, in the period that precedes the *Autobiographical Manuscripts*, she does not open up, in her letters, to anyone as much as to her sister Céline. Céline is «that other *myself*» (LT 90, 560), the «*sweet echo of my soul*» (LT 89, 556; 94, 577), «the SAME SOUL» (LT 65, 467), very simply «*my soul*» (LT 83, 541), «you are me» (LT 108, 629). Thérèse and Céline are the two «halves of a heart,» of the same heart (LT 102, 610). And Thérèse realizes that she opens herself to her in depth: «How easily I talk with you... It's as if I were speaking to my soul... Céline, it seems to me that I can say everything to you» (LT 96, 587), «I shall never come to an end with you.»[6] It is true that this correspondence presents a special difficulty: one must be able to illuminate it by the frequent conversations of the two sisters in the parlor of the monastery and by Céline's letters to Thérèse of which only fragments are preserved. But it nevertheless remains a marvelous source which reveals to us the soul of Thérèse. Unfortunately, when Céline entered Carmel on September 14, 1894, the letters or notes become much less numerous. Céline's *testimonies* are also precious, but they are no longer intended only for Thérèse.

4. Thérèse writes with her *heart*. She always remained gifted with a great sensitivity. This brings for example, at the age of sixteen, seventeen, eighteen years, a certain inclination toward romanticism, in the manner of youth in every age, but with characteristic

---

[6] LT 127, 724. We find many other expressions of the intimate union of the two sisters, see for example also: A 6 v-10 r, 78-84; 62r, 73; 69r, 185; 73 v, 193; 82r, 209 f.; LT 47, 423; 57, 448; 85, 546; 98, 590; 126, 722; 127, 724; 132, 740; 134, 747; 137, 760; 142, 794; 149, 826; 165, 860; 167, 870. See J. WU, «Thérèse et Céline,» in his book *Humanisme chinois, spiritualité chrétienne*, Castermann, 1965, pp. 161-180.

reference to the «evil of the century» of her time, mingled with a genuine nostalgia for Heaven amid great sufferings. However, Thérèse hates all insincerity[7] and one can be sure that she expresses herself as she is and as she feels.

The facsimile edition of the *Autobiographical Manuscripts* has the advantage of revealing, as it were, the degree of emotion with which Thérèse writes. Sometimes, one notices how the elipses [...] or exclamation marks increase on the same page, even up to sets of five or six and sometimes more; the writing enlarges or expands; Thérèse underlines, even several times; she distributes capital letters[8] generously. All these details are able to convey the atmosphere of certain passages, for example, of Manuscript B. In these cases, it can be useful to place in logical order the reflections which Thérèse causes to whirl about in an impetuous burst of feeling.

5. Let us pause for a moment on the words which Thérèse *underlines*: there we find a small methodological secret which will be useful to us. François de Sainte-Marie discerned it well: «The Saint underlines a great deal and sometimes in a surprising manner but almost always with a serious intention»; however he does not explain himself further.[9]

We believe we can indicate five reasons for which Thérèse ordinarily underlines or uses italics: to insist (several examples: A 81 r, 206-207); in antithesis: for example, little-big (A 16 r, 95; 66 r, 180), to dance-to walk (A 82 r, 208), far away-close by (A 82 v, 209); sometimes in the presence of words that have for her a personal value: this is especially the case with the word «little» (see Manuscript B), and sometimes Thérèse seems to have fun accumulating an underlined word[10]; nicknames, for example: «king, queen, fine

---

[7] «She would not lie for all the gold in the world,» writes Mrs. Martin of her youngest girl (A 11 r, 85). «I never lie,» said Thérèse at the boarding school, troubled that someone had doubted her (PO, p. 551). «She had a real horror for the least lies, even light-hearted ones,» testified Mother Agnès later (PO, p. 161).

[8] See Mss I, 55-56. According to FRANÇOIS DE SAINTE-MARIE, concerning the words endowed with a capital against the general rule: «These are for her "emotional words" loaded with significance and personal value.»

[9] Mss I, 56.

[10] For example LT 162, 85 2; A 66 r, 180; 77 r, 199.

pearl, diamond,» in letters to her father; «little ball» and «little toy» in letters to Sister Agnès; to indicate the borrowing of a phrase.

This last reason is by far the most important, because it permits us to track down several borrowed phrases and perhaps influences. Did they teach this rule to Thérèse at school, or is it, again, honesty which makes her flee the slightest hint of plagiarism? In any case, one hardly ever encounters in her writings a text from Sacred Scripture, from the *Imitation*, or from another author, without the text being set off by quotation marks, italics, a reference given in brackets, or underlining. (For these cases, cursive was moreover customary in a number of works of her time.) And Thérèse insists on it. She expressly gives instructions on her rough drafts: «The underlined words must be written in italic.»[11] How she followed the rule! Often there are only about two or three words underlined, but words which one will sometimes come across elsewhere in the same quotation reported more at length. These quotations are reflections which had impressed her and which return spontaneously to her mind: it is possible that their influence is rather important. Let us notice, lastly, that often her quotations are not exactly literal.[12]

6. In her autobiographical writings, Thérèse does not limit herself to the past. One finds there *a mixture of past and present*. She «narrates history,» in the same way as the title of Manuscript A announces it.[13] But, from the beginning, she calls attention to the «numerous digressions» that she will make: «It is not, then, my so-called life that I am going to write; it is my *thoughts* on the graces

[11] See Mss I, 16 (twice).

[12] Once she points out the «almost» of her words (C 28 v, 273).

[13] Thérèse possesses a lot of the qualities necessary to write about her beautiful «memories.» Her greatest academic successes were precisely in history and composition (A 37 v, 129), she is endowed with an excellent memory (CSG, p. 106; see also A 13 v, 90 and 37 v, 129), her intelligence opened at a very early age (A 4 v, 75), she experienced «deep» impressions (A 6 r, 77; 11 v , 86; 12 v, 88; 14 v. 91; 18 r, 97). Her interior world was much more vast than her outside world was restricted. As for the *dates* given explicitly, Thérèse is very precise. While still a child, she already liked to make personal chronologies (Mss I, 22 and 24), and later she will say: «since I've been at Carmel, I've had a good memory for dates» (LT 90, 560). As for the general datings (for example: «for four years,» «five years after»), they are usually only approximations.

that the Good God deigned to grant me» (A 3 r, 73). Constantly one comes across these present «reflections.» Thérèse describes the past, but she often compares it with the future and with the present: she points out contrasts, evolutions, or simply a continuity. She also speaks of the present without explicit relation with the past. Thus, she does not always follow the actual order of events.

It is very important to bear in mind the complex character of her autobiography and to know how to place everything in context: in this way one will avoid quite a number of incorrect interpretations. It is a history, but reflected in the mirror of the author's interior world at the time of writing. It is this which makes it a very rich source, but one that is sometimes delicate to use.

7. The *Poems* of Thérèse are also very interesting. They reveal a poetic soul — but not literarily poetic — and one sees in them how easily Thérèse embodies her reflections in symbols.[14] They illustrate many aspects of her spirituality: Jesus' love for us (manifested in His incarnation, His humanity, His death, the Eucharist), the love of Thérèse for Jesus (love concretized by the practice of virtues, the observance of religious vows, the imitation of Mary and of favorite saints). But of the fifty-four poems, six at the most were the fruit of an entirely personal inspiration[15]; the others were made on demand or for a special occasion. Thérèse is not a poet by nature and the constraint of the technique must have bothered her. Have no doubt about it: the arrangement in stanzas, the verses, the rhyme, the melody with which it was to be sung, made her often reject a word or a spontaneous sentence to look for others that were more in harmony: she «adjusted,» «composed.» In what sense does one find in these poems a faithful reflection of her thoughts?

In a letter of February 24, 1897, Thérèse answers us in a reassuring enough manner: «While composing them, I looked more at the substance than at the form, so the rules of versification are not always respected.» We therefore have a certain guarantee of the

[14] She also expresses herself in a very anthropomorphic manner about God. It is often just a way of speaking in symbols.

[15] This is especially the case with *Prayer of the Child of a Saint* (PN 8); *Living on Love* (PN 17); *To Théophane Vénard* (PN 47); *To my Little Brothers of Heaven* (PN 44); *To Joan of Arc* (PN 50); *Why I love you, O Mary* (PN 54).

personal nature of her reflections, but it is not the same with each of the expressions that she uses. And her reflections themselves have a flavor of idealization: they reveal «not what I am, but what I would like and ought to be,» they translate «my sentiments, [or rather the sentiments of the Carmelite]» (LT 220, 1058).

8. Thérèse loved *Sacred Scripture* very much and referred to it profusely, both in her writings and in her conversations.[16] Is she biblical, then? Yes, very biblical! Is she a good exegete? Let us determine whether or not she is. If it is a question of perceiving the main lines of Scripture, of reading into the «heart» of the Bible, of recognizing — as she said[17]— the «nature» of God Who reveals Himself in it, her exegesis is marvelous. And in this sense, there is no doubt that her spirituality is based solidly on the Bible. When it is a question of a particular text, then she usually interprets it and applies it very well. More than once, however, she goes beyond its immediate and concrete content. Let us explain.

First of all, one cannot expect that Thérèse, with her means and at her time, was never mistaken about the real meaning of a text. Translations of that time, based generally on the Vulgate, were imperfect. Thérèse knew this and was distressed by it (CSG, p. 107) but could not remedy it, and so she sometimes became attached to a meaning that was no longer the original, or at least that was not founded on this particular text.[18]

But there is more. Thérèse said of Holy Scripture: «All seems

---

[16] «It was believed that she knew [it] by heart,» says Marie of the Trinity (PA, p. 470), with a slight exaggeration. See some statistics in J. COURTÈS, «Les Citations bibliques dans la correspondance de Thérèse de Lisieux,» *Revue d'ascétique et de mystique*, 44 (1968), pp. 63-85 or VT, 7 (1967), pp. 38-47 and 95-103. See also FRANÇOIS DE SAINTE-MARIE, «Saint Thérèse de l'Enfant-Jésus et la Sainte Écriture,» *Cahiers Évangile*, Paris, new series n 2, 1951, pp. 41-56. Above all see *La Bible avec Thérèse* (Cerf/DDB, 1979).

[17] LT 161, 850. See Geneviève: «She scrutinized Sacred Scripture in order to know the nature of God» (PO, p. 275). See also CSG, p. 107.

[18] Let us take for example: Proverbs 9:4. This is for Thérèse a fundamental text in the spirituality of her «little way»; it is at the basis of her great discovery and at the head of a long chain of musings. The translation that Thérèse came across declared: «If someone is very little, let him come to Me.» (It is a question of an invitation of Wisdom to participate in the meal that she has prepared.) However, the Jerusalem Bible translated correctly: «Who is simple? That he passes by here!» Thérèse, who, besides, came across this verse isolated from its immediate context, was especially touched — as we shall see — by the word «little,» in truth «very little,» and attracted

luminous to me; a single word uncovers infinite horizons for my soul» (LT 226, 1092); and elsewhere, on the Gospels: «I am constantly discovering new lights in them, hidden and mysterious meanings» (A 83 v, 211). Thus, one notices that Thérèse sometimes immerses herself from the outset in «the horizon» and in «the hidden and mysterious meaning» that this or that text opened before her eyes. She had the tendency, then, to be allegorical. She understood the spirit of the Bible well. She knew the Lord of the Bible and her own Lord through the «science of Love» (B 1 r, 219) and so a single word evoked a lot more than what it contained if it was taken literally: she read «farther.» She said: «I have only to cast a glance in the Holy Gospels and immediately I breathe in the perfume of Jesus' life» (C 36 v, 285). It is good that such a «plenary» exegesis doesn't replace, but completes the exegesis of the letter. And vice versa.

II. THE TESTIMONY OF OTHERS

The unsystematic nature of Thérésian writings make external testimonies concerning her words and deeds a useful and even necessary complement.

1. Thérèse had to give a great deal of advice to others. One must understand her counsels in the light of a principle of interpretation that has been formulated well by André Combes: «Gifted with an uncommon psychological incisiveness and with a pedagogical tact which was natural and at the same time inspired, Thérèse always knew not only how to give to each of her novices the advice that, in the present circumstance, suited them, but also to adopt the very manner that would make it more comfortable to

---

by God's invitation («let him come *to Me*»). It is very unlikely that the reading of the original meaning had seized her. She must have waited for another moment of grace to be illuminated. That also shows the ways of the Lord! But let us not draw the conclusion from it that her «little way» is not founded on the Bible! The themes of childhood in the spiritual sense and divine mercy are manifest. Here, we touch upon the question of knowing how Sacred Scripture can speak to someone by means of a text or a translation that is not authentic. It is that the Inspirer of the Scriptures speaks not only through the letter, but through the entire context, and not only in the Book, but also in our heart.

understand or to accept. Hence there was a diversity going as far as contradiction in her statements relating to the application of her doctrine. To the childishness of one, she did not apply the same remedy as to the presumptuousness of another. For all matters relating to novices, a careful prudence was imperative. To attribute to each of these admonitions, and to all the formulas that express them, a value no less absolute than universal, was often to risk solidifying into doctrine the strokes of a very subtle art.»[19]

2. The testimonies which were given also constitute an object of study for an *historical critique*. In what measure do they faithfully report Thérèse's words? Are they a copy? Or do they offer the spirit of her words without rendering the letter? Or are they infiltrated with the witness' personal reaction, thus giving evidence of a new reflection? More than once, during the course of our research, comparison with «form criticism» in biblical exegesis was indispensable to us, even if only as the result of Sister Geneviève's remark warning us to no longer be «astonished by some variations of the Evangelists recalling the same event,» when she reported the *Last Conversations* in a slightly different manner than Mother Agnès did in the *Novissima Verba* (CSG, p. 222). One will perhaps smile at the thought of the problems that this «solution» raises.

But here the problem does not have the same importance nor the same scope, although it is not the simplest of all problems. Let us look into it a bit. While Thérèse was alive, and even in her presence, Mother Agnès recorded in writing some of the Saint's words.[20] Sister Geneviève, too, had already written down some of her remarks.[21] After Thérèse's death, she wrote, just as Sister Marie of the Trinity and others did, new recollections for the publication of the *Story of a Soul*. These were increased in the successive editions, which at the same time already present variations. More than six years after Thérèse's death, the sisters of Carmel once again lean

[19] «Saint Thérèse de Lisieux modèle de vie contemplative» *Ephemerides carmeliticae*, 13 (1962), p. 126. See also A. COMBES, *Sainte Thérèse de Lisieux et sa mission. Les grandes lois de la spiritualité thérésienne*, Paris-Brussels, 1954, p. 221. Combes' remarks are also appropriate for Thérèse's Letters.

[20] PO, p. 181. Thérèse benefited from it in order to complete, by this means, some of her teaching.

[21] Mss I, 32.

heavily on their memories in view of the Diocesan Process (1910-1911): the harvest is plentiful. In 1914-1915 the Apostolic Process followed; sometimes its testimonies varied with those of the previous process. Later, the sisters published separate compilations: *Conseils et Souvenirs* by Sister Geneviève (1952) and the *Novissima Verba* by Mother Agnès (1926).

This *Novissima Verba* has a longer history, which follows.[22] 1. First we had notes, taken while Thérèse was alive; unfortunately they are not preserved. 2. These notes were collected in a notebook, the «Black Notebook,» and today they, too, are destroyed (DCL). 3. This was followed by a new version, the «Green Notebooks,» in February of 1909; these are preserved. 4. They were re-worked for the *Novissima Verba* of the Process. 5. Between 1921 and 1924, Mother Agnès wrote and completed these notes again: the «Yellow Notebook.» 6. In 1927, the printed *Novissima Verba* finally followed. Let us point out the sizeable conformity between the *printed* texts: *Novissima Verba*, the «*Summarium*» of the Process, and the «*Conseils et Souvenirs*» from *Histoire d'une Âme*.

In all these testimonies of the Carmelites, Thérèse's words are recalled with rather numerous variations,[23] as much between the versions of different witnesses as between those of the same person. This demonstrates, especially in the case of Mother Agnès,[24] the danger of a personal «reaction» and this danger becomes much greater as the years pass — because it is a psychological law that memory has the tendency to alter facts as time separates us from them — and as they speak of Thérèse and think about her canonization. In order to reconstitute the authentic words of Thérèse, it will be necessary to compare the different versions in a critical manner, while favoring the oldest ones. A critical edition of the *Novissima Verba* is being prepared in Lisieux.[25] For the most important words of Thérèse, we examined them ourselves.

---

[22] Mss I, 30-32. We add to it the copy of the «Black Notebook» (2).

[23] One finds some examples in Mss I, 67-68.

[24] Up to a certain point, these annotations still reflect the psychology of Mother Agnès herself. It is she who often suggests the terminology of Thérèse, who sometimes determines the degree of tenderness in it, who chooses between the Saint's words depending on whether they impress her in the nature of her own psychology. Especially for the «last words» not yet published, this remark seems of value to us.

3. Our last remark directly concerns the depositions to the Process. The oath guarantees the veracity of the witnesses, but it goes without saying that it does not make them infallible. In fact, three questions arise from the beginning. Does the witness have a direct or indirect knowledge of the facts? Does he or she relate them accurately? Does he or she know how to situate them in their historical perspective?

There is yet another factor. While Therese was alive, numerous sisters appraised her as a holy religious, but no one imagined her eventual canonization.[26] However, soon, the reputation of holiness was broadcast extensively: *Histoire d'une Âme* (*Story of a Soul*) was read and re-read, people already spoke of miracles, pilgrimages to Lisieux had their modest beginnings; the question of beatification was beginning to impose itself. It is thus that reflection, already begun among the Carmelites during the remarkable life of Thérèse, became concentrated in an effort of recollection and penetration; the depositions to the Process were the fruits of this. But here are the dangers which, without being unavoidable, are inherent in the phenomenon. The first is that of «interpreting» and «understanding»[27] the actions and words of Thérèse in a subjective manner (be it individually or collectively following conversations[28]). The second danger — which is essentially a practical application of the first — is that of «arranging» and «accumulating» the facts, in a way leading to certain excessive accentuations. It is

---

[25] (*Note of 1994.*) These will be the *Derniers Entretiens* in two volumes, published in 1971 (Cerf/DDB). In the *Oeuvres complètes* in one volume, pp. 989-1191.

[26] See Mother Agnès, PA, p, for example, 209.

[27] Mother Agnès herself mentions this movement: «the religious... *understand perfectly now, in light of the events* [the italics are ours] everything that there was of heroism hidden in the life of which they were witnesses» (PA, p. 209). Here is a striking example of this «subjective interpretation.» (Let us remember that Thérèse's prayer was almost always very dry.) «When the Blessed Sacrament was exposed, her deep and inflamed look revealed her intimate feelings. An angel would not have contemplated with more love the One whom she contemplated under these veils made transparent by her faith. Also what ardent prayer in her simplicity: it was but an impetus, but it embraced all, the interests of God and those of souls.» (Thérèse of Saint Augustine, PA, p. 330).

[28] With respect to the (physical) face of Thérèse, FRANÇOIS DE SAINTE-MARIE notes: «The declarations of the Saint's sisters to the Process of Beatification, on which one would want to be able to lean entirely, are unfortunately tainted with a form of

thus, for example, that one notes in the second Process, conducted about five years after the first, a will, perhaps unconscious, to emphasize the suffering which Thérèse, directly or indirectly, endured because of Mother Marie de Gonzague. What results from this, it seems, is an exaggerated impression that needs to be corrected by other historical data.[29]

All this invites us to use a critical prudence and to prefer the writings of Thérèse herself to outside testimony, which nevertheless remains valuable.

---

partiality: that which is born of affection and admiration.» (VTL, *Notes et Introduction*, Lisieux, 1961, p. 17). Later he adds, still speaking of the Saint's *physical* appearance: «The Sisters of Carmel, living in an enclosed environment, where one was easily influenced by the written word, by imagery where the ideal had the tendency little by little to supplant the real. They also influenced one another until they finally arrived at a sort of common vision of Thérèse in which a large portion of projection entered» (*Ibid.*, p. 41).

[29] Some authors didn't know how to apply rules of the historical criticism to the depositions of the Processes. The works of A. BARRIOS MONEO suffer the same shortcoming. (See *La espiritualidad de santa Teresa de Lisieux a la luz de los Procesos de su canonización y de sus «Manuscritos autobiográficos»*, Madrid, 1958, 2 vol., 288 and 277 pp. Also *Santa Teresita modelo y martir de la vida religiosa. Historia documentada en los Procesos de su canonización y en sus Manuscritos autobiográficos*, Madrid, 1960, 418 pp.). It is also a weak point in the biography of G. PAPASOGLI, *S. Teresa di Lisieux*, Milan, 1967, 678 pp.

First Part

THE DISCOVERY

Thérèse could not have kept silent, in her autobiographical writings, about one of the greatest graces of her life. She related how a light suddenly came to shine on a troublesome question: how will I become holy, me, a weak human being? The solution did not come without preparation and yet it took on the form of a new discovery: Thérèse had discovered her «little way of spiritual childhood.»

Let us set out from there. Let us analyze the content of this grace in order to find in it the basic core that will have to direct our entire investigation, as much from the evolutionary as from the structural point of view: thus we shall avoid presenting a preconceived notion of Thérèse's way toward holiness. But the question immediately emerges of the chronological place which this experience occupies because Thérèse herself didn't put a date on it. An answer is crucial if we want to retrace its preparation and describe its unfolding.

However another question is of prime importance: in her narration, Thérèse speaks most of a «little way, short, straight and totally new»; is this actually the same as the «way of spiritual childhood»? This answer, too, has its importance and we are going to attempt to provide one.

Some readers will not find the pages in the first and the third chapters of this part to their liking since they are sometimes a little technical. They were nevertheless necessary in order to establish well the basis for all the development that follows. It is our desire that the joy of following Thérèse in her spiritual ascent and doctrine be realized as much as possible in the truth.

Chapter I

Thérèse and the Formula of «Spiritual Childhood»

Whereas «spiritual childhood» has been mentioned so often with relation to Thérèse of Lisieux, it is astonishing to learn that one scans her autobiographical writings, letters, and poems in vain to find this formula even a single time. It is entirely possible, however, that the nun used it in her oral teaching and, indeed, more than once we encounter it in the witnesses' depositions, and we come across it at the very heart of a solemn declaration regarding her mission. Do these provide us with a solid point of departure? Let us not forget the difficulties already mentioned regarding these testimonies. We will now examine a first example.

I. «SPIRITUAL CHILDHOOD» IN THE TESTIMONIES OF OTHERS

Let us begin with a very interesting little piece of dialogue between Mother Agnès and her sick sister as it is reported in the first edition of *Histoire d'une Âme* (1898).[1]

«What is this way you want to teach to souls?»

«Mother, it's *the way of confidence and total abandon*. I want to teach them the little means» (p. 241).

In six successive editions, it remains as such. But in 1907 it undergoes a modification. Now Mother Agnès asks what «little»

[1] Several of our first findings have already been established by FRANÇOIS DE SAINT-MARIE, Ch. BERNARD (see n. 2) and S. PIAT (*À la découverte…*, pp. 350-356). But it is good to recapture them systematically here and to reinforce them.

way Thérèse intends to teach. And her sister answers: «*It is the way of spiritual childhood, the way of confidence*» (p. 244). It is in this manner that our printed sources, including the *Summarium* and the *Novissima Verba*, express themselves thereafter. The unpublished sources (CV of February 1909 and CJ) on the contrary, are silent. Is there any way we can determine which is the authentic version?

Solely from the point of view of the literary critic, everything would lead us to believe that the words «the way of spiritual childhood» are interpolated. We cannot explain why such a beautiful formula would have been suppressed if it were original. And yet, if some omissions had to be made, how can we explain why the redactors would have gone so far as to leave out the certainly Thérésian expression «little way,» at Mother Agnès' request, when in fact it was used only eight lines above in the text in question? When the dialogue was reviewed, *additions* were made, not deletions.

If the expression in question is an addition, many reasons can be given to justify it. Thérèse had given full authority to her sister Agnès «to delete something, or to add, whatever she would have told her by word of mouth» (NV 16.7.2, see DE II, 164), and one could rightfully presume that this authorization was not limited to the autobiography alone. Furthermore, this formula made Thérésian doctrine synthetic: Thérèse had so often had recourse to the symbol of a child to illustrate her filial approach to God. She often used in her writings the expressions «childlike virtues» (PN 13; Pri 14) and «virtues of childhood» (PN 24). Besides, the formula had a pronounced evangelical accent and brought to mind a number of patristic, medieval, and modern spiritual references.[2] Therefore, it was both beautiful and effective. But there is another reason that prevents us from welcoming it as coming literally from Thérèse.

[2] See the valuable article «Enfance spirituelle» with bibliography, *Dictionnaire de spiritualité*, t. IV, cd. 682-714 (Ancien Testament, Nouveau Testament, Pères de l'Église by M.F. BERROUARD, Moyen Âge et temps modernes by FRANÇOIS DE SAINTE-MARIE and Ch. BERNARD). The formula «spiritual childhood» is encountered already in Julienne de Norwich († 1442), but J. ROBILLIARD («Sainte Thérèse de L'Enfant-Jésus et de la Sainte-Face, Sainte de lumière et de clarté,» *Revue des sciences philosophiques et théologiques*, 40 [1956], pp. 670-679) points it out beforehand in Adam de Perseigne († 1221) (PL 211, 651). Evidently, the formula in itself only has a very reduced value.

It is the concession of the witnesses. In fact, Sister Geneviève did not hesitate to declare: «She herself didn't call it "Spiritual Childhood," but rather "her Little Way," "her Little Doctrine".... Mother Agnès... thereafter popularized the "little way" under the name of spiritual childhood.»[3] François de Sainte-Marie and Stéphane Piat, both very informed individuals, speak in a similar manner.[4] We, in turn, collected the testimony of a contemporary of Mother Agnès; the latter (Mother Agnès) affirmed that she herself had introduced the formula; undoubtedly she had not suspected that even the small details regarding Thérèse would acquire such interest and she launched her sister's doctrine under a very appropriate term that would soon develop to the point of becoming part of the language of popes and theology.[5] Thérèse, who on earth would perhaps have recoiled for a moment before a title so solemn and already somewhat abstract, is probably rejoicing in Heaven.

The formula appears yet another time in Thérèse's words, re-

---

3 See M.-M. PHILIPON, «Comment ma Sainte petite Soeur eut l'idée de sa petite Voie d'Enfance spirituelle,» ED, 28 (1952), p. 195.

4 Refer to the works cited in notes 1 and 2.

5 Where had Mother Agnès drawn her inspiration? Had she heard this formula from a priest or a theologian? Had she developed it herself from Thérèse's spirit, according to the formula «spirit of childhood» that she had already used during her sister's life (see S. PIAT, *À la découverte...*, p. 353; the expression is found again in an 1889 poem by Mother Agnès — DCL) and that already appeared in HA 98, p. 227? Or was she following the expression the «way of childhood» that Mother Marie-Ange de l'Enfant-Jésus already used in 1906 (see her *obituary Circular*, p. 10)? It is also possible that the source is found with Bishop GAY, but not in the place that was mentioned by François de Sainte-Marie and S. Piat. In fact, in his well-known work *De la vie et des vertus chrétiennes considérées dans l'état religieux* (1874), he says regarding the state of abandonment (we quote and italicize from the eleventh edition of 1888, Paris-Poitiers, t. III, p. 180):

«Will I say the *last* name of this blessed and sublime state? It is the life of God's children, it is holy *spiritual childhood!* Oh, how perfect it is! more perfect, I already told you, than the love of suffering, because nothing immolates man so much as to be sincerely and peacefully little. Pride... the spirit of childhood kills it much more surely than the spirit of penance.» He again compares the abandoned soul to a child (p. 174 and 182) and says: «Childhood, the same as abandonment, is the grace proper to Christianity» (p. 181). If Mother Agnès didn't know these passages, others could have spoken of them to her. The comparison of these pages with Thérèse's way of «total abandonment,» which she, too, prefers to penance and in which she resorts to the image of the child, could have been at the origin of the new Lisieux formula.

corded by Mother Agnès.[6] But since it is missing in all the copies prior to 1910 (CV and all of the editions of HA after 1899), we must consider once more that it was interpolated, leaning again on the reasons that we have just set forth.[7]

As for the question of knowing whether the Process of beatification can subsequently inform us, we obviously face a great difficulty. Marie of the Trinity and Marie of the Angels affirm, in passing, that Thérèse used this expression.[8] But from whom did they hear it? Several years had already passed since the formula was introduced and had become commonly used. And even Mother Agnès and Sister Geneviève, who informed us of the real state of things, readily attributed the expression to Thérèse.[9] Regarding this, one therefore cannot use the depositions and, whatever the case may be, they yield before the more categorical confessions.

Here other findings are essential. If from now on Thérèse's message is inseparable from the beautiful formula of «spiritual childhood» — which has become classic and almost official — it is pointless to strive hard to find it in the Thérésian corpus, or to interpret it *a priori* or to interpret it *a priori* according to what it means at first glance or in the manner in which theologians and even Thérèse scholars have been able to elaborate on it. One must, on the contrary, by an assiduous examination and while collating the other formulations and descriptions of Thérèse, establish what «the child» symbolizes for her and therein deduce her notion of «spiritual childhood.»

---

[6] «With the virgins we shall be virgins [in Heaven]; with the doctors, doctors; with the martyrs, martyrs, because all the saints are our relatives; but those who've followed the way of spiritual childhood will always retain the charms of childhood» (NV 16.7.2; see DE II, 164). This text also appears in CJ (13.7.12; DE II, 258 s.) and PO, p. 192.

[7] One comes across the expression «way of childhood» again in another dialogue with Thérèse, but this time in a sentence of Mother Agnès: «You are very blessed to be chosen to show to souls the "Way of Childhood"!» (from HA 23, p. 269). Again, the formula is revealed as foreign to the original dialogue, because before it was a matter of being happy «to do good, to procure God's glory» (from HA 99, p. 274) or «to show a path of love and confidence» (CJ 21.7.5 and CV; it is not entirely certain whether this is a matter of the same dialogue here).

[8] Marie of the Trinity, PO, p. 467 and PA, p. 475. Marie of the Angels, PO, p. 414.

[9] Mother Agnès, PA, p. 165 and elsewhere. Sister Geneviève, PO, pp. 287, 301 and PA, p. 290.

II. «SPIRITUAL CHILDHOOD» AND «THE LITTLE WAY»

And is the formula «little way» literally Thérésian? Without a doubt! The surprise here is in the fact that one encounters it only a single time in Thérèse's entire output: in the writing of her discovery.[10] And although no outward sign (underlining, cursive writing, or quotation marks) gives it a particular emphasis, the word «little» doesn't seem to be a pure diminutive as one finds so often with Thérèse, but on the contrary it is presented in clear opposition with the way of saints who are not weak and little like Thérèse: it is therefore filled with a specific importance. Here the expression «little way» does not yet capture the *entire* Thérésian doctrine of spiritual childhood, but, placing itself at the center of this doctrine, it does contain its seed.[11] Besides, there is no legitimate reason to doubt that Thérèse verbalized it and did this again and again. The witnesses attest to it in abundance,[12] and one comes across the formula from the very first edition of *Histoire d' une Âme*.[13] Still, there is room to admit that, later on, and in order to designate the same reality, the formula crept in a certain number of times during the re-composition of Thérèse's dialogues; however, it is difficult and not that important to indicate these cases.[14]

But is the formula «little way» completely equivalent to that of «spiritual childhood»? The question has merit, because André Combes, an authoritative Thérèse theologian, has always refused to identify the two. We shall have to take up this exceptional posi-

[10] «I want to seek out a means of going to Heaven by a little way, a way that is very straight, very short, and totally new» (C 2 v, 237).

[11] What is the relationship between the words «little way» in the writings and the stereotypical formula of the same name? It is possible that the account had the same origin as the formula, which, in this case, would become more common in the following months. It is also possible that the formula came first and that Thérèse afterwards is referring to it. We do not know how things actually happened.

[12] For example PO, pp. 287, 289, 414, 456, 519-520; PA, pp. 165, 275, 290, 291, 303, 559... and CSG, pp. 38 and 56. Often the formula is joined to the other: «little way of [spiritual] childhood.»

[13] HA 98, 241. This is the only time it is used in this first edition.

[14] Another example can also illustrate this natural tendency to *clarify* Thérèse's images and formulas. CJ 7.7.3 gives: «I was a long time before settling into this degree of abandonment. Now, I am there! The good God took me in His arms and put me there!» However, all the editions of HA from 1898 (p. 321) did not use the words «in His arms.»

tion soon, but from now on it is undeniable that the entire Thérésian tradition, that of the witnesses,[15] that of the faithful, that of theologians[16] — with the exception of Combes — all unanimously affirm the identity of the two formulas. The analysis of the discovery will immediately prove the accuracy of this conclusion. It is a matter of the «little way *of* spiritual childhood.»

[15] Mother Agnès who introduced the formula «the way of spiritual childhood» gives it exactly in answer to the question: «What little way do you want to teach?,» as we have seen. In the same way, the witnesses at the Process speak readily of the «little way of spiritual childhood» (see n. 12). See also CSG, p. 56 and 57.

[16] We know of no exception but Combes. To cite only one witness, famous for his perspicacious mind and his careful judgments, let us quote the future Pope Pius XII, Cardinal PACELLI: «[Thérèse's doctrine] is contained in these two words: Spiritual Childhood, or in these two other equivalents: Little Way» (Speech of July 11, 1937). In his radio message of July 11, 1954, he speaks simply of the «little way of childhood» (See *Acta apostolicae sedis*, 46 [1954], p. 405).

CHAPTER II

Analysis of a Discovery

Thérèse described the discovery of her «little way of spiritual childhood» in Manuscript C, written in June 1897. However, this account clearly relates to a time already past. To analyze its content and to date the experience will be the object of the following pages.

The account (C 2 v-3 r, 237-238) is characteristic of Thérèse: simple and subtle at the same time. The coherence of ideas is clear; the abundance of images, on the contrary, involves difficulties of exegesis, especially when one aims to translate the language of metaphors and emotions into the language of concepts. If we want to free our minds of the images to which she closely adheres, we will have to know how to familiarize ourselves with this type of expression which, although sufficiently intelligible, has nevertheless become somewhat foreign in our time. Still, it is not without joy that one penetrates into the psychology of Thérèse Martin.

I. SYMBOLIC LANGUAGE AND SIGNIFIED REALITY

When Mother Marie de Gonzague ordered Sister Thérèse to write her autobiography, the nun readily acquiesced. Just as she had recognized the hand of God in the «strong» education that the prioress had given her at the beginning of her religious life, so she read the will of God in the present order. «How different are the ways by which the Lord leads souls!» Thérèse thought. Among the saints there are some who left no written memoirs; others, on the other hand, did publish the graces they received from God. But they all «followed the movement of the Holy Spirit» and so, «all is well, when one seeks only the will of Jesus.»

This is what immediately precedes the narration of the discovery of the «little way.» The transition is not very transparent. But it is perhaps her reflection on the «ways» and the «saints» that led the Carmelite to speak of her own way to holiness.

The narration contains five principal elements which we are going to describe one by one: a desire, a distance, an interior certitude, a search, and God's response.

1. The account begins by pointing out an old *desire*: «You know, Mother, I have always wanted to be a saint.» This is a very important confession. The ideal of holiness will dominate the entire narration: the invention — this term is from Thérèse herself — of the «little way» will only be a means of attaining this goal. Its *functional* character therefore imposes itself from this point on: the «little way» is not a goal in itself; it is a means, a «way.» What does this term «saint» mean here? Must it be taken in the sense of «little» saint, or of «great» saint, two other stereotyped formulas of Thérèse, which she already uses at this time and which have a very proper meaning? No, there are still no exterior motives here. Thérèse is simply thinking about the saints she has spoken of and of whom she will speak later: men and women either canonized or canonizable. In other words: she aspires to a very great love — that is the essential thing — which, according to her feeling, is still far beyond her.

2. She is therefore conscious of the great *distance* that still separates her from it: «But alas! I have always noticed that when I compared myself to the saints, there is between them and me the same difference that exists between a mountain whose summit is lost in the clouds and the obscure grain of sand trampled underfoot by passers-by.»[1] This observation is as old as the desire for holiness itself: having «always desired» holiness, she has «always noticed» the distance that separates her from it, even today. But... subjective impression and objective truth don't always agree.

3. An *interior certitude* keeps the nun from feeling troubled by

---

[1] See her letter of November 10, 1887: «How little I seemed in the presence of these gigantic mountains [of Switzerland]» (LT 31 A, 317).

her observations: «Instead of becoming discouraged, I said to myself: God cannot inspire unrealizable desires; I can, therefore, in spite of my littleness, aspire to holiness. It is impossible for me to grow up, and so I must put up with myself as I am with all my imperfections.» How beautiful it is to be able to say in all honesty of conscience: 'It is impossible for me to grow up.' One sees by this that Thérèse did everything in her power to fill the gap, but in vain: she sees herself as far from being holy, she always believes herself to be little in holiness and full of imperfections.[2] However, she also believes that this cannot validly prevent her from aspiring to her ideal. Obliged to accept her state of imperfection by the impossibility of growing up — that is, of growing up by her own power[3] — she holds on to the assurance that perfection is not out of reach for her. From where does this certainty come? From the fundamental conviction that «God cannot inspire unrealizable desires.» Later we will return to this conviction which seems to owe its origin to the authority of Saint John of the Cross. Let us point out only that it will appear again elsewhere as a true minor premise in Thérèse's reasoning. The conclusion that ensues from her statements is that a means of attaining perfection must exist.

4. Here is Thérèse in *search*: «But I want to seek out a means of going to Heaven by a little way, a way that is very straight, very short, and totally new. We are now living in an age of inventions, and we no longer need to take the trouble of climbing stairs, for, in the homes of the rich, an elevator replaces these very successfully. As for me, I would also like to find an elevator which would raise me to Jesus, because I am too small to climb the rough stairway of perfection.»

The fundamental thought is very simple: find a solution to the problem; find, in spite of irreparable weakness, a means of attaining holiness. Let us follow Thérèse for a moment in the flexibility of her depictions.

---

[2] Later, we will explain the nature of these «imperfections» and we will see if they remain, once one has become a «saint.» Here, Thérèse doesn't express her opinion.

[3] A. COMBES says it well: «The word of God for which she searches is a word that, defining the spiritual status of those who are irreparably little, teaches them in spite of everything how they can become saints.» (*Introduction à la spiritualité de sainte Thérèse de L'Enfant-Jésus*, Paris, 1948, 2nd ed., p. 295 — henceforth called *Introduction...*).

Why does she speak about going «to Heaven»? Is she explicitly thinking about beatitude? No. She always considers earthly holiness: there is the problem. Several factors seem to mingle here in her imagination: the image of the mountain (symbol of saints) «whose summit is lost in the clouds,» the image that she already has in mind of «the elevator» which rises, and especially the thought of Jesus Whom she pictures up there in Heaven.

She also specifies in a pleasing way her notion of holiness: it is «to be raised to Jesus,» that is to say, to be united to Him. To unite, and the union: two terms that will be repeated a number of times. The notion must be defined further, but here is a first attempt.

And why does she take an «elevator» and not the «stairway»? The image of the elevator, resulting from the solution that Thérèse found and which consists — it is again symbolism — in being carried by Jesus, is well chosen. The steep staircase requires a disproportionate effort from Thérèse, the «little one» — therein lies its «roughness.» But the other means does not require a great deal of strength: it is enough to take one's place in the elevator and to let oneself be carried. Here is a little way, very «straight» because it is entirely vertical, very «short» because it avoids the spirals of the staircase, «totally new»... at least at the time.[4]

5. Thérèse has *found* «the elevator» which she was seeking. God enlightened her in the reading of two scriptural texts. Let us read the passages. «I searched, then, in the Scriptures for some sign of this elevator, the object of my desires, and I read these words which came from the mouth of Eternal Wisdom: *Whoever is a* LITTLE ONE *let him come to me*. And so I succeeded. I felt that I had found what I was looking for; and wanting to know, O my God, what You would do to the very little one who answered Your call, I continued my search and this is what I found: — *As one whom a mother caresses, so I will comfort you; you shall be carried at the breasts, and upon the knees they shall dandle you!* Ah! Never did words more tender and more melodious come to give joy to my soul. The elevator which must raise me to Heaven is Your arms, O Jesus! And for this I had no need to grow up, but rather I had to remain little

[4] The image was *up-to-date* in her day! Today, would Thérèse speak of an escalator or... of a spaceship? Or... would she have not used these images?

and become this more and more. Oh my God, You have surpassed all my expectations, and I want only to sing of Your Mercies.»

Let us pause at the first biblical text (Proverbs 9:4). Why does this sentence impress Thérèse? First, because the nun feels that it concerns her personally: she is the «little one,» there is here a message for her. Then because she is invited to «come to Jesus,» to come near Him, that is to say, to unite herself to Him as she had dreamed of doing.[5]

In the writing of this verse, two words attract attention: *very little*. Writing in cursive, Thérèse also underlined them, as the photocopy shows. Was this from a nervous trait or deliberately? It is without a doubt that Thérèse acted consciously and intentionally here, because we will again encounter the same words on other occasions always highlighted.[6] It is a small detail that one cannot lose sight of, because it has a special importance.

In the reading of this text, Thérèse supposes that she is moving in the right direction and she «continues her search» until she finds Isaiah 66:12-13. Then the supposition becomes certainty! 'To be very little and to go to Jesus as a very little one' is the way to experience His maternal goodness, to be taken in His arms, raised up to His breast: 'the elevator is the arms of Jesus.' He Himself raises the little one up and unites her to Himself. It is precisely the means for which Thérèse was searching!

What, then, in conceptual language, are the dispositions of the two protagonists, hidden behind this cascade of images? On the one hand, God reveals Himself in Thérèse's eyes as the One Who loves the little one, Who invites the little one close to Him and

---

[5] It is possible that Thérèse found there the echo of an evangelical Gospel which she loved (CSG, p. 41, and PA, p. 165), and which even has a textual ring: «Let *the little children come to Me*» (Lk 18:16). Thérèse kept several holy pictures, even since her childhood, which represented this scene in the Gospel (DCL).

[6] See B 1 r, 220, where the two words are underlined; CSG, p. 43 (facsimile of the autograph), where they are written bigger. The verse from the Bible appears again on the autograph of Poem 44 (see Mss 1, 15), where the adjective is capitalized («very Little» — see French edition of DLTH, p. 224 — and not «Very Little,» as Mss gives). We come across the text a fifth time on a picture (see VTL, photo 43. Thérèse is holding it in her hands), but everything is written in capitals without highlighting. In an unpublished note from Mother Agnès to Thérèse (see chap. III, n. 2), the words are again highlighted.

Who, if the other accepts this invitation, fills her with a tender maternal love, an open, uniting love. Although the word «mercy» is not used in the two biblical texts, the notion is understood, because God describes Himself as a love that leans toward what is little and powerless. And, besides, Thérèse doesn't hesitate to see therein a reason to «sing of the mercies» of the Lord. For his part, man must accept his littleness, which implies a sincere humility: it is the condition required of those who are invited. And he must «come to God» like a child. What does this mean? For it is not, obviously, a question of a physical approach. To come to God in the consciousness of one's own littleness means to recognize that He is merciful, that is to say, to believe in Him, but more still to have confidence that this divine love will fill me in spite of my misery, and it is to embody this confidence in an act of surrender, through which I express my love.

Does powerlessness remain a hindrance, then? No, because it does not by any means prevent the confidence and surrender which are the conditions required for God Himself to give us His love, His grace which increases our love. «For this I had no need to grow up,» said Thérèse, «but rather I had to remain *little* and become more and more little.»

It is here that the mysterious emphasis on the words «very little» will reveal its secret. Thérèse had read that God invites the «very little» and that it is on his behalf, if he consents to it, that God puts His love to work. The conclusion? Thérèse is little, but 'she must *remain* little and *become more and more little*' to the point of being VERY little[7]! It is then that she will be able to perfectly receive God's love, which will live perfectly in her! It is there that the words «very little,» thanks to a very literal exegesis, describe for Thérèse an ideal, a true «way,» and we shall see that they become a formula of predilection and like a slogan, a leitmotiv. The two words «very little» do therefore contain much more than a

---

[7] On this fundamental point, we separate ourselves from A. COMBES, according to whom Thérèse would have gone beyond her text: «It is necessary,» declares Thérèse, while exceeding the requirements of her text, «to become more and more little» (*Introduction…*, p. 296). S. PIAT, on the other hand, limited his attention to this important account of the discovery to quote the most important passage (*À la découverte…*, p. 137). Farther on, he returns, it is true, to the symbol of the elevator (p. 296).

synonym of humility. They indicate the whole of all the tendencies that we have enumerated. It is an attitude of our entire being. One will easily understand that they do not imply a tolerance of wretchedness and imperfections: no, Thérèse will always press on towards the limit where «it is impossible to grow up.» But on the subject of this littleness, great as it is, she affirms that imperfections are not a hindrance, but very much the opposite.

We can now contain the «little way» in a first definition precisely as the account of the discovery suggests. It is a way toward holiness which consists in humbly recognizing one's state of imperfection and in having confidence in the mercy of God Who Himself will give us the grace of His love. This is a definition on the static plane. If we consider it on the dynamic plane, it consists in always progressing in this attitude, which Thérèse indicates with the expression «to become more and more little.»

Many nuances will yet attach themselves to this notion, stemming from other Thérésian descriptions. But here we have the core.

II. «THE ELEVATOR.»
ORIGIN AND RELATIVITY OF AN IMAGE

At this point, we must return to a question concerning the historical investigation that will shortly be in progress. This question also suggests the spirit in which we must conduct the examination.

In the first days of June 1897, the nun speaks then of an «elevator,» an image that she will use again in her letter of July 18. Is it at the same moment when she was in search of her way of holiness that she imagined it as such? Without a doubt, she was familiar with elevators: she had seen them in Paris and in Italy and sometimes she spoke of them to the other nuns.[8] Or is it only later, after the discovery of her «little way,» that she resorts to this image, perhaps at the time of the actual writing? The two hypotheses are plausible.

Everything seems to indicate that the second is in fact verified; this is the thesis to which André Combes came in the end[9] and

---

[8] Mss II, 67.

François de Sainte-Marie welcomed it with sympathy.[10] In fact, among Thérèse's «last words» appears an answer concerning a note of Mother Agnès, which bears this crucial passage: «You were telling me [in your note] that He [God] had not made me climb the rough stairway of perfection like others, but that He had placed me in an elevator so that I might be brought to Him more speedily.»[11] This statement is dated «May 21st to 26th.»[12] The actual note no longer exists. Now, in these days, on May 23rd, Thérèse writes to Mother Agnès: «[You are] the Angel whom Jesus sent before me *to prepare the way*, the way leading to Heaven, the elevator lifting me without fatigue to the infinite regions of love» (LT 229, 1098). Who used this image first? The internal critique seems to have to grant priority to Mother Agnès. In fact, Thérèse says that her sister has «prepared» the elevator for her, but overall she is content to evoke the image with a single word — which supposes that the recipient is already familiar with it and knows what it is about — whereas in the «last words» she believes it necessary to explain herself more fully.[13] Here there is an additional factor: previously one never encountered the image of the elevator with Thérèse, where she often speaks of being carried in Jesus' arms; after the exchanges of May 1897, the image returns. It appears likely, therefore, that Mother Agnès inspired the symbol and that Thérèse enthusiastically took hold of it; her correspondence showed, moreover, that she willingly returned to the ideas and symbols that others suggested to her.

Or must one surrender to the temptation to regard the symbol in Mother Agnès's note as interpolated afterwards?[14] In fact, the oldest versions of this note (HA from 1899, p. 227) do not give

---

[9] *Le Problème de l'Histoire d'une Âme et des Oeuvres complètes de sainte Thérèse de Lisieux*, Paris, 1950, pp. 103-109 — henceforth referred to as *Le Problème....*

[10] Mss II, 67.

[11] CJ 21-26.5.11. COMBES quotes with slight variations (*Le Problème...*, pp. 104-105) from another copy which was not preserved (DCL).

[12] In fact, see also HA 99, 227: «some days» before May 28th.

[13] In this case, the use of the indefinite article («*an* elevator») in the «Words,» and of the definite article («the elevator») in her letter of May 23, could confirm this interpretation.

[14] (*Note of 1994.*) Thus did we write, twenty-five years ago. The thorough research that was necessary for the critical edition of the *Oeuvres Complètes* of Thérèse (See

this passage (why omit it if it was original?), but: «You were telling me [that I was] on the verge of receiving from the hand [of God] the eternal crown.» Is not the introduction of the symbol of the elevator another example of this tendency (not entirely illegitimate), which we have noted before, to explain the text?

For now, let us disregard this problem. Already the very possibility of a delayed conception of the image of the elevator merely reminds us of a very important rule: the concept is not necessarily covered immediately by a symbol; the symbol can be attached to it much later.[15] Often we are overly concerned with finding this or that symbol, this or that symbolic action in Thérèse's spiritual itinerary. We should on the contrary, before all else, establish the conceptual core of her representations (symbolic or not): if we find this core, we must not preoccupy ourselves with not finding its symbol; on the other hand, if we find a symbol, let us first examine the reality it designates, because some symbols can have more than one meaning. It is therefore possible that Thérèse, at the time of discovering an answer to the means of becoming holy, did not think of an elevator and a staircase, nor of a way that was straight, short and new. Perhaps she also did not compare herself to an obscure grain of sand, or to the saints, to whom she knew herself to be inferior, or to some mountains, etc. All this can easily be a symbolic expression which her thought assumed only later and even at the time of writing.[16]

DE, words from 21/26.5.11 with the note d, and LT 229 with the note c) now allows us to think that Mother Agnès' «note» in question, and which, in any case, is not preserved, had actually never existed. In fact, why would this note not have been preserved by Thérèse, who had preserved others of much less significance? By the expression «little word,» Mother Agnès undoubtedly condensed some oral communications. Our problem shifts, then, in two ways: 1. Did Mother Agnès interpolate her first annotation, prepared for the edition of HA, while later introducing the symbol of the elevator to it? That appears very likely. 2. Has there been, in the *oral* exchanges, priority for Mother Agnès in the use of the symbol? From the way in which Thérèse speaks of it in LT 229, we think so.

[15] See (Mss II, 67): «Moreover, a reality always surpasses the symbol that expresses it and the image, as adequate as it is, ordinarily does not come but rather late to fulfill its role of explanation.»

[16] «It is not the image [of the elevator] that is important, but the concept.» Thus GABRIEL DE SAINTE-MARIE-MADELEINE, «Settimana di studio su Santa Teresa del B.G. Risultati,» *Rivista di Vita Spirituale,* 2 (1948), p. 216.

III. IN DIRECT SERVICE OF THE SANCTIFICATION OF OTHERS?

We have just enumerated several symbols, separable from the moment of the discovery. The symbol of the *child* is not to be found on the list. Since the discovery of the way of holiness came with the reading of the two verses of the Bible which expressed themselves with the help of the symbol of a child, this symbol cannot be historically separated, at the time of the discovery, from the reality symbolized. Thérèse was compelled by the scriptural passages themselves to *think* of the «very little,» of «the child,» and to compare herself to it.

This symbol is therefore of great value. By its presence alone, it can recall right away the entire perspective of the «little way.» (But it is also possible that it reveals but one aspect of it; one must study its real significance.) We have done well, then, to see in this discovery of the «little way» the discovery of «spiritual childhood» itself.[17]

However, since 1950, André Combes has been opposed to this way of thinking. According to him, it is a question of two experiences and two different spiritual discoveries. The discovery of the «little way» had to answer to the problem of personal sanctification (we are in agreement on this point!), while the discovery of «spiritual childhood» had to answer to the problem of the sanctification of others.[18] In order to establish this second thesis, Combes

---

[17] See also Mss II, 66.

[18] Here is a clear explanation of COMBES: «Let's try, now, to disassemble the mechanism of the two Thérésian inventions...: the *elevator* and *spiritual childhood*. Before considering each of these two inventions in itself, let's note that they must be treated one and the other as techniques.... Any error, on one or on the other, threatens in the most direct and most serious way the interpretation of the Thérésian message. Therefore, these two inventions are bound together by affinities of such nature that no one can flatter himself to understand one well if he is mistaken about the other. They are alike, first of all, in this, that one and the other were necessary for Thérèse in order for an inherent impossibility in her spiritual itinerary to become surmountable. The elevator appeared in line with her personal sanctification: without it, Thérèse declares to us, it would have been impossible. Spiritual childhood — whatever one could have believed and could have said on this subject — presented itself as a solution to a radically different problem: the problem of supernatural and apostolic action» (*Sainte Thérèse de l'Enfant-Jésus. Contemplation et apostolat*, Bonne Press, 1950, pp. 118-119. See also pp. 125 and 143). Although the author seems to avoid, in this book, calling «the elevator» the «little way,» the identification is automatically made since Thérèse herself considers them as synonyms.

supports himself with a text of Thérèse written in 1897, which, according to him, refers to an experience of February 1893, when her sister Agnès, the new prioress, asked Thérèse to look after the novices. Here is the passage in question: «My dear Mother [this is Mother Marie de Gonzague], I have recalled to you the first work that Jesus and you saw fit to accomplish through me; this was only the prelude of those which were to be entrusted to me. When I was given the office of entering into the sanctuary of souls, I immediately saw that the task was beyond my strength. Then I threw myself into the arms of God like a little child and, hiding my face in His hair [!], I said: Lord, I am too little to nourish your children; if you wish to give them through me what is suitable for each one, fill my little hand and, without leaving your arms or turning my head, I shall give Your treasures to the soul who will come and ask for nourishment» (C 22 r-v, 264-265). The thesis is too important and its defender too qualified for us not to lend him our attention.

Of course, the quoted text deals with a problem other than that of sanctification proper. But several reasons prevent us from going along with the opinion which sees, in the solution of this problem, the discovery of «spiritual childhood.» For, as we have already said, in the discovery of «the elevator,» the symbol of the child was inherent in the sources themselves. On the other hand, while receiving the order to look after the novices, it is hardly sure that Thérèse compared herself explicitly to a little child. It is possible that only later, even at the time of recalling this episode, she would have consciously referred herself to the symbols of the child and the father who carries her. (The symbol of the *elevator* was perhaps an analogous case, as we have seen.) Why refuse Thérèse the right to also use here a symbol, imagined later, to express a

---

Besides, there is no reason to doubt the thought of Combes. He himself said elsewhere on «the elevator»: «There is nothing more typically Thérésian nor more central to the doctrine of the little way» (*Le Problème*..., p. 105). The distinction willingly returns in the author's later works: see *Sainte Thérèse de Lisieux et sa Mission*..., pp. 83-84 and 213 and «Un exemple à proposer: l'espérance dans la prière de Sainte Thérèse de Lisieux,» *Lumen vitae*, 9 (1954), p. 513 (implicitly) and «Sainte Thérèse de Lisieux modèle de vie contemplative,» *Ephemerides carmeliticae*, 13 (1962), p. 105.

(*Note of 1994.*) Let us also add the work of which we only had knowledge subsequently, *De doctrina spirituali sanctae Theresiae a Jesu Infante* (Coll. Spiritualités, 6), Rome-Paris, 1967, pp. 125, 135 and 259.

previous experience? At the discovery of her insufficiency, perhaps Thérèse could have thought only to ask, with humility and great confidence, for the help, love, and goodness of God, the source of all good, joining with this request the resolution to always keep herself united to Him alone.[19] Connections with the symbols were perhaps made afterwards. This is a real possibility, which gives André Combes' opinion a less solid basis.

But above all, it appears arbitrary to want to recognize «spiritual childhood» behind the symbol of the child in God's arms (C 22 r, 264), and to refuse it where the same symbol is as much present, and in an intrinsic way (C 3 r, 238). All of tradition has, unanimously and with reason, turned to the last case to recognize in it the invention of «the elevator» and of the «little way,» and of «spiritual childhood.» This is why André Combes' first interpretation, which permitted him to use the three terms equally, was preferable.[20]

According to Combes — and also according to us, but in a different way — Thérèse's decision concerning her duty to the novices takes place *after* the discovery of the «little way.» But it is not necessary here to turn to a new Thérésian invention: it is only a question of an *application to a particular case* of the fundamental attitude «of spiritual childhood» towards God.[21] The solution that the Saint found to the problem of her own sanctification now extends itself to the sanctification of others. Besides, one need not separate the two too much: to sanctify others is for Thérèse to obey God's will and therefore to sanctify oneself at the same time.

This point of view strongly imposes itself if one interprets the quoted text about the novices as having reference, not to the pe-

---

[19] Moreover, we do not understand why it would be necessary to join the discovery of «spiritual childhood» to the experience of February 1893 (at least, this is the date that Combes proposes) and not to an identical experience in the days of her father's illness (from the beginning of 1889). According to CJ 13.7.9, Thérèse «soon» understands that she was «incapable» of consoling a soul (it is also a question of apostolic action), but conscious of her «helplessness,» she simply «asks Jesus to supply for her weakness» and she also states that God «answers her.» Nothing is missing, except the image of the child, but it is not an image that is decisive.

[20] See *Introduction…*, pp. 300-302.

[21] Thus it is also M.D. DE PETTER, «Theresiana,» *Tijdschrift voor geestelijk leven*, 14 (1958), p. 59, who criticizes Combes' rigid position.

riod of February 1893, but to that of *March 1896*, when Thérèse received her appointment to be responsible for the novices, not from Mother Agnès, but from Mother Marie de Gonzague, who had again become prioress. And at this moment, Thérèse's spirituality is already saturated with the idea of «spiritual childhood,» as we shall see. In our opinion, the internal critique of Manuscript C indisputably asserts the relationship of the quoted text with an experience, not of 1893, but of 1896. Due to the technical character of our reasoning, we have preferred to justify our position in an Appendix (see p. 355, Appendix I). We note here that the interpretation of Combes (erroneously attributing this text of Manuscript C to the year 1893, instead of 1896) has influenced many authors (we shall return to this) in their exegeses. It is time to attempt to date the discovery of the «little way *of* spiritual childhood.»

CHAPTER III

The Discovery and Its Chronological Place

Nowhere did Thérèse give us a chronological indication of her great discovery. From her writings, it emerges only as having been in the past, before the month of June 1897. This is very little. And yet it is of great importance to know its historical place. Not only is it a matter of an extremely remarkable event in a saint's spiritual journey, but its dating is simply *essential* in order to be able to define, to follow, and to understand the periods of its preparation and its development. In a certain way, all our work depends on its structuring and on its exegesis of this answer. How much richer a meaning can be revealed, for example, from terms like «child,» «father,» «mercy,» and others, if one finds them written by Thérèse *after* the discovery of her «little way.»

In order to date the discovery, we are obliged to follow an indirect path, even at the cost of some effort. However, the first step is comforting; it is easy, and it at once carries us back to the month of September 1896, when we again find united together in her «little doctrine» of Manuscript B the two biblical texts that were at the basis of the great discovery, and this in a context that indicates somewhat more clearly the perspectives of the «little way.»[1] It is not impossible that one may even go back as far as Easter 1896, and perhaps as far as Easter 1895.[2]

---

[1] See B 1 r-v, 220.

[2] An unpublished note, written by Mother Agnès, recalls one of the two texts: «Hallelujah. Rejoice my faithful Spouse in thinking of this word that I pronounced by the mouth of a prophet: "If someone is very little, let him come to me..." Be yourself this *very little* one and I will take you into my arms during the time of your

As for the rest, we must feel our way along. The path cannot be marked out beforehand. It is only after having met the objective, that we will be able to retrace the way that led to it. Here is the itinerary, laid out in hindsight, that we present. First we are going to establish the historical core just as it is given in the account of the discovery: it is the reading of the two biblical verses, in their original content. Thanks to the examination of the sources which Thérèse had available and which may contain these verses, we manage to identify the one that the Saint used, to the exclusion of all others. After which the road is easy, at least as far as the *terminus post quem*, that is to say, the establishing of the date *after* which Thérèse used this source.

As regards the *terminus ante quem*, little by little, with the help of internal critique, we will close the doors on a well determined time period. Thus we will finally be able to establish the time frame in which Thérèse discovered her «little way.» Fortunately, this period is very short.

This seemed to us the *only* way to determine, not only with some probability, but with the greatest possible degree of certainty, the chronological place of a major grace in the life of Saint Thérèse. A single isolated argument will not be able to convince, but we believe that the convergence of all the arguments is convincing.

This detailed itinerary will also permit us to anticipate the objections that one might bring.

I. THE HISTORICAL CORE

We have already taken up the two issues of reality and symbolism, of past and of present in the narration of the discovery. Let us examine the text again, this time to establish what is certainly historical, that is to say, what in fact happened.

---

exile and you will be for all eternity on my knees at the feast of the eternal Easter.» On the envelope, Mother Agnès later wrote: «Note made up by our little Thérèse the day of Easter at the refectory in 1895 or 1896» (DCL). The phrase «made up» can indicate a fictitious presentation: Mother Agnès would use this formula again. Does this note suppose a previous secret on the part of Thérèse who would have communicated her discovery to Mother Agnès?

To this core surely belongs the action of reading: «I read» «in the holy books.» Then, Thérèse continued her search from the first text to the second: «I continued my search» (always in the holy books). Therefore, her discovery does not arise by chance: Thérèse intentionally searches and she does this while reading.

«The holy books,» what are they? Everybody will answer: Sacred Scripture, inasmuch as Thérèse finds scriptural texts. However, it is not necessary that it be the whole Bible; it could also be a matter of an abridged edition or an anthology. To set our minds at rest that we have not overlooked anything, we also add liturgical books, and even those of spiritual reading, containing some biblical texts.

Thérèse read two scriptural texts and she cites them. But one knows that she sometimes quotes in a rather free manner. Let us try to see if the two texts of interest are faithful to the content in which Thérèse read them originally.

Two psychological reasons already suggest — although they do not yet compel it — a strong fidelity to the original reading. It is first a question of two texts which impressed the nun greatly. One still feels it from afar: «Never did words more tender and more melodious come to give joy to my soul» (C 3 r, 238). Furthermore, Thérèse is in an attitude of seeking, of listening, of waiting, of receptiveness. In such psychological circumstances, the answer must have inscribed itself deeply in her mind. Besides, these texts serve as a basis for a series of ideas (which, moreover, are very spontaneous and intuitive), for a complete way.

Let us next compare the quotations one with the other, as Thérèse repeats them in different places. Five times, and once with Mother Agnès,[3] we encounter, at various times, Proverbs 9:4 («Whoever is a little one, let him come to Me»), quoted precisely the same way. Until further notice, then, one can be sure that this is how Thérèse read it.

Isaiah 66:13-12 («As a mother caresses her child, so I will comfort you, I will carry you on my bosom and I will dandle you on my knees») is in its turn almost completely identical, the two fur-

[3] See *supra*, chap. II n. 6.

ther times when Thérèse quotes it.[4] But, these two times the words «will dandle» are replaced by «will caress.» And thus it is that the original version must be read. In fact, besides the greater number — two times versus one — which argues for «will caress» and by the fact that this term appears in the oldest copy, stands the argument that the Vulgate — from which was made, at the time, most all of the popular editions of the Bible — also uses the word *blandiri* (to caress) twice: it would appear normal that the translation also repeated it. We can conclude, then, that Thérèse came across the text just as it is determined above. However, let us bear in mind the fact — altogether accessory, besides, for it is a matter of two juxtaposed sentences — that Thérèse could have inverted the two verses of Isaiah. In fact, she quotes verse 13 before verse 12. Moreover, in consulting the Vulgate and other translations of the time, it is possible that Thérèse could have changed the passive form into the active form, that is to say, «you shall be carried,» etc., to «I will carry you», etc. This change is also very accidental and, if need be, Thérèse would have done it to logically link the verse of Isaiah to Proverbs 9:4, which was written in the active form.

II. THE TRUE SOURCE

1. The Bible, the liturgy, and spiritual readings

Thérèse had therefore read «the holy books.» Let us look for the source. Let us immediately go to the two copies of the Bible that existed at the Carmel of Lisieux.[5] But a general rule, then in use at

---

[4] See B 1 r, 220 and CSG, p. 43. That this text accompanies Pr 9:4 every time shows how very much Thérèse considers them and interprets them as inseparable. One might again find an echo of Is 66:12-13 in a letter of Christmas 1896 (LT 211, 1038); it is God's Mother who speaks: «You will take your place on the knees of my beloved Jesus and I will also take you in my arms and I will shower you with caresses, because I am your *Mother.*» The passage from «to caress» to «to dandle» probably took place on the basis of a personal meditation of Thérèse, imagining how God «dandled» her, very much like her father used to «dandle» her on his knees. (See A 18 r, 97 and *Prayer of a Child of a Saint*, PN 8.)

[5] See their description in Mss II, 5. It is obvious that the discovery was made *at Carmel*. At the age of fifteen, Thérèse didn't as yet have the long and intense experience of her powerlessness (C 2 v, 237); very much to the contrary, she is consumed with conquering the summit of holiness.

the monastery, presents us with an initial disappointment: the young sisters were not allowed to read a complete Bible.[6] Besides, the Glaire translation as well as that of Le Maistre de Sacy express themselves in a manner too different for one to be able to recognize the source of Thérèse's quotations.[7]

Let us move on, then, to the spiritual books that Thérèse had either read or glanced through and that deserve consideration.[8] However, it was in vain that we examined her dear *Imitation of Christ;* the books of Arminjon, Monsignor de Ségur, Surin, Suso, Faber and Argentan; the *Discourse* of Saint Bernard with appendices; *The Little Breviary of the Sacred Heart of Jesus*; the *Treasure of Carmel; The Sacred Banquet; The Life and Works of Blessed Margaret Mary Alacoque*; the *Meditations on the Mysteries of the Faith and on the Epistles and Gospels; The Insinuations of the Divine Pity.*[9] The works of her venerated master, Saint John of the Cross, however, contain a ray of light, but not enough. Indeed, they explain the text of Isaiah

---

[6] CSG, p. 105, n. 1. Sister Geneviève, as well, in the note of «Céline's Notebook» of which we will soon speak and P. DESCOUVEMONT, *Sainte Thérèse de l'Enfant-Jésus et son prochain*, p. 253. In the pages that follow, we again refer to this book , which contains a supplement, *Les Lectures de Sainte Thérèse* (pp. 243-259), made in direct collaboration with the Carmel of Lisieux.

[7] The Glaire edition translates Proverbs 9:4 exactly as Thérèse quotes it, but Is 66:13-12 differs considerably (we underline the differences from the triple quotation of Thérèse): «As a mother *who* caresses *some one* [of her children], *in the same way* I will comfort you. *At the breast* you will be carried, and on the knees they will caress you.» Le Maistre de Sacy, on the other hand, provides a translation of Is 66:13-12 that is rather similar to Thérèse's quotation: «As a mother caresses her *little* child, so I will comfort you. They will carry you *at the breast* [without the conjunction «and» of Thérèse], they will caress you on their knees.» But Pr 9:4 could not have inspired Thérèse, especially because of the words «very little» that are missing: «*Whoever* is *simple*, let him come to me.» And yet is it likely that the nun would have glanced through the hundreds of pages that separate Pr 9:4 from Is 66:12-13 in her search that appears to have been accomplished in the same psychological thrust and in a rather short time span?

[8] A large number of them can be eliminated, mainly because of their biographical character or because Thérèse read them well before her entrance into Carmel, or after the writing of Manuscript B where she already appears clearly in possession of her «little way.» Moreover, the nun did not have the leisure nor frequent desire to read so many books: after the age of eighteen, she writes in 1895, «all books left me in aridity» (A 83 r, 210).

[9] (*Note of 1994.*) See the description of these books in the *Supplément* to the work of P. Descouvemont and in *La Bible avec Thérèse de Lisieux*, Ed. du Cerf-Desclée De Brouwer, 1979, pp. 307-311.

and quote it, but only partially,[10] and everywhere they lack the verse from Proverbs. Moreover, it is not from the text of Isaiah to that of Proverbs that Thérèse would have passed, but just the reverse.

Perhaps the liturgy will inform us of it? Be that as it may, it will not be the *Missal Roman-carmélitain,* since it does not contain either of the two texts. The *breviary,* on the other hand, does contain the two biblical texts. In fact, Proverbs 9:4 appeared no less than nine times a year,[11] the text of Isaiah only once.[12]

Evidently, Thérèse knew very little Latin, but there existed translations, and every evening in the refectory they would read the lessons of Matins.[13] At the end of Thérèse's life, they used the Dom Gréa edition to do the reading of the lessons, but the author warns that the translations of the biblical texts were based on the Glaire edition, which carries with it the inconveniences that we have indicated. Unfortunately, we are no longer able to establish what translation was used before, but it appears *a posteriori* highly unlikely that it would present the biblical verses precisely as Thérèse, who — as we shall see — in her turn, uses a dependent source for our two texts from two *different* translations.[14] Three reasons seem, moreover, to make it impossible that Thérèse was inspired by a translation from the breviary: during her short religious life, only once had the verse of Isaiah been read during the Office and therefore in the refectory[15]; the narration of the discovery does

[10] See CS, str. 27: «You will be carried at the breast and they will caress you on their knees,» in the translation that Thérèse had at her disposal.

[11] This verse appears in the third lesson of the first Nocturne of the Common of the Virgin Mary. It was recited (several feasts have been omitted since then) January 29, July 16, August 5, September 24, November 21 and 28, the Sunday of the octave of the Nativity of the Virgin, the first and the last Sunday of October.

[12] Friday of the fourth week of Advent, lessons of Matins.

[13] If this translation from the breviary gives Pr 9:4, as Thérèse quotes it, she therefore heard her favorite text many times, without having given it particular attention. But we are unaware of the translation used.

[14] We have examined many French translations of the Bible, but we did not find any that gave the two texts, taken together, as Thérèse gave them.

[15] In fact, it is necessary that Christmas fall on a Sunday so that one can still read during the Office the lessons of the Friday of the fourth week of Advent. It only happened in 1892. This part of our work was already written when we became aware of A. COMBES's recent book, *De doctrina spirituali Sanctae Theresiae a Jesu Infante,* Rome-Paris, 1967, 263 pp. The author insists on texts from the breviary and concludes that

not speak of a hearing, brought on by chance, but of a reading, done deliberately («to search for»); the verse of Isaiah is found at the beginning of the breviary, that of Proverbs farther on; if Thérèse had searched there for her solution, she would have had to browse her way backwards.

Let us also add Dom Guéranger's *Liturgical Year*, a very well known and beloved monumental work in the Martin's home and at the Carmel of Lisieux. But Proverbs 9:4 is missing there.[16]

2. «*Céline's Notebook*»

A single source for us to solve the problem confronting us — the one we have hitherto concealed — remains: the best source of all! When Céline entered Carmel, she in fact brought with her a small biblical anthology which she passed on to Thérèse.[17] Let us read the note that Céline wrote in this very notebook on January 31, 1945: «Upon entering Carmel, on the 14th of September, 1894, I brought this small notebook that I had copied while still in the world, based on the translation of the Vulgate by Bourassé et Janvier [*Bible de luxe*, Mame, 1872] and especially on the translation of Le Maistre de Sacy. Saint Thérèse of the Child Jesus used this notebook with enthusiasm and couldn't separate herself from it, so much so that Sister Marie of the Eucharist began to copy it for her. But it is from this one that she borrowed several beautiful texts, notably: "If someone is very little..." [Proverbs 9:4, then, other texts come after]. I think that she also borrowed this passage from it: "As a mother caresses her child..." [Isaiah], but it was, under

all data seem to converge toward this Friday, December 22, 1892, as the date of the discovery of «the elevator.» Whatever the case may be, «it is beyond doubt,» he says, that Thérèse's discovery does not take place after the beginning of 1893. See pp. 147-159, especially p. 159. As we shall see, we cannot make this chronology of Combes our own.

16 Is 66:12-13 translates thus: «They will carry you *at the breast* and they will caress you on their knees, as a mother caresses her child; so I will comfort you.» Note also the punctuation. See the fourth Friday of Advent. (Ed. 1880, I, p. 274.)

17 Henceforth we will refer to this manuscript as Céline's Notebook. An appendix of this work indicates the excerpts from the Bible that it contains and of which Thérèse freely made use. It is to this source that Thérèse will thereafter draw her quotations of the Old Testament.

her pen, a free quotation, hence a variant.... As for the complete Bible, it was not, at that time, in the hands of the nuns, it was especially unknown to the youngest.»

This first class testimony, which is categorical in the case of Thérèse's first quotation and suggestive for the second, is corroborated by the exclusion of all other sources within the Saint's reach and confirmed by the internal criticism.

In the Notebook, we in fact encounter among the excerpts from Proverbs: «If someone is very little, let him come to Me.»[18] The underlining of the words «very little» was Thérèse's own work. Farther on, we find Isaiah 66:12-13: «You will be carried at the breast, and they will caress you on their knees. As a mother caresses her child, so I will comfort you.» So Thérèse inverted verses 12 and 13, and changed the passive form («you will be» carried) into the active («I» will carry you). But apart from these incidental details, the remainder is rendered word for word. Thérèse even repeats the word «breast,» which is a rather exceptional translation.[19]

The other conditions fall into place marvelously. The expression «holy books» applies itself without difficulty to this anthology of sixteen biblical and only biblical books. And to arrive, in her search, from Proverbs 9:4 to Isaiah 66:12-13, Thérèse only has to scan 26 pages, 3 x 5 inches in size.

This, then, is how we put together the arguments, either by the exclusion of all other sources at the Saint's disposal, or by the

---

[18] It is neither Le Maistre de Sacy («whoever is simple») nor Bourassé et Janvier («whoever is little») that provide this translation. Céline would therefore have drawn from yet other sources while composing her notebook!

(*Note of 1994.*) See *La Bible avec Thérèse de Lisieux*, Paris, 1979, p. 310: «... correct the affirmation of the preliminary note of Sister Geneviève: in fact, she followed the Glaire translation for all her texts, except for Isaiah, which she copied from Bourassé et Janvier.»

[19] This is the translation from Bourassé et Janvier. Thérèse's exegesis is good. It is true, the one who carries at the breast and caresses (v. 12) is not directly God, but Jerusalem. However it is God who comforts *by means* of Jerusalem; because Yahweh immediately says: «As a mother caresses her child, so I will comfort you, and you will find your consolation in Jerusalem» (v. 13, see also v. 9). Thérèse therefore rightly attributes the action of verse 12 to Yahweh Himself. In the Notebook the passage Is 66:9-15 was copied in its entirety. It is all a vivid description of God's maternal love (by means of Jerusalem). Thérèse who had read God's invitation to the little one, attracted by these sentences, discerned in them a definitive answer. (For Pr 9:4 see our Introductory Chapter, n. 18.)

internal critique of the true source, to conclude with certainty: it is in Céline's Notebook that Thérèse read the two texts which revealed her «little way of spiritual childhood» to her. Let us now try to date this privileged moment.

III. THE DATE OF THE DISCOVERY

1. *After September 14, 1894*

Since Céline «brought» the Notebook upon entering Carmel, it is clear that it is after this date, that is, after September 14, 1894, that Thérèse discovered her «little way.» But did it take her a long time to arrive at the source? According to another testimony,[20] Céline specified that it was «at the very moment of [her] entrance» that Thérèse had «particularly relished» the text of Proverbs 9:4. Is that not the reason why Thérèse «used this notebook with enthusiasm and could not separate herself from it»? This text, continues Céline, «had opened the door, so to speak, to her investigations on the fatherhood of God. This idea enlightened her and gave her heart an enthusiasm until then unknown.»

There is another factor which suggests that the renewing discovery is situated soon after September 14, 1894. Thérèse already loved Sacred Scripture very much and she frequently quotes it in her letters. How extraordinary, then, that she should have fallen upon this treasure, when she had at her disposal a pretty little book with «the most beautiful texts» of the Old Testament, which until then had been in large part forbidden to her![21] Unfortunately, the following months provide us with few documents to verify this hypothesis.

---

[20] From February 16, 1951, cited in S. PIAT, *À la découverte...*, p. 137.

[21] It is possible that Thérèse, distressed by her own problem, set herself to reading the Notebook, from the first page. It did not require a lot of time to arrive at Pr 9:4, which could be found 50 pages further on in this small sized notebook. It is also possible that Thérèse, wanting to have a divine answer, opened the Notebook *blindly*, just as Saint Francis of Assisi had done — whose life she had read in her childhood. There are, in fact, several examples of Thérèse acting in this way where she finds an answer as she remembers a text from the Bible. See LT 143 for example, 800; 193, 977; 230, 1100; HA 55, chap. XII, 185; A 2 r, 71: she opens the Gospels, her eyes fall on a certain text, and «there, for sure, is the mystery»!

2. Before 1895

Let us now seek to specify the *terminus ante quem* of the discovery.

It is certainly not necessary to go beyond June 9, 1895. Thérèse had then composed her *Act of Oblation to Merciful Love,* which is absolutely faithful to the structures of her «little way,» as we shall see. One is also tempted to recognize in a letter of *April 28* the fundamental inspiration of «spiritual childhood.» In it, Thérèse compares her abandonment of 1890 with the present time, and points out an evolution. Now she thinks that Jesus has many souls «full of sublime virtues,» but that her own soul is poor 'and like a toy of no value.' But Jesus finds some joys in it, different from the former ones. «Then,» concluded Thérèse, «I rejoiced at being poor, I wanted to become more and more poor each day, so that every day Jesus would take more delight in *playing* with me» (LT 176, 902). Thérèse has already understood God's specific inclination toward the poor (this is mercy); in her poverty she finds her joy, her wealth and a motive to grow ever more in the recognition of her poverty.

A small detail, which is already well known and which returns with a mysterious persistence, obliges us to retrace our steps, that is, until *February 24, 1895*. It also permits us to record with Thérèse the psychological repercussion of Proverbs 9:4 and of the ideal that it placed before her eyes.

It is a matter of the expression «very little.» We have said how Thérèse cannot speak of Proverbs 9:4 without highlighting these two words, and the analysis of her account of the discovery has shown to what degree they condense the way that is opening up: she, the little one, will become the *very* little one, more so each day, so that mercy showers down upon her always more. Now, the formula «very little,» by its innovation, its abundance, its context, and the manner of its presentation, constitutes, in 1895, a sufficiently singular phenomenon to be studied.

In fact, Thérèse suddenly begins to call herself «very little.» It is in her letter of February 24, 1895 (LT 175, 899). It is new, but the gesture will repeat itself: in the following letter (April 28), and in a third one (July 20-21). A small note without the formula intervenes. But the formula returns in the following letter (October 14-17). Again a small note, and again the formula on November 16.

This means that, from February 24 to November 16, in the five letters considered, Thérèse calls herself «very little» five times.

But the phenomenon is not limited to this. It is always at the end, in the final formula of the letter, that Thérèse gives herself this qualification, except the fourth time where it is right at the beginning. (That the expression is missing in two notes finds its explanation perhaps in the absence of the final formula.) This is full of significance, because it is there that one most often condenses one's personal feelings; it is thus that one presents oneself a last time to the eyes of the other. Thérèse had never before done it this way!

But there is a final characteristic: she underlines the two words (with the exception once again of the fourth time). This already conveys a special emphasis, which becomes still more meaningful when one puts it alongside the highlighting that Thérèse gives to these same two words while quoting Proverbs 9:4. We have said it elsewhere: often an underlining indicates, with Thérèse, a quotation or a borrowed formula.[22] Strangely enough, at the same time Thérèse uses the words «very little» in her Manuscript A without underlining them: she seems to do it only when they have a personal and spiritual meaning.[23]

The novelty,[24] the abundant use after 1895, the context, and

---

[22] See our Introductory Chapter, pp. LVII-LVIII.

[23] Thus «very little thimble» (A 19 v, 99), «three very little children» (A 52 v, 156), herself when she was «very little» (A 41 r, 135 and 72 r, 191). Once she underlines «my *very little* purse» (A 66 r, 180), but it is because of the contrast with the «*huge* purses.» See our Introductory Chapter, pp. LVII-LVIII.

[24] To tell the truth, in the three hundred pages of the Letters of Thérèse before 1895, one already comes across these two words three times, but let's not forget that the use of «very» before an adjective is a typical French twist, and is quite frequently used by Thérèse: for example a way «very/totally new» (C 2 v, 237). It is in this sense that we interpret these three cases. So it is in 1890, when she calls herself «a very little flower» in the crown of her sister Marie (LT 113, 661). So too, on February 20, 1893, when she declares herself to be «a very *little* lyre» of Mother Agnès (LT 140, 781): the accent doesn't fall on «very little» but on *little* (underlined); thirteen words later, she speaks again of «your *little* lyre.» We shall see, in fact, how much the theme of littleness was always noteworthy for Thérèse, but until the discovery of «spiritual childhood,» littleness is synonymous with weakness and especially with humility, while afterwards, littleness indicates above all an attitude of confidence in divine mercy. Also the third case, that of December 27, 1893, doesn't present any more difficulty: «During the month of dear little Jesus, ask Him that I remain always little, *very little*!...» (LT 154, 835). The sentence that follows explains well how one must interpret the two words, whose underlining indicates the increasing intensity: «I will offer the same prayer to Him for you, because I know your

the underlining make the presence of the formula «very little» in 1895 a factor that is only explained in light of the great discovery of the «little way»: Thérèse had already read Proverbs 9:4 and in the words «very little» she had found her ideal, her program, her title of nobility. It is to this word of God that thenceforth she referred her entire existence and she alluded to it constantly.

From then on, the formula freely returned, and more so during the final months preceding Thérèse's death.[25] It is not without interest to note that it also appeared in the notebook of her autobiography (Manuscript A): it is the «Notebook of obedience belonging to the very little white flower.» Unfortunately, we are unaware if it was at the beginning, in the month of January 1895, therefore, that Thérèse wrote these words.[26] Thus, it is not certain whether a deeper significance must be given to the expression.

Can we go back also to the documents of the month of December 1894? Probably. However, since the question is a subtle one, it is preferable to defer all analysis: one must already have studied the interior world of Thérèse before this date, in order to perceive the new lines of strength that would eventually begin to be drawn. But even if some of the poems of the month of December 1894 do not yet reveal the perspectives of the «little way» — which does not exclude that Thérèse already possessed them — the prologue of Manuscript A, written in the month of January 1895, no longer leaves any reasonable doubt.

It is therefore the period that runs between September 14 and the beginning of 1895 that we shall speak of, when hereafter we shall use comprehensive expressions like «toward the end of 1894» or «before 1895.»

Against the conclusion of this chapter, one could still make

---

desires and I know that humility is your favorite virtue.» It is not enough to find the two words together! Otherwise, everything would have already been accomplished when Mother Agnès writes to Thérèse, in preparation for her First Communion: «To you who are still very little, Jesus will give Himself as very little» (See CG I, LC 28).

[25] For example LT 186, 950 and 190, 958 (twice the «very little lamb,» that is the more taken on the knees of the divine Shepherd); 191, 965; 220, 1058; 224, 1083; 225, 1090; 230, 1100; C 20 v, 262. Also PN 32. It is not surprising if she signs Manuscript B, the account of her «little doctrine,» with «the *very little*...» (B 5 v, 232).

[26] See the facsimile in the edition of the Mss: it concerns the cover of one of the two original notebooks of Manuscript A. We are unaware if it is the first. The other cover is very mutilated and only bears that it is the «Notebook of obedience...» (DCL).

an objection[27] which at first sight appears rather serious. Thérèse seems to have said that she wanted Céline to enter Carmel «so that she would follow [her] little way» (NV 16.7.1; DE II, 78-79). It would follow that she would already have discovered this way before her sister's entrance and before the reading of the Notebook. But this text from *Novissima Verba* does not pass the test of textual criticism. In fact, other sources show that it is once more a case of some posthumous attribution,[28] an elucidation which is inaccurate this time. Thérèse will only have expressed her desire to see Céline walk in the same way as she (the religious, Carmelite, spiritual way) without specifying further. It is in the same manner that she expresses her desire in Manuscript A: «to live under the same roof, to share the joys and pains of my childhood companion» (A 82 r, 208).

Before going on to the Second Part , we probably should again do a general survey of the opinions of others about the chronological question of the discovery. But since it is a matter of the arguments of internal criticism, it appears more useful for us to deal with it at the time of touching upon these particular points, while describing the preparation and the partial outlines of the «little way» before 1895.[29]

---

[27] See A. COMBES, *De doctrina...*, p. 150.

[28] Several variations of the text of NV, which is also found in the *Summarium*, are preserved. CJ 16.7.2 gives: «so that she walk our way.» CV states: «She spoke to me of her desire... to form her in the religious life.» Yet another source, quoted in the old edition of the Letters (1948, p. 275, n. 2) says: «so that she might be similar to us.» The Carmel of Lisieux informs us that it is indeed the last version that is authentic. Also see [French] DE, p. 80, n. 81.

[29] Let us not forget that A. COMBES' interpretation of the text of Manuscript C concerning spiritual childhood, and approaching according to him February of 1893 instead of 1896, has had a lot of influence. S. PIAT had situated the reading of the two biblical verses well toward the end of 1894 (*À la découverte...*, p. 136). But he only assigns a *complementary* value to it. All of Chapter 5 («At the discovery of spiritual childhood»), which deals with the years 1891- 1894, suggests it and the author didn't highlight this date: it is not central in his work, but it comes from the third phase, that of «research and adjustment (1891-1896).» The fourth phase, that of «blossoming and radiance,» begins only in 1896. Although the author underlines the synthetic autobiographical nature of the narration, written later, where the plans sometimes overlap (p. 130), he hasn't perhaps sufficiently kept track of the historical core that they contain and expose. In a later book, S. PIAT says: «In this year 1893, Thérèse, who had recently become an auxiliary mistress of the novitiate, is already in full possession of the first elements that will constitute her spirituality; she has discovered in the Scriptures the strong notions that will underlie her "little doctrine"» (*Léonie Martin. Une Soeur de Sainte Thérèse à la Visitation*, Lisieux, 1966, p. 88). This seems premature to us.

SECOND PART

THE GOAL

(1873-1894)

The discovery of the «little way» is not an isolated event in Thérèse's spiritual journey. It fits into a search for holiness which she had undertaken a long time earlier and into the no longer new experience of her own insufficiency. Thus, the discovery and its preparation shed light on each other.

The second part of this study is dedicated to the years 1873-1894, those preceding the «little way.» Actually, it is not simply a matter of «the Thérésian journey» which is very short (this one is more extensive), although we may constantly speak of its central themes. Our attention centers in the first place on the «little way,» considered from the point of view of its development. Thanks to the investigation which preceded, we now know how to point out the elements we will need to follow above all: in their birth and in their growth, to the point where they can be taken up, enriched, and reassessed in a new synthesis.

For the «little way» does not use any entirely new materials. Several of its typical elements are found scattered along Thérèse's spiritual path. After having gathered them, we will better understand the real impact of the discovery at the end of the year 1894: whether it is a matter of a prepared moment or of an unforeseen moment, of a simple confirmation of the followed path, of a new synthesis, of an enrichment or an abrupt change of course. It is only upon the backdrop of the past that the picture of «spiritual childhood» is painted with all that is implied of both old and new in it. It is possible that the reader will not always understand in detail the reason for this recomposition of the background. At times we had to first describe the overall structure of Thérèse's «little doctrine» so that the reader could recognize the fine lines which, as they enlarge, run toward it, sometimes from afar. In this way, the reader will be able to see more clearly the difference between the period before 1895 and the period that followed, even if the resemblances are still numerous. But it is part of the human condition not to be able to say everything in a single word. He who explains will need patience. He who listens will at times need to trust.

At the center of this retrospective survey is found the theme of Thérèse Martin's holiness. There is the goal of all her efforts, the goal which attracts her, for which she constantly longs, which she reaches only par-

tially however, and which will remain the same even when she comes to discover new means. We are going to follow the birth of this ideal, the forms that it borrows, the progress that Thérèse makes in its direction, and the means that she uses to reach it. It goes without saying that our subject involves the study of love, which with Thérèse is at the same time both the ideal and the way. But other factors which prepare for the discovery of the «little way» must be examined: humility; the choice of ordinary settings; faithfulness to the demands of God, even small ones; confidence and abandonment, together with suffering which is like their existential environment; the weakness that temporarily holds the ideal out of reach. All of the symbols which one day will help Thérèse to explain her doctrine of «spiritual childhood» also deserve to be considered. The last chapter will present the synthesis of this part.

For a larger biographical setting (we wanted ours to be elementary but clear), we willingly refer you to the work of Thérèse or to the work of Fr. Piat. Here, we only draw the lines that converge in some way toward the discovery of the «little way.» We have divided this itinerary into periods, because, in preparation for «spiritual childhood,» it marks new turning points. But to record these points of emphasis is a delicate thing. Often it is only after a certain period of time that one recognizes the changes and can, on the one hand, search for their roots, and on the other hand, follow their progress.

Chapter I

The Call

(September 1873-1887)

M. and Mme. Martin, who took their vocation to holiness seriously, sought successfully to communicate the same ideal to their children. They thus established a fertile beginning. Thérèse was nine years old when she received a clearer call. She was fifteen years old when this call irresistibly resounded again. Therein are the two great stages of this chapter, whose intentions, beyond those already enumerated, are to present the personality who will one day walk in the «way of spiritual childhood,» and to carefully outline the chronology of the slow maturation, through the sufferings and the days of grace, of her ideal of holiness.

I. THE FIRST CALL

1. The Seed

Psychology has revealed the importance of the beginnings of each life. It likes to examine closely this period of subconsciousness or spontaneity to uncover a person's temperament. Let us pause for a moment, then, at the case of Thérèse and at the milieu of her first Christian initiation. This is the soil where God sows. Thérèse distinguishes three separate phases[1] in the story of her life.

[1] A 4 v, 75. Thérèse speaks here of three periods until *her entrance into Carmel*, but farther on, they will become the three periods of her entire life (A 13 r, 89 and 45 v, 142).

The first lasts until her mother's death, when she was four years and eight months old. These were the «sunny years.» «Oh! everything truly smiled upon me on this earth: I found flowers under each of my steps and my happy disposition also contributed to making my life pleasant» (A 11 v and 12 r, 86-87). Thérèse's mother and the Saint herself, who freely express themselves with a certain vigor, will provide us with many details of her early childhood.[2]

Thérèse has «parents without equal,» she receives «smiles and the most tender caresses,» and she has a little «loving and sensitive» heart, «a heart of gold.» She is «very affectionate,» but at the same time «very honest» and «very open.» This does not prevent her from being inclined to observe and to think: «Without appearing to do so,» she said, «I paid close attention to everything that was said and done around me; it seems to me that I was judging things then as I do now.» She is «very intelligent and she remembers everything.» She is «a charming child,» said her mother, «very sensitive and very lively.» She is very happy and it was said that she had a bit of «Heaven in her eyes.»[3] In short, Thérèse would have been a most likable imp.

However, she is not without faults. She is «very nervous,» «easily brought to tears,» knows how to throw herself «into frightful tantrums,» and the little girl from Normandy sometimes gives evidence «of an almost unconquerable stubbornness.»[4]

Already God's gift begins to bloom in this rich soil. What a beautiful testimony Thérèse gives in 1896: «Our Lord wanting my first glance for Himself alone, saw fit to ask for my heart right from the cradle, if I can so express myself» (LT 201, 1013). Again «without knowing too much what it meant,» she decides at the age of two years, once and for all, to become a nun like Pauline (A 6 r,

---

[2] See for the following details A 4 v-13 r, 75-89. The mother's testimonies, cited here, are all recorded in Thérèse's autobiography. One finds some others in Zélie MARTIN, *Correspondance familiale* (1863- 1878), Lisieux, 1958, 463 pp.

[3] Sister Geneviève, PA, p. 300. In fact, her cousin Jeanne Guérin later seems to like to tease Thérèse on her «fascinating» eyes (LT 24, 274).

[4] When Mother Agnès will later find that these testimonies are exaggerated by Mme. Martin, anxious to make her letters more interesting, Thérèse will simply agree: «I believe that you are right» (DE II 27.5.2). Let us note however that NV is the only source to report these words.

77); indeed, she will be the Mother of the monastery![5] At the age of three years and ten months, she already applies herself with fervor to making small sacrifices. Four months later, Mme. Martin writes: «She speaks only about God and wouldn't miss her prayers for anything.»

Is this simply a case of an impersonal imitation of her environment, a very pious source of inspiration? Thérèse clearly recognizes the beneficial influence of her environment (A 8 v, 82), but what she writes, at the mature age of twenty-two years, certainly makes one reflect: «Already... virtue had its charming qualities for me and I was, it seems to me, in the same dispositions then as I am now, already enjoying a firm control over my actions.» Thus, for example, she has already formed «the good habit of never complaining,» even when treated unjustly, and she corrects herself at the first word.

Her parents teach her to have confidence in God: there again is precious seed! «Confidence in God,» Céline will say, «and total abandonment to Him, were family virtues in our home.»[6] One of Thérèse's first desires as a child was 'to hide herself beneath the shadow of the virginal mantle of the Mother of God' (A 57 r, 164).

2. *First encounters with suffering*

The child is four years and eight months old, when her mother's death causes a trauma in her that will leave deep marks in her psyche. She is going «to pass through the winter of trial» (A 12 r, 87) as she enters the second period of her life which extends until the end of her thirteenth year. It is the beginning of a long encounter with misery and weakness, an experience that will open her to divine mercy.

Deprived of the affection of an «incomparable mother» (A 4v, 75), Thérèse feels an acute injury from it. «After Mamma's death,» she admits, «my happy disposition changed completely; I, once so full of life and so open, became timid and retiring, sensitive to the

---

5 See Pauline's letter of April 4, 1877 (LD, CG I, p. 108).

6 See M.-M. PHILIPON, «Comment ma Sainte Petite Soeur eut l'idée de sa petite Voie d'Enfance Spirituelle», ED, 28 (1952), p. 194.

extreme. One glance was often enough to reduce me to tears and I was happy only when left alone completely. I couldn't bear the company of strangers and found my joy only within the intimacy of the family» (A 13r, 89). Elsewhere, she declares herself at that time to be «timid and sensitive» (A 22v, 104), «sweet, but much given to crying» (A 24r, 106), rather clumsy (A 37v, 129; 44v, 140-141), yes «intolerable» (A 44 v, 141). But, if we can believe witnesses, this last judgment is undoubtedly extreme, although her hypersensitivity may at times have been annoying, even for others.[7]

However, immediately after her mother's death, Thérèse's life goes on in a rather «peaceful and happy» way for a period of four years (A 22r, 103), hidden as she is in the intimacy of Les Buissonnets, the new home in Lisieux. Thérèse is surrounded by the love of her sisters and especially of her father, whose «very *affectionate* heart… seemed to be enriched with a truly maternal love» (A 13 r, 89). Moreover, the Martin family belonged to the rich middle class and did not know material worries.[8]

The little girl intensifies her virtuous life: «I loved God very much and I offered my heart to Him very often, using the little formula that Mamma had taught me» (A 15 v, 93). The liturgical feasts, Sundays, and nature carry her to God and make her long for Heaven, «the eternal feast» which «the exile» of the earth does not know how to procure.

She is five years and seven months old, when she admires, one evening, the light that the sun, disappearing on the horizon, cast over the water of the sea: «I contemplated this luminous trail for a long time,» Thérèse will say later, «and saw it as a picture of grace shedding its light across the path that the little white-sailed vessel had to travel.… Sitting by your side, Pauline, I resolved never to let my soul wander away from the gaze of Jesus, so that it could sail peacefully toward the Homeland of Heaven!»[9]

---

[7] The maid of the Guérin family will testify: «She was very happy and very open in her family and with us. One saw that she was compensating for the uneasiness that the boarding school environment imposed on her» (PO, p. 362).

[8] See for example S. PIAT, *Histoire d'une famille*, 1948, p. 41 (footnote 6) and p. 378 (footnote 4), on their economic situation.

[9] A 22 r, 103. For the date, see Mss II, 14. Thérèse expresses herself approximately: «I was 6 or 7 years old.»

She is six or seven years old, when she confesses herself for the first time. 'Never had she felt so much joy in her soul.'[10] She also promises to redouble her fondness for the Blessed Virgin.

The date of May 13, 1880 is a notable one; Thérèse is then seven years and four months old. It is the day of the First Communion of her most dear sister, Céline. This event produces on Thérèse «an impression similar» to that of her own First Communion. She decides «to start living a new life.» She feels filled to overflowing with divine benevolence: «I believe that I received great graces that day and I consider it as one of most *beautiful* of my life» (A 25 v, 108). She also begins to conscientiously prepare for the day when she herself will receive the Eucharist for the first time.[11]

Thérèse Martin is eight years and nine months old when she leaves the little paradise of Les Buissonnets to attend as a half-boarder the school of the Abbey of the Benedictines in Lisieux. The five years that she spends there will be the «saddest of [her] life» (A 22r, 103). She is the youngest of her class (and yet the first in her class). They tease her, but she does not know how to defend herself and cries without saying a word. She appears to lack vitality and dynamism, but actually her inner inhibitions are too great for her to overcome them. She does not know how to play anymore, does not consider herself «a pleasant companion,» and gets very bored. She feels her weakness deeply: «I didn't have sufficient virtue to rise above these miseries of life and so my poor little heart suffered very much.» It is to her benefit that her dear Céline accompanies her and that every evening she returns to 'her own home where her heart unfolds again' (A 22r-23r, 104-105).

Her piety and her generosity, although still insufficient to master her sensitivity, have not stopped growing. It is to this child and at this moment that God addresses His clear call to perfection.

---

[10] A 16 v-17 r, 95. See also Mss II, 12-13. Pauline, who was preparing Thérèse for this confession, will say later: «I was very embarrassed to find no sin in her, never having seen her disobey or commit any fault» (PO, p. 151).

[11] A 25 v, 108. She lamented the fact that she was not born two days earlier, in order to be able to make her First Communion one year earlier (PA, p. 265). One day she had wanted to stop the Bishop of Bayeux to ask for the permission (PO, p. 241). Even as a small child, she asks to be able to go to the Christmas midnight Mass: «I, too, would go to Communion, and I would slip myself in among the others, so no one would notice. Could I do that?» (*Ibid.*).

It is an important moment. Here, Thérèse not only proposes to herself the goal that her «way of spiritual childhood» will later seek to attain, but one already encounters, on the level of means, a first hardly noticeable change which her life takes on.

3. *The clear call*

At first, it is difficult to assign with certainty the chronological place of this grace and therefore to insert it at a precise moment in Thérèse's religious development. But, upon our examination, it follows her entrance into the school of the Abbey[12] and precedes Pauline's entrance into Carmel.[13] The new insight is therefore situated in the year following the Saint's age of eight years and nine months, that is, between October 1881 and October 1882.

What is this grace (A 32r, 119) which she counts among 'the greatest in her life'? Thérèse explains it to us. «While reading the stories about the patriotic deeds of the great French heroines, especially that of the *Venerable* JOAN OF ARC, I felt a great desire to imitate them; and I seemed to feel within me the same burning zeal with which they were animated, the same Heavenly inspiration.

---

[12] The grace links itself to the reading «of the patriotic actions of the French heroines», especially of Joan of Arc (A 32 r, 1194): that is to say, «when I began to learn the history of France,» as she specifies elsewhere (LT 224, 1083). This refers to school, to lessons, to study («to learning the history of France»). So, it is unlikely that it is a question here of Pauline's lessons at Les Buissonnets. (Thérèse mentions reading, writing, catechism, grammar, *sacred* history: A 13 v, 90; did secular history find room there?) It is more likely that she is referring to the period where she is already attending the Abbey school, therefore after her eight years and nine months. In any event, there is a more certain indication. Thérèse says that God «didn't *delay*» in removing her ideal of 'holiness without suffering' conceived in the reading about Joan of Arc, precisely by sending her the trial of Pauline's entrance (A 32 r, 120). The grace can therefore not precede this suffering by much. Besides, Thérèse affirms that the strength which comes from suffering as a means to achieve holiness is always part of the period «when perfection was set before her» (A 10 r, 84).

[13] Actually, Thérèse announces that she will tell a few small details of her childhood before Pauline's entrance into Carmel, on October 2, 1882 (A 31 v, 118). Then she immediately begins to speak of her readings up until her own entrance into Carmel (A 31 v-32 r, 119). Has she therefore crossed the boundaries? No, because at the time of the grace, Thérèse still doesn't think of having to suffer very much, but on this point God soon illuminates her by sending her trials (that are therefore subsequent), and which relate precisely to the *entrance of Pauline* into Carmel (A 32 r, 120). It is even especially starting from this moment that suffering explodes (A 13 r, 89).

Then I received a grace which I have always looked upon as one of the greatest of my life.... I considered that I was born for *glory*» — «It seemed to me that the Lord was also destining me for great things,» she will say in a letter to Maurice Bellière[14] — «and in seeking the means of attaining it, God inspired in me the feelings that I have just described.» What sentiments are they? Thérèse hardly explains them: «It is true that in reading certain tales of chivalry, I didn't always understand *the realities of life*; but soon God made me realize that true glory is that which will last eternally and that, to achieve it, it is not necessary to perform outstanding deeds but to hide oneself and practice virtue in such a way that the left hand does not know what the right is doing» (Mt 6:3). And Thérèse applies herself to this principle of true glory: «He made me understand also that my own *glory* would not be evident to the eyes of mortals, that it would consist in becoming a great *Saint*!!!» But a long path remains for her to travel: «This desire could certainly appear daring if one were to consider how weak and imperfect I was.»[15]

She discovers God's plan for her life and understands that she, too, was born for glory, true glory, and that this will consist in becoming holy, a great saint. It is a clear call of God, not only to an ideal, but a call where a basically outlined way is already being drawn up: a way that does not require outstanding works (in the manner of Joan of Arc, of heroines, of tales of chivalry), a way that is not seen by the eyes of men, that is hidden, and that hides its own virtues to itself (this is what Thérèse wants to say with Mt 6:3). We see here a realization which is remarkable for its clarity; it is also undeniable that it helps to orient the young girl toward a cloistered, hidden life, which a little later she in fact decides to embrace. Without a doubt, this way in which outstanding works already are

---

[14] LT 224, 1083. Compare the confession of Edith STEIN: «In my dreams [as a child] I always saw before me a bright future. I dreamed of happiness and glory, because I was convinced that I was destined for something great and that I was not made at all for the narrow and bourgeois setting in which I had been born» (*Aus dem Leben einer Jüdischen Familie* (*Oeuvres*, t. VII), Louvain-Fribourg, 1965, p. 45).

[15] Here follows a very important paragraph to which we will return later, since it contains a reflection concerning the state of her soul in 1895.

revealed as relative and in which one advances in obscurity, constitutes a beautiful prelude to the «little way.»

Nevertheless, Thérèse's way is, for the moment, still missing this character of the 'realities of life': she does not yet think «[one must] suffer very much to attain holiness.» Soon reality itself convinces her of this necessity: «The Good God was not long in showing me this was so by sending me trials,» in the first place that of Pauline's departure.

Another important confession reflects the state of Thérèse's soul in the following months, around the time when she was ten years old, when this new vision is already integrated: «When I understood what perfection was, I realized that to become *a saint* one had to suffer much, to seek out always the most perfect thing to do, and to forget oneself [this last expression better expresses what 'to hide oneself' means]; I understood, too, that there were many degrees of perfection and that each soul was free to respond to the advances of Our Lord, to do little or much for Him, in other words to *choose* among the sacrifices for which He asks. Then, as in the days of my childhood, I cried out: My God, *"I choose all.*[16]*"* I don't want to be a *half saint*, I am not afraid to suffer for You, I fear only one thing: to keep my *own will*. So take it, for *"I choose all"* that You want!» (A 10 v, 84-85).

Thérèse therefore has become more realistic: she now suffers, but in suffering she perceives a secret message of God and she takes it upon herself «to suffer much» in her program of holiness. The wisdom of this approach will illuminate her entire life. This increase of light, which could terrify a weak child, actually invited Thérèse Martin to a new and more comprehensive option. Basically, Thérèse shows herself to be determined and will emerge from her trials with a more realistic perspective and a more strengthened will.

Let us examine for a moment these sufferings which follow her first decision to become holy. They show how Thérèse's prayers were heard.

---

[16] Thérèse attributes the present reflection to an anecdote that she has just told, when she «chooses» all of a sudden her sister Léonie's entire basket, with all it contains.

4. The invasion of suffering

Thérèse is nine and a half years old, then, when she learns suddenly, unexpectedly, and because of some negligence on Pauline's part, that her older sister is getting ready to leave her for Carmel (A 25v-26r, 109). The shock comes hard, very hard! For Pauline is her «second mother,» her dear «*Mamma,*» she is the one 'who received all her intimate confidences and cleared up all her doubts' (A 19r, 99)! The wound, caused by the loss of her first mother and never healed, is further torn as if by «a sword» in the loss of this other mother. Every dream vanishes within a few seconds: «How can I express the anguish of my heart?... In one instant I understood what life was; ... I saw that it was nothing but a continual suffering and separation.»

For God, to take is to give. By tearing Pauline from her, He is giving Himself to her in an unexpected way. When Pauline explains the life of Carmel to her, Thérèse hears a new irresistible call, not to holiness this time, but to the place where she will sanctify herself. «I felt that Carmel was the *desert* where God wanted me to go also to hide myself... I felt this with so much force that there wasn't the least doubt in my heart: it was not the dream of a child who lets himself be led along, but the *certitude* of a Divine call; I wanted to go to Carmel not for *Pauline* but for *Jesus alone....*» How many times this refrain will again resound: «Jesus alone.»

Yet, there is no doubt that here God uses Pauline, Thérèse's «ideal from childhood» (A 6 r, 77) and that Thérèse, both consciously and unconsciously, experiences her influence.[17] Moreover, Thérèse Martin's life admirably shows how God wants to bestow his graces on mankind *through* the multiple exterior and interior circumstances of one's existence. Reflecting on her life, Thérèse grasps this law well. Moreover, all her generous correspondence to the moves of this divine economy stems after all from a *feeling* which was endlessly sustained and nurtured, from a natural sen-

[17] Pauline will always remain a help for Thérèse (see also Mss II, 3 4). But let us notice with what firmness the Saint, who, at the time of narrating this episode, was twenty-two years old and possessed a long and lucid experience of human nature, reveals the motive that drove her.

sitivity enhanced by her education and completed by the grace granted to her in response to her generosity.

But the perspective of Carmel does not soothe the suffering very much, because Thérèse is still «FAR from being *mature*» (A 27r, 111). Having entered the monastery, her second mother is simply «lost» to her (*ibid.*), and it is especially from this date on that the second period of her life becomes truly painful (A 13r, 89). Hitherto, suffering passed through her heart gently and drop by drop, so to speak, but now it is going «to break» her heart (A 25v, 108). Each visit to her second mother behind the grilles causes a new rending. Soon the delicate constitution of the little girl collapses under the strain: «It is surprising to see how much my spirit developed in the midst of suffering; it developed to such a degree that it wasn't long until I became sick.»

Thérèse's «strange sickness» in which she believes that she recognizes the role of the devil, and her healing following a vision of the Virgin Mary — the reality of which she is convinced even on her deathbed (PA, p. 247) — are sufficiently known so that we do not have to speak of them.[18] But the suffering, changed into joy by the vision and the cure, changes itself into suffering again; Thérèse will undergo serious and persistent doubts of conscience concerning her own responsibility in the mysterious phenomenon of her illness and concerning the supernatural nature of the Virgin's intervention. We will come back to this. Let us notice, however, that the year beginning when she was eleven years and four months old, that is to say, from May 1884 until May 1885, was a year of great peace.

5. The sky «without clouds»

Thérèse reaches the age of eleven years and four months and finally she is allowed to make her First Holy Communion. It is a time of great happiness. «The time of my First Communion remains engraved in my heart as a memory without any clouds. It seems to me that I could not have been better disposed than I was, and

[18] See A 27r-30v, 111-117 and here p. XXXI.

all my spiritual trials left me for nearly a whole year after that. Jesus wanted to make me taste a joy as perfect as possible» (A 32 v, 121). «The year following my First Communion passed almost entirely without any interior trials for my soul.»[19]

Already Thérèse is a soul of prayer and it is an interior need that urges her on. Let us glance through her past for an instant. While still very little, she already loves to sit down in nature alone, her thoughts become «very profound and,» adds the Carmelite now that she has experienced it, «without knowing what it was to meditate, my soul was absorbed in real prayer» (A 14 v, 91). During common prayers, her exterior attitude reflects her interior attention.[20] She liked to play «alone» (A 23 r, 105) and would have even wanted to live in a faraway desert place (with Pauline! A 25 v, 109). She spends hours looking at holy pictures and finds in them «the sweetest joys and strongest impressions» (A 31v, 119). It is in bed that she makes «her deepest prayers,» and unlike the bride in the Canticle of Canticles, she always finds «her Beloved» there (A 31r, 118). Sometimes, she hides herself behind the bed-curtain and then «thinks» about God, about life, about eternity: «I understand now,» writes the contemplative in 1895, «that I was making mental prayer without knowing it and that God was already instructing me in secret» (A 33v, 122). She is ten years old when she asks her sister Marie for permission to make a half-hour of prayer every day, and then, a quarter of an hour, but her sister refuses.[21] It is at the Abbey finally that Sister Henriette will explain to her this mysterious exercise which is called prayer or meditation: to make prayer is very simple; it is to place oneself in the presence of God, our Father, with the same love of a child as Thérèse loves her own father; it is to tell

---

19 A 39 r, 132. It is not known what «nearly a whole year» and «almost entirely» refer to in these passages. Was she thinking about her sufferings at the Abbey and, one presumes, about those caused by the absence of Pauline?

20 PO, pp. 352-353; PA, pp. 403, 277. Mlle. Philippe, who took care of the sacristy and was therefore well placed to observe the girl in church, is going to even predict her destiny: «Thérèse Martin is a real angel. I would be very surprised if she lived a long time: but if she does live, you will see that we will speak of her later, because she will become a saint» (PA, pp. 208-209). Provided that Mother Agnès, who gives us this detail, recalls it accurately.

21 PO, p. 249. It was «around the time of her First Communion,» says Marie. A 33 v, 122 suggests the same time.

Him everything, one's joys and pains; it is to make oneself very little; in short, it is «with the heart» that one makes prayer. Thérèse thanks her and goes to consult an expert, her Carmelite sister. Pauline approves.[22]

Thus the long-awaited and long-prepared-for day of her First Communion arrives. During the three months that still separate her from it, Thérèse's preparation for it intensifies; it is a «new thrust» (A 33r, 121). Pauline sends her an «attractive little book,» which Thérèse uses with enthusiasm, as we learn from a letter of February 1884: «every day I try to perform as many practices [that is, sacrifices] as I can, and I do my best not to let a single opportunity slip by. I say the little prayers from the bottom of my heart... and as often as I can» (LT 11, 190). This is radical language! Thérèse will record in this notebook 1,960 sacrifices and 2,773 ejaculations, for a period of sixty days.[23] She has already understood that love has no need «of striking works,» and she resolutely profits from the least opportunities! Marie repeats it to her: «She showed me the means of becoming *holy* through fidelity to the most little things» (A 33 r, 122). The echo of this teaching, divine or human, will express itself in the full spirituality of the «way of spiritual childhood.» Finally, May 8, 1884, the most «beautiful day of all days,» «this Heavenly day» of «unspeakable memories» and «interior peace» arrives (see A 34v-35v, 124-126). The psychological resonance is great in her soul, because the long separation has sharpened her desire and her consciousness of the reality of what it is. «How sweet was that first kiss of Jesus to my soul!... It was a kiss of *love*, I *felt* that I was *loved*, and I said: "I love You, and I give myself to You forever!"» There were no demands made, no struggles, no sacrifices; for a long time before, Jesus and poor little Thérèse had *looked* at each other and understood each other.... That day, it was no longer simply a *look*, but a *fusion*. They no longer were *two*;

---

[22] See *La Petite Thérèse à l'abbaye. Souvenirs inédits recueillis par une ancienne maîtresse*, N.-D. du Pré, 1930, p. 35.

[23] (*Note completed in 1994.*) See CG I, p. 182; also A. COMBES, *L'Amour de Jésus chez sainte Thérèse de Lisieux*, Paris, 1951, 2nd ed., p. 29. This «attractive little book» which was handwritten and revised, has been published with illustrations, under the title *Deux mois et neuf jours de préparation à ma Première Communion*, Paris, 1909, 96 pp.

Thérèse had disappeared like a drop of water that loses itself in the immensity of the ocean. Jesus alone remained, He was the Master, the King. Had not Thérèse asked Him to take away her *liberty*, for her *liberty* frightened her? She felt so weak and fragile that she wanted to be united forever to the Divine Strength! That same afternoon, she consecrates herself to the Virgin Mary «as a child throwing itself into the arms of its Mother, asking her to watch over it.» Thérèse radiates joy.[24]

Shortly thereafter, on June 14, 1884, she receives the sacrament of Confirmation, the coming of the Holy Spirit, prepared for and welcomed with love (A 36 v, 128).

This year of peace and joy is rich in graces, especially Eucharistic ones.[25] For example the second time that she receives the Eucharist, she experiences moments of «ineffable» union (A 36 v, 127).

Another Eucharistic encounter will exercise a lasting influence (A 36r, 127). One day, during her period of thanksgiving, Thérèse reflects upon what Marie had told her the evening before: Thérèse probably would not walk the way of suffering, God would always carry her as a child. At this moment, she understands forever that to suffer and to be a child are not mutually exclusive. «I felt born within my heart a *great desire* to *suffer* and at the same time the interior assurance that Jesus was reserving a great number of crosses for me; I felt myself flooded with consolations so *great* that I look upon them as among the *greatest* graces of my life. Suffering became my attraction; it had charms about it which ravished me without my understanding them very well. Up until this time, I had suffered without *loving* suffering, but since this day I felt a real love for it.» Although it was at first an object of fear and aversion, suffering becomes a desire and attraction, a charm, and it received a loving welcome. Later, it will cross over to a third degree of evolution by becoming a joy.

But suffering is desired in order to be able to love and to make

---

[24] Many witnesses are said to have noticed the exterior reflection of this interior jubilation: PO, pp. 241, 266, 543; PA, pp. 229, 259, 373, 387, 391. Later, Thérèse will say, about her consecration to Mary: «[I chose her] for my Mother in a special way» (LT 70, 482, of 1888).

[25] Thérèse received Communion sixteen times in this year until the crisis of scruples. See Mss II, 24.

love exclusive. It is another effect of her Communions: «I also felt the desire to love only God, to find my joy only in Him. Often during my Communions, I repeated these words from *The Imitation* [III, 26, 3]: "O Jesus! unspeakable *sweetness*, change all the consolations of this earth into *bitterness* for me." This prayer fell from my lips without effort, without constraint; it seemed to me that I repeated it not by my own will, but like a child who repeats the words that a person she loves has inspired in her.»[26] This will not prevent the child from quivering when she sees how the «person she loves» takes her at her word.

6. *Interior torment*

Thérèse is twelve years and four months old, when she is assailed by «the terrible sickness of scruples» that will last an eternity: a year and half. «One would have to pass through this martyrdom in order to understand it well: for me to express what I suffered for *a year and a half* would be impossible…» (A 39 r, 132), and, in fact, she does not linger very much on this point. This crisis is designed to emphasize in her the awareness of her fundamental fragility, and it is in this way that God wanted to prepare her for the great graces that await her. In addition, this is a basic element for her entire life, no less than for her «little way» which will come later on. This awareness must grow, but it would not have become what it did become without these experiences of her youth.

This terrible assault surprises her in a retreat, between the 17th and the 21st of May, 1885. It is likely that a negative and pedagogically deficient[27] catechesis had awakened in Thérèse this state of

[26] A 36 v, 127. «Shortly after her First Communion,» she will tell the maid of the Guérin family: «suffering, united to the love of God… will make one grow in perfection» (PO, p. 366).

[27] See Mss II, 26-27. In a small notebook, Thérèse made some summaries of the instructions. Here it is on mortal sin (we follow her lack of punctuation, A 13 v, 90): «What Father said to us was very frightening he spoke to us of mortal sin he depicted to us the state of the soul in sin and how much God hates it.» Note that the preacher, Father Domin, was «a very honorable priest, but scrupulous and fearful» (Mss II, 22). We also read what the poor child says about an instruction during the retreat for her *First* Communion, the previous year (*ibid.*): «Tonight the instruction

anguish and insecurity, this «interior martyrdom,» which she had already experienced in connection with her mysterious illness and healing two years earlier, and, further back, the feeling of insecurity which began with her mother's death. If now she was also going to lose her Jesus! Let us first study for a moment these doubts of conscience which we have already sketched and which are emerging again.

The first concerns her illness: «For a long time after my cure, I believed that I had become ill on purpose and this was a *real martyrdom* for my soul» (A 28 v, 113). In spite of the reassuring words of Marie and the confessor, this «*interior martyrdom,*» which occurred immediately after her recovery (*ibid.*), lasted for five years, until Father Pichon freed her from it at Carmel «as with the wave of his hand.» «Ever since then,» added Thérèse in 1895, «I am perfectly calm.»[28]

This first doubt immediately finds an ally! Disturbed by indiscreet questions about her vision of the Virgin, the child's happiness caused by the apparition of her Heavenly Mother changes into bitterness: «For four years the memory of the ineffable grace I had received was a real *spiritual trial* for me.... I thought that I *had lied*.... I was unable to look at myself without a feeling of *profound horror*... Ah! I shall not be able to say what I suffered except in Heaven!» (A 30v- 31r, 117-118). After four years and four months, at Our Lady of Victories in Paris, 'the Blessed Virgin made her feel that it was *really She Herself Who had smiled on her and had cured her*' (A 56 v, 164). Only then was the happiness which she had first experienced restored to her in all its fullness (A 30 v, 117). The two heavy simultaneous trials which imprint in her soul the acute feeling of vulnerability will also leave the feeling of a profound humility. It is in this sense that Thérèse understands God's intention:

---

was on hell Father showed us the tortures that one suffers in hell he told us that our First Communion was going to determine if we went to Heaven or to hell, I myself am preparing well I hope to go to Heaven.» And again on another «instruction» from the same retreat: «Father has spoken to us of the 1st sacrilegious Communion. He said things to us that made me very frightened.»

[28] A 28 v, 113. See also Mss II, 47. Father Pichon was in Lisieux at the end of May 1888. This is when he will declare that Thérèse never committed a mortal sin (A 70 r, 187). We shall return to this later.

to humble her (A 28 v, 113), to give her humiliations instead of honors (A 31 r, 118).

But in the meantime, the little girl of thirteen is still afflicted with scruples on many other points. She herself suggests that her scruples were general: «All my most simple thoughts and actions became the cause of trouble for me» (A 39 r, 132). She doesn't explain further, but it appears certain that one — not the only — of the sources of her difficulties was made up of doubts concerning chastity, doubts that were actually *unfounded*.[29] Thérèse seems to never have committed the least sin in this domain and perhaps was never even stricken by any temptation that was truly carnal. But, because of her education and the lack of instruction, and therefore the lack of intellectual clarity, she was bound to experience many spiritual anxieties, which could have been avoided but only served to purify her of self indulgence and to deepen the feeling of her weakness, and to make her progress in the love of Jesus; she progressed, while defending her treasure with jealous zeal, in the midst of flames which tormented her grievously but had no objective reality. What is at bottom here is a striking interplay of nature and grace, of the human shot through with the divine.

During this long crisis of scruples, Thérèse will sometimes taste «an instant of peace» after having confided in tears — a gesture so often repeated! — her scruples to her sister Marie; but this peace is as ephemeral as a «flash of lightning» (*ibid.*). She will nevertheless obey Marie so well that her confessor never suspected that he was dealing with a child who was ill: «I could have passed as being the least scrupulous soul on earth, in spite of the fact that I was scrupulous to the highest degree...» (A 41v, 136). One can guess at the inner tragedy mingled with heroic obedience, while reading her own confession: «She, too, [Thérèse] has passed through the *martyrdom* of scruples, but Jesus has given her the grace to receive Communion just the same, even when she believed that she had committed great sins...» (LT 92, 567).

It is not surprising that her health breaks down again. She must leave the Abbey and take private lessons. Two afternoons a

[29] We have studied this particular point and have come to these conclusions; see Appendix III, p. 361.

week she goes back to the boarding school — motivated at once by her love of the Virgin and by a concern not to displease her (A 40 v, 134) — to obtain her enrollment in a Marian association. Then, when the work lessons end, she goes up to the choir of the chapel and there, alone, she prays for an hour, an hour and a half, two hours,[30] until her father comes to fetch her. «This was my only consolation, for was not Jesus my *only Friend*?… I knew how to speak only to Him, and conversations with creatures, even pious conversations, wearied my soul… I felt that it was far more valuable to speak to God than to speak about God, for so much self-love intermingles with spiritual conversations!…» (*ibid.*).

Suffering continues its work of stripping the soul and separating it from earthly pleasures. Her sister Marie, 'without whom she could not live,' who is 'indispensable' to her, who is her 'sole oracle,' her only support in her trial of scruples, decides to enter Carmel herself. Thérèse resolves «to take no pleasure on earth.» In her room she hangs 'a large wooden cross without Christ': a symbolic and meaningful gesture of someone who loves very much.[31]

Compelled to live alone, Thérèse is delivered from her scruples after Marie's entrance (October 15, 1886) when she prays to her little brothers and sisters who have died: «Soon peace came to flood my soul with its delightful streams» (A 44 r, 140).

But Thérèse is flooded by many others «streams» — streams of tears. She remains hypersensitive and tearful like a little child. Basically, she has still kept in her psyche some impediment, some childishness, something she does not manage to overcome in spite of her real and great generosity. It is with pain that she looks at herself «still in *the swaddling clothes of a child*» (A 44 v, 141). She is twelve and a half years old when her father's absence, during a journey to Constantinople, causes her «much grief» (A 41 v, 136). She was thirteen and a half when a holiday of two or three days at her aunt's place near the sea, away from the company of Céline, is enough to make her sick with nostalgia (A 42 v, 137). She is thirteen years and nine months old when she pours a cascade of tears

[30] «One hour and sometimes two hours» (PA, p. 387), «an hour or an hour and a half» (PO, p. 548), say the nuns of the Abbey.

[31] For all these details, see A 41 r-42 v, pp. 135-137.

on her mother's grave because she forgot a bouquet of cornflowers; and during this stay so full «of sadness and bitterness,» people in Alençon are whispering that she has a weak character (A 43 r-v, 138-139). She is not yet «accustomed to doing things for herself» and she doesn't do «any housework whatsoever»; she tries however to make a bed sometimes or to bring in pots of flowers, but if Céline forgets to show surprise, this child of thirteen years cries... (A 44 v, 141).

The feeling of her powerlessness is very acute at this time; let us note this with insistence. Just look at the severity with which Thérèse judges herself: «I was really unbearable because of my extreme sensitiveness; if I happened to cause someone I loved a little trouble, even involuntarily, instead of rising above it and not *crying*, which would only make matters worse, I *cried* like a Magdalene, and then when I would begin to cheer up, I'd *cry all over again for having cried*.... No amount of reasoning with me did me any good and I couldn't manage to correct this terrible fault» (*ibid.*). Thérèse is turning in «a very narrow circle... not knowing how to get out of it» (A 46v, 145). «Up to the age of fourteen,» she will say later, «I practiced virtue without experiencing its sweetness, and I gathered none of its fruits. My soul was like a tree whose blossoms had scarcely opened when they fell» (CSG, p. 37). Thérèse had remained a child and «God needed to perform a small miracle to make [her] *grow up* in an instant» (A 44 v, 141).

But God will perform this very miracle! Will Thérèse ever be able to attribute it to anything else but Mercy? The existential milieu that we have described suggests not. Here is an experience and a lesson for her entire life! The «way of spiritual childhood» will benefit from it later on.

II. THE SECOND CALL

1. *The «grace of Christmas»*

Up to this point, it seems to be in secret that divine strength sustained Thérèse Martin during dark and difficult days. Now it finally shows its true face by becoming known and almost tangible. Thérèse is at the end of her fourteenth year and enters into a period of nine months that will remain engraved in her mind as an unforgettable memory, a time full of freshness and enthusiasm, a second call, the worthy beginning of «the third period of [her] life, the most beautiful of all and the most filled with graces from Heaven» (A 45 v, 142).

This period starts with what has been called the «grace of Christmas» 1886 (A 44v-45r, 141-142). The effect of it was as marvelous as the cause was banal: a word of annoyance on the part of her father, noting that it was eternally necessary to treat his big girl «like a baby.» Once again, Thérèse finds herself faced with the flagrant truth, more painful this time because of the fact that it is her beloved father who puts his finger on the wound: it is necessary «to rid oneself of the faults of childhood.» Will she repeat the classic gesture and run away in sadness? Here is the miracle of strength! Thérèse who has just received at midnight Mass «the *strong* and *powerful* God,» learns how to take possession of herself, to drive back her tears, to appear totally happy. That which a short time ago was impossible suddenly becomes «a sweet reality.» The victory obtained, after long years of effort, from a new «act of courage» (DE II 8.8.3) and from grace, gives her the healthy confidence in herself that will continue to prevail. There occurs in her «a sort of psychological crystallization which in one instant gave evidence of a 'state' which had been slowly preparing in her subconscious.»[32]

It is on this humble psychological foundation of a single instant, prepared in its turn by the 'good will of ten years,' that God builds a new life for her: «On this *night* (Christmas) when He made himself *weak* and suffering for love of me, He made me *strong* and courageous.» Thérèse 'begins to run as a giant and will no longer be defeated in any fight, but will march from victory to victory.' She receives «strength of soul forever,» «the grace of her complete conversion,» «the grace of leaving childhood.» This last expression dismisses forever a false idea of authentic «spiritual» childhood.

But this is not the only remarkable thing for her and for us. The axis that joins the two poles is mercy: on the one hand, there

[32] GREGORIO DE JESÚS CRUCIFICADO, «Les Nuits sanjuanistes vécues par sainte Thérèse de l'Enfant-Jésus,» *Supplément de La Vie spirituelle*, 63 (1962), p. 619.

are *ten years* of weakness, on the other there is this *single instant* of merciful omnipotence that suffices: «The work that I had been unable to do in ten years was done by Jesus in one instant, contenting Himself with my *good will.*» Thérèse, like the apostles, had fished without catching anything. Now, Jesus, «more merciful for me than He was for His disciples,» casts the net Himself.

Arriving at this point in her autobiography, the levels of her life superimpose and Thérèse moves on, almost unnoticeably, to an image that is similar, that of the fisher of souls: in short, it will not be long before *charity*, the love of sinners, will «enter into her heart,» as she says. But it is important to grasp clearly, if we want to understand Thérèse's journey, that here it is a matter of *subsequent* graces, as we shall demonstrate. Often the events of Christmas have been interpreted along the line of charity. But in fact the grace of Christmas 1886 is the encounter with the *Strength* of the God of love; it is the leaving behind of the «swaddling clothes of childhood» — in 1896 she explains herself again in these terms[33] — it is being taken away from the influence of hypersensitivity.[34]

It is incontestable that this grace is extremely important and that it prepares her for many others. No longer paralyzed by her

[33] «I received the grace of leaving my childhood,» it is «in a word, the grace of my complete conversion.» The miracle is performed to make her «*grow up*» (A 44 v-45 r, 141). On November 1, 1896, she will describe her «conversion» as follows: «Jesus who made Himself a child out of love for me, saw fit to have me come forth from the swaddling clothes and the imperfections of childhood... [He] clothed me in His divine strength» (LT 201, 1013).

[34] It is necessary to understand clearly the significance of this grace. Thérèse will always have a very sensitive nature, which will appear again in tears of sorrow: especially in the beginning (for example: A 54 r, 159; 54 v, 161; 63 v, 176; 68 r, 184), but also at Carmel (for example: A 77 r, 199; CSG, pp. 20, 201, 223). Nearly one year after Christmas 1886, she still feels her «great timidity» (A 53 v, 158); before her journey to Rome, she was «so timid that [she] usually hardly dared to speak» (A 57 r, 165). Some months before her death, she admits, one day, to being very intimidated in the parlor and adds: «My timidity comes from an extreme shyness that I feel when anyone pays any attention to me» (DE II 30.6.2). However, after the Christmas grace, it is no longer a question of *hyper*-sensitivity. Thérèse's strength of soul will appear more and more and with great evidence, while tears will only come «rarely and with difficulty» (A 45 r, 141). And when they do come, reason, or rather virtue, soon is able «to take the upper hand» (A 44 v, 141). She knows how to hide her feelings (for example: A 65 r, 179; 65 v, 180; 66 r, 180; 69 r, 186; 70 r, 187), and how this lovable Saint has learned this!... Nothing that is passing will ever again get her down, she vows in 1895 (A 43 r, 139).

excessive sensitiveness, Thérèse begins to 'come out of the narrow circle of herself' (A 46 v, 145). Freed from worry about her own person which she imposed on herself although as if in spite of herself, she opens herself more to others, and discoveries in this change of direction will not long be delayed. But the turn that her spiritual journey takes is not accomplished on that Christmas night alone. A great increase in the love of God has to be achieved in her, a love that will spread to the love of others. As time goes on, freed from withdrawing into herself, Thérèse makes great progress in the love of neighbor. Already, she says, referring to the summer months of 1887, she possesses «the desire to work for the conversion of sinners,» but this desire is not felt «as strongly» as it will be after the great apostolic graces which await her.[35]

2. The love of Jesus

Before coming to this new attraction to her neighbor, Thérèse experiences a great burst of love for God in the months that follow her «Christmas grace.»

Her desire for Carmel becomes intense. It is true that, while Thérèse's spirit was developing greatly, — this explains itself again after the Christmas liberation! — she feels an intense desire for learning, but she is not overwhelmed by it (A 46 v, 145). She already «burns» to follow her two sisters, says M. Martin on March 19, 1887 (PO, p. 515). Thérèse confides later: «Without this change [of Christmas], I would have had to remain in the world for many more years» (LT 201, 1013). But everything is changed! With Céline, who had become her intimate confidante, she now experiences here «on earth the *Ideal* of happiness,» they enjoy «the most beautiful life that young girls could dream about» (A 49 r, 150). Yet the younger sister feels that neither this sisterly love nor any trial that may come will be able to keep her out of Carmel: «The divine call had [become] so strong that, had I been forced to *pass through flames*, I would have done it to be faithful to Jesus…» (A 49 r, 149.)

It is effortlessly that, on May 29, 1887, the day of Pentecost,

[35] A 45 v, 143. See: «She had zeal for souls since her childhood, making prayers and sacrifices to save them» (Mother Agnès, PA, p. 175).

she receives permission from her father to enter the monastery. The two of them were walking a long time together in the garden of Les Buissonnets that afternoon, until the father at length plucks a little white flower from the wall and explains with what care God had preserved it until that very day. For Thérèse, inwardly touched, it is a «*symbolic*» scene that takes place here: 'she believes she was hearing her own story' (and later she will understand it even better!). She accepts the little flower as a relic and puts it in her *Imitation*, at the chapter «How one must love Jesus above all things»: a gesture that expresses a response.[36]

Thérèse's love of Jesus becomes very strong at this time. Quoting Ezekiel freely (16:8-13), she declares: «Passing close to me, Jesus saw that the time had come for me to be loved.» To the *Imitation* is added now «in abundance» a new food for her love: the book of Father Arminjon, *Fin du monde présent et mystères de la vie future*,[37] which Thérèse read in the months of May and June.[38] She reveals the importance of this reading: it «was one of the greatest graces in my life… a happiness that was not of this world… I already experienced what God has in store for those who love Him (not with the eye but with the heart) and seeing that the eternal rewards had no proportion to the small sacrifices of this life, I wanted to *love*, to *love* Jesus with a *passion*, to give Him a thousand proofs of my love while I still could.… I repeated over and over the words of love burning in my heart» (A 47 v, 146).

---

[36] See A 50 r-v, 151-152. Thérèse then knew by heart nearly all the chapters of the *Imitation*, which never left her (A 47 r, 146). But this chapter spoke volumes to her. «On the day of her entrance into Carmel, Mother Marie de Gonzague will ask her: "It appears that you know the *Imitation* by heart? Can you tell me a chapter?" Sister Thérèse of the Child Jesus immediately began Chapter VII of Book II: *How one must love God above all things* and continued it without lapse of memory all the way until the end» (DCL). In 1895, the little flower remains still in the same place in the *Imitation* (A 50 r, 152), like a faithful reminder.

[37] *"The End of the Present World and the Mysteries of the Future Life"* — English translation forthcoming.

[38] See A 47 r-v, 146. It is a question of the second edition of Bordeaux, Paris, Bar-le-Duc, Fribourg, 1882. (In 1964, the book was republished in Lyon.) One can read in Mss II, 32-33 three passages, copied by Thérèse, of which especially the second will often resound in her writings. The book contains nine conferences. On May 30, 1887, Thérèse copied an excerpt from the fifth; on June 4 and 5, excerpts from the seventh. It is therefore in these months that she was in the process of reading the work, probably in the second half of May and the first of June.

This reading coincides with the «conversations in the belvédère [their upstairs room with the beautiful view],» which were already taking place between Thérèse and Céline.[39] «From our lips came aspirations of love inspired by [Jesus],» says the Saint. «It seems to me that we were receiving graces as noble as those granted to the great saints.... Doubt was not possible. Faith and Hope were no longer necessary, and *Love* was allowing us to find on earth the One whom we were seeking.»[40]

She realizes what is happening in her: «I was growing in the love of God; I felt within my heart outbursts unknown until then, and at times I had true transports of love.» Sometimes she did not know 'how to tell Jesus that she loved Him and how much she longed for Him to be loved and glorified everywhere.'[41] Ten years later, she will again remember these «transports of love.» «Ah! how I loved God!» she then exclaimed (DE II 7.7.2).

A rapid transformation takes place in her soul: «graces as great as these could not remain without fruit, and the fruit was abundant; the practice of virtue became sweet and natural to us. At the beginning, my face often betrayed the struggle, but little by little this impression vanished and renunciation became easy to me, even from the first instant» (A 48 r, 148).

---

[39] A 47 v-48 r, 146 f. The volume of *Letters*, published during the lifetime of Céline, places them during the spring and the summer of 1887 (LT 24, 274). Thérèse suggests that they had already begun before the month of May, because the progress in virtue *that they encouraged* is precisely the basis of the authorization given to her in the month of May to receive communion four times per week (A 48r-v, 148). They certainly were prolonged to the month of June, because they adopted Arminjon's theme «Now, my turn!». Thérèse had copied this passage on June 4 (see CSG, p. 18 and Mss II, 32).

[40] A 48 r, 147-148. «I don't know if I'm mistaken, but it seems to me that the outpouring of our souls was similar to that of Saint Monica» and Augustine at Ostia. However, Thérèse didn't have an ecstasy, in the technical sense of the word (CSG, 2nd ed., 1954, p. 218; CSG p. 18). The description doesn't permit us to doubt the mystical character of these graces.

[41] A 52 r, 155-156. According to its physical place in Manuscript A, this passage would refer itself directly to the last days of October. But we see in it, with François de Saint-Marie (Mss II, 35), a digression that deals with the previous states and facts. The fundamental reality already dates back to some months earlier.

3. The love of sinners: co-natural grace

It is in this climate of intense love for Jesus that the new apostolic graces are inserted. «Insert» is the word to use here, because Thérèse's zeal looks above all to the love of Jesus, 'to quench His thirst.' The sight of a picture of Jesus on the Cross was at the source of this new thrust. In 1926, Mother Agnès situated this grace on a Sunday in July, 1887 (DE II 1.8.1), but this very tardy choice of a date does not appear to be accurate. François de Sainte-Marie prefers to see it as «an expansion of the Christmas conversion.»[42] He is followed by Stéphane Piat who calls the new grace «a corollary and as it were an enlargement» of the grace of December 25, 1886, and he places it «at the beginning of the year 1887.»[43] We gladly subscribe to this *co-natural* character of Thérèse's apostolic graces, but we can attach them only to the thrusts of her love for Jesus during the spring and summer of 1887, believing that the well-stocked data furnished by Thérèse are sufficient not to situate «the grace of the Crucified» and the zeal for souls that it causes, before the month of July. Let us listen to Thérèse describe and situate this expansion of her ideal (A 45 v-46 v, 142-145).

After having told about her Christmas grace, she continues: «[Jesus] made of me a fisher of *souls*, I felt a great desire to work for the conversion of sinners, a desire I hadn't felt as intensely before… I felt *charity* enter into my heart, and the need to forget myself in order to please others; since then I've been happy!» When did this love of souls enter into her heart? Further on, Thérèse answers: it was «before the *wounds* of *Jesus*, while seeing his Divine *Blood* flow that the thirst for souls had entered into my heart.» This is a clear allusion to the «grace of the Crucified» which Thérèse describes in these terms: «one Sunday while looking at a picture of Our Lord on the Cross, I was struck by the Blood flowing from one of his Divine Hands,[44] I felt a great pang of sorrow in thinking

---

[42] Mss II, 30.

[43] *À la découverte…*, p. 48. J. LAFRANCE also inclines toward this solution. See «La grace "unique" de mai 1887,» VT, 7 (1967), pp. 123- 124.

[44] On the reproduction that Thérèse looked at, there is no blood flowing from the hands of Jesus and falling to the ground. It is therefore a matter of an entirely interior, exclusively spiritual way of looking. See A. COMBES, *De doctrina…*, p. 57, n. 1.

that this Blood was falling to the ground without anyone hastening to gather it up, and I resolved to remain in spirit at the foot of [the] Cross to receive the Divine dew flowing from it; I understood that I was then to pour it out upon souls....» Another stimulus is attached (like a spontaneous reaction): «The cry of Jesus on the Cross also resounded continually in my heart: *"I thirst!"* These words ignited within me a new and very intense longing... I wanted to give my Beloved to drink and I felt myself consumed with a *thirst* for *souls*.» And to specify the category that she was then considering: «[The souls of] *great sinners*; I *burned* with the desire to snatch them from the eternal flames.»

The difficulty now consists in situating the «grace of the Crucified.» Thérèse brings it closer to the conversion of Pranzini. Pranzini is her «first child.» And to encourage herself in her apostolic action, Thérèse begs for a sign from God (even when she has «so much confidence in the infinite mercy of Jesus,» because we are after the experience of Christmas 1886!). The prayer for Pranzini follows, therefore, very near the «grace of the Crucified»; it is indeed unthinkable that, «burning» to save great sinners, she would have lingered very long to put herself to work. However, when she heard about Pranzini, he already «had just been condemned to death»; we are therefore *after July 13*, the day of his sentence. And already «everything led to believe that he would die without repenting,» which could suggest that one is not far from August 31, the day of his execution.[45] It follows, then, that the «grace of the Crucified» happened in July, maybe in August.

After a holy crusade of prayers and sacrifices, Thérèse learns, on September 1, 1887, of the conversion of her «first child.» The requested sign is granted. And in what a way! Pranzini, brought up on the scaffold, «seizes a *crucifix*... and *kisses* the *sacred wounds three*

[45] See Mss II, 30-31. Thus, we come back to the date that Mother Agnès proposed. Certainly, her testimony is not decisive, but it demonstrates nevertheless that she did not believe that she must situate the grace elsewhere. That she situated, since 1898 (HA, p. 71), the conversion of Pranzini «soon» after the event of the Crucified, reveals the same feeling. See also A. COMBES, *De doctrina...*, pp. 59-63. Thérèse will continue to pray for Pranzini. She will tell the Carmel: «It is for my child: after the tricks he played, he must need it!... I mustn't now abandon him » (Sister Geneviève, PO, p. 283).

times.» For the young apostle, this gesture is once again a symbol, it contains a mystical significance: Jesus reminds her by this sign, of her *own* «grace of the Crucified»! Because, exclaims Thérèse, «this sign was the perfect replica of the graces that Jesus had given me in order to attract me to pray for sinners,» when she herself saw the Blood of the Lord flowing from his wounds. «What an unspeakably sweet response!...»

This symbolic answer is a new grace, which will not fail to have a profound effect. «Ah! Ever since this unique grace, my desire to save souls grew each day, and I seemed to hear Jesus say to me what He said to the Samaritan woman: "Give me to drink!" It was a real exchange of love; to souls I gave the *Blood* of Jesus, and to Jesus I offered these same souls refreshed by his *Divine dew*. Thus it seemed I quenched His thirst, and the more I gave him to *drink*, the more the thirst of my poor little soul increased, and it was this ardent thirst that He was giving me as the most delightful drink of his love.»

A look back at the months that passed since Christmas 1886 is sufficient to remark, with the Saint, that she learned how to come out of her old «narrow circle» in a very short time. Her spiritual interest grows in width and in depth. At the age where «every young girl feels born within her the first vibrations of the heart of a wife and the heart of a mother,»[46] it is on a supernatural plane that Thérèse achieves her personality. It seems to her now — but, later, she will understand her mistake — «impossible to understand perfection better» (A 74 r, 194). She would have confounded the learned with her understanding of the «secrets of perfection.» Jesus instructs her «secretly in the *things* of His *love*» (A 49 r, 149), He serves her «the delicious and strong wine» of it (A 48 r, 147). Her way at this moment is so straight and so clear that she needs no other guide but Jesus (A 48 v, 148-149). It is a time of great idealism.

Now, more than before, comes the dawn of full realization. Trials await her, but they are those which will enrich Thérèse's way with new nuances, thus preparing her definitive way, the «little»

[46] ALBERT DU SACRÉ-COEUR, *Approches...*, p. 110.

one, which reveals its structure and its characteristics completely only at the heart of Thérèse's entire existence, while preserving many of the traits of her youth. It was proper to show how, in 1887, Thérèse put the finishing touch on conceiving the *goal* to which she will continue to aim until her death and how she dreamed of it in all the freshness of her adolescence.

Chapter II

The Discovery of Abandonment

(October 1887-March 1888)

If Thérèse believed that she was able «to fly away without fear to Carmel» (A 50 v, 152) to realize in peace her project of holiness there, very painful trials would first have to purify her desire and give to her vocation a greater stability. She who loves to do the will of Jesus will from now on be forbidden to require that the will of Jesus be conformed to hers: she must rather learn to make Jesus' will her own, whatever it is, even if it affects the time when she will be able to sacrifice herself in the monastery. In the month of March 1888, she will make this remark on the rough draft of a letter to Pauline: «I believe that God is sending me these trials so that I may desire nothing, not even what I believe to be the best» (LT 43 A).

Thérèse will therefore be invited to abandon herself and it is the grace of this period that she succeeds in this and discovers the values contained in this interior disposition.[1] It is possible that for a biographer, the six months from October 1887 to April 9, 1888, which still separate her from Carmel, do not constitute a separate chapter; but if one applies oneself to studying the preparation of the «little way,» this brief period of the painful awakening to abandonment does reveal itself as a new chapter and as a very impor-

[1] Not long before, Thérèse had encountered other burdensome trials, and one can not deny that she accepted them with a certain abandonment. But it was really that she submitted to sufferings and endured them than that she welcomed them through resignation, and turned them into a positive gift.

tant turning-point in the spiritual journey leading to the way of «spiritual childhood,» which Thérèse defined as «the way of total abandonment.» However, it must be pointed out that the abandonment of 1887 differs on more than one point from that which Thérèse will know later.

Rather than give an account of the exterior obstacles which stand in the way of the immediate realization of her Carmelite vocation and which Thérèse is called to overcome,[2] we will follow her interior history, the slow germination of the seed of abandonment watered with many tears.

I. BEFORE THE FAILURE

It is a brutal shock when, on October 8, 1887, M. Guérin, Thérèse's guardian, energetically opposes her entrance into Carmel which the young girl plans for December 25, the first birthday of her «Christmas grace.» Thérèse withdraws, «her heart plunged into the most profound bitterness.»[3] But she prays. «As far as God is concerned, these obstacles don't exist,» she writes on the same day. «In spite of everything, I feel that I am filled with courage; I am very sure that God is not going to abandon me» (LT 27, 288). From October 19 to 22, she passes through «a very painful martyrdom,» a «deep night of the soul»: like Jesus in the garden of agony, she feels alone, apparently forsaken, while Jesus «sleeps.»[4] On October 22, her Guérin uncle gives his consent; for Thérèse, there

---

[2] See, among others, A. COMBES, «Sainte Thérèse de l'Enfant-Jésus du Jardin des Buissonnets aux pieds de Léon XIII (29 mai - 20 novembre 1887,» *Mélanges offerts au R.P. Ferdinand Cavallera*, Toulouse, 1948, pp. 471-495 and Mss II, 34 f.

[3] A 51 r, 153. ALBERT DU SACRÉ-COEUR minimizes it too much when he says: «Small test, to tell the truth, very small test!» (*Approches…*, p. 123), but he is right when he points out in Thérèse a tendency to dramatize. This is why she has need of the repeated trials to lead her to a new attitude.

[4] A 51 r, 153. On the morning of the 22nd, she told Pauline: «I have never suffered so much; if this continues, I will die of sadness… but it seems to me that God always asks only for possible things, and He is asking this from me… Oh Pauline, I have only one hope, and it is prayer; I am praying and praying: if you only knew with what fervor! … I have been sorely tried this week, I have suffered very much.» See LD, pp. 294-296. It is the moment to note with S. PIAT (*À la découverte…*, pp. 53-54) that this insistence on entering Carmel is not explained by the unconscious need to recover a mother in the person of Pauline. The difficulties will be so serious, their

is rejoicing, the night has passed, Jesus has awakened. But, probably on October 25, she learns of the categorical *veto* from the superior of Carmel; she visits her: to no avail, and there are tears. On October 31, she has personal recourse to the bishop of Bayeux; she pleads without result; again, there are tears: «It seemed to me that my future was forever ruined.... My soul was plunged into bitterness, but also into peace, for I was only seeking God's will» (A 54 v, 158).

'Determined to reach her objective,' Thérèse conceives the idea to have recourse to the Pope, during her coming pilgrimage to Rome.[5] This journey, from November 4 to December 2, is important because of four experiences: *Firstly*, the «Marian» graces in Paris, which also mark the end of her doubts of conscience concerning the vision and the marvelous cure at the age of ten; Thérèse understands still better the maternal goodness of Mary.[6] *Secondly*, her contact with priests, which leads to her realization of their «extreme need for prayers,» since they remain always «weak and fragile» men (A 56 r, 163). *Thirdly*, clearer light on «the vanity of everything that passes.»[7] *Fourthly*, the invitation to abandonment in trial. It is this point that presently draws our full attention.

The journey unfolds, beautiful and happy. But, on November 20, her recourse to the Pope, her «only plank of salvation» (A

---

repercussion in Thérèse's soul so bitter that, in this case, she might have quickly abandoned her desire. The psychological factors that incline her to the convent will have had their influence, but, in the last analysis, it is the will to execute what she believes to be God's plans, that governs her perseverance. It is in this love of Jesus that the Saint herself, from the distance of several years, recognizes the motive behind her actions (See A 53 v, 158).

5 It was she who first thought of it: see A 52 r, 155 and especially LT 32: «before Pauline wrote me, I thought of it.»

6 «I understood that she was watching over me, that I was *her* child, and I could no longer give her any other name but *Mamma* for this seemed even so much more tender than Mother...» (A 56 v-57 r, 164). We will return to Mary's place in the spirituality of Thérèse. Here is a testimony again, caught live: «I was very happy at Our Lady of Victories» (LT 30, 307 from Paris, of November 6).

7 «[This journey] taught me more than long years of study, it showed me the vanity of everything that happens» (A 55 v, 162). She watches like an unbiased observer: «What an interesting study the world is when one is close to leaving it» (A 59 r, 168). She was already familiar with the world and its vanities (at the age of ten years, A 32 v, 120-121; at the age of fourteen years, A 53 v, 158), but this was not as it is now: «one month... during which I learned more than during several years» (A 67 r, 182).

62 r, 173), is a failure. Thérèse's prayer is nevertheless ardent and she points out to friends from Lisieux: «I have such a great confidence in Him [God] that He will not be able to abandon me; I'm leaving everything in His Hands» (LT 32, 332). But no, the cross is her portion.[8] She cries. All the attraction of her journey disappears (A 64 r, 177).

Interiorly, how does she greet the bitter disappointment? «At the bottom of my heart I felt a great peace, since I had done absolutely everything in my power to respond to what God was asking of me; but this *peace* was only at the *bottom* and bitterness *filled* my soul, for Jesus was silent. He seemed to be absent and nothing revealed His presence to me» (A 64 r, 177). Let us listen also to her confession on the day of the failure: «Oh! Pauline, I cannot tell you what I felt. I was crushed. I felt abandoned, and, then, I am so far, so far.... I was crying a lot while writing this letter; my heart is very heavy. However, God cannot give me trials that are beyond my strength.... I have only God, Him alone, Him alone!» (LT 36, 353).

II. AFTER THE FAILURE

At the time when she is invited to abandonment, an apt symbol to express her dispositions comes back to her mind: to be in the Hands of Jesus like a toy in a child's hands, completely surrendered and disposed to any kind of treatment. And this comes to pass with a seriousness that is way out of proportion to this childish symbol. Already before her encounter with the Pope, she had offered herself as «a little ball of no value,» to serve the «childish whims» of the Infant Jesus, «to amuse Him,» and «to please» Him.[9] But secretly she hoped that Jesus would accomplish His will for her and, like a wise child, would make His little ball roll to Car-

---

[8] See A 60 v, 170; 62 v, 174; 63 r. 175.

[9] See A 64 r, 177. This symbol, very likely borrowed from a poem of the time (*Le Jouet de Jésus*, by Dom J. LÉONARD, Trappist and abbot) is used in a letter from Mother Agnès to Thérèse, of November 8 (and also in her letters of the 9th and 10th), but presumably it had already been used in previous conversations. Thérèse returns to it in her letter of the 14th (see Mss II, 42-43 and CG II, p. 1169). It will become very familiar to her at this time.

mel: «This has to be possible [that is, to ask the Pope for permission to enter Carmel]; it has to be Little Jesus who is preparing everything, so that His *little ball* has only to roll where He wills.»[10] We should read: where *she* wills. The disillusionment will be all the greater.

But it does not take long for the future saint to understand and be reasonable. Jesus, she thinks, has pierced His toy in order to examine it in depth, but if then He dropped it, one day He will take it in His Hands forever.[11] Thérèse understood that He is the Master: if He «wishes to break His *toy*, He is free to do so. Yes, I truly desire everything that He wills,» she writes, again in tears, on the same evening as her failure in Rome (LT 36, 353). «Sad to see herself *on the ground*,» she becomes capable of «hoping against all hope» (A 64 v, 178). The example of Saint Cecilia, for whom she feels «the real *tenderness of a friend*» since Saint Cecilia experienced her confidence in the midst of the dangers that threatened her virginity,[12] must have encouraged her.

Thérèse's abandonment, if it does not succeed in giving her back her joy at the bottom of her heart,[13] nevertheless leaves her with the hope of «becoming a prisoner» in time for December 25; but, we must say it with her: her hope is founded on God alone.[14]

Upon her return to Lisieux, she 'surrenders herself completely, having done everything that had depended on her' (A 67r, 182), but on the advice of Sister Agnès, she does not hesitate to write to the bishop of Bayeux. The post office is the source of 'a new dis-

---

[10] LT 34, 335 of November 14, 1887.

[11] See A 64 r-v, 177. The detailed description at this place, that dates from 1895, was inspired by a letter of Mother Agnès of November 23, 1887 (LC 66). Only, Thérèse expresses herself with more soberness.

[12] A 61 v, 172-173. Saint Cecilia will become her «saint of predilection, her intimate confidante.» But when Thérèse writes, in 1895: «Everything in her delights me, especially her *abandonment*, her limitless *confidence*,» we believe that it is here a matter of a present reflection, of which the seed, it is true, dates from 1887. The relationship between verbs in this paragraph suggests, as we see it, that the word «delights» is a present tense, and not a simple past. Moreover, Thérèse immediately continues in the present tense: «Saint Cecilia is like....» See also n. 21 of chapter V of this part.

[13] A 65 r, 179. «The earth... appeared to me like an arid desert without water» (A 66 r, 180).

[14] A 67 r, 182 and 66 r, 180.

appointment' to her each morning [as she hoped to find a letter of response from the bishop], but this 'didn't shake her faith' (A 67v, 183).

Arriving at this point, it is good to ask ourselves what pushes the girl to this astonishing perseverance. Is it the obstinacy of her will which is «always so ready to impose itself,» as she will say one day, very humbly of course (A 68 v, 185)? With the same humility, two years before her death, Thérèse analyzes her conduct as being motivated by «only the love of Jesus,» by the decision to love Him alone, and by the desire to not displease Him for anything on earth.[15] Let us listen to her plead her case in a letter to Bishop Hugonin, of December 16, 1887 (LT 38 B, 381): «Little Jesus made me feel so much that He wanted me for Christmas that I cannot resist the grace that He has given me,» and Thérèse is not afraid to remind His Excellency that it is a question of «the accomplishment of God's will.» The letter to Father Révérony, the man who, in Rome, encouraged the failure, is no less eloquent: «there are only eight days from now until Christmas! But, the more time advances, the more I hope; this is perhaps temerity, but nevertheless, it seems to me that it is Jesus Himself who is speaking within me. All the distractions of the trip to Rome were not able to chase from my mind for one instant the ardent desire of uniting myself to Jesus. Ah! Why call me so strongly if it is only to make me languish far from Him?» (LT 39, 388). Her vocation is obvious to her own eyes — so obvious that she never thought to submit it to a spiritual director.[16]

III. A SECOND «GRACE OF CHRISTMAS»

Christmas 1887 arrives and Thérèse is not behind the grilles of the Carmel of Lisieux. Jesus sleeps in His manger and in 'the broken heart' of Thérèse; on the little 'toy remaining on the ground' He does not seem to cast a glance anymore.[17] But the bonds that

---

[15] See A 49 r, 149; 53 v, 158; 58 r, 167; LT 112, 658.

[16] Mother Agnès, PO, p. 164 and Sister Geneviève, PA, p. 259.

[17] See for these details, as well as for next one, A 67 v-68 r, 183- 184.

God wants to break this day are those same ones that attach the future saint, not to the world, but to her own will: «I begged Jesus to break my bonds, and He broke them, but in a way totally different from what I expected....»

It will be truly a second «grace of Christmas» to understand it! This trial «was very great for my faith, but *the One whose heart watches even when He sleeps*, made me understand that to those whose faith is like that of a *mustard seed*, He grants *miracles* and moves mountains in order to strengthen such a small faith; but for His *intimate friends*, for His *Mother*, He doesn't work any miracles *before having tested their faith*.» Forced by this harsh reality — which is a grace from Jesus, because it causes light to spring forth — Thérèse then understands that Jesus asks of her a subsequent step in the nakedness of faith and abandonment, before granting her the miracle of her entrance. Subtle hints from Céline and the nuns of Carmel point in this same direction on this day. For Thérèse, here again is a message from Jesus.

But when the new year brings the painful news that Mother Marie de Gonzague, now provided the bishop's authorization, decided[18] to delay Thérèse's entrance for three months, the cross is heavy and painful to the point of causing tears.

Still Thérèse accepts it again and it is this «very great» trial of the three-month delay, «so rich in graces,» that makes her «*grow* very much in abandonment and in the other virtues.» This time will pass under the sign of waiting and of conscientious preparation by «a *serious* and *mortified* life.»

Here Thérèse offers a precious testimony concerning the kind of mortification she practiced until then. «When I say mortified, this is not to give the impression that I performed acts of penance. Alas! I *never made any*. Far from resembling the beautiful souls who practiced every kind of mortification since their childhood, I felt no attraction for this; ... I could have, like Céline, found a thousand little ways to make myself suffer.... My mortifications consisted in breaking my will, which was always so ready to impose itself, in

[18] This decision was made at the demand of Sister Agnès... ! This resulted in the «very particular characteristic» (A 68 r, 184) of this trial for Thérèse. But by gentleness for her «little mother» she won't lay stress on it in her autobiography (DCL).

holding back a reply, in rendering little services without any recognition, in not leaning back when seated, etc., etc.» She will never use penitential instruments before her entrance into Carmel (CSG, p. 186). It is «the practice of these mere *nothings*» that is mortification to her. All this is the continuation of the «practices» (small sacrifices) of her childhood and this «fidelity in the little things» that Marie had proposed to her as a program. Céline described in these terms the period that lasts until the grace of Christmas 1886: «Even in this period of her life, she was actually really strong, in spite of the apparent weakness produced by her extreme sensitivity. This remarkable strength is clear to me from the fact that these sadnesses never diverted her in the least from her duties. As for my part, she never surprised me, even in this period, with a change of character, a quick word, or a lessening of virtue: she was mortified at every moment and in the smallest things. It seems to me that she let no opportunity escape to offer sacrifices to God.»[19]

What is there to say, then, of her renunciation *after* Christmas 1886, now that she desires to give to Jesus «a thousand proofs of her love» (A 47 v, 146)? With a gentleness and a new vigilance, she has shown herself to be generous in a thousand ways and in the least of opportunities. Of course, few people ever suspected the extraordinary spiritual flight which she was taking in such an ordinary setting. Thérèse Martin remained as she always was at the Abbey school: she stayed there «without attracting attention, entirely hidden, as the Child Jesus had passed through Nazareth.»[20] But her Guérin uncle had a discerning eye: «This child will do great things,»[21] he said.

Before following Thérèse as a Carmelite, we must make note of the three characteristics of the kind of abandonment that was born in her soul through contact with her recent difficulties. 1. The abandonment from October 1887 to March 1888 *is born* of trials; it is therein that it finds its starting point. 2. It is accompanied by *sadness*. 3. It is still *limited* to the realm of encountered difficulties. Later

[19] PO, p. 268. Perhaps we must here take the part of reverence.

[20] *La Petite Thérèse à l'Abbaye…*, p. 17.

[21] Jeanne Guérin, PA, p. 515.

Thérésian abandonment will go through a profound evolution. Then, in the «little way,» it will be born of a determined vision of God Himself, it will be a source of joy, and it will expand to a general disposition of soul. It would be a mistake to exaggerate the contrasts, but the differences are nonetheless considerable.

An existential line has been drawn and it will be extended. The discovery of the «little way» will not make an abstraction out of past experiences and dispositions already lived. When Thérèse will be fascinated by new realizations through understanding that God is maternal mercy by biblical definition, the present experiences — the goodness of Jesus who has nevertheless taken the «little ball» which He at first had rejected, and also Thérèse's blind waiting — will serve, together with other old and new factors, to form the bed[22] through which a new river will pass.

[22] It is in this sense that we can understand A. COMBES' affirmation that the Christmas grace of 1887 constitutes «the [it would be better to say *a*] starting point of the Thérésian little way of spiritual childhood» (*Contemplation et Apostolat*..., p. 90) and also the affirmation of S. PIAT, according to whom, «timid and clumsy, but already implied clearly, the [it would be better to say: *some of the*] musical themes that will in the future constitute the "little way"» already appear (*À la découverte*..., p. 71). But the assertion that already «the outline of childhood is impressed on her heart» (*ibid.*, pp. 66-68) seems premature to us.

CHAPTER III

To Disappear in Order to Love

(April 1888-1892)

On April 9, 1888, Thérèse Martin, entering into «the prison [that she preferred] to all the palaces on this earth» (LT 201, 1013), becomes involved in a new situation. Not only does her farewell to the «world» inevitably have great psychological repercussions, but spiritually, her way changes considerably. She now follows the evangelical counsels, she devotes herself to an austere life in a purely contemplative setting, she espouses the Carmelite spiritual tradition. A new period begins that will last approximately five years.

Thérèse herself stresses this number, when she says, regarding suffering, that 'for five years this way was hers' (A 69 v, 187) and she notes additionally that it was «especially» since the day of the election of her dear blood-sister Pauline as Superior — Thérèse had at that time been at Carmel for five years all but a few weeks — that she «flew» with love (A 80 v, 206). We will see in fact, in 1893, certain themes become attenuated in her writings and others present themselves.

What is the spiritual climate of her beginnings at Carmel? It is love, we know; love as an ideal and as a way but with this nuance that it shows up above all in the desire to disappear, in the quest for littleness-humility. Mother Agnès gives the same explanation when she assigns the characteristic of «humility» to this time period, «the care to be faithful down to the smallest things» (PO, p. 143).

This period is too complex to allow us to follow Thérèse day by day. Besides, although ninety-three letters, thirty-one of which are to her intimate confidante [Céline], are preserved and will serve us well, they do not form a journal. When Thérèse will describe this period later in her autobiography, she will often speak of it in a summary fashion. We thought therefore that it would be good to look over these years from different angles — always, however, keeping our purpose in mind. The examination of this long period constitutes a unit that we divide into two chapters, by reason of the broadness of the subject.

In the first chapter we shall examine Thérèse's new environment and the suffering that she encounters in it: there where abandonment blossomed not long ago, new riches await her. Then we will describe her dream of love or, in other words, her ideal of perfection, which she assiduously tries to achieve. In light of these facts, we shall be able to interpret in the second chapter Thérèse's search for littleness and its relationship with — its contribution to and its difference from — the subsequent «way of spiritual childhood.» Indeed, some texts could, at a first reading, give the impression that Thérèse was already walking in her «little way.»

We have entitled these two chapters «To Disappear in Order to Love.» This, it seems to us, characterizes the spirit which governs that period. In fact, Thérésian littleness is here mostly synonymous with humility and is pursued to support love for God. In «spiritual childhood,» on the contrary, littleness is mostly synonymous with confidence and it is sought in the perspective of God's merciful love for us. The contrasts, slightly exaggerated, nevertheless denote the differences.

I. IN THE CRUCIBLE OF SUFFERING

When she begins her autobiography, Thérèse of Lisieux writes: «I find myself at a time in my life when I can cast a glance upon the past; my soul has matured in the crucible of exterior and interior trials» (A 3r, 73). These words pertain primarily to the years of which we speak.

1. The «desert» of Carmel

The premonition of Thérèse as a child, identifying Carmel with 'the *desert* where God wanted her to go hide herself' (A 26 r, 109), turns out to be well founded the moment she crosses over the cloister-wall: «I felt as though I had been transported into a desert.»[1] To hide herself to the eyes of her brothers and sisters of the whole world whom she will not be able to forget, is for her but a means of hiding herself entirely in God, forgetting herself. To disappear from her own eyes: the spirituality of Carmel teaches her nothing else. The solitude, and the exterior detachment, to which is added a nearly constant aridity and great trials, will invite her to become a little grain of sand in the desert that she chose.

This desert «delights» her, of course. The girl who had believed that in this desert 'all the aspirations of her soul would be fulfilled' (A 54 v, 160) cannot stop repeating in her heart: «I am here forever and ever!» (A 69 v, 187). But is this not a romantic and ephemeral happiness which had already disappointed many a postulant? No, not another sound will be heard in the following months: Thérèse feels 'entirely in her element' (LT 58, 451), she is 'very, very happy and at the height of her desires' (LT 69, 480). After seven and a half years she will be able to testify that the intimate peace, which she tasted upon entering, 'remained her portion, even in the midst of the greatest trials.'[2]

This is because Thérèse possessed a spiritual realism of the highest degree upon entering the monastery.[3] If she resolutely preferred the cloistered life to the missionary life, it was 'to suffer more

---

[1] A 69 v, 186. «The comparison [of Charles de Foucauld] with Saint Thérèse of the Child Jesus is striking: Thérèse lives in the open Normandy city of Lisieux, far from any material desert, but the enclosure of Carmel is a bulwark of desert that definitively isolates her from her city, in order for her to live only in contemplation of God. In the Sahara, on the contrary, Brother Charles wants to live united with the inhabitants of the desert, as Jesus lived with the inhabitants of Nazareth.» See M. CARROUGES, *Le Père de Foucauld et les Fraternitiés aujourd'hui*, Paris, 1963, p. 99. But basically, it is one and the same love of Jesus and mankind that inspired these two heroic lives. See also ID., «Soeur Thérèse et Frère Charles,» VT, 1966, pp. 6-13.

[2] See A 69 r, 186, and 65 r, 179.

[3] See VICTOR DE LA VIERGE, *Réalisme Spirituel de Sainte Thérèse de Lisieux*, Paris, 1956, ix-201 pp.

through the monotony of an austere life, without ever seeing the fruit of her labors.'[4] She knew the religious life «*exactly as it is* with its *self-mastery*, its small sacrifices carried out in the shadows» (A 58 r, 166). If Carmel did not cause her any disillusionment, it is because, upon entering, she did not create any illusions for herself (A 69 v, 186). Let us listen to the realistic tone of her dreams a few days before her entrance: «I want to give myself totally to Him, I want to live only for Him. Oh! no, I shall not fear His blows, for even in the most bitter sufferings, I always feel that it is His gentle hand that is striking.... I desire only one thing when I shall be in Carmel, that is to suffer always for Jesus.»[5] Soon she will even be persuaded that «a day of a Carmelite spent without suffering is a day lost» (LT 47, 423). If her spiritual mother, Saint Teresa of Avila, had compared life to «a night spent in a bad inn,» Thérèse truly wishes that hers is spent «in a hotel that is *entirely* bad [rather] than in one that is only half-bad» (LT 49, 427).

There is Thérèse Martin's «spirituality of the desert»: idealism filled with realism, happiness conquered by the sword which Christ came to bring (LT 57, 448). She will remain unchanged.

2. «*Suffering opened wide its arms to me*»

Behind the prioress and nuns who embrace the postulant amiably upon her entrance into Carmel, an invisible host approaches (the master of the «bad inn»!); Thérèse recognizes him and greets him lovingly: «Suffering opened wide its arms to me and I threw myself into them with love.» Since her first steps, which 'will meet with more thorns than roses,' she commits herself to the way of

---

[4] See CSG, p. 147 and 193.

[5] LT 43 B, 400. Pauline, who is so engaged in enabling Thérèse to enter, doesn't appear less clear-sighted when she invites her, in a letter at this time (LC 78), to follow along the way of Mount Calvary «the Spouse of Blood.» This last expression was dear to Father Pichon, who had preached a retreat at the Carmel of Lisieux in 1887. The notes taken on this occasion will serve Thérèse later as well. The sentences on suffering seem to have touched her especially (for example: LT 89, 556). S. PIAT indicated several excerpts that could have influenced Thérèse (See «Père Pichon et Sainte Thérèse», VT, 1962, p. 14-21 and above all DCL, «Le Père Pichon et la Famille Martin jusqu'à la mort de Sainte Thérèse», VT, 7 (1967), pp. 187-204; 8 (1968), pp. 49-69 and 114-140). Thérèse herself will use the expression «Spouse of Blood» again (LT 82, 536; 112, 658; 165, 860).

the cross which, she says, «was my way for five years. But on the outside, nothing revealed my suffering which was all the more painful since I alone was aware of it.» Those with whom she was intimate can be informed, however: for example, Father Pichon, who was very surprised at the time of his visit seven weeks after Thérèse's entrance 'to see what God was doing in her soul: her way was anything but sweet and childish' (A 70 r, 187). Or Céline, who will paint this portrait: «It is a fact that I always noticed in the life of God's Handmaid, that the Divine Master served her trial after trial, tribulation after tribulation. Everything always went awry or so poorly that it was constantly necessary for her to practice patience and abandonment» (PO, p. 294). Thérèse of Saint Augustine will also collect a morsel of Thérèse's confessions: «I assure you that I had many struggles and that I was not a single day without suffering, not a single one!»[6]

Although it is important to be aware of this environment of suffering, because of the rich fruits which it causes to ripen and also because it provides us with a basis for understanding certain declarations of Thérèse, it does not seem necessary to us to dwell on all the details. The most important ones will be given as a footnote.

The most painful element is the humiliating and agonizing illness of Thérèse's father. We shall return to this. The second place belongs, it seems, to Mother Marie de Gonzague, although actually the prioress's conduct was not the only source of suffering nor the greatest. During the 'five years of suffering' coinciding with this superior's leadership, it is difficult to see anything in this indication other than a veiled allusion to Marie de Gonzague. The terms in which Thérèse describes the attitude of the superior in her regard are sparing but clear: «*without her even being aware of it* [and the facts seem to prove that it was not here just a matter of stating things in a kindly way, but that Thérèse had a shrewd insight into the psychology of the other[7]] she [was] VERY SEVERE. I could not

---

[6] PA, p. 337. We are unaware of the time of this statement.

[7] A 70 v, 188. It is indeed surprising to see that the entire first edition of HA, prepared under the authority of Marie de Gonzague, who was prioress once again, not only doesn't soften the quoted words of Thérèse in the least, but adds four paragraphs of reminiscences (p. 112-113). This suggests that the prioress didn't doubt that her conduct was just. Although she highly esteemed her — «she is a treasure for Carmel,» she will tell Father Pichon (PA, p. 1181); «not a word to tell him, everything

meet her without kissing the floor.» If this education was «strong and maternal» at the same time, as Thérèse reminds her later,[8] it was the strong side that prevailed!

Another trial from the first years consists in her inability to open herself up to her confessor and her superiors. The reasons seem to be the following. Thérèse is a simple soul, already illuminated with a strong spirituality: her «difficulties» are not «problems»; she herself glimpses their solution. She is lacking a «technique.» «Not being accustomed to speaking about my soul, I didn't know how to express what was happening within it»[9]; she thinks and feels «deeply»: very often — sometimes maybe a little too readily — she confesses her inability to express herself with «the language of this earth.»[10] This trial, which seems to have lasted several years, surely by 1895 belongs to the past: by this time, Thérèse already possesses «a very great ease» in expressing herself.[11]

---

is perfect,» she writes to the Guérin family (PA, p. 517) — she suspected in Thérèse a hidden pride (Mother Agnès, PA, p. 194) and wrote to Thérèse (end of 1890?): «I don't believe my little lamb is without faults; far from it, I know very well that she has her failings» (LC 144). May we add that Thérèse was very sensitive and, besides, did not let her sufferings show.

[8] C 1 v, 236. This woman combined a real charm and good qualities with some great imperfections, among which jealousy and touchiness were prominent. She also had a very unstable character. It is undoubtedly on her bad days that Thérèse had much to suffer. Once she even threw herself into the arms of her novice mistress to confide to her that «her heart was breaking, without letting, however, the least whisper escape» (PO, p. 398). But then, it is on her good days that she clung to the banister of the staircase in order not to turn back to seek in her «beloved mother» some crumbs of pleasure (C 22 r, 263-264).... Several times, in her correspondence, Thérèse speaks of her with great kindliness (LT 93, 575; 129, 728; 167, 870).

[9] A 70 v, 188. Toward the age of fourteen, she never said a word about her interior feelings to the confessor (A 48 v, 148).

[10] See, for example, LT 32, 332; 59, 453; 84, 544; 90, 560; 106, 620; 123, 712; 124, 713; 139, 765; 152, 832; 154, 835; 178, 907; 181, 921; 202, 1021; 255, 1145; A 14 v, 91; 26 r, 109; 35 r, 124-125; 50 v, 152; 56 v, 164; 60 r, 170. The powerlessness to express her affection for her aunt shows in nearly all the letters she writes to her: it is like a cliché. Here is present the normal psychology of the teenager, who is often unable to express herself. See LOUIS DE SAINT-THÉRÈSE, «Saint Thérèse de l'Enfant-Jésus et la direction,» in *Direction spirituelle et psychologie*, coll. «Études carmélitaines,» 1951, p. 256.

[11] A 71 r, 189. Thérèse already mentions this difficulty with respect to her confession to Father Pichon, at the end of May 1888 (A 70 r, 187). As for her relationship with her mistress of novices, her 'soul didn't expand,' and she had to 'make a great effort' (A 70 v, 188), which she did in fact make (see for example: A 70 r, 187 and 74 v,

And then there is the austere life of the Carmelites of Lisieux, with all its deprivations that can make a teenager feel lonely, community life with its rules, its setting, and its members — of which she was not «the pet» (A 70 v, 188)! — and mortification in rest, food, and heating. Then there is the company of Thérèse's own sisters, of whom she hastened to say «that this had to be the cause of continual suffering... when one wishes to grant nothing to one's natural inclinations.»[12] And there are so many other details which would require many pages, Thérèse said, «but these pages will never be read on this earth» (A 75 r, 196), and she refers us to the last judgment to become acquainted with all the subtleties of her sufferings (A 70 r, 187)!

In some places the book nevertheless was open and those pages suggest to us the tone of the others. We will read in these pages, for example, her pain in seeing her profession postponed for eight months (A 73 v, 194) or the confusion of her soul in a 'storm as she had never seen the likes of before' when, on the eve of her profession, the devil instills in her «the assurance» of not having a vocation (A 76 r, 198). In the same way, we will notice her disillusion and her misunderstood tears in her father's absence on the day of her reception of the Veil.[13] In the same way, too, she is extremely tested during a night when she no longer knows if she is loved by God[14] or the period that precedes her encounter (in October 1891) with Father Prou, when Thérèse is overwhelmed by

---

195). This «real trial» (A 70 v, 189) will last «maybe two years» (see Mss II, 49). We see the same difficulty with Marie de Gonzague: rare directions, A 70 v, 188; without understanding how she could correct the shortcomings for which she was reproached, HA 98, p, 112. Thérèse writes in January 1889: «I can't tell her what is taking place in my soul. I leave without joy after having entered without joy!» (LT 78, 511.) Let us notice also that in the month of October 1891, she enters the confessional of Father Prou, «prepared to say nothing of [her] feelings, not knowing how to express them» (A 80 v, 205).

[12] C 8 v, 245. For two years (1889-1890, see CJ 13.7.18) she works with Pauline in the refectory: this nearness will be a cause of suffering, because Thérèse loves silence (A 75 r, 196). «You had come to the point where you no longer knew me,» she will tell her «little Mother» later (CJ 13.7.18). As for Marie who initiated her into the mysterious meanderings of the breviary, the fervent Thérèse dismisses it after a few weeks; she will thereafter ask for her forgiveness (see LT 49, 427, and n. 1).

[13] A 75 r, 196; 77 r, 199-200 and LT 120, 683.

[14] A 78 r, 201. This test certainly precedes December 5, 1891, the day of Mother Geneviève's death. See Mss II, 46.

«great interior trials of all sorts, even to the point of sometimes asking [herself] if Heaven really exists» (A 80 v, 205).

These last two confessions, revealed incidentally, take on therefore an even greater significance and make one suspect that there are similar trials. They are better explained when one studies Thérèse's prayer life in these years. After a brief period when she prays perhaps with less difficulty,[15] '(spiritual) aridity became her daily bread and she was deprived of all consolation' (A 73 v, 193). The situation in 1895, extending over nearly all her religious life up until that time, is identical: she slept during prayer and during her thanksgivings 'for seven years'[16]; retreats, especially preached retreats, were «of great aridity»: that of her Profession took place in «the most absolute aridity and almost total abandonment,» and Thérèse adds these very meaningful words: «Jesus was sleeping *as always*.»[17] André Combes perfectly summarized Thérèse's prayer when he said it was «the meeting of two sleeps: the sleep of Jesus and the sleep of Thérèse.»[18] However, a trial of

---

[15] Toward the *end* of 1895, she says that «for seven years» sleep overtakes her during prayer (A 75 v, 197). Also she seems to say that aridities are («soon») joined by sufferings of the heart caused by her father's transfer to Caen, in February 1889 (A 73 r, 193). The great aridity will therefore start after several months at Carmel. But it is certain that, already prior to the month of February 1889, Thérèse had experience of aridity in prayer (see LT 57, 448 and letters from her retreat in January 1889). Father Pichon also notes, in May 1888, her «aridity» and «spiritual trials» (PA, p. 114-115 and PO, p. 381).

[16] A 75 v, 197 and 79 v, 204. Letters from her superior reveal in turn the misery that Thérèse experiences in her prayers: «My Nightingale from Paradise must know that she is not the only one who is dry, very dry with God» (letter from her novice mistress). And Mother Marie de Gonzague, more in a manly way: «Do not be disturbed by the prayer of Saint Peter» (who slept during the agony of Jesus in the garden) (LC 91 and 144).

[17] A 75 v, 197. Our emphasis.

[18] «Sainte Thérèse de Lisieux, modèle de vie contemplative,» in *Ephemerides carmeliticae*, 13 (1962), p. 83. This definition is indeed owed to COMBES (see *Introduction...*, p. 257). It is necessary to note however that this looks rather at the hours of official prayer. Thérèse was a very recollected soul and one of habitual prayer, also knowing the sweetest aspirations of love (for example: CSG, p. 167-168); it is unanimously confirmed by eye-witnesses, but more still by her writings, where so often she begins totally spontaneously to speak with Jesus. We will return to Thérèse's prayer (see here Part IV, chap. vi). Let us recall here a word from the chaplain of Carmel, Father Youf, instructed by Mother Agnès (PA, p. 209): «[Thérèse] always makes me think about these blessed candles that burn in churches before the Blessed Sacrament and of which the sight alone leads one to prayer and recollection.»

this sort for a Carmelite must not be underestimated: to know to what heights God can call, to feel the duty of always disposing oneself to His call, to apprehend the example of the two founders of the reformed Carmel — and to spend hours, day by day, in mental prayer that is thoroughly arid.

3. *«Three years of martyrdom»*

This already impressive list of sufferings needs to be completed by her supreme trial: the slow agony of this «incomparable father,» with whose heart Thérèse's own heart beats in unison. This is the main element that determines the duration of the period we are treating.

What are we dealing with here?[19] After the appearance of extremely alarming events which by necessity caused a painful tension in the postulant Thérèse, M. Martin, once again gravely disturbed psychologically, had to be transferred, on February 12, 1889, to a mental hospital in Caen. He will remain there for more than three years, until May 10, 1892, when physically paralyzed he was returned to Lisieux. Before completely losing his lucidity, this friend of God understood and accepted this humiliating sacrifice. He died on July 29, 1894.

But why will Thérèse speak of a martyrdom of *three years* when the illness had already appeared before his transfer to Caen and it was prolonged for two more years after his return to Lisieux? The trial is measured here from an exterior circumstance that came with this illness and that had a great emotional effect on Thérèse. In fact, before his transfer to Caen, Thérèse was already suffering a great deal: «Now, we no longer have anything to hope for on earth, no longer anything but suffering and more suffering. When we have finished, suffering will still be there extending its arms to us.»[20] But the heavy blow of February 12 is 'the greatest cross that she could have imagined' (LT 155, 836). It is now that the Spouse of Blood «wants for Himself *all* the blood of her heart»; now «it is

---

[19] See the touching chapter XIV, «Le Sacrifice du Père,» of S. PIAT, *Histoire d'une famille...*, pp. 375-419.

[20] LT 83, from the beginning of February, 1889.

martyrdom that begins,» she says in the first letter that follows this indelible date.[21]

Because, to the eyes of Thérèse, her father's trial and her own consists above all in the humiliation of the mental hospital (and we must remember that at that time this matter was judged differently than today): there, her «king» is far from his loved ones, entrusted to good but strange hands, in the company of others who are afflicted, perhaps treated by force, still lucid enough to suffer from his state, stirring up on the part of the people of Lisieux — and even in Carmel — indelicate remarks which sometimes are expressed to his own daughters, and to Thérèse in particular.[22] It is in this sense that she repeatedly referred to the 'martyrdom of three years.'[23] When her father left the mental hospital and returned to the care of his family, although he was still sick, Thérèse will express her joy and her satisfaction.[24]

February 12, 1889 therefore remains a noteworthy date for Thérèse's spiritual journey, because her father's martyrdom is no less the martyrdom of Thérèse: «This passion was not his alone; just as the sufferings of Jesus pierced the Heart of His Divine Mother with a sword of sorrow, so our hearts felt the sufferings of the one we cherished most tenderly on earth.» When she declared, in June 1888, that she had 'suffered very much, but could still bear even greater trials,' she didn't imagine those of February 12, 1889, in which her father drank from the «*most bitter* and most humiliating of all chalices.» Now she would say 'she could not have suffered more; words could not express her anguish.'

---

[21] *Ibid*. And some weeks later: Jesus «is offering us a chalice as bitter as our weak nature can bear» (LT 87, 552). Eighteen months later, for the day of her profession, she wants someone to light the candles that her father had given her for her reception of the Habit. Then, they were pink and fresh, now pink no longer exists here on earth (LT 116, 671).

[22] See Mother Agnès, PO, p. 167, and PA, p. 189. Those inquisitive about psychiatry said, even in Thérèse's presence, that it was especially her entrance that had been the cause of the illness (PO, p. 167).

[23] She speaks of «the very sad trial of *Caen*» (LT 137, 760, we italicize), where the father was in «exile» (LT 138, 763). These letters date from October-November 1892, when her father returned to Lisieux. The dregs of the chalice were, for her, to leave this dear father «over there» (LT 107, 621), to be separated from him and to entrust him to religious but 'strange' hands (LT 261, 1163).

[24] See LT 138, 763; 146, 810; 155, 836.

What was the effect of these three years? In 1895, Thérèse is happy to have endured these «glorious trials.» «Yes Papa's three years of martyrdom appear to me as the most lovable, the most fruitful of all our life [that is, until 1895]; I wouldn't exchange them for all the ecstasies and revelations of the Saints. My heart overflows with gratitude when I think about this inestimable *treasure*.... We were no longer walking in the way of perfection, we were flying.» This February 12 will remain the day of «great riches.»[25] Yet her attraction to suffering, fulfilled in one instant, did not diminish, says Thérèse (A 73 r, 193); and, participating in a movement already put in motion from the time of her entrance into Carmel, «my attraction for suffering grew in proportion to its increase» (A 69 v, 187).

4. *The Fruits*

Good suffering makes a person strong and generous, but also humble and small. Not only did its persistence already confirm Thérèse in the way of abandonment and provide her with the means to nourish moment after moment the fire of her love — like «a gold mine to be exploited» (LT 82, 536) — but it greatly encouraged her desire to disappear in the esteem of others and of herself, in order to love Jesus more purely and more exclusively. At the same time, she found in her suffering a plentiful opportunity to experience her weakness. The sketch of the sad situation of the years 1888-1892 is the backdrop against which we must look at certain confidences of Thérèse and their connection with her «little way.» Soon we shall speak of that *more fully*.

Suffering bore other fruits as well. The first is the deepened awareness of the fleeting nature of time and the relative value («the vanity» was Thérèse's word) of all that is earthly, coupled with a great desire for Heaven. We will not delay here on what might be called her eschatological vision. Let us merely point out the great lines of her thought: the temporary nature of earthly things; life is but an instant, an illusion, a dream, one night, a mirage; the earth

---

[25] See A 86 r, 215. For the previous facts, see A 73 r, 193.

is exile — how many times must we hear it! — and bitterness[26]; Heaven is the true homeland (the new Les Buissonnets!) which is approaching and from where, in the meantime, Jesus watches over us; the value of every moment, because it prepares us for eternity.[27] In all of this, it is not a matter of disdaining what is created.[28] But, setting aside the romanticism which leaves no adolescent untouched, her sometimes unilateral formulation must be understood in the context of her education and her surroundings, her contemplative vocation, her love of Jesus — blind like all passionate love — and especially the painful trial through which she passes. On the other hand, we must take into account that saints see more clearly than we.... So for now let us leave this topic, but first let us underscore what is important for our subject: this vision greatly encouraged the nun in her way of generosity and of making self

---

[26] All these reflections are scattered liberally throughout the letters of this time. Also see A 79 r, 203. Let's quote a text: the things of this earth are «this *mud* so unworthy of an immortal soul» (LT 81, 529). This judgment, probably the strongest that Thérèse made, was pronounced during the month of January 1889, when the aggravated illness of their father causes bitter sufferings to Thérèse and Céline, the recipient of this letter. Another personal factor could have exercised an influence, perhaps unconsciously: «From my childhood [the Good God] saw fit to give me the intimate conviction that my course here below would be short» (LT 258, 1151). It is not impossible that this conviction contributed to gnawing little by little at Thérèse's physical strength.

[27] J. GUITTON highlighted the positive content of these Thérésian reflections: see «Le Génie de sainte Thérèse de l'Enfant-Jésus,» VT, 1964, pp. 103-125. See also «Sainte Thérèse et la vie éternelle,» VT, 1965, pp. 2-10, where he points out the influence of Arminjon on Thérèse. The influence of the *Imitation* was also great.

[28] One is correct to assume that our contemplative thought very deeply, as in 1893, when she revealed her little theology of creatures. (Is there not, all the same, a change in the direction of an approach to creatures that is more «benign»?) («*The flowers by the roadside* are the *pure pleasures* of life, there is no evil in enjoying them» (the words underlined by Thérèse are borrowed from the *Spiritual Canticle* of Saint John of the Cross (*Oeuvres*, IV, p. 142. There is moreover a strong Sanjuanist resonance, it seems, in this entire passage). But, she explains, creatures reflect the Beloved as a mirror reflects the sun, but they are not the sun itself. It is sort of an «indirect way.» It is why Thérèse sees in the trials that occur to her a sign of the jealous love of God, Who desires that she has «not even the time to breathe at ease, so to speak, [and that her] heart may turn toward Him, Who alone, she says, is our Sun and our joy...» (LT 149, 826). Three years later, she explains, putting the words in God's mouth: it is not a question of «separating ourselves *completely* from creatures and despising their love, their kindness, but on the contrary of *accepting* them in order to please Me, *of using them as so many steps,*» in order to attach oneself to Him alone (LT 190, 958). Let us notice that this letter is addressed to Marie de Gonzague to encourage her and to delicately correct her in her sadness after her difficult reelection.

disappear. Thérèse and Céline «dreamed of things of *eternity* and in order to soon enjoy this happiness without end, they chose here below for their only portion "suffering and contempt."»[29]

Another fruit of her trials is the conviction, deeply engraved in Thérèse's spirit, that suffering is a privilege of love. This thought, which takes its deep roots as far back as 1887,[30] is as encouraging as that of the good things that await us in the future: besides, the two are intimately united.[31] It will appear with great frequency in her letters of the years 1888-1892, then become more rare — as suffering decreases — and return with more regularity toward the end of the Saint's life. It contributed, and we emphasize this, to making Thérèse better understand Jesus' love for her: it is a special love, since it is a matter of *privilege*. This conception brings out the gratuity of His love and thereby highlights the idea of *mercy*.

What an anthology one could compose here! But let us be satisfied with a single text, taken from the first letter written after the «wound of love» (LT 82, 536) of February 28, 1889: «Far from complaining to Jesus about the Cross that He is sending us, I cannot understand the *infinite* love that has drawn Him to treat us this way. Our dear Father must be dearly loved by Jesus to have to suffer this way! But don't you find that the misfortune that is striking him is really the complement of his beautiful life? I feel... that I am speaking real follies to you, but that doesn't matter; I still think very many other things about the love of Jesus which are perhaps much stronger... What a joy to be humbled! It is the only thing that makes

---

29 A 73 v, 194. The quotation is a phrase from Saint John of the Cross.

30 It may be that it is again Pauline who enriched her sister on this point, when she encourages her in the trials preceding her entrance. Thus, she writes her on November 20, 1887: «Jesus never sends anything but crosses to His loved ones.... To those who don't love Him completely, He sends roses, [because they] would not love Him at all unless He did this.» And three days later: «Aren't you blessed by the *distinct preference* that Jesus is showing you?» (See LC 64 and 66). In any event, the grace that Thérèse receives on Christmas 1887 (See A 67 v, 183) was surely a contribution. Thérèse then understands that *intimate ones* of Jesus must first be tested before seeing miracles. Is the influence of Saint John of the Cross later added to it? (See here n. 43.)

31 For example, LT 108, 629: «Time is only a mirage, a dream; already God *sees us in glory*, He *takes delight* in our *eternal beatitude*! Ah! What good this thought does my soul! I understand now why He is not bargaining with us.... He feels that we *understand* Him and He is treating us as His friends, as His dearest spouses....»

saints!... Can we doubt now the will of Jesus concerning our souls?»[32]

Let us finish this sketch of the painful situation from the years 1888-1892. When Thérèse encouraged her sister Céline, through motives which were as admirable as they were unusual, to enter her Carmel, she will be able to speak with the authority of experience: «fear nothing, here you will find more than anywhere else the cross and *martyrdom*!» (LT 167, 870).

II. THE BEAUTIFUL DREAM OF LOVE

In a sense, one could characterize the spiritual life of our Carmelite at this time as the beautiful dream of love, a dream which she is convinced is achievable. Let us pause at this ideal and at the means of attaining it: love will remain the ideal of her «little way,» which will assume and enrich the means that Thérèse is presently using.

1. *«To love Him more than He has ever been loved»*

At the doorstep of the religious life, Thérèse could not have formulated her intentions more clearly: «*I want to be a saint*.... I am

[32] LT 82, 536. (note the word «to be humbled,» in the feminine. Thérèse and Céline take part in their father's humiliation.) See also, for 1888: LT 43 B, 400; 59, 453; 65, 467; 67, 477; 68, 479. And for 1889-1891: LT 81, 529; 82, 536; 83, 541; 84, 544; 89, 556; 94, 577; 100, 600; 107, 621; 108, 629; 112, 658; 127, 724; 129, 728. It is in this line of thought that we interpret the sentence: «Papa is God's little child» (LT 91, 563, of May 1889). The context clearly demonstrates it: M. Martin is God's little child, because, while sending him suffering, «the Lord loves Papa incomparably better than we love him»: while granting him this privilege, God singled him out as a child. This is totally the predominant idea of this period. Therefore, it is not here a question of an active attitude that consists in raising oneself like a child into God's hands. An allusion is perhaps attached to the fading of M. Martin's mental faculties, which also makes him like a child, but God will take very good care of him. Except for the term, which has many meanings, there is nothing in common with the notion «of spiritual childhood,» except the relationship (similar to the other indicated texts) of the privilege of suffering with the idea of mercy, as we have said. Note that the humbled state of M. Martin gave to his daughters a maternal feeling in his regard. It is very strong in Céline in 1892-1894: she will speak of her father as «her baby» (LD, from Céline to Marie of the Sacred Heart, around July 20, 1893).

not perfect but I WANT to become perfect.»[33] Until the day of her reception of the Habit, we encounter this resolution twice like a driving force in her life: «To become a great saint.»[34] If she doesn't succeed at this, «it will really be her own fault» (LT 72, 493); in any case, the fault will not be that of the Lord: «There is nothing that is impossible for Him. He does not want to set any limit to the SANCTITY of His lily [that is to say, of Céline, and quite evidently of Thérèse herself]... His limit is that there is no limit!» The present sufferings are like a pledge: they are favors «just as He gave to the greatest saints» (LT 83, 541). But it is not primarily for herself that she envisages holiness. It is for Jesus (and Thérèse, while knowing that He needs nothing, loves to present Him very humanly, as thirsty, afflicted, etc.); it is for love of Him and for love of her brothers and sisters, humankind. Her writings abound in this double sense that, after all, is not double for Thérèse except in appearance. Let us listen to this declaration which precedes her entrance by a short while: «If at the moment of my death, I could have a soul to offer to Jesus, how happy I would be! It would be a soul that would have been snatched from the fire of hell and would bless God for all eternity» (LT 43 B, 400).

To become holy is to follow the path of the total gift of oneself. Thérèse never thinks otherwise: «Jesus is asking ALL, ALL, ALL from you — as much as He can ask from the greatest saints» (LT 57, 448). «I want to give all to Jesus, and I don't want to give to the creature even one *atom* of my heart.... He wants that *all* be for Himself! Ah well! *all* will be for Him, all! Even when I feel that I am able to offer Him nothing, then, like this evening, I will give Him this *nothing*!» (LT 76, 5 03). Just days before her reception of the Habit, she said: «I would so much like to love Him! ... To love Him more than He has ever been loved» (LT 74, 499).

Has she therefore decided to rival her spiritual mother, the great Teresa of Avila, who said that she could never abide that anyone should love her Lord more than she? Thérèse, the little one,

[33] LT 45, 406, of March 27, 1888. The second sentence is attributed to Saint Augustine.

[34] LT 52, 433; 80, 519.

could read this text on a picture on the wall of her cell, and it is in this direction that she was encouraged to go.[35]

2. *On bold desires*

In May 1890 it seems,[36] Thérèse will confide to Father Blino, S.J.: «Father, I want to become a saint; I want to love God as much as Saint Teresa.» The preacher thinks he can see a hidden pride and presumption in what he calls her «bold desires.» However, Sister Thérèse replies: «But, Father, I don't think that these are bold desires, since Our Lord said: 'Be perfect as your Heavenly Father is perfect....'» There seems to be an echo of this encounter in a letter to Céline, in which Thérèse expresses a notion of holiness which betrays some personal experience: «Céline, do you think that Saint Teresa received more graces than you? ... As for myself, I won't tell you to aim for her *seraphic* holiness, but rather *to be perfect as your Heavenly Father is perfect*! Ah! Céline, our *infinite desires* are not, then, either dreams or fancies, since Jesus Himself gave us this *commandment*!» Even a nun gifted with much discernment like Mother Geneviève of Saint Teresa is taken aback by the audacity of Thérèse's desires and she warns Sister Agnès of the need to moderate the young enthusiast somewhat.[37]

But let us not be afraid: Thérèse of the Child Jesus is a very realistic idealist. She knows that the way of holiness passes through humiliation (LT 82, 536), that it «consists in suffering *everything*»

---

[35] See DLTH, p. 131. The ingenious Thérèse of Lisieux knew so well how to draw profit from every detail in order to love! For example, on the occasion of the marriage of Jeanne Guérin (in the beginning the month of October), she listens «eagerly» to everything she can learn about the delicate attentions of the young spouse, for, she says, «I didn't want to do less for my beloved Jesus» (A 77 r, 200). Marie de Gonzague encouraged the young enthusiast, by repeated notes, to follow the steps of their *Mother*: «to walk in our Mother's footprints!»; to become «another Saint Teresa»; to become «a great and holy Thérèse of Jesus» (LC 118, LC 144, CG II, 1097).

[36] One proposes this date, based on the letter to Céline, of May 1890, that we are going to quote and that contains, it seems, an allusion to conversations with Father Blino (see LT 107, 621, and n. 5). The content of this meeting is revealed by Mother Agnès, PA, p. 159.

[37] See *La Fondation du Carmel de Lisieux et sa Fondatrice, la Révérende Mère Geneviève de Sainte-Thérèse*, Lisieux, 1912, p. 88 and the La *«Petite Mère» de sainte Thérèse de Lisieux, Mère Agnès de Jésus*, Lisieux, 1953, p. 53.

(LT 89, 556) and in loving: «Let all the moments of our life be for Him alone,» she writes in 1889 on the feast of her Patron; «let creatures touch us only in passing.... There is only one thing to do during the night of this life, the one night which will come *only once*, and this is to love, to *love* Jesus with all the strength of our heart and to save souls for Him so that He may be *loved*.... Oh! to make Jesus loved!» (LT 96, 587).

The strong desires of 1887 do not appear diminished at all, then. Thérèse dreams of loving «unto folly,»[38] «to infinity» (LT 127, 724), «with passion» (LT 94, 577), «with all her power to love» (LT 104, 615), and «with a *jealous* care»![39]

It is not surprising if Thérèse, in this end-of-the-century France, begins to dream of martyrdom: «This was the dream of my youth and this dream has grown with me within Carmel's cloisters» (B 3 r, 225). But we must not get lost in the unreal: «Meanwhile, let us begin our martyrdom, let us allow Jesus to *tear away* from us everything that is most dear to us and let us refuse Him nothing. Before dying by the sword, let us die by pinpricks» (LT 86, 551); «if this is not through blood, it must be through love,»[40] 'but without feeling the sweetness of this love perhaps this is still martyrdom' (LT 94, 577). Notice the spiritual realism of the one who affirms: «[More than] ecstasies, I prefer the monotony of sacrifice» (LT 106, 620)! But she understands the divine economy that governs the «great wound» of February 12, 1889: «to detach her from all that is created» (LT 94, 577), to make her be 'alone with Him alone in order that He may unite Himself more intimately with her' (LT 120, 683), so that He might lead her to the true 'Father, who art in Heaven.'[41]

---

[38] For example: LT 93, 575; 96, 587.

[39] LT 95, 579. See also LT 101, 601. On the other hand, Jesus is no less jealous of her love: this is why He adds a little bitterness to every earthly joy (LT 149, 826); His hand is «*divinely jealous*!» (LT 120, 683). It is true, Thérèse Martin knows well how to manipulate the language of passionate love!

[40] LT 54, 440. See also LT 55, 442; 96, 587; 132, 740 and the *Note of profession* (Pri 2), where she asks for martyrdom of the body and heart. This martyrdom of the *heart* was given to her plentifully, because according to her own assessment, «Exterior crosses, what are they? ... What is a real cross is the martyrdom of the heart, the interior suffering of the soul» (LT 167, 870).

[41] See LT 127,724 and A 75 v, 197.

The consistency of Thérèse's love proceeds also from her deep faith in Christ, the first Truth and Beauty. «There is only Jesus who *is*: all the rest *is not*.... Let us love Him, then, unto folly» (LT 96, 587). «There is no other support to seek outside of Jesus, for He alone is *unchangeable*» (LT 104, 615). «Everything created, which is nothing, makes room for the uncreated, which is reality» (LT 116, 671). «[Jesus] alone is ravishing in the full STRENGTH of the word.... Beauty itself ... , He alone is perfect happiness» (LT 76, 503), «even when He is *silent*... even when He *hides Himself*» (LT 111, 654).

3. *A master of love: Saint John of the Cross*

Who taught her this sound doctrine of love? One of her masters is the friend whom she has recently «discovered»: Saint John of the Cross. He tells her marvelous things about their common Friend and about the way to love. Thérèse and John meet with each other more than often: «at the age of 17 and 18 years [in 1890 and 1891, then] I had no other spiritual nourishment.» But Thérèse had already been reading him before this, and later she will remain faithful to him. «How many lights have I not drawn from [his] Works,» she was able to say.[42]

«How many lights,» that is to say, a lot of light! In our opinion, after the Holy Spirit, Who speaks to Thérèse through the Scriptures and through illuminations of the faith, no one exerted as much influence on her as John of the Cross. His works never failed to pro-

[42] A 83 r, 210. The affirmation «at the age of 17 and 18 years» doesn't exclude a reading in the preceding years (one finds several quotations in fact in 1889) or in the years that follow (where we find many other quotations as well). We are not sure whether this «later,» when all books left her in aridity (*ibid.*), begins immediately after her eighteenth year. However, John of the Cross seems to always have enjoyed a certain favor with her: Thérèse continues to quote him and he is also one of her rare readings on her deathbed (see Mss II, 57). Sister Geneviève affirms that «even later (that is, after 1891), she especially appreciated the works of Saint John of the Cross» (CSG, p. 105). The edition that Thérèse will use was the translation (rather free and made after the Spanish edition of Séville in 1702) of the Carmelites of Paris (Paris and Poitiers, 1875-1880). We shall always quote from this edition, without explicitly mentioning it. See also Mss II, pp. 24-25, where it is said that Thérèse had for her personal use *The Spiritual Canticle* and *The Living Flame of Love*, hardcover in a single volume.

vide her with his leading ideas in her search for Christian perfection (there is, of course, nothing unusual about this in Carmel). Thérèse was nourished by the doctrine of John of the Cross on the necessity of blind faith, of total detachment, and of the benefit of suffering. A passage from *The Living Flame of Love*, dealing with this last point, gave her great interior strength.[43] But, there are two areas where the influence of the mystical Doctor is more apparent, understanding of course that the concept of «influence» does not refer only to the «contribution» that he made to her thought, but it refers also to the «support» he gave her, by encouraging and affirming her.

In any case, the greatest influence of Saint John of the Cross was exercised on Thérèse's conception of the ideal of love under its multiple aspects. «He is the saint of love *par excellence*,» she said of her spiritual father.[44] It is on this subject that Sanjuanist quotations are most numerous, for example in the letter of March 12, 1889: «Jesus' love for Céline can be understood only by Jesus! ... Jesus has done *foolish things* for Céline.... Let Céline do *foolish things* for Jesus.... *Love is repaid by love alone* and *the wounds of love are healed only by love.*»[45]

Another domain where the Sanjuanist influence is unquestionable is the Thérésian ideology of desire. We already touched upon this topic and we shall now examine how, at two crucial moments (the discovery of the «little way,» and the Offering to

---

[43] It is Marie of the Trinity who testifies to this (see PA, p. 471, in her obituary Circular, p. 11 and Mss II, 58). It deals with the explanation of the fifth verse («Pay all debt») of the second stanza of VF (*Oeuvres*, v, pp. 187-188), where it is a question of the necessity of suffering and the most interior pains by which God rewards the one who endured the most exterior pains well. According to these «intimate notes,» quoted in Mss II, Thérèse «lost her breath» when she read this passage. She explained with enthusiasm to Marie of the Trinity: «So, to welcome suffering well merits us the grace of a greater suffering or rather of a deeper purification to arrive at the perfect union of love. Ah! when I had understood that, strength was given to me to suffer everything.» «This passage,» said Marie of the Trinity, «fortified her marvelously at the time of her great trials.»

[44] Cf. Mss II, 58.

[45] LT 85, 546. The two quotations (underlined by Thérèse) are taken from the ninth and the eleventh stanzas of CS (*Oeuvres*, IV, p. 179 and 200). Thérèse alters the perspectives of Saint John of the Cross: with her, it is the soul that desires to be paid and healed. But there is the common principle of reciprocal dynamism in the love of friendship.

Merciful Love), a premise in the reasoning of Thérèse seems to be borrowed from Saint John of the Cross, notably: 'God does not inspire unrealizable desires.'[46]

4. The concrete realization

Thérèse therefore dreams of a great love. How will she attain it? We have already said something about this, but here is an answer that sums up everything and is, besides, quite characteristic of this time: «As for myself, I know no other means of reaching perfection but love.»[47] In her beloved *Imitation*, Thérèse read it and reread it: «Love can do all things; and *the most impossible things don't appear difficult to it*.»[48] And what a joy it was for the young nun to know that — following *Mother Teresa* — «*Jesus does not look so much at the greatness of actions* or even at their difficulty *as at the love which goes to make up these actions*.»[49] This is not the only lesson of this time period from which the «little way» will draw profit!

The entire chorus of eye-witnesses attests unanimously to how Thérèse puts herself to work with an admirable generosity. The Saint, in face of death, will confess how happy she was «for having deprived herself from the very beginning of her religious life» (C 22 r, 264). While still a novice, she makes a private vow of chastity[50] and she is faithful to the 'abundant lights that she received, since her reception of the Habit, regarding religious perfection, principally with regard to (the Vow of) Poverty' (A 74r, 194). The nuns consider her as «a very fervent novice and they never saw in her the smallest infidelity to the rule.»[51] Certainly,

---

[46] See here Part IV, chap. III.

[47] LT 109, 640, of July 1889.

[48] LT 65, 467 of October 20, 1888. Read all of this remarkable chapter V of Book III of the *Imitation of Christ*. Thérèse will quote it again, for example, in A 53 v, 158; 75 v, 197.

[49] LT 65, 467. For the quotation by Saint Teresa of Avila, see *Interior Castle*, the Seventh Mansion, chap. IV, at the end. Around this time, Marie de Gonzague writes to Thérèse: «My darling angel must know that Jesus isn't so much concerned about the value, the grandeur, or the size of the gifts that we offer to Him, as He is with our way of offering Him this gift» (LC 95).

[50] It results from a response from Father Pichon, of April 27, 1889 (LC 111).

Thérèse's «little practices» do cost her a lot in the beginning (A 74 v, 195), but she looks at the great Crucified One in the courtyard[52]: can she still refuse? Later, she becomes much stronger: «I floated so far above all those things that I was going along strengthened by humiliations; there was no one so brave as I in the line of fire» (CJ 22. 9.1). And what a testimony this contemplative gave on her entire religious life: «I wanted my soul to dwell in the Heavens, so that it looks upon the things of earth only from a distance» (C 9 r, 246).

Another name for this fidelity could be: *the untiring search for God's will*. Let us take the example of her profession. The long delay of eight months that precedes it is a 'great sacrifice very difficult to accept,' but it is enough for her to discover in her desire a «great self-love,» «a great search for oneself» by which she wants to impose her will on that of Jesus — a tendency already observed in the past. It is enough for her to understand this to cause her to decide to wait for 'as long as Jesus desires' in humility and «total abandonment,» and it is enough for her to regain her feeling of peace and truth.[53] The same ambition shows itself during her retreat — «underground»! — which she made to prepare for her profession: abandonment in obscure paths, «provided that [Jesus] is pleased,» and in this way Thérèse exercises «the most sublime virtues,» she seeks Jesus «alone, Him alone,» for «love of *Him alone* and not because of His gifts» and it is thus that she climbs «the mountain of love.»[54] The same day of her profession, Thérèse said: «I offered myself to Jesus in order for Him to accomplish His *will* perfectly in me, without creatures ever being able to place any obstacle in the way.» She expresses the same longings in a note that

---

[51] Marie of the Sacred Heart, PO, p. 244. Let's listen also to Marie of the Angels, PO, p, 416: «Her mortification was summarized in these words: to suffer everything without ever complaining.» There is an element of exaltation perhaps in one or the other of the numerous testimonies, but their unanimity is impressive.

[52] See HA 1907, p. 230.

[53] See A 73 v-74 r, 194 and LT 176, 902.

[54] See LT 110, 651; 111, 654; 115, 667 and A 76 r-v, 197-199. Also, in the brief crisis of vocation, on the eve of her profession, it is the search for God's will that is the supreme rule (A 76 v, 198). *Im*, 1, 3, 7, said insistently that love doesn't look at the gifts of the beloved, but at the beloved himself.

she carries on her heart: that she may attain «love, infinite love without any limits other than Yourself… love which is no longer I but You, my Jesus.»[55] Abandonment, and through it suffering, thus become Thérèse's happiness (LT 76, 503), her consolation, her strength, her peace, and her joy (LT 78, 511). However, it is a matter of a joy that is found in faith: «The other day, while reflecting on it,» she writes during the course of her great trials, «I found the secret of suffering in peace. The one who says *peace* is not saying *joy*, or at least *felt joy*.… To suffer in peace, it is enough to will all that Jesus wills» (LT 87, 552). But it is possible that «this *unfelt* joy [is] above every other joy» (LT 85, 546), that it becomes «a refined joy» (LT 78, 511). Thus, Thérèse became able to give thanks (A 73 r, 193). «God must love us very much to treat us like this,» she writes to Father Pichon. And to Marie of the Trinity she will say later: «These trials are for me occasions of perpetual thanksgivings.» With what happiness she sings in choir: «*In te, Domine, speravi*! ["In You, O Lord, I have hoped!" Psalm 70:1]»[56] «The ocean of suffering» was able to become «an ocean of graces and love» (LT 127, 724). In fact, one finds in Thérèse a dialectic of suffering and love: suffering begets love, and love contains suffering.[57] But suffering comes from the One who is 'admirable and especially lovable' (LT 94, 577). It is for Thérèse a sign of confidence if He sends her trials: «I am only too happy that He doesn't bother with me, for He is showing me that I am not a stranger when He treats me this way» (LT 74, 499). Whatever He does, Jesus remains a friend! With her, He is at home: He can «take a rest without a lot of ceremony!» (LT 104, 615). It is not difficult to understand that, in this perspective, confidence develops in her — a confidence which «works miracles»[58] and the lack of which offends Jesus.[59]

The love of Jesus and of others leads Thérèse more than ever

[55] See A 111, 417 and the *Note of profession* (Pri 2).

[56] See PA, p. 115, 483 and CJ 23.7.7 respectively.

[57] LT 81, 529; 83, 541; 89, 556.

[58] LT 129, 728. The context is that of the prayer to obtain the conversion of Hyacinth Loyson. Compare with the letter of Mother Agnès of November 8, 1887: «Pray for our Léonie with fervor and *confidence*, for prayer obtains all» (LD 8.11.87, p. 309).

[59] LT 92, 567. The context is that of scruples.

to fidelity in the smallest circumstances. «Let us profit, let us profit from the shortest moments, let us act like misers, and let us be jealous of the littlest things for the Beloved!» (LT 101, 601). One notices that it is not a matter here of a lack of magnanimity by which one wants to accomplish only small sacrifices alone! Elsewhere Thérèse affirms: «Love for mortification [in the sense of «bodily penances»] was given to me also, and it was all the greater because I was allowed nothing by way of satisfying it.» Then, while embracing penances of the Rule joyously, even bodily ones,[60] she orients herself decidedly, at the incitement of her superior, toward the mortification of her self-love instead of taking on penances that are not required. She applies herself «especially to practicing little virtues, not having the capacity of practicing the great ones»; she renders her sisters «all the little services» that she can; these are her «little practices.» And so she puts her self-love «in its proper place, that is, under her feet.» Thérèse also profited from an «inestimable grace» of living in the company of Mother Geneviève, «a *Saint* who was not inimitable, but one made holy by the practice of hidden and ordinary virtues.»[61]

The description of Thérèse's response to the love of Jesus is far from being finished. We have not seen anything yet of all her very characteristic efforts to grow in littleness, to imitate the Suffering Servant of Yahweh, or to avoid the least sin. But we needed the sketch of the environment in which she lived, and we needed to know her dream in order to be able to interpret these points well and to measure their relationship to the future «way of spiritual childhood.» As far as the genesis of the «little way» is concerned, progress has already come from the things we have described. The suffering and humiliations that the nun encounters in these first five years at Carmel make her grow a great deal in humility, abandonment, and her correspondence with the divine will. According

[60] Three times per week they took "the discipline." For three days they wore a penitential instrument for two or three hours. See here Part IV, chap. VI. However it is possible that Thérèse didn't wear this instrument of penance, which was not required in the beginning of her religious life. It is possible since the refusal of permissions related precisely to this point (DCL).

[61] Concerning mortification, see A 74 v, 195. On Mother Geneviève, see A 78 r, 201. We shall return to these two points with more details (Part IV, chap. VI).

to her, it is a privilege to be able to suffer and thus she further convinces herself of God's love for her. Her dream of love, her audacious desire or, in other words, her ideal of perfection, is very great. This perspective and, at the same time, the weight of daily suffering will increase her impression of remaining short of her ideal. To remedy it, she will later resort to her «little doctrine,» but in the meantime her way clearly remains a way of love: «I know of no other means» (LT 109, 640). In this way she makes progress in practicing, for instance, faithfulness to the «little things.»

Chapter IV

To Disappear in Order to Love
(Continuation)

With a slight exaggeration, one could characterize the present period (April 1888-1892) in another way: as the discovery of humility.

Surely, Thérèse had already been directed in this way before by her educators, and humiliating trials had kept her on that path. She had understood the relativity of what is dazzling and she had acted accordingly, with enthusiasm even for a hidden life. But all of this concerned the exterior contours rather than a real spirituality of littleness in her own eyes; it concerned her relationship to others more than to herself and to God. At any rate, one notices a remarkable intensifying of her humility. Before the «grace of Christmas,» Thérèse suffered from being unable to leave the things of childhood: how could she be enthusiastic, then, for what must be discarded at all cost? But freed from her quandary, having found the «desert» in which to hide herself, surrounded with great sufferings and feeling her own weakness, Thérèse right now is strongly convinced that in order to rise, one must descend; in order to grow, one must decrease. «He must increase and I must decrease» (Jn 3:30) says it perfectly.

Is this way of «becoming more and more little,» as Thérèse puts it, already the «little way,» where 'one must remain little and become more little each day'? Do «littleness» and «spiritual childhood» already overlap?

Actually, the desire to be little can raise several concerns, have other motives, express diverse attitudes. One must therefore examine what Thérésian littleness aims at in this period in order to be able to answer the questions at hand. One must even analyze some of her formulations which are similar to that of «spiritual childhood,» to be able to understand clearly what «littleness» means right now. As for a presence of the «way of spiritual childhood,» our conclusion will be negative, yet not entirely. In fact, the line of littleness-humility will hardly fade away, very much the contrary, when later on Thérèse will live her «little way» which is essentially littleness-confidence.

I. TO GROW IN LITTLENESS

1. *«To become more and more little»*

A few days before entering the monastery, Thérèse had received a letter from Pauline which seems to be at the origin of a new symbol and a new tendency in this fifteen-year-old girl: «I desire that Jesus' little Toy be not admired by anyone in this world,» writes Pauline. «If Jesus wants to play with a grain of sand, He is free to do so, the whole earth is His.... Jesus loves humility. Jesus loves what does not appear before the eyes of men, what they trample down underfoot, what they despise.... I am sure that the little grain of sand understands me and that it will not ever wish to become a mountain, but, on the contrary, always littler, lighter, in order to be lifted more easily by the breeze of love.»[1]

---

[1] LC 76, March 18, 1888. The symbol of the grain of sand (see also LT 45, 406, note 4) is found in a prayer of the General of Sonis, quoted by Father Pichon in a retreat to Carmelites, and perhaps it came through this route to Sister Agnès (see Mss II, 66). Nevertheless, S. PIAT notes (*À la découverte...* , pp. 68-69) that Thérèse could have read it before in one of her books. This symbol, as well as that of the «little ball,» finds a great success in Thérèse. But practically, neither of them seems to survive the year 1890, except in memories of the past (A and LT 176, 902 and in a stanza of the *Pious Recreation* of Christmas 1895, RP 5. — C 2 v, 237 where the latter doesn't seem to us to have the power of a symbol, but is simply a comparison). It is therefore possible that Thérèse no longer preserved the same enthusiasm for these kinds of symbols, maybe by reason of their passive, inanimate, impersonal, and (as for her «ball») too childish character. Let us note that it is especially (but not exclusively) in writings addressed to Pauline, the inspirer, that Thérèse uses them, perhaps as a kindness, and rather spontaneously. She will compare herself also to a reed, a lyre, a drop of dew, a flower, before coming to the symbol of the child, which will convey all. To encourage others, her novices in particular, she will also borrow this or that image from the world of games (for example: the top, see LT 212, 1039, with

Thérèse's reaction is most enthusiastic! «Oh! Pauline, I desire always to be a *little* grain of sand.... How much good your letter did me! If you only knew how much it has been at the bottom of my heart! I would like to say many things regarding the little grain of sand, but I haven't any time.... *I want to be a saint*» (LT 45, 406).

At Carmel, the movement toward lowliness intensifies. Thérèse understands that what is needed is not to *be* little, but to *become* always more little in order to be little. «That [the little and very obscure grain of sand: herself] may become smaller and smaller, that it may be reduced to *nothing*...» (LT 49, 427), that it may «become an ATOM» (LT 74, 499). It is her sadness to not yet be a «little enough or light enough» grain of sand (LT 54, 440). And on the day of her profession, the nun adds to the note which she carries on her heart: «Let me be looked upon as one to be trampled underfoot, forgotten like Your little grain of sand, Jesus» (Pri 2). Two months later: «In everything, [I want] very much to be the last and the littlest» (LT 125, 715).

This same tendency toward humility comes up when she compares herself with others. Marie is an eagle, Thérèse a reed (LT 49, 427). Céline a «Lily-"*immortelle*,"» Thérèse a «weak» lily (LT 57, 448). Céline is a beautiful dazzling lily and a diamond, while Thérèse is a poor daisy and a little pearl (LT 127, 724). It is her own desire that she is projecting, when she invites Céline to be 'the little shadow of Jesus' (LT 86, 551) or a little flower unknown on earth.[2]

What pushes her to this continuous self-abasement? Two things: the need to be truthful in face of the daily experience of her weakness and the need to love God more purely and more exclusively (which is, by the way, only another expression of the truth). This is what we wish to explain.

2. *Being weak*

The youngest of the Martins will become a great saint and yet she will never stop confessing her wretchedness and her imper-

---

explanatory note). Let us take this opportunity to say that a study of the symbolism in Thérèse of Lisieux would not be fruitless for the understanding of her psychology and certain nuances of her doctrine.

2 LT 123, 712; 124, 713; 127, 724.

fection. What must be said, then, of her first beginnings at Carmel, where a great torrent of suffering floods her immediately? Let us glean some expressions of her weakness: they are not difficult to find.

She was in the convent of Lisieux for three and a half months: «Life is often burdensome. What bitterness, but what sweetness! Yes, life is painful for us. It is hard to begin a day of work.... If only we could feel Jesus present, oh! then we would really do all for Him..., but no, He seems a thousand leagues away and we are all alone with ourselves; oh! what annoying company when Jesus is not there!» (LT 57, 448).

A collection of five intimate letters (LT 74-79, 499-514), written to her Carmelite sisters in a span of three days and in the silence of a retreat, sheds light on her interior situation and lets us observe her usual state (because Thérèse already began the «seven years» — and more — of aridity in prayer and sleepiness). In January of 1889 therefore, she speaks of «pinpricks» with which she feels «riddled» to the point of «being unable to stand it any longer.» «She doesn't understand anything about Jesus' conduct»; 'even more than before, if that were possible, she was deprived of all consolation.' 'Near Jesus: aridity! sleep!' What passionate dialogue: «[Thérèse] can say nothing to Jesus and, above all, Jesus says absolutely nothing to her»; «He makes no effort to carry on a conversation with me....» She is 'immersed in darkness'! First conclusion: 'she has great need of borrowing from her sister a little strength and courage, that courage which overcomes all things.' Second conclusion: «The *toy* of Jesus is weakness itself; if Jesus does not carry it, or He does not Himself throw His *little ball*, it will remain there inert in the same place.»[3]

Evidently, the experience of her weakness does not diminish when, after the transfer of M. Martin to a mental hospital, her suffering becomes greater. Five months later, a letter testifies to it: «Oh!

[3] It is superfluous to say that it is not here a question of the «little way.» Thérèse only expresses the observation that she is incapable of progressing by her own strength and that it is God Himself who must make her advance. However, the conviction of her own weakness is precious, it has to be extended, to deepen itself, and one day Thérèse will find her «little way» that will reveal to her *how much* God wants to make her progress. Soon we shall return to the expression «to carry.»

how hard it is to live, to remain on this earth of bitterness and anguish. [...But let us love God enough] to suffer for Him all that He wills, *even* spiritual pains, aridities, anxieties, apparent coldness...» (LT 94, 577). And so that we do not think these trials are always surmounted valiantly, the Carmelite assures us: «You are mistaken... if you believe that your little Thérèse walks always with fervor on the path of virtue; she is weak and very weak, and everyday she has a new experience of this weakness» (LT 109, 640). One can suppose that the feeling of weakness and imperfection (A 70 r, 187) or of the insufficiency of her own strength (A 77 r, 200) which Thérèse emphasizes at times, extends throughout the whole period of which we are speaking.

II. TO LOVE BETTER

That Thérèse was on fire with the desire for littleness comes, therefore, on the one hand from her thirst to be true and, on the other hand from her intuition of the chances that the humble acceptance of weakness for the sake of love generally provides.

We have seen that at this time love, for Thérèse, is at once an ideal and a way: it follows logically that her self-abasement will inject itself into this synthesis. Actually, Thérèse assures us of it repeatedly. She wants to become more and more little in order to love: to love more, to love more exclusively, and to love more purely, and weakness will be an effective means of reaching these three facets of the same love for Jesus. «You will always carry out those ardent desires for sanctity, for the apostolate, by aiming at nothingness out of love for God,» Father Pichon had written to her in June 1888 (LC 82, 436); «in your little nothingness, you will find the great ALL! And with Him what can you not do? Love for love! That is your motto. Try to rival Him. You will always be conquered.» And in October 1888, echoing a letter of Thérèse unfortunately lost: «To feel our nothingness and to rejoice in being only a poor little nothing is indeed a great grace. Profit!» Let us see how she has «profited» from her nothingness; it suffices to listen attentively.

1. To love more

«When I think that if God were to give us the entire universe with all its treasures, this would not be comparable to the *lightest* suffering!» writes Thérèse. But ordinarily it will be difficult to prove our love by suffering without failing: then our weakness, increasing the suffering, increases the possibilities of proving our love! «What a grace when, in the morning, we feel no courage, no strength to practice virtue.... Instead of wasting our time gathering gold-dust, we can draw in diamonds. What a profit at the end of the day!....» It is true that, sometimes «our poor and feeble little love» fails to react; this is followed then by «the difficult moment, when we are tempted to leave everything behind.» But this sluggishness can be transformed into a stepping stone toward a beyond not yet reached: «In one act of love, even *unfelt* love, all is repaired and behind us» (LT 65, 467). Three months later, the idea is repeated in the presence of Céline: to be willing «to fall a hundred times, if necessary, to prove your love [for Jesus], rising with greater strength after your fall!» (LT 81, 529). How Céline convinces herself of it because, after one month — after the «martyrdom» of the father and their own martyrdom began — Thérèse insists again: «How it costs to give Jesus what He asks! What *joy* that it does cost! What an unspeakable joy to carry our Crosses FEEBLY!... It is a gold-mine to be exploited» (LT 82, 536). One will remember the privilege of suffering; this Thérésian conviction finds here its explanation!

2. To love more purely

But let us not interrupt our little theologian of love: she explains further how the search for littleness and the exploitation of our weakness open the door to love.

First of all, they make it more exclusive of all love that is foreign. This is the reason why Thérèse wants to be this «very obscure grain of sand»: so that it will be «truly hidden from all eyes, that Jesus alone may be able to see it» (LT 49, 42 7), «seen only by the eyes of Jesus!» (LT 74, 499). It is this undivided love that is always her dream: «Jesus alone!... Nothing but Him! *the grain of sand* is so little that, if it wanted to place someone [according to the notes of *Letters*, the 'someone' is Mother Marie de Gonzague!] other than Him in its heart, there would be no more room for Jesus» (LT 54, 440). No, Thérèse wants to be anonymous, «in her place, that is to say, under the feet of all,» but «*seen by Jesus*» (LT 95, 579)! She wants to pass unseen to the eyes of others, so that her love goes directly and completely to Jesus.

If consideration from others must not be sought, self-consideration must also be avoided, and our misery helps us here. Thérèse writes to her cousin: «You must lose your little nothingness in His [Jesus'] *infinite All* and think only of this uniquely lovable *All*.... You must no longer desire to see the fruit of your efforts, [... Thérèse is also very weak, but] Jesus is pleased to teach her, as He did Saint Paul, the science of *rejoicing in her infirmities*. This is a great grace.... When we see ourselves as so miserable, then we no longer wish to consider ourselves and we look only at the unique Beloved!» (LT 109, 640).

Here "more exclusive" is synonymous with "more pure." That weakness plays a role in this regard is at least the experience of the novice of Lisieux: «The *grain of sand* wants to get to work without *joy*, without *courage*, without *strength*, and it is all these titles which will facilitate the undertaking; it wants to work through love» (LT 82, 536).

There is no better way to sum up the advantages that Thérèse sees in her weakness, than to mention the double wish that she herself formulated regarding her faults: that they might have no other result than «to humble and to make love stronger» (LT 114, 662).

3. *Already strong from her weakness?*

It goes without saying that Thérèse sought courage in the company of Jesus by faith in His provident love which remains faithful even if we only love feebly. Her letters give testimony to it: 'Jesus has done foolish things for us' (LT 85, 546): 'He is aware of our poverty and weakness much better than we ourselves are aware of them' (LT 109, 640); «when we don't have the strength for it, it is then that Jesus fights for us» (LT 57, 448); «He is helping us without seeming to do so» (LT 65, 467); and if He seems to forget Thérèse: «He will more quickly grow tired of making me wait than I shall grow tired of waiting for Him!» (LT 103, 612).

Is it in the light of these expressions that we must interpret this sentence of 1889: «It is its weakness which gives rise to all its confidence» (LT 55, 442)? Let us study this more closely.

In her letter, Thérèse compares herself to a reed. Some of her garments were, in fact, marked with this distinctive sign[4] and Thérèse, so sensitive to the symbolic, had immediately «seen» the hidden meaning behind it! However, in her letter, she says that she does not fear the «agonies of the heart» and the «pinpricks» — by now we understand this language — because she said «what does it matter to the *little reed* if it bends? It is not afraid of breaking because it has been planted at the edge of the waters. Instead of touching the ground when it bends, it only encounters a beneficent wave which strengthens it and makes it want another storm to come and pass over its frail head. It is its weakness which gives rise to all its confidence.» This last sentence comes at the end of an allegorical description and it is from this context that one must interpret it: the weakness of the reed, that is to say, its resilience, its «supple» character, is its confidence; in other words, «it is not afraid of breaking» but is sure of coming out of the storm stronger. Thérèse immediately adds: «[The reed] cannot break since, no matter what happens to it, it wants only to see the gentle hand of its Jesus.»[5] Therefore suffering won't break Thérèse; Jesus will take care of her! The aforementioned sentence about weakness expresses, as other sentences which were mentioned earlier expressed more implicitly, Thérèse's confidence in Jesus.

One should therefore not see here a kind of synthesis of «spiritual childhood.» It would be something else if Jesus Himself were the «water» or the «stream» that strengthens: thus the weakness of the reed would be a means of drawing from God's strength.[6] But

---

4 See LT 54, 440 and n. 3.

5 She loves this expression: the «gentle hand» of Jesus (see also LT 43 B, 400 and 74, 499).

6 It would be something else again if Thérèse had written: it is *my* weakness that gives rise to all *my* strength, in the same way as the old edition of the letters presented it before 1948. In this case, Thérèse would have departed from her allegory, to speak directly and in clear terms of herself, of the non-symbolized reality. The authors

the context shows that this is not the case: Jesus strikes and presses down; He is therefore not to be identified with the stream itself which is below![7] Thérèse's allegorical twists, often as supple as the reed that she describes so lyrically, are limited here! Besides, if Thérèse referred to 2 Cor 12:9-12 (which we do not accept), one should not see in it a veiled description of the «little way,» because when she quotes this Pauline chapter one year later, she still interprets the benefit of her weakness as a chance for her to love Jesus more exclusively (LT 109, 640). Soon, this state of mind will become more manifest, when we will speak of the famous letter [to Céline] of April 26, 1889.

4. In the wake of the suffering Christ

Thérèse's ambitions at this time concentrate on her devotion towards Christ's Holy Face. The two aspects of her devotion are united here: (1) to love Jesus, whose suffering Face is for Thérèse the mirror of His love, and (2) to imitate Him in His profound humility. This piety in inverse order provides a basis for interpreting Thérèse's ideals in these years.

---

who based their work on the old text, interpreted it therefore differently than us, that is to say, in a Pauline sense. Thus, for example, M.-M. PHILIPON, *Sainte Thérèse de Lisieux...*, p. 70, also in the edition of 1958; see also ID., «Het geestelijk kindschap,» *Tijdschrift voor Geestelijk Leven*, 3 (1947), t. II, p. 178 (Here it is a question of the translation of a conference given at the Thérésian convention in Paris in 1947). See also, again in 1955 (at any rate this study was published at that time, but it had also been given as a lecture in Paris in 1947), LUCIEN-MARIE DE SAINT-JOSEPH, «La Pauvreté spirituelle chez sainte Thérèse de l'Enfant-Jésus,» *Carmel* (France), 1955, p. 183; he adds: «This word *weakness*, in spite of the early date of this letter, already has the resonance that it will have in the way of childhood.» A. COMBES, basing his work on the authentic text, sees in it not only a Pauline reminiscence but the development of this one, and according to him it is a matter of a «psychological disposition... inscribed into her weakness itself... it is in this deficiency itself that she knows how to discover the grounds of a confidence that can only grow with her» (*En retraite avec sainte Thérèse de Lisieux*, Paris, 1952, pp. 86-87). We don't see how we can make these interpretations our own.

[7] There is perhaps another indication in the fact that Thérèse constantly writes the symbols of Jesus with a capital letter: see for example, LT 89, 556; 102, 610; 103, 612; 141, 783; 142, 794. However, «water» and «stream» are written here with a lowercase letter. On this point, it is perhaps interesting to point out another feature, one of the numerous ones which reveal to us the soul of Thérèse: very generally she adorns the symbols of others with a capital, reserving for her own a humble lowercase!

It is also the suffering of M. Martin,[8] a great servant of God, which intensifies devotion to the Holy Face among the Martin sisters (M. Martin himself had a fervent reverence for this devotion). The Holy Face became «our family's symbol,» Thérèse will say (LT 102, 610). The addition of «the Holy Face» to her religious name, the day of her reception of the Habit and upon her own request, is a first trace of it (LT 80, 519). Shortly before or shortly after,[9] she «fathomed the depths of the treasures hidden in the Holy Face» and «the mysteries of love hidden in the Face of our Spouse,» which were explained to her by Sister Agnès. Let us listen to her reaction, which demonstrates at the same time the personal character that she knew how to imprint on her own «spirit of reparation.» «I understood what *real glory* was. He whose Kingdom is not of this world showed me that true wisdom consists in 'desiring to be unknown and counted as nothing' [*Im*, I, 2, 3], in 'placing one's joy in the contempt of self' [*ibid.*, III, 49, 7]... Ah! Like the Face of Jesus, I desired that: 'my face be truly hidden, that no one on earth would know me' [Is 53:3]. I thirsted after suffering and I longed to be forgotten.»[10]

There is an interesting comparison to make here! At the time of her first clear call to holiness, Thérèse also understood what «true glory» was: to hide oneself, to forget oneself — without brilliant works being necessary — and, as a final element that was attached to it shortly afterwards, to suffer.[11] Here is added the emphasis of being «forgotten,» «unknown,» «counted as nothing»: there is all the tendency already triggered by the «grain of sand.» Thus, the two devotions, if one can use this term, blend. Of course, the Face

---

[8] In our work *Les Mains vides* (Cerf, new edition, 1988, pp. 58-66), we explained in what sense the suffering of Thérèse concerning her father brought her to better support her faith on Christ, crucified and resurrected.

[9] One would believe in the last hypothesis while listening to Mother Agnès' account: it is while explaining to Thérèse «her name of the Holy Face» that she communicates this devotion to her. See *La «Petite Mère» de Sainte Thérèse de Lisieux*, p. 60. The comparison of the Holy Face and the «vision» that Thérèse had about her father, «at the age of 6 or 7 years,» will be made only in 1893 or in 1894, «after 14 years» (A 20 v, 101).

[10] A 71 r, 189.The three quotations are at another time united in a letter of August 2, 1893 (LT 145, 808). Other quotations are added to it.

[11] See here Part II, chap. II.

remains an eloquent testimony: «Look in His Face.... *There, you will see how He loves us.*»[12]

Thérèse's walk in the footsteps of the suffering Christ will undergo nuances, however. The heroic disciple first wanted «to be despised,» as John of the Cross had desired.[13] But a letter of May 1890 makes us aware of an evolution: now, the «grain of sand» «longs to be reduced to nothing, to be unknown by all creatures. Poor little thing, it desires nothing any longer, nothing but to be FORGOTTEN.... Not contempt, insults, this would be too glorious for a *grain of sand*. Were one to despise it, one would have to see it, but to be FORGOTTEN!.... Yes, I want to be forgotten, and this, not only by creatures, but also by *myself*. I would like to be reduced to such an extent as to have no desire whatsoever.... The glory of my Jesus, that is all! As for my own glory, I abandon it to Him» (LT 103, 612).

Everything leads us to believe that it is in 1890 that Thérèse does her most intensive 'fathoming of the hidden depths of the Holy Face.' Her allusions multiply freely in her letters, and she quotes for the first time this passage from the *Imitation*: «to BE FORGOTTEN, counted as nothing» — while repeating that she prefers oblivion to humiliation[14] — and, in the month of July, she quotes for the first time Isaiah 53:15 which she will later on indicate as the foundation of her devotion to the Holy Face (DE 5.8.9).

III. A DOCUMENT ON THE «WAY OF SPIRITUAL CHILDHOOD»?

A letter from Thérèse, of April 26, 1889, serves to confirm our progress and thought process. It is an illustration and sort of another summary of many of the aspects already set forth. It has the

12 LT 87, 552. Thérèse also mentions other expressions of the love of the suffering Jesus for us: His falls (LT 81, 529), the crown of thorns and the effusion of blood (LT 87, 552). The old theme of Jesus' thirst on the cross returns: for example, LT 107, 621; 108, 629; 109, 640; 141, 783; 145, 808; 149, 826.

13 See, for example, LT 8l, 529 of January 1889. Also A 73 v, 193, which referred to a later period.

14 LT 95, 579. See also LT 176, 902 where she quotes this text (I, 2. 3), as well as the *Imitation*, III, 49, 7, in relation to the delay of her profession (end 1889-August 1890).

advantage of formulating a notion of holiness, as Thérèse then conceives it. What is more, its very content obliges us to think about its connection with the doctrine of the «little way.» At the same time, it constitutes a point of departure for some clarifications concerning Thérésian symbolism and the preparatory elements of «spiritual childhood.» This is why it has attracted the attention of several authors.

1. The text

Let us read this text (LT 89, 556) in its context and comment on it; we must go back far enough to come to its central passage. Remember that Thérèse and Céline, in whom she confides, are both suffering very much. The theme of the letter immediately concentrates on love.

«Oh! let us allow nothing... nothing in our heart except Jesus!» Whoever wants the end must desire the means: «let us not believe that we can love without suffering, without suffering much.» This is easier said than done: «Our *poor* nature is there and it isn't there for nothing!» But since one cannot love without suffering, poor nature offers us a rich chance to love: «It is our riches, our means of earning our bread! It is so precious that Jesus came to earth purposely to take possession of it. Let us suffer the bitter pain, without courage!... 'Jesus suffered with *sadness*; without sadness would the soul suffer?' [Thérèse is quoting Father Pichon here and continues.] And we would like to suffer generously, grandly... Céline!... What an illusion!... We would never want to fall? — What does it matter, my Jesus, if I fall at every moment; I *see* my weakness through this and this is a great gain for me.» This from

[15] See LT 108, 629. In reading Thérèse, one has the impression that the texts she puts together on a page still have their first freshness, and that Céline doesn't know them (see LT 108). One of the quoted texts is John of the Cross; all the other excerpts are in the breviary of the feasts, now omitted except one, that of the Passion, the Fridays of Lent. (Let us note here that the breviary and the missal contained, at least at this time, the entire Canticle of Canticles, evidently cited on many feasts. Following so many saints, Thérèse often quotes this biblical book.) She could have quoted from somewhere else, for example from Saint John of the Cross. From now on, she will quote Is 53:3 («the hidden face») often: LT 116, 671; 137, 760; 140, 781; 145, 808: 165, 860; 216, 1046; and in her Pri 12.

the weak Thérèse. Her «gain» is based on the previously established principle that suffering is very useful, if not necessary, in order to love. During the course of her epistolary exchanges with Céline, Thérèse had explained to her and did so often, as we have seen: human weakness can make one humbler (more of a «grain of sand,» unconsidered by others and oneself), and it can serve the cause of love, increasing the frequency and the quality of actions after the falls and hesitations of nature, thus arriving at an exclusivity and a purity which are greater. And on Jesus' side?

«*You can see* through this what I can do and now You will be more tempted to carry me in Your arms....» (This terminology is analogous to that of «spiritual childhood.») Thérèse's reasoning is clear: if Jesus wants her to advance without «falling at every moment» and notices that she does not have strength for it, He must logically conclude that He will have to carry her forward Himself! This is what she had already insinuated, in the previous month of January: 'if God does not carry her, she will remain there inert in the same place' (LT 79, 514).

But the Carmelite bears in mind — and it is important to note this — a possible withholding of help: «If You do not do it, it is because it pleases You to see me *on the ground....*» What God wants is worth more to her, for Thérèse is convinced of His love; and, consequently, her confidence, which she really expresses here, will not falter: «Then I am not going to be worried, but I shall always stretch out my arms toward You, suppliant and filled with love! I cannot believe that You would abandon me!...» With the help of a new quotation from Father Pichon on the well-known theme of the privilege of suffering, she supported her attitude of confidence: «When the saints,» said Pichon, «were at the feet of Our Lord, it was *then* that they encountered their Crosses.» How well Céline understands that misery, far from hindering sanctification, opens a door to her by the suffering that it increases. «If you only knew my misery.... Oh! if you only knew!» That's a very meaningful confession! but... «Sanctity does not consist in saying beautiful things, it does not even consist in thinking them or in feeling them; it consists in *suffering* and suffering *everything*.» And to quote a third time the authority of Father Pichon, to support her notion: «Sanctity! We must conquer it at the point of the sword, we must *suffer... we must agonize!*»

2. A draft of the «way of spiritual childhood»?

Are we in the presence of a real draft of the «little way» here, as André Combes and Stéphane Piat have suggested?[16] Let us be precise. Our search is not for an image or a mere expression, but for a reality. Moreover, Thérèse had already described herself as 'carried by [the arms] of Jesus.'[17] Also, it is not a question of locating this or that element which is also part of the doctrine of «spiritual childhood.» Love, abandonment, confidence, humility, fidelity: these are many of the aspects of it that we already find in Thérèse; otherwise, it would be regrettable and hardly Christian if they were not there! But to assume — which is not proven and in fact was not the case — that all the elements are already present in 1889 and do not have to evolve any further, does not mean that they make up the «whole,» the order, the hierarchy, the *doctrine*. A pile of stones does not make a house! Eventually one would have to make a third clarification: the presence, one time only, of a single text that describes a truth or a determined attitude, does not yet offer a final proof that we are dealing with a real «way» — something which is normally followed, lived, assimilated, directive of a life, and representing a spirituality. Obviously, this is a delicate matter, but, happily, it is not an issue here.

There are many differences between the letter just quoted and the «way of spiritual childhood,» even if one sees in the letter the materials that will serve the way later on. In the last analysis, the variations all come from the same core that we shall presently examine from different angles and under different lighting.

1. Having failed in all the other ways in which she did not «grow,» Thérèse will later see the «little way» as the only way possible, the absolutely *necessary* way to become holy. In this letter of April 26, 1889, on the contrary, the so-called «little way,» which is that of the intervention of God carrying the weak in His arms, is

---

[16] If it is useful, one can remember the content of the «way of spiritual childhood» as Thérèse described it in the narration of her discovery. See here Part I, chap. II. As for the interpretation of the present text by Combes and Piat, see farther on.

[17] LT 79, 514. To be carried or to be left on the ground were also the alternatives of her spirituality of the «little ball» for a year and a half. Her sister Marie used it while instructing Thérèse (A 36 r, 127). The expression is a secular one carried over into the language of piety.

presented as *optional*, chancy: Thérèse foresees in fact the possibility of a non-intervention of God. If this possibility is realized, she 'hardly worries': holiness remains secure, provided one wants «to suffer and to suffer *everything*.»

Her attention therefore focuses on different areas: the «little way» is concerned with the way of holiness, whereas the letter is concerned with a psychological method, external to the way of holiness: how to suffer deeply while falling at every moment or, thanks to God's intervention, how to advance valiantly without falling. One understands why, in the first case, Thérèse readily accepts remaining «on the ground,» whereas, later she will be anxious to find a solution to not remaining as she is: 'at the foot of the mountain.' Then there will be a different problem, one of great importance and ontological significance, for it will concern the very growth of divine life in her. As for the way of holiness, two remarks are yet to be made. Suffering, which predominates in the letter, will have a more secondary place in the «little way.» Then, Thérèse will clearly see how holiness is a grace from God that one must «receive»; here, on the other hand, one has to «conquer» it.

2. «Spiritual childhood,» according to Thérèse, will show us a vision which is very different from the divine *mercy* in 1889. Upon contact with the biblical description, Thérèse will understand that God is mercy *par excellence* to such a degree that He overflows with goodness, that He bends down over misery which recognizes itself as such and which entrusts itself to Him. Once these two conditions of humility and confidence are satisfied, Thérèse has no shadow of a doubt about God's intervention.

But in her letter of April 26, 1889, this deepened vision is still missing. Thérèse willingly confesses her misery and, with confidence, she stretches out her arms; however, even when she does, she doesn't consider God's intervention necessary: perhaps He will not intervene. To be sure, there is in the letter a sense of the faithfulness of God (Who will not abandon her) and of His goodness (by which He will be tempted to intervene at the sight of her misery, though maybe He won't do so every time). But in the «little way» this mercy will be condescending by nature, irresistibly condescending if one opens the door to it. Thérèse can no longer conceive, as she still does here, that God might be 'pleased to leave her on the ground.'

3. *Confidence*, too, is not the same in the two cases. In the letter, it is present, but it does not go to the point of actually anticipating God's intervention. In «spiritual childhood,» on the contrary, Thérèse's confidence will be such that God's intervention will appear to her as certain. Then, she will no longer be able to conceive that God would not take initiatives, because she has become convinced that «God cannot inspire unrealizable desires» (C 2 v, 237).

4. Let us say it again another way, from the point of view of *weakness*. The doctrine of «spiritual childhood» sees human misery, accepted and opening to God through confidence, in the light of the divine mercy which stoops toward it, in order to transform it. In other words, God's intervention depends on the attitude of the one who experiences misery: the person recognizes it and «approaches» God, trusting in His mercy; human weakness therefore, through the mediation of confidence, provokes the intervention of God.

On April 26, 1889, on the other hand, and all in the spirit of this period, Thérèse sees weakness in terms of humility and especially of love: so that finally one may love better. God's intervention — if it happens! — is provoked by the simple presence of misery and not by seeing it as Thérèse does when she sees it in the light of confidence in divine mercy. For, in the letter, there is not a causal relationship between the first sentence where Thérèse recognizes her weakness and the second sentence where God intervenes.[18] The cause of the «gain» from weakness is specifically different.

Let us conclude. The letter of April 26, 1889 does not outline the «little way.»[19] The problem which it deals with is different and

---

[18] The two sentences are simply juxtaposed, without any causal relation between them. This becomes clear here; in fact, Thérèse refers in each sentence (by means of the words «through this») to a third given fact: «to fall at every moment.» The «through this» which will eventually provoke God's intervention doesn't indicate, then, on Thérèse's part, the recognition of her weakness and her confidence. Besides, «what I can do» from the second sentence clearly refers to her continual falls and not to her humility or her confidence.

[19] We disagree, therefore, with the interpretation of A. COMBES (see *Contemplation et apostolat*, pp. 101-115 and 123-125), who suggests that the only difference between the spirituality of the letter and the doctrine of the «little way» is in the goal to attain: holiness, instead of to suffer much. However, we have seen, there are other more important differences. Here is what the author says: «Definitely, one would

so are its perspectives. One could say that the two protagonists of «spiritual childhood,» God and Thérèse, are both missing. This does not mean that Thérèse doesn't love intensely in her weakness, but that she exploits it in a way different from the way she will do it later. Her ideas will have evolved then and her conscience will be structured differently; her weakness will have become a greater «gain,» thanks to the new road which her love travels. Thérèse must first experience that she is even weaker than she thinks and that she succeeds less in transforming her misery into love than she now imagines. It is in discovering better how high perfect love is elevated that she will feel her powerlessness to attain it. Then she will conceive her way toward perfect love in another manner: this will be the «little way.» Understanding the mercy of God better, its primacy, and its dynamism, she will draw into this knowledge

---

force this essential text if one said that it already contains, in fewer words, the Thérésian elevator [that is, also for Combes, the «little way»], since it doesn't pose the whole of the problem of holiness, but only that of suffering. It is no less true that one would blind oneself to its existence and its significance, if one failed to observe that, since this date, Thérèse no longer has to discover the elevator that will excuse her from trying to attempt the impossible while exhausting herself in useless efforts: the elevator is already installed there. This observation is fundamental, because, to suppose that the problem of holiness is not yet resolved in all clarity in Thérèse's mind, the main part of the solution is an actuality and already so well acquired that it will henceforth be a question only of extension, confirmation or adaptation» (p. 124). It is also difficult to maintain that henceforth Thérèse «counts» on Jesus' arms (*ibid.*, pp. 124, 125), since she has in mind the possibility of the non-intervention of Jesus, which does not worry her. As we see it, Combes' mistake was to see the confidence of Thérèse, 'stretching out her suppliant arms' not as relative to suffering, but as an insistence (in spite of Thérèse's own declarations) to be 'carried by the arms of Jesus.' Here is the text of A. COMBES: «Thérèse still confesses that she always stretches out toward Him "her arms suppliant and filled with love." The attitude is rather meaningful. The motive that Thérèse immediately gives for it is still more (meaningful). Why, in fact, this permanent supplication and one that inspires love? For an extremely remarkable reason. Because, so long as Jesus' arms won't have raised her from earth in giving her this interior strength that her nature cannot give to her, Thérèse will judge herself practically "abandoned." However, that Jesus leaves her to her own resources is something that her faith cannot admit. Her last word therefore announces the triumphs of the mystical by Jesus' transforming intervention as indubitable» (p. 113). For the same reason, the interpretation of S. PIAT (*À la découverte...*, p. 101) doesn't satisfy us: «Like a first antiphon of the "little doctrine" of which the Saint will be the herald.... This calm misery which entrusts itself, this argument that the soul pulls from it in order to touch God, this gesture of confident calling, in short, this certainty of divine condescension: is this not — outlined awkwardly, like in a first intuition of it — the parable of the elevator?»

another dynamism: that of the confidence of the «little way» which, finally, will lead to holiness, not by «conquering» it, but by «receiving» it. Weakness will be changed into love, not through a direct way — a way that, after all, did not succeed — but through the mediation of confidence in the divine mercy which bends down to the littleness of the one who is confident. Weakness, opportunity that it was, will become a pledge.

At this time, there is less a contradiction in Thérèse's idea of «spiritual childhood» than simply an absence of it. The «little doctrine» is yet to be born; it will make use of elements which, in 1889, are still in evolution.

One could not better show the difference between Thérèse's spirituality during this period and the period after the discovery of the «little way» than by putting two formulations together. In the month of July 1890 — that is, more than one year after the letter of April 26, 1889, Thérèse will write to Marie Guérin: «My dear little Marie, as for myself, I know no other means of reaching perfection but love... Love, how well our heart is made for that!...» (LT 109, 640). More than six years later, about twenty months after the discovery of her «little way,» she will write to her sister Marie, and complete the exposition of her «little doctrine.» «It is *confidence* and nothing but *confidence* that must lead us to love» (LT 197, 998) [The italics are ours]. This way is obviously not opposed to a way of love; nor does it exclude it in the least. Love remains the soul of the «little way,» but its face changes into loving confidence. Psychologically and existentially, it is a different way to reach the goal, which remains perfect love. As a *goal*, love will always remain the center; as a *means* of progress, the center will become confidence — loving confidence, of course. And insofar as love is already present, it will want to prove itself.

But first, in the spirit of Thérèse, we need a slow re-examination of spiritual values, a new organization.

IV. THE MEANING OF A LIBERATING ENCOUNTER (OCTOBER 1891)

The picture of this period would remain unfinished if we did not speak of a reality which silently tended to hinder the flight of

Thérèse: we mean to say her anxiety over sin. Regarding this, she will have, after three and a half years of religious life, a very beneficial encounter with the Franciscan Alexis Prou. One should not hesitate to also connect this encounter with the «way of spiritual childhood.»

1. The fear of sin

When she entered Carmel, Thérèse still had the same sharpness of conscience, the same horror of sin that she had when she was a child.[20] At the same time, her education and her crisis of scruples, although the latter had passed, did not fail to leave in her a residue of fear. The fact that her doubts about her personal responsibility in her strange and unexpected illness at the age of ten persisted, even after the period of her scruples, already shows that, on this point, she did not recover a perfect balance. Her joy will be great when Father Pichon reassures her (A 28 v, 113).

This conversation, which takes place a little more than one month after her entrance into Carmel, is not limited there. In fact, after a general confession, Thérèse is told that she had never committed «A SINGLE MORTAL SIN.» This declaration and the fullness of joy that it caused in Thérèse must be understood in the light of what she has revealed to us: «I had such a great fear of soiling my Baptismal robe» (A 70 r, 188).

In Carmel, her delicateness of conscience is further accentuated by several factors. First, there is the growth of her ideal of love which increases her vigilance against every voluntary fault. There is also the continuous presence of her weakness and the aridity of her prayers which makes her wonder: am I faithful enough? And unfortunately, it is also the negative influence of certain preachers who sometimes said «that it was very easy to offend God and to lose one's purity of conscience»[21] and that easily «one can fall into mortal sin, even by a simple thought.» Mother Agnès described Thérèse's reactions: «During the entire course of these exercises, I

[20] See here Part IV, chap. I.

[21] Mother Agnès, PO, p. 155.

saw her pale and defeated, she could no longer eat or sleep, and would have fallen sick if it had lasted.»[22]

It is very likely that, under these influences, Thérèse was again anguishing over her past in 1889. Father Pichon, whose style of writing certainly gives one the impression of clear answers to questions from his correspondents, had written to her on October 4, 1889: «I forbid you in the name of God to call into question your being in the state of grace. The devil is laughing heartily at you. I protest against this ugly mistrust. Believe obstinately that Jesus loves you» (LC 117, 585).

A certain trouble seems nevertheless to persist simultaneously with a new intuition.[23] Let us listen to her avowals during the last days when she is preparing for the irrevocable gift of herself: «Tell Him [Jesus] to take me on the day of my Profession if I must still [this word is suggestive!] offend Him afterward, for I would like to carry to Heaven the white robe of my second baptism without any stain on it. But it seems to me that Jesus can easily give me the grace of no longer offending Him or committing faults that DON'T OFFEND Him» (LT 114, 662). And here is her reaction after the Sacrament of Confession: «Really pray in order that Jesus may leave me the *peace* which He HAS *GIVEN* ME. I was very happy to receive absolution on Saturday» (LT 112, 658). On September 8, she formulates, on the note that she carries on her person, this wish, that is the first: «[Jesus] take me before I can commit the slightest voluntary fault.»

---

[22] PA, p. 163. See a deposition of her novice-mistress: «This saying: "no one knows whether one is worthy of love or hatred" caused her to shed many tears one day, until she was consoled by the explanation that was given to her» (PA, p. 352). There is an echo of this text (Ec 9:1) in a letter of July 8, 1891: «no one knows if she is just or a sinner,» but Thérèse probes nevertheless: «But, Céline, Jesus gives us the grace of feeling at the bottom of our heart that we would prefer to die rather than to offend Him» (LT 129, 728). A letter from her novice-mistress, in the month of November 1889, also reflects (and urgently) a question of Thérèse, the one that she will always pose to herself (for example, B 2 v, 223, in a dream!): «Yes, my beloved little daughter, Jesus is very, very pleased with you» (LC 120).

[23] Let us notice this sentence from the month of May 1890 again: «[Hidden in Jesus], the poor atom will no longer have anything to fear, it will be *sure* of *no longer sinning*!...» (LT 95, 579). Thérèse herself underscores.

2. The encounter with Father Prou

Soon her intuition will receive the confirmation provided by the authority which it needed.[24] It is during the retreat of October 1891 that Thérèse receives «great graces.» Determined to say nothing about her «interior dispositions» — she then has «great interior trials of all sorts» — she enters the confessional of Father Prou and, to her surprise, she feels 'expanded, understood in a marvelous way, even fathomed. Her soul was like an open book for the Father.' What is the reaction of the confessor after the reading of this beautiful book? «He launched me full sail upon the waves of *confidence* and *love* which attracted me so strongly, but upon which I hadn't dared to advance... He told me that *my faults caused God no pain*, and that, *holding as he did God's place*, he was telling me in *His Name* that God was very much pleased with me....» Thérèse is very happy, because «never had I heard that our faults *could not cause God any pain*,» however «I felt at the bottom of my heart that this was really so, for God is more tender than a Mother.»[25]

It is clear, at least to us, that it is necessary to interpret 'the strong' attraction that confidence and love exert and the liberation that Father Prou brings about in the area of the question of faults. Thérèse herself explains why she felt attracted, when she says that she had already felt in her heart the keen desire to behave according to the permission that Father Prou will grant her. However, as we have seen, this previous interior feeling really concerned her faults and it is in this way that she explains it again in Manuscript A: it is a question of «little indelicacies.» When, later, Thérèse reminds Mother Agnès, twice, of her joy caused by the confessor's words, it is because the latter «taught her that her imperfections, all of human frailty, caused God no pain... because the fear of offending God had become an obsession in her life.» And others testify in the same way.[26] That the Father now 'launches her full sail

---

[24] Thérèse underlines (literally) that Father Prou speaks to her while *holding the place* of Jesus and in His Name. The account of this conversation is A 80 v, 205-206.

[25] Is the *comparison* between God and a mother contemporaneous with her feeling of God's goodness, or is it a later elucidation?

[26] PO, p. 155. See also Mother Agnès, PA, p. 163 and Marie of the Sacred Heart, PA, p. 235.

on the waves of confidence and love' stems directly from her behavior in the face of *sin and faults*: do not feel rejected because of your faults, do not break your stride, do not believe that God loves you less and that your own love is less sincere and that your confidence is not justified or hypocritical; trust yourself and love without the least reservation.

One must therefore not identify the movement of confidence and love, authorized by Father Prou, with «spiritual childhood.» Certainly, there is a progress in confidence, indeed considerable progress, and it will not fail to have its repercussion on a broader scale than the single domain of faults. But the element of confidence in God's goodness does not yet constitute the «little doctrine,» which has a specific motivation and construction; we explained it earlier and we will return to it. It would be sufficient to compare the two attitudes relative to her weakness: here, Thérèse advances, no longer trapped by her misery, but *in spite of it*. In the «little way,» she will advance, so to speak, *thanks* to it, having understood that it is because she is in misery, that God is all the more eager to help her in a special way, if she recognizes her nothingness and trusts in *this* mercy.[27]

She must still progress in confidence and in the understanding of divine mercy to get to the fullness of her «way of spiritual childhood.» We can perhaps still infer that the grace of October 1891 is not comparable to that of the discovery of the «little way» from the fact that we did not find any traces of it in the letters of the fol-

---

[27] We therefore distance ourselves from what S. PIAT wrote (in the chapter «À la découverte de l'enfance spirituelle,» *À la découverte…)* with respect to the conversations with Father Prou: «A turn is taken. Mother Agnès of Jesus emphasizes it before the ecclesiastical tribunal: "Ever since this retreat, she gave herself entirely to confidence in God and she looked in the holy books for the approval of her audacity. She repeated the words of Saint John of the Cross: 'One obtains from God as much as one hopes to receive from Him.' Father Prou had not revealed her way to her; he had approved it definitely» (p. 125). As for the testimony of Mother Agnès, it is lacking, we think, in historical perspective. Mother Agnès herself has moreover indicated as characteristic of the period lasting until her election to the office of prioress (February 20, 1893, therefore sixteen months after the retreat of October 1891) *humility* and *faithfulness in little things* (PO, p. 143). ALBERT DU SACRÉ-COEUR (*Approches…*, p. 173) suggests also that it is following her encounter with Father Prou that Thérèse engages herself in her 'little way' of confidence and abandonment.

---

[28] LC 151. The letter is of January 20, 1893.

lowing year. It remains rather surprising that Thérèse falls again — for one instant? a long time? to what degree? we do not know — into anxiety concerning her being in a state of grace, and this is much more than the problem of knowing if her faults 'cause God any pain.' Here is an answer of Pichon which mirrors one of Thérèse's letters from around the end of 1892: «Dear Child of my soul [!], listen well to what I am about to tell you in the Name and on the part of Our Lord: No, no, you have not committed any mortal sins. I swear it. No, we cannot sin gravely without knowing it. No, after absolution, we must not doubt about our state of grace.... Banish your worries, therefore. God wills it, and I command it. Take my word for it: never, never, never have you committed a mortal sin.»[28] Besides, if Father Prou 'launches her full sail' on the waves of love, Thérèse notices that it is «especially since the blessed day» of Sister Agnès' election, on February 20, 1893, that is to say, one year and four months after her encounter with Prou, that she «flew in the ways of love» (A 80 v, 206). Let us now follow this flight.

Chapter V

«It Is Jesus Who Is Doing All»

(1893-1894)

A certain obscurity hovers over this new period. It is probably the least known of all, the least studied by authors. And Thérèse's autobiography hardly tells us much about it. Why did she remind Agnès of the recent facts which the new prioress knew as well as Thérèse did? And the manuscript already counts a modest hundred and sixty pages.... Without dallying over the details, the Carmelite flies through the last three years 1893-1895, to arrive at the end in the four following pages.

Yet, occasional information is not missing. The inventory of 1893-1894 contains two Pious Recreations, fifteen Poems and the Correspondence. The latter is especially valuable. About thirty letters are preserved and among them there are thirteen, most of them lengthy, which are addressed to Céline: they fill about thirty-four large printed pages. The whole soul of our Contemplative is undoubtedly poured into these letters. She opens herself up to the friend to whom she can say: «I believe that God has not often made two souls who understand each other so well» (LT 142, 794). However, being in no way methodical, these exchanges do not readily surrender their secrets and it is only after careful reading that one can pull the main ideas out of them.

The year 1893 marks another turning point in Thérése's progress toward the «way of spiritual childhood.» However, it's difficult to say when this change begins. In the month of October 1892, the shared martyrdom of «Caen» having ended in May, Thérèse understands that her purification will now reach a more interior level. Her exterior suffering subsides even more when Sister Agnès is elected superior, on February 20, 1893; for Thérèse, she who was her mother 'in the secret of her heart' is at this moment *publicly* consecrated as 'her mother': she shows her enthusiastic reaction on the same day (LT 140, 781). Nearly three years later, she will confide that it is especially '*since* Pauline became her living Jesus, her book of Love, that she flies in the ways of love' (A 80 v, 206). These external events and their psychological repercussion had also fostered the determined spiritual atmosphere to which a trilogy of letters will finally testify in July 1893. It is therefore with a certain margin of imprecision that we point in an overall way to the beginning of 1893 as the point of departure of the new approach of the «little way.»

The change is not staggering. It is the old desire to disappear which prompts in Thérèse an awareness, already present, but now pushed into the foreground, and which will remain in her insistently. At the time when her exterior trials were lessened, the humble and fervent nun — who wanted to hide herself from the eyes of all in order to be seen only by Jesus — concentrated more on the *interior* dimension of her vocation of humility: to seek to do nothing that magnified her in her *own* eyes; to want to possess nothing of which she could boast. And she will insist at the same time on faithfulness to little things, and logically, on the refusal of whatever might seem remarkable. Even with regard to her effort to search for God, the same attitude clearly appears[1]: the effort is made, and is made very generously, but Thérèse attributes the beginning and the end of it to God alone; she wants to surrender to Him, to the very limit, whatever can make her «something» and an owner. «It is Jesus who is doing all and I am doing nothing.» In Thérèse's own words, there is the new perspective of abandonment, which surpasses, in extension and in depth, Thérése's abandonment at the time when obstacles piled up against her entrance into the cloister. During this same time, the symbols that Thérèse will later use to express her «little doctrine» emerge more and more.

---

[1] This interiorization of renunciation is moreover a very frequent phenomenon in the courageous seekers of God. After years of effort (and results, as small as they are!), they begin to discover the «subtlety» of their pride and their self-love.

But let us not rush to our conclusions. It is at the end that we will better distinguish what is new and what is still missing in order to arrive at Thérése's «spiritual childhood.» It is only a short step away. A final discovery is in the air.

I. A MILDER CLIMATE

1. *The Events*

What are the various facts? Some important events take place, although they are rare. Since May 10, 1892, M. Martin returned to the bosom of the family in Lisieux. A great exterior cross is taken away, and one sees its effect on Thérèse: she is happy about her father's new situation,[2] the theme of the privilege of suffering receives less immediate attention, and the desire to disappear takes a new track.

In fact, a letter of October 19, 1892, written to Céline, contains this important declaration, which is the fruit of her retreat reflections and which will be confirmed thereafter: «Jesus is telling us to descend! ... This is where we must descend in order that we may serve as an abode for Jesus: *to be so poor that we do not have any place to rest our head*. This, my dear Céline, is what Jesus has done in my soul during my retreat.... You understand that it is a question here of the interior. Besides, has not the exterior already been reduced to nothing by the painful trial of Caen.... In our beloved father, Jesus has stricken us in the most sensitive exterior part of our heart; now let us allow Him to act, He can complete His work in our souls.... Jesus desires that we receive Him into our hearts. No doubt, they are already empty of creatures, but alas! I feel that mine is not entirely empty of myself and it is for this reason that Jesus

---

[2] Although he is still sick, his return to the family is «a very sweet consolation» (LT 138, 763, of November 17, 1892). In the eyes of Thérèse, her father is like Job: «After having humbled him, [God] is showering His favors upon him» (LT 146, 810, of August 10, 1893). Now «Our Lord came to sweeten... the chalice of sorrow» (LT 155, 836, of December 29, 1893).

tells me to descend.»[3] Some months after her father's return home, Thérèse meditated therefore, in a quiet moment, on what henceforth awaits her: she recognized that, the exterior trials being lessened,[4] Jesus wants to purify a more hidden area, winning especially «the interior,» the «me» of Thérèse, after having already won and purified (in part, because this work constantly repeats itself and intensifies) her exterior ties. Actually, we shall see how Thérèse insists on the necessity of a total renunciation of herself. In this sense and while taking the essence of the quoted text, it would not be too venturesome to formulate the characteristic mark of the period 1893-1894 as one of a deepened discovery of spiritual poverty.

The election of Sister Agnès allows Thérèse to take a breath. The date is important also because the new Superior asks Thérèse to take care discreetly of her two colleagues who are still in the novitiate.[5] This is a very light task for a year and a half. It will become heavier when, on June 16, 1894, Marie of the Trinity enters the Carmel of Lisieux, followed three months later by Céline. In the meantime, M. Martin passed away on July 29: for Thérèse this is an additional joy, for she has the impression of finding her father

---

[3] LT 137, 760. It is obvious that detachment from oneself which Thérèse describes here is not an absolute beginning: she had already considered it before and it is intrinsic to all detachment of will, even when it concerns exterior things. But it is here a question of attention and accentuation. Concerning detachment, considered on a general level: see LT 76 for example, 503; 74, 499; 78, 511; 94, 577, and A 74 v-7 r, 195. All of this is prior to 1892.

[4] She suggests it again on July 6, 1893 (LT 142, 794).

[5] See Appendix I, p. 355. At the same time, we note that many authors, mistaken about the intention of a passage from Manuscript C, situated the discovery of «spiritual childhood» before or on the occasion of the demand of Mother Agnès, in the month of February 1893. Thus A. COMBES (*Introduction…*, pp. 296-297; *Contemplation et apostolat*, p. 119; «Sainte Thérèse de Lisieux, modèle de vie contemplative,» *Ephemerides carmeliticae*, 13 [1962], p. 105; *De doctrina*, pp. 149-159), and after him, LUCIEN MARIE DE SAINT-JOSEPH («Sainte Thérèse de l'Enfant-Jésus, ou l'Enfance unie à la maturité,» *La Vie spirituelle*, 85 [1951], p. 320), C. BEAUVALET («La Thème de l'enfance chez sainte Thérèse de Lisieux,» ED, 29 [19 53], p. 69), DOMINGO DE SANTA TERESA («La doctrina de la Infancia Espiritual. Génesis y évolución en la vida y pensiamento de Santa Teresa del Niño Jésus,» *El Monte Carmelo*, 61 [1953], pp. 21, 25- 26, 45-46) and S. PIAT (*À la découverte…*, p. 132). It goes without saying that this erroneous chronological position had greatly influenced these authors to interpret in the sense of «spiritual childhood» Thérésian texts from 1889-1894 where it is a question of «to carry,» of «arms» or of «child.»

again.[6] With regard to her physical constitution, she still claims «an iron health,»[7] in July of 1894.

2. *«Thérèse is not in the heights»*

The present period seems to be the least eventful of all her religious life, although it is, down deep, very intense. However, it is no longer the bitter suffering[8] which inspires an attachment to God's purifying work in her, but, among other things, the longer periods of aridity in her prayers and, for this reason, the experience of her weakness. During her two hours of daily prayer, her thanksgivings and her retreats she is plagued by sleep and aridity, just as before. Her spiritual readings? 'Even the most beautiful books said nothing to her, her heart contracts, her mind comes to a standstill' (A 83 r, 211). The *Imitation* and Sacred Scripture come to her rescue and give her a strong and very pure nourishment and a great deal of enlightenment,[9] but it happens that this source too runs dry.[10] Thérèse no longer seems to have escaped this law of religious psychology according to which the natural enthusiasm of the beginning does not last: monotony tends to take its place. One is more aware of the miserable side of «one's self» and how

[6] «After a *death* of five years, what joy to find him once more always the same» (LT 169, 881, of August 19, 1894). «Papa's death does not give me the impression of a death, but of a real *life*. I am finding him once more after an absence of six years, I feel him around *me*, looking at me and protecting me...» (LT 170, 884, of August 20, 1894). And in the beginning of the month of January 1895: «Do you not find, as I do, that our beloved Father's departure has brought us closer to Heaven?» (LT 173, 896). See also A 82 v, 209.

[7] LT 167, 870. However, it is «toward 1894» that she begins to suffer throat pains (Mother Agnès, PA, p. 203). It is therefore possible that, in the letter, Thérèse wants to reassure her relatives, but that, in fact, she thinks about it further....

[8] This is not to say that exterior trials are missing completely! Thérèse feels equally and deeply the difficulties that Mother Agnès sometimes encounters in the community. There is also the possibility in 1893 of a departure for the missions with the consequent separation from loved ones (see LT 167, 503) and the relative difficulties surrounding the entrance of Céline (see LT 167, 870 and A 82 v, 208).

[9] A 83 r, 211. The letters testify to several illuminations found in Scripture: for example, LT 135, 752 on her apostolic cooperation as a contemplative; LT 137, 760 (quoted) about detachment.

[10] Let's read this passage of 1894: «The *vast field of the Scriptures*, which has so many times opened before us to pour out its rich treasures in our favor; this *vast field* seems to us to be a *desert*, arid and without water...» (LT 165, 860).

far one is from the ideal. One experiences one's weakness more readily especially because one perceives it much better.

Against this backdrop are added to Thérèse's life, like so many confirmations, lots of details gathered from her correspondence which are very suggestive! On July 6, 1893: 'Thérèse is not in the heights at this moment, Jesus withdraws from her His tangible presence and if He leads her to (Mount) Tabor, it is for a few moments.' She also speaks of her 'imperfections.' On July 18: 'Sometimes she is incapable of praying and practicing virtue, the fire of love seems to have gone out;' «oh! no, I am not always faithful.» On July 23: a chaplet of practices that, in principle, does not appeal to her, is nevertheless very useful to her 'in her present state of soul.' On August 2: «Jesus hides Himself, wraps Himself in darkness, is silent.» On October 20: «We do not see Him, He is hiding, He veils His divine hand.» On November 17: Thérèse experiences 'helplessness' in her prayer; she only has her 'good will.' Let us move on to April 3, 1894: Jesus «is almost always *sleeping*.... Poor Thérèse's Jesus does not caress her as He used to caress her Holy Mother» [Thérèse had a picture of Saint Teresa of Avila being embraced by the Divine Child]. On July 7: sometimes, there is «turmoil or at least darkness.... At times, we believe ourselves abandoned.»

There is no doubt that this state of aridity and frequent helplessness led Thérèse to surrender all to Jesus even more. In her letters to Céline, she is more insistent, because the correspondent is also experiencing aridity, difficulties, distress.[11] However, these pains are common, Thérèse says: «It is incredible how we always have the same trials» (LT 167, 870).

II. A TRILOGY ON ABANDONMENT IN A PERSPECTIVE THAT IS NEW

From April 25 to August 13, six long letters to Céline follow one after the other. The second, third, and fourth, written in a time span of eighteen days, form a true trilogy. They contain the most notable reflections of Thérèse at this moment. Their analysis will

[11] See LT 142, 794; 143, 800; 145, 808; 147, 813; 149, 826; 157, 841; 161, 850; 165, 860; 169, 881.

be difficult, but the reader will find their synthesis farther on.

The letter that precedes them, that of April 25, is like a «preface» to them, summarizing in a way the previous search for humility and love, while showing how much this ideal had become pure, with a strong emphasis on the more 'subtle' renunciation of oneself. Thérèse reveals her desires relative to *Céline*, but at the same time she suggests her desires with regard to herself: she wants, for her part, «to realize what Jesus made her understand.» It is true that she develops her reflections in the perspective of their common vocation to a purely contemplative life,[12] and this is the reason for which she affirms that «Jesus doesn't call all souls» to follow the proposed ideal and that all will not understand it. But on the other hand, this perspective has the advantage of clearly distinguishing the core of Thérèse's ideal from its exterior forms, which can vary according to vocations.

Thérèse and Céline must therefore always be and must remain like a 'drop of dew hidden in the chalice of the Flower of flowers.' What can this mysterious expression mean? It is to exist «for Jesus alone [and] to be His, one must remain little, little like a drop of dew»! This littleness is sought at three levels. The first: to be hidden from all 'human view: Jesus alone will know its freshness.' The second is more interior: 'neither to consider nor to envy things that cause human admiration.' The third is 'to forget oneself,' to 'not know one's own value,' 'to deem oneself as beneath others.' This is their way: «to respond to it, how *simple* we must remain.»

Logically, Thérèse insists on a conviction, which in principle is already old:[13] God «has no need of our beautiful thoughts and our dazzling works... or our sublime thoughts»; for all this He has

---

[12] One of her more intimate desires was Céline's entrance into Carmel (A 82 r, 208).

[13] We already mentioned the relativity of «striking works» (A 32 r, 119) and of «beautiful thoughts» (LT 89, 556). We can place the belief, which Thérèse expresses here, in relation to an analogous and contemporary experience (A 81 r-v, 206-208), while we cannot determine the chronological sequence. «For three years» — the correction made in the manuscript was first defined as a personal retouching (Mss II, 102), then as foreign by P. François — since 1892 therefore, Thérèse has, among other things, experienced the vanity of certain desires: they made her paint (since June 1892, see Mss II, 56), write poems and pieces (the first poetry dates from February 2, 1893), but she recognized «from EXPERIENCE [an allusion to the reactions of

His Angels, said the Carmelite, and we could add: especially Himself. But straightaway she notices that 'all are not called' to this ideal, that God 'wills that others be esteemed and that they comfort men in their needs.' The one theme that runs through all of Thérèse's reflections is the fundamental attitude of a love which has the tendency to forget itself completely for God, and an obedience to the divine will which determines its concrete ways. But as for herself, her very elevated ideal has helped her greatly to understand the relativity of everything that is human, to probe deeply her duty of withdrawing from everything that makes her great in her own eyes, and to abandon herself to God alone from whom all things, after all, come.[14]

Then comes the trilogy of letters from the month of July 1893. The first, written on July 6, takes up the theme of merit, progress, and sanctity. Replying to a possible objection of Céline that: 'I have more consolations and consequently less merits,' Thérèse opposes the principle: «Merit does not consist in doing or giving much, but rather in receiving, in loving much» and a little farther on: «When Jesus wills to take *for Himself the sweetness of giving*, it would not be gracious to refuse. Let us allow Him to take and give everything He wills, for perfection consists in doing His will.» (LT 142).

How far we already are from the famous definition of April 26, 1889! «Sanctity... consists in *suffering* and suffering *everything*,» she says, with recourse to the authority of Pichon who recommends 'conquest at the point of the sword, suffering, agony' (LT 89). Personal activity is put back in its true place, it is placed under the sign

---

the 'greatly astonished' sisters?] that happiness consists only in hiding oneself, in remaining ignorant of created things. I understood that without *love*, all works are nothing, even the most dazzling, such as raising the dead to life or converting peoples.»

[14] Describing the fate of the «drop of dew,» Thérèse writes that, at the time of her death 'the divine star [this is Jesus, who is the calyx of the flower containing the drop of dew and at the same time the sun that attracts her above!] will attract her toward Him, to Heaven' (LT 141, 783). «A first explanation of the little way» has been seen there, already announcing its discovery (UNE MONIALE BÉNÉDICTINE, «Sainte Thérèse de l'Enfant-Jesus et le Mystère pascal,» VT, 1963, July, pp. 18-20). But Thérèse is thinking here only of death and eternal life, and she doesn't describe the way to travel through life to reach holiness. We need to insist again and again that a symbol can have many meanings and it is necessary to study the particular meaning it has in an author's concrete thought.

of God's will, because, as Thérèse is well aware, merit comes from Him and therefore holiness consists above all in receiving. The ideal of love — Thérèse expresses it: «to love much»[15] — remained intact, but, once again, the preoccupation is displaced: «How easy it is to please Jesus, to delight His Heart! one has only to love Him, without looking at one's self, without examining one's faults too much.»

Is the last statement not a little disturbing? Did Thérèse, who formerly was so careful to avoid infidelities and to transform her faults through love, yield with the years to a decrease in generosity? No, but she looks at her faults in another way: it is God who must do everything and our love consists in always abandoning everything to Him — including our shortcomings — with a blind faith, based on Him and not on the absence of mistakes nor prevented by their presence (this is why Thérèse refuses to examine her faults too much)! Let us read this suggestive passage which follows the last quoted text: «Your Thérèse is not in the heights at this moment, but Jesus is teaching her *to draw profit from everything, from the good and the bad that she finds in herself.*[16] He is teaching her to play at the bank of love, or rather He plays for her and does not tell her how He goes about it, for that is His business and not Thérèse's. What she must do is abandon herself, surrender herself, without keeping anything, not even the joy of knowing how much the bank is returning to her.»

A little further on, she summarizes all this and explains herself again: «Ah! Let us be always Jesus' *drop* of dew. In that is happiness, perfection....» The symbol is already familiar to us, but let us notice that, this time — as we will immediately see — it is not used in the perspective of a contemplative life, at least in this place,[17]

---

[15] When, on July 29, 1894, Thérèse happened to come across a note which described a discontinued practice of loving everywhere one is, she experienced in it 'an extreme pleasure' and said to Marie of the Trinity: «[This note] is the echo of my soul, for a long time I have understood love and have trained myself to practice it in this way» (PA, pp. 473-474).

[16] The words in italics are borrowed from a poem of Saint John of the Cross (*Oeuvres*, I, p. 488). Thérèse will rely also on this text, the meditation on which may have contributed to her new awareness.

[17] The perspective of the contemplative life *seems* to return in the following paragraph, where the «drop of dew» declines being appreciated by others (LT 142, 794).

but in that of the aforesaid abandonment and of total renunciation which gives all and renounces even having something in oneself of which one can boast. Thérèse understands well that she is taking a clear position with her attitude, she has never said it with so much conviction. Let us listen to it: «[This language of the drop of dew], I admit that it is true for only a few souls. In fact, directors have others advance in perfection by having them perform a great number of acts of virtue, and they are right; but my director, who is Jesus, teaches me not to count up my acts.[18] He teaches me to do *all* through love, to refuse Him nothing, to be content when He gives me a chance of proving to Him that I love Him; but this is done in peace, in *abandonment*,[19] it is Jesus who is doing all in me and I am doing nothing.»

The second letter of our trilogy, that of July 18, repeats in a subdued way the same theme: Jesus who works for her, abandonment on her part, humble renunciation of trying to make herself grow and, consequently, insistence on «little» acts of love.

Now Thérèse makes us listen: «Now I want to tell you what is taking place in my *own* soul.... Céline, God is no longer asking anything from me... [that is to say, according to the context, referring to new kinds of sacrifices]. In the beginning, He was asking for an infinity of things from me. I thought, at times, that now, since Jesus was no longer asking anything from me, I had to go along quietly in peace and love, doing only what He was asking me,[20] but I experienced a light.» What is this light? Thérèse explains it by a liberal appeal to a comparison made by Teresa of Avila. Love is a fire which we must maintain: the wood for it might be out of our reach, but we will always have little pieces of straw at our disposal. These little pieces of straw are an attentiveness which pleases the Lord and — let us note well Jesus' role compared to that of Thérèse again — «then [Jesus Himself] throws on the fire a lot of wood.» We feel 'the *strength* that love's warmth gives.' «I have ex-

[18] This is why Thérèse will say, fifteen days later, that 'a chaplet of practices hardly pleases her' in principle, although it is at that moment very useful.

[19] (*Note of 1994.*) It is very characteristic: the noun *abandonment* appears here for the very first time in the writings of Thérèse, considered in their chronological order.

[20] Thus the original text. Céline later added the words «in the beginning» after «asking me» (see CG II, pp. 707-708) to make the sentence clearer.

perienced it,» says Thérèse, and she begins to describe her «little pieces of straw» to her: «when I am *feeling* nothing, when I am INCAPABLE of praying, of practicing virtue, then is the moment for seeking little opportunities, *nothings*.... For example, a smile, a friendly word, when I would like to say nothing or put on a look of annoyance.... I want at least to tell Him frequently that I love Him; this is not difficult and it keeps the *fire* going [... and even if this fire of love seems to have gone out] Jesus could then relight it.» However, «Jesus is really powerful enough to keep the fire going by Himself.»

«Little opportunities».... Because one could still make oneself grow by means of them and cultivate the spirit of possession, Thérèse warns expressly: «My dear Céline, do you understand? This is not for the purpose of weaving my crown or gaining merits; it is in order to please Jesus.»[21]

The last consequence that Thérèse draws from this spiritual poverty and from the priority of Jesus' action has to do with her attitude after an infidelity: «Oh! no, I am not always faithful, but I never get discouraged; I abandon myself into the arms of Jesus [and there, the little drop of dew] finds again all it has lost and indeed even much more.» We see that the bank of love in her view yields generous returns!

The third letter of the trilogy, that of July 23, contains an interesting symbol, but let us examine its context: «I am not surprised that you don't understand anything about what is happening in your soul. *A* LITTLE *child all alone* on the sea, in a boat lost in the midst of the stormy waves, could she know whether she is near or far from port?» As long as she still sees the shore, she knows how far she has gone: she sees that she is progressing, but entering into the full sea, she does not have any point of reference, she must abandon herself: then «the little child's *knowledge* is reduced to nothing, she no longer knows where her boat is going. Not knowing how to control the rudder, the only thing she can do is abandon herself and allow her sail to flutter in the wind.» ... So it is with Céline! «Céline, the *little child* of Jesus, is all alone..., she no longer

---

[21] On the evolution that Thérèse underwent in her conception of merit, see here Part IV, chap. IV.

knows where she is going, whether she is advancing or if she is going backward.» But Jesus is there, sleeping as in days gone by in the boat of the twelve! In an instant and with a single word He can bring about calm and brightness in the night's storm. Thérèse therefore encourages Céline again to practice abandonment.

We also find some complementary aspects in Thérèse's correspondence with Céline. The two successive letters — the «appendices» one could call them! — contain some very instructive remarks on Thérèse's spiritual poverty and they show clearly how pure love is the goal of it. «If Jesus had willed to show Himself to all souls with His ineffable gifts,» said the nun, «no one would have despised Him. If Céline were to see Jesus' love for her, she would die in an ecstasy of happiness.» But «He does not want us to love Him for His gifts; *He Himself* must be our *reward*.»[22] And Thérèse concludes with Saint John of the Cross (*Canticle*, str. 1), then, 'in order to find something that is hidden, this hidden treasure that is Jesus, one must hide oneself: one's face must be hidden like that of the Man of Sorrows; to be unknown and counted as nothing, to leave oneself, and to place one's joy in the contempt of oneself, to say it with the *Imitation*' (LT 145, 808). Shortly after, Thérèse explains the same thing, but from a more passive point of view: Jesus makes the external gifts that others can see in us disappear; He completely despoils those whom He loves. «When seeing themselves in such great poverty, these poor little souls are fearful; it seems to them that they are good for nothing, since they receive all from others and can give nothing; but this is not so: the *essence* of their *being* is working in secret.» And God «is pleased to show them their nothingness and His power. In order to reach them, He makes use of the *lowliest* instruments so as to show them that indeed He alone is working» (LT 147, 813). One would think the Spanish mystical Doctor himself were speaking! Besides, the main lines of his doctrine could not have passed unobserved by the one who found in it 'so much light'!

---

[22] This is not the first time that she expresses this thought! In the month of May 1890 for example, she declares herself «happy to follow her Fiancé because of her love for *Him alone* and not because of His gifts» (LT 111, 654). She does not watch the hands of her Lord in order to discover gifts or watch His face to gather a smile, but looks rather at His tears (LT 115, 667).

One will already have understood how much these letters contain certain elements which will soon be assumed in her «little way of spiritual childhood.» The preparation is coming to its end: some elements and the final structure are still missing. We will return to that soon, while also presenting a synthesis of this analysis.

III. THE CONSOLIDATION

The rest of her writings from 1893-1894 (letters and poems) take up and reinforce the themes she has already discussed, but the thought does not seem to evolve any further before the end of the year 1894. The consciousness of the primacy of God's action, which was already placed in the foreground, remains lively. «*If the Lord does not build the house Himself, in vain do those work who build it* [Ps 126:1]. All the most beautiful discourses of the greatest saints would be incapable of making even *a single* act of love come from a heart that Jesus did not possess» (LT 147, 813). This same conviction resounds in related themes.

In her letters to Céline, who is suffering, Thérèse returns to abandonment. It is not necessary «to fear,» she says, «it is not the precipices that we must avoid, we are in the arms of Jesus» (LT 149, 826). She proposes to her «the abandonment» of Saint Cecilia who, in the midst of dangers that threatened her virginal vocation, did not tremble or weep, but sang (*ibid.*). For Céline's birthday, she composes a poem about Cecilia, «the *Saint* of ABANDONMENT,» 'whose story is Céline's story too,' since she is in the midst of difficulties as well. «I would need a language other than that of this earth,» said Thérèse, «to express the beauty of a soul's abandonment into the hands of Jesus; my heart was able only to babble what it feels…» (LT 1 61, 850). Abandonment is revealed in this poem as an expression of love and a victory over fear, through confidence. Here is its central passage:

> *You sang this sublime canticle to the Lord*:
> «Keep my heart pure, Jesus, my tender Spouse.»
> *Ineffable Abandonment! divine melody!*
> *You disclose your love through your celestial song.*

Love that fears not, that falls asleep and forgets itself
On the Heart of its God, like a little child....

[And the end:]

Obtain for me to taste perfect abandonment,
That sweet fruit of love, on this foreign shore.[23]

The abandonment that Thérèse contemplates in Saint Cecilia is in a sense less rich than that of which she speaks in letters from the month of July 1893: it expects from God only protection and not, as before, the perfection of love. However, it better sketches the totally confident atmosphere in which it is born: that of a child in her father's arms (we will come back to this point). This confidence is explained well when one sees how many times Thérèse affirms that God loves us, that He wants to help us, that He is near to us.[24] But three months later, Thérèse speaks again of abandonment in a richer sense (in relation with 'the groanings of the Spirit within us' from Rm 8:26): «We have, then, only to surrender our soul, to *abandon* it to our great God» (LT 165, 860).

Abandonment evokes humility in Thérèse. God cannot do His work in a soul and bestow His gifts on it, if it is not humble. It is in order to make it humble that He allows trials: while «we were no longer daring *even to look at ourselves*, so much did we consider ourselves to be without splendor and adornment... Jesus calls us» (*ibid.*, 861), but first He wanted us to become like 'an empty tent' (*ibid.*, 863).

Thus the old theme of humility is expanded. «Ask [Jesus] that I remain always little, *very little*,» she writes to Léonie, of whom

---

[23] PN 3. It should be noted that, before 1893, Saint Cecilia is always mentioned as an example of *love* (LT 87, 552; 54, 440; 55, 442; PO, p. 413). Since 1893, Thérèse sees her as an example of *abandonment*.

[24] Jesus' silence is a melody for her (LT 145, 808), Jesus understands when nothing answers us (LT 149, 826), His Heart watches (LT 160, 848; 171, 888), He is content with our good will (LT 152, 832; 167, 870), He is close to us (LT 149, 826), at our side (LT 149), He does not hide Himself in such a way that He does not allow Himself to be divined (LT 147, 813), and finally, He is there looking at us through the window (LT 157, 841).

she is actually «the last and *littlest*» sister.[25] And again: «Which [of us two] will be the more fervent? The one who will be the most humble» (LT 164, 854).

It is in the humble that God can do great things. As in the case of Joan of Arc. Thérèse addresses to her, through the words of Saint Marguerite, this praise, an echo of the *quia respexit humilitatem meam* of the Mother of God [*"... because He has looked upon the humility of His handmaid,"* the Mother of God (*Magnificat*)]: «It is the humility of your life that makes Him [God] descend toward you.» Joan answers: «My life is poor and hidden, it is very true! Now, I understand why Our Lord wanted to be born in poverty in order to practice the humility that is so dear to Him. I want to always remain very little, very humble, in order to resemble Jesus and to deserve that He make of me His abode.» It is therefore to God alone that «belongs all glory [and] to show it, He fortifies an arm of a child,» a «weak and timid child.»[26] In order to protect His divine glory: there is the intention that Thérèse reads in the trials and weakness which overwhelm Céline: «[Jesus] is happy that you are feeling your weakness; *He* is the one placing in your soul sentiments of mistrust of itself [... He wants to prove, as to the apostles who had fished all night without catching anything], that He alone can give us something. He willed that the apostles *humble themselves* [... and then He rewarded them]. This is indeed the *character* of Jesus: He gives as God, but He wills *humility* of heart» (LT 161, 850).

Humility does not try to make itself admired by others. That is why Thérèse returns to fidelity in «little opportunities,»[27] also indicating their role of psychological and theological preparation for

---

[25] LT 154, 835. This «very little» is situated well in the line of *humility*: See here Part I, chap. III, n. 24. In the same sense, Marie of the Angels wrote to Thérèse on September 8, 1890: «Make yourself little, very little too, so well hidden,» etc. (LC 141).

[26] See RP 1, «The Mission of Joan of Arc.» While reading these pages, one senses how much Thérèse reveals her own heart.

[27] It is likely that Thérèse found a support for her convictions about «little things» in Saint John of the Cross, an indisputable authority for her, who says in the twenty-ninth stanza of CS: «[In this state] the smallest movement of pure love has more value in God's eyes ... and it is more profitable to the Church than all works combined together.» She certainly had already read this sentence which she will quote several times: B 4 v, 229; LT 221, 1069; 245, 1128 and in the rough draft of a prayer (see Pri 12). It should be noted however that John of the Cross speaks here of an act of love completely purified, as is possible only after the dark nights of the soul.

greater crosses (LT 148, 815). But, in spite of this appraisal of «little things,» the greatest deeds are not excluded (LT 164, 854). Whatever the case may be, their value comes from love: the loving «attentiveness» of little «nothings» «pleases Jesus more than mastery of the world or even martyrdom suffered with generosity» (LT 143, 800) and «the smallest thing [given with love] is precious in His divine eyes» (LT 145, 808); «everything is so big in religion.... To pick up a pin out of love can convert a soul!» (LT 164, 854). But Thérèse understands well that, at a deeper level, this value depends on God alone: «It is Jesus alone who can give such a value to our actions» (*ibid.*). And maybe the reward will be the ability to accomplish the 'great things of love' with the strength that it gives: «If you always remain faithful in pleasing Him in *little* things, He will find Himself OBLIGED to help you in GREAT things...» (LT 161, 850).

IV. THE SYMBOLIC CASING

You will have noticed that, as abandonment and humility grow stronger, the symbols of the «arm» of Jesus and of «the child» appear again, and the adjective «little» is used frequently. In our opinion, they encompass certain factors that will play a role, and a very important role, once the Carmelite will have fully worked out the structuring of her «little way of spiritual childhood.» That is why we have to stop here for a moment.

Earlier, we noted how old are the symbols of arms or hands which carry, and consequently the expressions «to confide,» «to give oneself,» and «to abandon oneself into the arms of someone»; they have existed since there have been mothers. Thérèse herself quotes Psalm 90:12 where the symbol is used: «[An angel of Jesus] *carries you in his hands lest your foot strike against a stone*» (LT 161, 850). She will also refer to the symbol of God's arms (LT 147, 813) in order to express her confidence in Him and her abandonment: an attitude that she is cultivating intensely at this time. She compares the abandonment of Saint Cecilia to the love of a little child who falls asleep on the Heart of her God. It should be noted moreover that she herself in her childhood loved it when others carried her, and she will recall this later with pleasure.[28] How could one not think that little Thérèse had sometimes compared herself to the child whom Jesus blessed and took into His arms, as she could see in the holy pictures which she possessed[29] of this Gospel scene? In 1893-1894, the use of such a symbol still does not cover the entire doctrine of «spiritual childhood»[30] necessarily. In fact, Thérèse had already used, in 1889 — in a less rich context than in 1893, it is true — the expression 'to be carried [in the arms] of Jesus.'[31]

What we have just said could be summarized in this way: if we could lean on the symbol alone and what this symbol expresses *in an overall way*, perhaps we could say that the essential step is cleared in the case «of spiritual childhood» when Sister Agnès writes to Thérèse, on September 3, 1890: «[God] isn't giving you any consolation because you are in His arms, and you are not walking, He is carrying you.... Does the child in its Father's arms need any other consolation?» (LC 137).

Our previous remarks and this last sentence of Mother Agnès inspire a certain prudence in the interpretation of the symbol of the «child» which is sometimes used at this time, especially in the letter of July 23, 1893 to Céline. There it expresses powerlessness and ignorance at the same time — indeed, Céline 'doesn't understand anything that is taking place in her soul,' she is like a child, alone

---

[28] See A 5 v, 76; 7 r, 79; 35 v, 126 (She throws herself into the arms of the Virgin Mary, like a child in her Mother's arms; however, it is possible that we are dealing with an explanation which came subsequent to the experience). Thérèse recalls with pleasure that she was taken *on the knees* of someone (and therefore in someone's arms): A 18 r, 97; 22 v, 104 (of her father!), 28 v, 113; 33 v, 121; 36 r, 127; 62 r, 174 (of her sisters).

[29] LC 137. The child's abandonment on the heart of her father (or of her mother) was a theme of the entire Visitandine tradition and the devotion to the Sacred Heart, in which the Martin sisters were immersed. This is also the ambiance of all the prose in the lacework pictures that they loved.

[30] We disagree therefore with A. COMBES (among others), when he says: «The same solution, that she symbolizes by the metaphor of the elevator, Thérèse expresses in its spiritual reality, after July 18, 1893 [LT 144, 803], in letter CXXII to Céline: "I never get discouraged, I abandon myself into the arms of Jesus."» (*Contemplation et apostolat*, p. 123).

[31] LT 79, 514; 89, 556. As we have said, the alternative, either to be carried in the hands of Jesus or be rejected, is also an allegory of the spirituality of the «little ball.» It is not impossible that the use of the symbol of the «arm» results here from a transposition of her «drop of dew» *in the calyx* of the Flower of flowers, by the transition from impersonal to *personal* things.

on the dark and stormy sea. But Jesus is taking care of her, her boat will not drift away: Céline is «the little *child* of Jesus.» She must have confidence in Him and show Him the «heart of a *child*.» In short, powerlessness,[32] confidence, and the solicitude of Jesus are the theme of the letter of July 23 and the meaning of the symbol. Besides, does not everyone quite often spontaneously have recourse to the well-known symbol of the child to express these realities? Nor is it impossible that Thérèse used this symbol in view of Céline's *simplicity*, a character trait emphasized repeatedly.[33] It should also be noted that Thérèse had already called Céline a «poor little child» in 1889 (LT 81, 529) on account of her helplessness. Finally, we should point out that Thérèse sometimes calls herself a child in relation to people who in some way act as a mother to her.[34]

As for the adjective «little,» used a great number of times, it is loaded with value for Thérèse,[35] whether it expresses her search for humility in its many manifestations, emphasizes her abandonment, or arises from affection and even affectation.

Where are we, then, after the period 1893-1894, with respect to «the way of spiritual childhood»? It has seemed preferable to us to delay the answer until the following chapter.

---

[32] It is in this sense of powerlessness (but a powerlessness which God makes strong), that Thérèse in her compositions compares Joan of Arc to a «child.» In her first poem, of February 2, 1893 (PN 1), the word «childhood» must be taken in the same sense: Thérèse, a «weak child,» sees in the Host only the white color, the color of milk, but, she says, «it is milk that suits childhood,» and therefore suits her, thus making an allusion to the spiritual food that the Eucharist provides. We differ, then, from C. BEAUVALET (*Le Thème de l'enfance...*, p. 69), who surmises that in this poem «the first indications of spiritual childhood have been timidly heard,» and from S. PIAT (*À la découverte...*, p. 131) who goes in the same direction.

[33] «It is always simplicity that is presented to me as the distinctive characteristic of your heart» (LT 141, 783, of April 25, 1893). One year later, she praises her 'docility and childlike candor' and she assures Céline that Jesus cannot misguide «a *little child* like *you*» (LT 168, 877). See also PN 13.

[34] Thus relative to her aunt (LT 139, 765), to Pauline (LT 140, 781), to her superiors.

[35] Let us notice, for example, its repetition and underlining: «*Little* picture painted by *little* Thérèse for the twenty-five years of *little* Céline with the permission of *little* Mother Prioress» (LT 162, 852).

Chapter VI

In the «Way of Spiritual Childhood»?

(End of 1894)

I. WHERE ARE WE IN IT?

We have followed the genesis of the «little way» step by step, and have arrived at the last months of 1894, the time when Thérèse made her great discovery. Let us briefly summarize the route we have covered. Having been born in a very Christian environment, Thérèse hears at the age of nine a first clear call to perfection. At the same time, she understands the relativity of «striking works» and the importance of renunciation, humility, suffering, and the hidden life. The conception of her ideal of love, love of God and humanity, is developed during the course of the nine intensive months that follow the «grace of Christmas 1886.» In the face of opposition to her intention to enter Carmel soon, she opens herself up to abandonment to the will of Jesus. Having entered Carmel, her dream of love does not weaken at all in the midst of great exterior and interior sufferings. The only means that she knows of arriving at perfection is love, but love by its own choice travels the way of humility, of life hidden to the eyes of all in order to be seen solely by the One Whom she wants to love most intensely and most exclusively. Her weakness helps her in that respect. The Holy Face of Jesus is her mirror.

Her exterior suffering being greatly lessened, Thérèse concentrates further on the more interior renunciation of herself. She applies herself with heightened attention to disappear from her own eyes, to withdraw from everything that can exalt her in any way.

Thus, she further insists on the love of «little things,» a way to which she had committed herself since her childhood. She expects merit, progress, and holiness not from herself, but from God. Her weakness appears to her now less as something that must be «transformed» into love than as something which Jesus will decide how to use. She abandons herself to Him in everything, including the area of love. This is the great overall realization of the year 1893: God must do all. The long-lasting experience of her weakness and her powerlessness to be as she would like to be, and a marvelous understanding of the priority of the love of God, all these have facilitated this new perspective of abandonment, this new ranking of values, this psychological restructuring of her notion of holiness. Personal activities become more clearly cooperations with the initiative of God. Thérèse understands better the divine phase into which her acts of love, imperfect love, enter: it is He who must perfect them, prolong them, and make them «yield a return.» In this dialogue, Thérèse listens to the word of Jesus much more attentively. She becomes in that sense more passive.

It was toward the end of the year 1894 that Thérèse received the great grace — a grace equally charismatic, although she was not conscious of it at the time — of discovering her «little way of spiritual childhood.» But did there in fact still remain something to discover after the insights of the year 1893? Thérèse had already become little, she knew her weakness, she was humble, she had confidence in God, she knew that everything must come from Him, she loved «little» acts of love.... What more would be necessary besides this? Is all this not already spiritual childhood? Yes, it is a kind of spiritual childhood, but this is not yet the *Thérésian* way of spiritual childhood! The aforementioned elements have all had their importance on the level of origination and they already form a synthesis, but the discovery of the «little way,» still more than being a new synthesis, implies new realizations about particular elements. If it is allowable for us to use Thérésian terminology from the month of July 1893, we could express it as follows: if, beforehand, Thérèse realized the divine 'play' in her search for holiness — this is 'the goal'! — without yet knowing «how [Jesus] goes about» making her love «yield a return» (LT 142, 794), now, in revealing to her the «little way,» Jesus also reveals to her «*how* He goes about it» in order to sanctify her, and Thérèse, illuminated, will fully commit herself and will adapt herself to God's game. It is a new discovery, a new psychological structuring of her «way,» and a new impetus in the way.

Let us explain. What was the light shed by the two biblical texts which were the foundation of her great discovery? To believe Thérèse's account of this discovery concerning it, this light is neither the knowledge of her weakness nor the conviction that her sanctification can not be the result of her own efforts. Thérèse's testimonies, even in the previous years, seem to confirm it wonderfully: she no longer needs to discover it! The discovery relates more to God, it is a penetration of the divine mystery: it is the discovery of mercy as *mercy*. Thérèse understood God's love for her, His forbearance, His goodness, His help. But what she understands in light of these two scriptural verses is not simply that God's love is real, prior to ours, and faithful, but that it is a love which comes down from above to below, a love which descends, which seeks the little one and especially *because* he or she is little, in order to *fill* them. Thérèse discovers that mercy is *for* the little, that it is what it is *because* one is little, and *how great* it is for the little.

This light is a new principle for understanding her entire way. In divine mercy, even with the help of her weakness, Thérèse discovers the dynamism of her sanctification, triggered from her side by confidence in this mercy. To approach God as a little one no longer means, then, to humble oneself, to disappear so that He alone is the Beloved. That continues, but as a basis for further soaring: after she accepts her nothingness, Thérèse entrusts herself to mercy, sure that it will fill her with its grace. Littleness, instead of being mainly humility, becomes mainly *confidence*. Under the light of mercy and subjected to God by confidence, powerlessness becomes in a way a pledge of divine intervention. The new way of holiness, the «little way» which Thérèse discovered, certainly generates a new thrust. Thérèse has now understood the way between God and herself and rushes into it. How much better one will travel on a road that is all lit up! *Implicitly* she has already progressed along this path: because the «little way» that she discovers is so essentially Christian that every good way toward holiness in a certain sense contains it.[1] But Thérèse was advancing along this way without knowing it, like a blind person, slowly, hesitantly, and making mistakes — which is what such a way imposes. The illumination that God gives her on His mercy will henceforth light the way by which she will advance toward Him. We must return to all this again.

II. THE FIRST TRACES OF THE «WAY OF SPIRITUAL CHILDHOOD» (END OF 1894)?

In our first part, we showed that it was after September 14, 1894 that Thérèse lived this privileged moment, when she read Proverbs 9:4, and Isaiah 66:12-13. If one can believe a testimony of Céline about it, quoted during her lifetime, the discovery would be situated *soon* after September 14. The preceding analysis showed sufficiently that the Carmelite was now ripe for the reception of the new light. Some years earlier, she would have perhaps read these texts without penetrating them and without relating them to her own existence.

One will easily understand that the new intuition, at the beginning, is as yet embryonic. It is therefore not very easy to locate its presence with certainty. In our first part, we had already found a sure indication of it on February 24, 1895. Soon we will see that the prologue of Manuscript A allows us to go back as far as the month of January. Can we cross the threshold of the year 1894?[2] In

---

[1] And this is the reason for which one recognized somewhat of a «basic» likeness between Thérésian spirituality and that of one or another saint or school.

[2] We left out of consideration here a note of Thérèse to Sister Martha, placed in the volume of *Letters* at the end of 1894, but the date of which has remained *uncertain*. Thérèse recommends that she express, in misery, her love to Jesus and she adds: «This is the way to *force* Jesus to help you, to carry you like a little child too feeble to walk» (LT 241, 1117; CG II, 1005 prefers to situate this note which is not dated rather in June 1897). The idea of the merciful intervention of Jesus and the picture could be characteristic. In a letter to Léonie of the beginning of January 1895, Thérèse says, while speaking of herself: «That she be like you, happy to be everywhere the littlest, the last!» (LT 173, 896). It is not necessary to see here an allusion to the «way of childhood». Recalling her place in the family, Thérèse uses this idea several times in her correspondence with Léonie, but in the context of humility (see also LT 154, 835; 164, 854; 170, 884). A passage of a letter from Father Pichon of February 25, 1895 (LC 161), probably responding to a letter of Thérèse of the end of 1894 or the beginning of 1895, is very suggestive: «I am grateful to the good Master for inspiring you with so much confidence.»

the week that precedes Christmas 1894, Thérèse composed three Poems and a Pious Recreation.[3] This last composition highlights the clemency of Christ, curbing the desires of vengeance of «the Angel of the last judgment.» We again hear Jesus say: «I made them [souls] for Myself, / I made their infinite desires; / The littlest soul that loves Me / Becomes paradise for Me.»[4] But all this seems to us too vague to draw conclusions with certainty as far as a presence of the «little doctrine» is concerned.

On the other hand, a poem for Céline — the postulant to whom Thérèse does not fail to give her good counsel — offers more of interest. The Virgin Mary says there:

But, to shelter you always
Under my veil, close to Jesus,
You must remain little,
Adorned with childlike virtues.[5]

It is not the image of the child in Mary's arms that strikes us; besides it is not new.[6] It is rather the expression of «childlike virtues,» that is to say, the virtues suited to the child. And one must practice these virtues *in order* to experience the benevolence of Heaven. However, Thérèse had understood the same condition as the fundamental rule of progress in her «little way»: in order to be carried by the arms of Jesus, «I must remain *little*» (C 3 r, 238). Is this a spontaneous Christmas theme, in poetry, or an allusion to a way that has been discovered? Let us compare this stanza to a poem of December 18, 1894.[7] It was written for the other postulant, Marie of the Trinity, on the occasion of her reception of the Habit. Here is the third stanza:

---

[3] See RP 2.

[4] *Ibid.*

[5] PN 13, str. 5.

[6] See already PN 1 of February 2, 1893; LT 162, 852 of April 26, 1894; PN 5 of June 1, 1894. It is a question of the image of someone hidden under Mary's veil.

[7] PN 11 and the volume of Poetry of the [French] critical edition, [pp. 324-327]. This poem, kept in the state of a rough draft, doesn't have any punctuation.

Your Son's [the Son of Mary] ineffable glance
Has deigned to lower itself to my poor soul.
I have searched for His adorable Face,
And in Him I want to hide myself.
I will have to always remain little
To be worthy of His glances,
But I'll grow very quickly in virtue
Under the brightness of this star of Heaven.

Here, it is not a question of being carried by God. Nevertheless, it concerns the same reality: to experience the loving help of God in order to gain a beneficial effect. What is this effect? «To grow in virtue,» and even to grow «very quickly»! And the condition? «I will have to always remain little»: the same condition as in the poem of the following week. But here the help of God, conditioned by a conscious attitude of littleness, is applied to the problem of sanctification itself: to grow in virtue, that is to say, to become holy. And here a first rough draft reveals something interesting: under the words «I will have to,» Thérèse had written a first version, then abandoned it: «In holiness»! That indeed proves that she thought about progress in holiness. Besides, the poem expresses the merciful character of God's love. It is in remaining little that Thérèse «is worthy of» this glance: that is to say, that she touches the sensitive chord, that she knows how to attract the «brightness» of God.

It is very likely that this poem reflects the «little way,» already discovered. In order to become holy, Thérèse knows both the way and the results of following it, and she seems to place everything under the rubric of mercy. Does she still have new things to discover? Is it necessary to find a solution for what is no longer a problem? However, the danger of reading too much into the words, vague in spite of everything and written for another person, is not imaginary. We therefore do not want to see a definitive proof here of the presence of spiritual childhood. This does not prevent us from thinking that Thérèse had already discovered her way, even several weeks before, without actually describing it here. The clues, moreover, are not yet exhausted.

III. THE WORD «MERCY»

If it is true that Thérèse filled herself with the idea of divine mercy, could we not find traces of it in her terminology? Out of the abundance of the heart the mouth speaks! But we are due for a surprise here. In the Thérésian corpus of writings before 1895, which came to about 350 pages, we came across the word «mercy-merciful» only twice, and we came across it in an account that is not the most personal,[8] while in Manuscript A alone, of 1895, it occurs about twenty times. Does this tell us something?

Let us be prudent with our conclusions. That Thérèse had often thought about divine mercy is beyond the shadow of a doubt. The Psalms that she used to recite every day sing constantly of it. The Saint will have reflected time and again on God's paternal goodness, experienced by her all through her life. She was implicitly praising His mercy when she insinuated that God had 'forgiven her sins in advance'[9] or that 'with exquisite delicacy, He walked ahead of her, tossing aside the stones and reptiles.'[10] And we have cited other examples.

But Thérèse subsumed all that under the word «love,» tender love. This word, contrary to «mercy,» does not necessarily indicate an inequality of level between the lover and the beloved, it does not imply condescension in one of the partners. Certainly Thérèse understood her inferiority in relation to Jesus, but psychologically she seems to have continued to look at Him, in a certain sense, as an equal: He is her Spouse, her Brother, her Friend, her Beloved, Whom she therefore sees as Someone Who is strong, faithful, good, and forbearing toward her weakness.

It seems permissible for us to think that the discovery of the «little way,» in which Thérèse has so well understood that God is

---

[8] See LT 129, 728: Is it about the prayer for Hyacinth Loyson, ex- Carmelite: «...so that our brother, a son of the Blessed Virgin, return vanquished to throw himself beneath the mantle of the most merciful of Mothers» (allusion to *Mater misericordiae* in the *Hail Holy Queen*?). See also LT 147, 813 where she speaks of the shortcomings of Céline Martin's maid, Thérèse says: «For every sin, mercy.» That sounds like an impersonal proverb.

[9] LT 130, 731 of July 23, 1891.

[10] LT 149, 826 of October 1893.

like a mother filled with condescension for His very helpless little child, so affected her psychologically that the word «mercy» came to her lips frequently. Whatever the case may be, in 1895, Thérèse is fully aware of the basic inequality between the level of her love and that of God; Manuscript A testifies to this ever since the prologue of January.

Before passing on to a third part of our study, which deals with the development of the «way of spiritual childhood» after she had discovered it, we would like to make two remarks regarding method: first, the memories of two of the most important witnesses, Sister Geneviève and Sister Marie of the Trinity, who entered Carmel shortly before, have dealt almost without exception with the period which follows the discovery; and secondly, since the discovery of the «little way» consists above all in a new inner vision, which, for Thérèse, virtually excludes all other ways of seeing things, it follows that while many of the ascetic elements of her previous life will remain the same, they will be seen in a fresh light. Thus, they can become elements typical of the «little way.» From this point of view, Thérèse's whole manner of living will reveal her «way of childhood.»

THIRD PART

THE UNFOLDING

(1895-1897)

On January 2, 1895, Sister Thérèse celebrated her twenty-second birthday. The girl had become a woman. She is happy, energetic, full of enthusiasm, and rich in experience. Inside her body, however, tuberculosis is silently doing its work of destruction. Only thirty-three months remain for her to live.

Her spiritual journey is far from finished. More than ever it will become intensive and will pick up speed. Is it also beautiful? Certainly not always in the eyes of Thérèse who, as she ascends, seems to sometimes get lost in the dense fog. But surely it is in the eyes of those who are watching the unfolding of her dauntless ascent at this time. We do not lack documentation for this period. The grace with which Sister Thérèse knows how to converse with her sisters, to enliven their little domestic feasts, and to express her feelings in a way that is more sincere than poetic, will provide us with three Autobiographical Manuscripts, *six* Pious Recreations, *some* Prayers *and about forty* Poems. *Her fraternal duties and her apostolic zeal result in her sending about eighty letters. And her work with the fascinated novices inspired the countless memories they kept of her. As far as the «way of spiritual childhood» is concerned, there is no doubt that these factors strongly pushed her to conceive it, to develop it, and to communicate it, better.*

Because the discovery of the «little way» was not an end in itself, Thérèse will continue her discovery while living it. She must now draw the outline of it more clearly, make the seed grow, and release the energies pent up inside the uncovered core. In other words, a threefold task awaits her: to psychologically and practically assimilate her discovery, to understand the depth of it, and to formulate it. It is the time of its unfolding.

It is not our intention to gather in this third part all the available materials which have to do with the «way of childhood.» It is better to save them for the description of its structure. The developmental aspect will always engage our attention, but, more than previously, the structural aspect will enter into our account. In fact, at the basis of the entire structure of the «way of childhood» are two synthesis-like manifestations of it: the Act of Offering to Merciful Love *and* Manuscript B, *appar-*

ently so different from each other and from the narration of the discovery! We must analyze them with care.

In this part, we shall concentrate on three points, situating them in their Thérésian context, which is as much historical as it is spiritual: first, the full invasion of the idea of divine mercy; secondly, Manuscript B*; and finally, the realization by Thérèse of her mission in the Church as it advances towards its characteristic formulation.*

CHAPTER I

In the Embrace of Mercy

(1895-March 1896)

1895 is not only the year when Thérèse writes the «Book of Mercies,» it is above all for her the year of mercy itself. Still dazzled by the light perceived at the time of her great discovery, she sees the reflection of it everywhere while writing her autobiography: throughout her entire life, God's mercy had followed her! While writing, she brings her past to life again and, more remarkable still than that, she herself is brought to life again by it. This lengthy meditation becomes, in her mind, the backdrop against which the greatness of God's merciful love will come to stand out clearly «more than ever» some time later. To this love she offers herself as a prey and she experiences very lively effects from it. It is for her like a new departure.

I. THE «BOOK OF MERCIES»

Providentially Thérèse begins to recount her memories of childhood one evening in recreation with an affability that will cost her dearly: Mother Agnès orders her to set them down in writing. Thérèse obeys with simplicity, in spite of a certain initial confusion. The result will be two little child's copybooks worth a sou, which soon will win a place of honor in worldwide spiritual literature.

Three things demand our attention here. In the first place, Manuscript A is not a simple account of past events. About a dozen times Thérèse is caught up in her *present* experiences. Then, from the very first lines of the manuscript, the writer goes beyond the proposed theme. Describing, it is true, the «memories of childhood,» she serves notice that she is basically setting forth 'her thoughts on the graces that God deigned to grant her' (A 3 r, 73). This is the true theme, then: «the *Mercies of the Lord*» (A 2 r, 71). It is an autobiography *of a kind all its own*: the numerous adventures of love which describe her personal experiences are describing as well the vital role of the Beloved. In short, the writing, almost all finished in a single year, is done always in light of divine mercy, but this light shines much more brightly after the graces of June 9-11, the time when she composed the Offering to Merciful Love.

As for the «way of spiritual childhood,» Manuscript A reveals its presence sporadically and sketches a description of it. But that is saying too little, because the recent discovery of the «little way» projected, it seems to us, in Thérèse's soul a beam of light which permitted her to see her entire past life as a single act of divine *mercy*. It is possible that the Carmelite, choosing for a theme «the *Mercies of the Lord*!!! ...» (notice the exclamation marks and the suspension points), was inspired by the liturgy or the example of Mother Teresa of Avila.[1] But it is without doubt her important and recent discovery which gave the theme the luster that it will have and which especially sustains it during the course of the long narration.

As for the dates of Manuscript A, it was begun in January 1895, probably toward the end of the month, and was finished in the same year, but not necessarily at the very end of the year. We do not have any other chronological reference points. We do not know if Thérèse wrote with regularity.[2]

---

[1] Ps 88. In 1897, Thérèse will write verse 1 of Ps 88 on a copy of PN 48 (see the French critical ed. of *Poems II*, p. 272). Teresa of Avila wrote, in a letter of November 19, 1581 to Don Pedro de Castro y Nero, with respect to her autobiography: «*Intitulé este libro "De las misericordias de Dios"*.» This is something well known at Carmel. Sister Agnès, for example, will recall this sentence in a letter of 1886 to her father (See *La «Petite Mère...»*, p. 42).

[2] Thérèse wrote on the first page: «January 1895.» We thought at one time that Thérèse had written it in 1896, thinking that the 6 on the photocopy was original and the 5 was written over it by a strange hand in the course of the exploits of which the manuscript was the principal protagonist. Thus Thérèse would have told us nothing about the time of composition, but she would have added the date of the submission of the manuscript (exactly as she had dated her Pious Recreations and sev-

II. THE PROLOGUE OF MANUSCRIPT A: MEDITATION ON MERCY

Several factors bestow a special value on the prologue of Manuscript A (A 2r - 4r, 71-77). (1) Not only does Thérèse make known her intentions and the theme of the book, but, summarizing her life in a few words, she describes the spiritual climate of the time and collects her «thoughts» on God's action in her regard; (2) A certain time of hesitation and consequently reflection and maturation elapsed since the day of the prioress's order; (3) These pages contain the answer to a problem which has intrigued the nun for «a long time»; (4) The prologue has something solemn, and special about it: before writing, she prays, then she consults the Gospel.[3] Let us study its content now.

eral Poems with the date when they were recited or when she submitted them). Thus it can be better explained how Thérèse can say, hardly two pages after the beginning, that «seven years had passed» since she had entered Carmel: this would therefore be after April 9. But the Carmel of Lisieux really wanted to inform us that, contrary to the appearance of the photocopy, the 5 is original and the 6 an overprint: wanting to assign the whole of the Manuscripts to the three year term of Mother Marie de Gonzague (forgetting that this began in *March* 1896), they had simply added, at the top, the curve of the 6 and, and at the bottom, closed the lower loop of the 5. Later, they tried to erase the additions. This is what the autograph reveals. Consequently, a possible point of hesitation on the original date: January 1895. The «seven years» are an approximate indication. But this shows that it is necessary to allow a very large measure of imprecision to the other chronological reference points of Manuscript A: «After seven years» in religion (32 r, 73) and «for seven and a half years» (69 v, 186). Whatever the case may be, the manuscript ends in 1895 (one is unaware of the exact day), because on the last folio, while telling about her offering, she speaks of «this» year. We believe that Thérèse began the manuscript toward *the end* of the month of January 1895. In fact, the prioress's order having been given at the beginning of the year (Mother Agnès, PO, p. 146, and PA, p. 201), a certain period of perplexity elapsed (see A 2 r, 71), and for the 21st, the feast of the prioress, Thérèse had to compose her second Pious Recreation on Joan of Arc, a notebook of fifty pages (see RP 3). This belated date makes it even more likely that the writing of Manuscript A *followed* her discovery of the «way of childhood.»

3 She must have repeated this gesture during the course of the prologue, because the four times that she quotes the Bible, she gives the complete reference (chapter and verse) on three occasions and once the chapter. This (especially the indication of the verse) is very exceptional.

1. Mercy in the life of Thérèse

For two years now our Carmelite passes through a period of «beautiful calm» — if it is allowable to use an expression from Elizabeth of the Trinity, herself a fourteen year old girl at this time. Thérèse has the impression of being on a watch-tower. «I find myself at a period in my life when I can cast a glance upon the past; my soul has matured in the crucible of exterior and interior trials.» We recall the weak reed that bowed low under the strong gusts of wind. All that is over now: «Like a flower strengthened by the storm, I can raise my head and see the words of Psalm 22 realized in me.» And she quotes this biblical prayer which, in a description full of poetry, exalts the protection of the Shepherd. What she had to believe blindly at the hour of the trial, Thérèse then «sees.» The past is illuminated by the present, which on this account strengthens her for the future: «Yes, certainly Your goodness and Your mercy will accompany me all the days of my life!» And, although her autobiography does not transcribe this final verse of the quoted psalm, it copies this other, equivalent one: «I will fear no evil, for Thou art with me»; to which she adds (Psalm 102:8): «To me the Lord has always been full of gentleness and compassion.... Slow to punish and abundant in mercy!» One might be surprised that she does not quote verse 13 («as a father has tenderness for his children») as she will in her letter of May 9, 1897, but as far as getting things formulated is concerned the Saint is not yet at the end of her journey.

From this point of view, one can easily understand why Thérèse chooses as the leitmotiv of her book «the mercies of the Lord.» An autobiography? In her eyes, it is a recitation of «blessings,» its purpose is «to publish the totally gratuitous gifts of Jesus.» Gratuitous? It does not even cross her mind to take account of her very generous correspondence (since she is playing at the «bank of love,» her bookkeeping is not kept up-to-date!). «She knows that nothing in herself was capable of attracting the divine glances and that His mercy alone brought about everything that is good in her.» And Thérèse explains how 'God had her born in a holy soil and preserved her in order to take her for Himself to Carmel.'

It would be wrong to separate these graces. Opening the Holy

Gospels before beginning to write the Manuscript, her eyes fell on Micah 3:13, and she highlights what touched her: Jesus «called to Him those whom He *pleases,*» and not «those who are worthy of it,» she added with a reference to Romans 9:15 and 16 («He will have mercy on whom He will have mercy»). This is the keystone of her entire existence: «This is the mystery of my vocation, my whole life, and especially the mystery of the privileges Jesus showered upon my soul....»

Yet, it is Thérèse's vision of mercy in *God* that makes us discover the last characteristic of His merciful work in her.

2. Mercy in God

Thérèse did not always understand the secrets of divine mercy. But the light came: in two phases, it seems.

On the one hand, she saw men like Saint Paul and Saint Augustine whom God 'forces to accept the extraordinary favors which He showers on them,' or others 'to whom He grants such favors' that they are not able, so to speak, to put brakes on their race toward perfection. On the other hand, there is the uncultivated, primitive man who dies without having heard the name of God. (Thérèse cites him as an *example*, thus she is also thinking of others who are less privileged. Meanwhile, she herself, without identifying herself with the first category, nevertheless has ample reason to rank herself in their company.) This observation for a long time caused a problem in her mind, or rather astonishment: «I wondered for a long time why God had preferences, why all souls didn't receive an equal amount of graces.»

She ended up understanding: «Jesus saw fit to enlighten me about this mystery. He set before me the book of nature,» a book that had instructed her more than once.[4] She understood that in

[4] In nature she discovered for example «the things of life» (Mother Agnès, PA, p. 190). She relies on it in order to better understand her unity with Céline (LT 134, 747) or the role of suffering (LT 132, 740). This sentence is significant: «I understood that if, in the order of nature, Jesus is pleased to sow beneath our feet such delightful marvels, it is only to aid us in reading into the more hidden mysteries of a superior order that He is working at times in souls...» (LT 134, 747 of April 26, 1892). Love creates new sensitivities, a dimension that cold reason doesn't succeed in acquiring.

the wonderful variety of flowers, as great as it was, 'all are beautiful' and all have a role in making the beauty of the whole complete. It is the same in the supernatural order. There are 'the great saints' and there are 'the smaller saints.' These latter ones 'must be content to be flowers that give joy to the Lord whenever He looks down at His feet.' Are they less perfect for that? No, says Thérèse, because according to her notion of perfection (a notion which is a real gem, remarkable for its clarity, soberness, and precision): «Perfection consists in doing His will, in being what He wills us to be....» The first part of this definition is not news to us, because it already appeared in the letter of July 6, 1893, but while there it had to do with action, here it applies to being: it goes to a much deeper level.[5] This first insight is completed by another one which further illuminates God's plan for those who are little. Thérèse begins with a statement which is a step forward: «I understood, too, that Our Lord's love is revealed just as perfectly in the simplest soul that resists His grace in nothing, as in the most sublime soul,» and it proves her assertion by appealing to a law that is essential in that it is proper to love: «In fact, the nature of love [is] to humble oneself.» She seems to hold on to this notion, for she will repeat it twenty months later (B 3 v, 227). Let us be specific here. One cannot apply this definition to all love. I love a friend: but I do not have the impression of humbling myself; on the contrary the friend uplifts me. Likewise, the love among the three Persons of the Holy Trinity does not imply any inequality among Them. It follows, then, that Thérèse was thinking directly of the love that God has for us and it is in this case that she can see it as a condescension. In short, in this context and this prologue, she is speaking of that love which is mercy.

At first glance, one could say of God's love for the little ones that, what He loses in glory by withholding «extraordinary favors,»

[5] It is only in the [French] critical edition of 1956 that the second clause reappeared in the text.... Before, one read: «The more the flowers are happy to do His will, the more they are perfected.» Let us compare Thérèse's definition of perfection with this word of Saint Francis de Sales: «Don't desire to not be what you are, but desire very strongly to be what you are» (Éd. d'Annecy, t. 13, p. 291). See E. SCHILLEBEECKX, «Theologische bezinning op de geestelijke begeleiding,» *Tijdschrift voor geestelijk leven*, 20 (1964), p. 522.

He regains by the depth of His condescension, since God reveals Himself «just as perfectly» in them. And then, «if all souls resembled those of the holy Doctors who illumined the Church with the clarity of their teachings, it seems that God would not descend low enough when coming to their heart.» (It follows therefore that God's love is condescension also for the doctors.) This is why He created the child and the poor savage «and it is to their hearts that He deigns to lower Himself, these are His wild flowers whose simplicity delights Him....[6] When coming down in this way, God manifests His infinite grandeur.»

Between the child or the aborigine and the great saints, there is found a whole range of human beings who in various degrees manifest divine mercy in a specific manner. But, let us notice that in order for 'the simplest soul to reveal God's love as perfectly as the great saint,'[7] this soul must «resist His grace in nothing»! The smallest soul will be the full manifestation of divine condescension, if it is all docility, all acceptance. Then it is 'as God wills it to be': perfect and holy. In it, holiness and the full revelation of divine mercy in its regard coincide. It will open itself to God's personal love which Thérèse describes as follows: «Just as the sun shines simultaneously on the tall cedars and on each little flower as though it were alone on the earth, so Our Lord looks after each soul as if it had no equal; and just as in nature all the seasons are arranged in such a way as to make the humblest daisy blossom at the appointed time, in the same way, everything works out for the good of each soul.» Always provided that this one in no way resists His grace.

---

6 The ways of possessing and manifesting God are obviously different here. The child (baptized, she seems to say, because God 'descends to its heart') doesn't manifest it in a conscious manner. Likewise, the poor savage, «having nothing but natural law to guide him,» will be less conscious of his state of friendship and of the Trinity dwelling within him (which are real, if he observes the natural law) than the «holy Doctors.» But Thérèse puts herself simply in the place of the spectator who follows, by faith, these movements of mercy. The candor with which she already believed that God descends even to the heart of the «savage» is remarkable. This sound theological conviction probably comes from her intuitions concerning divine condescension.

7 The «holy Doctors» also owe everything to God's mercy, Thérèse doesn't deny it, but she always looks at the outside. The Doctors make better use of the potential of their natural gifts or the «extraordinary favors.» The little ones, on the contrary, are poorer by nature and the *manifestation* of Mercy as such will therefore be more eloquent in them. This is what Thérèse emphasizes.

3. *Thérèse's option in face of mercy*

Toward what side will our Carmelite lean? Will she see herself among the «beautiful flowers,» or among the «little flowers» in which mercy manifests itself more? We cannot but count her among the latter. For a long time Thérèse recognized herself as the littlest and that is what she wanted to be. Comparing herself to others, she easily found herself inferior, and in the prologue she appraises herself as a «little flower»[8] compared to her sisters, the «lilies.» Why would she change her opinion later on? For a long time now («I have always noticed,» C 2 v, 237) she sees herself as far removed from the «saints,» and she recognizes 'that it is impossible for her to grow up.' It is psychologically unthinkable for her now to rank herself anywhere else but among the «little souls.» Besides, as Thérèse immediately suggests, she also benefited from the divine condescension to the little ones: «These are my *thoughts* on the graces that God deigned to grant me,» she states, thus setting forth the little theology of her life. There is no doubt that she counts herself strictly among the simple souls, conscious of the work of mercy in them.

As for the «little way,» would it still be reasonable to situate its discovery after this prologue of Manuscript A? The Carmelite no longer has a problem seeing the distance that separates her from the «saints.» Clearly, she already knows that perfection is within reach of little ones. And even the way to it is suggested: to open oneself to the mercy that fills one, if one places no obstacle in its way. With full awareness, Thérèse ranks herself among the little

[8] See also LT 224, 1083. This title, which she gives herself about thirty times in Manuscript A, was perhaps inspired by the holy picture of «*the little flower* of the Divine Prisoner» which evoked for her, in her childhood, «so many things that I became deeply recollected» (A 31 v, 119); but what she added to it is the much greater influence of the symbolic gesture of M. Martin on the day of Pentecost 1887, when he gave her a «*little white flower*» and explained to her God's special care for that one (A 50 v, 152). In fact, Thérèse calls herself the little white flower (for example in the very title of Manuscript A) and she does this in light of God's mercy. It goes without saying that her father's little flower, which she kept forever, reminds her of God's mercy much more vividly in 1895 than in 1887. Nothing is more susceptible to evolution than a symbol! Thérèse will recall her father's gesture in a poem (PN 8, str. 8) and again on the tenth anniversary of the event (DE 7.6.2). On the picture where she had glued the little flower, she will inscribe her last written words (see Pri 21).

ones.[9] It is true, there is no obvious or complete description of the «little way» here, but the principle of an interplay between mercy and littleness in relation to perfection is consciously present. It is impossible to see how any hesitation on her way toward holiness could still exist in Thérèse. And if it does exist, in what would the new discovery consist?

Thérèse will remain faithful to her choice: she will remain little, in order to be favored with mercy. From February 24th on, she signs her letters with the addition of «*very little*,» thereby secretly alluding to Proverbs 9:4; and perhaps she would have adopted this usage earlier, had her correspondence been more frequent in the previous weeks.[10] On April 28th, she reaffirms her choice, indicating the evolution that she underwent in her thoughts:[11] she does not want to be among the «souls full of sublime virtues,» but to be «a *little* toy without value,» which Jesus can use as He wishes. With this in mind, Thérèse said «I rejoiced at being *poor*, I wanted to become poorer and poorer every day, so that every day Jesus may take more delight *in playing* with me.» She therefore offers herself to be loved by Him, and as a consequence to love Him. Repeatedly, the idea of divine condescension attracted by human poverty returns in Manuscript A: it is 'because Jesus knows she is too feeble that He does not expose her to temptation' (A 38 v, 131); it is 'because He knows how weak she is' that He called her quickly to Carmel (A 44 r, 140); it is 'because she is little and weak that He lowers Himself toward her and that He wants to make His mercy shine in her' (A 49 r, 149). In order 'to be instructed in the secrets of perfection, one must be poor in spirit' (*ibid.*), she says again. And she considers as 'the only good thing: to love God with all her heart and to be poor in spirit here on earth' (32 v, 121).

---

[9] It is possible — but we can say no more than that — that Thérèse's intuitions about mercy are positively a consequence of her discovery of the «little way». It is impossible to determine if they make up part of what Thérèse read in «the book of nature,» although Thérèse says at the beginning of a new paragraph: «I understood *again*....» As for this light she received from nature, we are unaware of the dates of it.

[10] The letter of February 24 is the first since the first days of the year. For the use of «very little,» see here Part I, chap. III.

[11] «Now again..., only I thought...» (LT 176, 902).

Such insights prove how deeply she is penetrated by the idea of mercy. In 1895, her life opens up to this condescending Love more and more. And, in the process, a new experience strengthens her in her way.

III. THE «LITTLE WAY» AND THE IMMOLATION TO MERCIFUL LOVE

1. *The intuition*

It took place on Sunday, June 9, 1895, in the choir of the Carmelites, while they were celebrating the Eucharist (CSG, p. 89). Six months later, Thérèse will describe what happened then, unknown to others (A 84 r-v, 212). «This year on June 9, the feast of the Holy Trinity, I received the grace to understand more than ever before how much Jesus desires to be loved.» These last words do not yet disclose that the perspectives of love will actually be reversed here: for Jesus, to be loved is to love; for Thérèse, to love means to let herself be loved. She goes on to explain herself: «I was thinking about the souls who offer themselves as victims of God's Justice in order to divert the punishments reserved for sinners and to draw them upon themselves[12]; this offering seemed great and

---

[12] Two questions: (1) What made her think about these souls? We don't know. Perhaps it was that, feeling an interior attraction to a deeper immolation, a first reflection made her think of making the offering to Justice, a well known spiritual practice at the time. (2) About whom was she thinking? There were in Lisieux two nuns who had offered themselves as victims: Sister Marie of the Cross and Mother Geneviève. (See A. COMBES «Note sur la signification historique de l'offrande thérésienne à l'Amour miséricordieux,» *Mélanges Marcel Viller, Revue d'ascétique et de mystique*, 25 [1949], pp. 494-496.) But let's note that these immolations weren't made expressly to justice nor for the purposes that Thérèse indicates; besides, she considered Mother Geneviève «a *Saint* not at all inimitable» (A 78 r, 201). The existence of such an immolation to justice was not unknown to her: the *Treasure of Carmel*, for example, mentioned it as an aim of the Carmelite order. (See A. COMBES, *ibid.*, pp. 496-497 or Mss II, 59 or S. PIAT, *À la découverte…*, pp. 77-80, who gives large excerpts which reveal what the author calls an «overly-severe, not to say terrorist, spirit.») To say of this last offering «that it was constantly proposed to the generosity [of Thérèse and that] after the spiritual doctrine that reigns in her monastery, it was the very essence of her vocation» (A. COMBES, «Sainte Thérèse de Lisieux modèle de vie contemplative,» *Ephemerides carmeliticae*, 13 [1962], p. 108) is

very generous to me [and one can take her word for it that she respects the way of others], but I was far from feeling attracted to making it.»

What gives rise to the hesitations of this generous woman? They are explained when one puts them back in the psychological context of this year 1895. The nun had already found her «little way.» For a long time she had felt her powerlessness very keenly: how would she venture to take upon her weak shoulders «the punishments reserved for sinners»? But it is not so much a matter of shirking an excessive burden and reacting against a sacrifice offered to justice[13]; it is rather that she is attracted elsewhere. She has already discovered divine mercy — henceforth the motive of her entire spiritual journey — and she grasped the dynamism of a condescending God. For more than four months, she relies regularly on the little gray notebook where she meditates upon «the mercies of the Lord» towards her, through the whole course of her life. She therefore already possesses a lively and experiential awareness of the merciful Lover, but now she understands it «more than ever»! The light of this spring-tide morning is utterly clear! Her own formulas indicate this fact: «O my God! I cried out from the depths of my heart, will Your Justice alone find souls willing to immolate themselves as victims?.... Does not Your Merciful *Love* need them

---

to exaggerate somewhat. The Carmel of Lisieux was imbued, even in its austere life, with a tender devotion to the Sacred Heart. The cult of the Holy Face also sought to make reparation by «consoling.» The tone of letters by which her colleagues encouraged Thérèse, also expressed a confident approach to Jesus.

(*Note of 1994.*) Even if we cannot draw a conclusion that is certain, we are tempted to think that Thérèse could have been impressed by the example of a Carmelite who had offered herself as a victim to divine justice and whose obituary notice had arrived at the Carmel of Lisieux just the day before, on June 8. (The notices were read in the refectory as soon as possible; they sometimes spoke of them at recreation.) Sister Marie of Jesus, a Carmelite of Luçon had «very often offered herself as a victim to divine Justice,» her circular revealed. Her agony of Good Friday 1895 was dreadful. The dying Sister lets this cry of anguish escape: «I am bearing the harshness of divine Justice… divine Justice! … divine Justice! …» And again: «I don't have enough merits, I must acquire more of them.» (See the French critical edition of the *Pious Recreations and Prayers*, p. 558; p. 84 of the current French edition of *Prayers*.)

[13] It seems «very great and generous» to her! One must not make Thérèse too much of a revolutionary. She reacts rather little *contra*. Nearly all her movement, all her originality, come from the depths of a *pro*.

too?.... On every side this love is unknown, rejected; those hearts upon whom You would lavish it turn to creatures seeking happiness from them with their miserable affection; they do this instead of throwing themselves into Your arms and accepting Your infinite *Love*....» The allure of this reflection suggests Thérèse's answer: not to reject this prodigal Lover, but 'to throw herself into His arms.' Ever since she discovered her «little way,» she approaches Jesus as a very little child who abandons herself into her mother's arms: with more intensity than ever, she is now going to repeat this movement! «O my God!,» she again cries out, «is your disdained Love going to remain closed up within your Heart? It seems to me [we understand why] that if You were to find souls offering themselves as Victims of holocausts to Your Love, You would consume them rapidly; it seems to me, too, that You would be happy not to hold back the waves of infinite tenderness within You.... If Your Justice loves to release itself, this Justice *which extends only over the earth*, how much more does Your Merciful Love desire to *set souls on fire*, since Your Mercy *reaches to the Heavens*.[14] ... O my Jesus! let *me* be this happy victim; consume Your holocaust with the fire of Your Divine Love!»

2. *The Act of Offering*

That this offering was envisaged in a serious and definitive way, we have proof in the fact that Thérèse thought she was obliged to ask permission before engaging herself in it. Once she received authorization, «full of emotion» she declares to Céline that she is going «to put her thoughts in writing and compose an act of obla-

[14] See Ps 35:6-7 in the translation of the *Manuel du chrétien* used by Thérèse: «Your mercy, Lord, reaches as high as the Heavens... Your justice is similar to the highest mountains» (DCL). One sees how Thérèse had continued to shore up, in her own manner, her convictions concerning mercy. We should also mention that mercy is a central theme in the liturgical text of the Mass of the Most Holy Trinity. The Introit, Offertory, and Communion repeat: «For He has shown us mercy.» Thérèse didn't know Latin and could no longer follow the Mass in a translation since, at this time, the choir was in darkness during Mass (DCL). But she could have read the translation at another time. Whatever the case may be, they had read in the refectory the translation and commentary of Dom Guéranger. One can neither verify nor exclude an immediate influence.

tion» (CSG, p. 89), which is a further proof of the gravity of her decision. Two days later, she pronounces with her sister her «Offering of myself as Victim of holocaust to the Merciful Love of God.»[15]

This document is of great value, not only because it marks a privileged moment of the spiritual journey of our Carmelite, but also because the reflection which preceded the writing ensures a faithful reproduction of Thérèse's thought. One will have perhaps noticed the precision of the title of the Act, which is almost official: indicating briefly and clearly the object of her offering, her method, and her recipient. But this precision is not consistently maintained, as André Combes has noted. Thérèse «proceeds toward her personal oblation by a path which winds a little, and which baffles an analysis that is too strictly logical. There is a succession and superimposing of the themes of offering, thanksgiving, and prayers which contribute to justifying her request for authorization and to putting her sacrifice of holocaust to merciful Love in its place, while at the same time illuminating it.»[16] We shall dwell a bit on the leading ideas which further articulate this document, for they have a direct relationship with the topic of our study.

1. The first paragraph establishes the goal of her immolation: «I desire to *Love* You and to make You *Loved.*» Thérèse expresses this goal: apostolic desires, the perfect accomplishment of the divine will, obtaining the degree of glory that is prepared for her.... But all is summarized in one statement: «In a word, I desire to be a Saint.» Further on, she will indicate as the more immediate goal of her offering: «to live in one single act of perfect Love.»

---

[15] Two autograph copies are preserved. The original, dated June 9, has been published among the «added fragments» of the edition in facsimile. One sees where Thérèse later added two reference to the Sacred Heart (to please her sister Marie of the Sacred Heart) and other small additions, struck out a superfluous sentence (because of repetition) and changed «infinite desires» to «immense desires.» This correction was imposed by Father Lemonnier, whom she consulted at the time of the retreat in the month of October. «Immense» was theologically more exact, said the Father. That didn't prevent him from declaring later that encounters with Thérèse had caused in him an «infinite» joy! The second autograph copy has been reproduced in the *Petit catéchisme de l'acte d'offrande de sainte Thérèse de l'Enfant-Jésus comme victime d'holocauste à l'amour miséricordieux du bon Dieu*, Lisieux, s.d., 44 pp. It is this definitive text that we follow. It is found in Pri 6.

However — and this observation has already been made — desire and reality do not amount to the same thing: «But I feel my helplessness.» This is why she resorts to merciful Love: «...and I beg You, O my God! to be Yourself my *Sanctity*.»

These initial lines show a small evolution. According to the first thought, described in Manuscript A — unless there be at that point a certain reticence — the offering was considered as a response to God Who desires to communicate Himself. But spontaneously Thérèse situates it in the perspective of her own sanctification. There is no trace of a selfish betrayal there, because for God to communicate His love and for us to love God with that same received love, means in fact for us to become holy.

2. After having stated her goal, she comes to the grounds that legitimize her demand. The first is the promise that the Father gave us in the humanity of Christ: «Since You [God] loved me so much as to give me Your only Son as my Savior and my Spouse, the infinite treasures of His merits are mine; I offer them to You with gladness, begging You to look upon me only in the Face of Jesus and [there follows now a later addition] in His Heart burning with *Love*.» To the merits of the Mediator she joins those of the saints in Heaven and on earth, of the angels, and of the Virgin Mary.[17] The second ground that she gives for her «certainty» of being heard is Jesus' word: «Whatsoever you ask the Father in my name He will give it to you!» (Jn 16:23). The third is intrinsic to her desire itself and it is protected by the authority of Saint John of the Cross: «I know, O my God! that *the more You want to give, the more You make us desire*.»[18] She can thus conclude: «I feel in my heart immense desires and it is with confidence that I ask You to come and take possession of my soul.»

3. Then a few somewhat mysterious sentences about Holy Communion follow, to which we will return later, as well as to

---

[16] *Introduction...*, pp. 187-188

[17] «It is to Her that I abandon my offering asking Her to present it to you,» writes Thérèse. In fact, she pronounced her act kneeling before the statue of the Virgin of the Smile (CSG, p. 89).

[18] Letter to Mother Éléonore (*Oeuvres*, I, p. 335): «The more [God] wants to give, the more He makes us desire, so far as to make the emptiness in our soul complete, to fill us with His treasures.» It is Thérèse who underlines — as is often the case — her quotation.

some sentences about her request for the stigmata in Heaven; then thanksgiving for all her graces, especially the «crucible of suffering,» and a statement of her desire 'to console the Lord for the ingratitude of the wicked.' On this subject, the Carmelite begs God «to take away her freedom to displease [Him].» To displease voluntarily, one ought to say, because she has the realistic expectation of her falls in weakness and pays in advance for them with the prayer of her Offering: «If through weakness, I sometimes fall, may Your *Divine Glance* cleanse my soul immediately, consuming all my imperfections like fire that transforms everything into itself....»

4. Here Thérèse begins to look at the present life in the light of the future life. It is an opportunity to reaffirm her absolute dependence on divine mercy: «I do not want to lay up merits for Heaven, I want to work for your *Love alone*.» She will remain poor: «In the evening of this life, I shall appear before You with empty hands, for I do not ask You, Lord, to count my works.» Necessarily poor, since «all our justice is stained in Your eyes,» she will depend on Merciful Love alone: «I wish, then, to be clothed in Your own *Justice*, and to receive from Your *Love* the eternal possession of *Yourself*. I want no other *Throne* and no other *Crown* but *You*, O my *Beloved*!» And Jesus transcends our efforts: «You can, then, in one instant prepare me to appear before You.»

5. After the confident Carmelite has described her goal and the grounds which justify her act, she takes the means to reach her objective, she draws up her offering. This is the heart of this document, the cardinal point of the grace of June 9. «In order to live in one single act of perfect Love, I OFFER MYSELF AS A VICTIM OF HOLOCAUST TO YOUR MERCIFUL LOVE, asking You to consume me incessantly, allowing the waves of *infinite tenderness* pent up within You to overflow into my soul, that thus I may become a *Martyr* of Your *Love*, O my God!....»

The effects that she expects from her offering clearly explain the word «victim,» inspired by the reference to the «victims of Justice.» In the two cases, there is a similar task: to submit to the action of a superior power, so as to die little by little from this action; but for Thérèse all will be mercy, infinite tenderness, consummation, and a martyrdom of love. She will lose her own life to live

God's life. Her martyrdom will consist less in enduring than in receiving without being able to contain. Two symbols illustrate this: the fire that «consumes» a «holocaust» and the irresistible river of which the «waves» «overflow.» 'May this martyrdom,'[19] Thérèse hopes, 'finally cause me to die and prepare me to encounter without any delay [in purgatory] Your Merciful Love in an eternal face-to-face.' In the meantime, she wants to 'renew her offering at every beat of her heart.'[20]

3. *The «Little Way»*

And now where are we in the «way of spiritual childhood»? Analyzing the graces of June 9 and 11, we did not digress from the proposed theme! The oblation to Merciful Love was achieved in the «little way» and the two descriptions reveal a basic agreement. But it is good to clarify.

First of all, the goal is a common one: sanctity, which transcends one's own human possibilities. In discovering her way, Thérèse recognized in herself the keenly felt powerlessness «to grow up.» In writing her Act, she reveals a similar experience: she feels her helplessness, she is weak and will fall, she has empty hands, and all her justice is tainted; but the act underlines further that this poverty is also the fruit of a voluntary attitude. In the two cases, the determination to pursue the way further really rests, although not solely, on a similar conviction: 'God cannot inspire unrealizable desires' (C 2 v, 237). God Himself 'makes me desire, therefore He wants to give' (Act); from this flows the confidence necessary to forge ahead. Against this backdrop the object of

---

[19] This martyrdom is therefore not directly considered as a martyrdom of suffering. This is what the Saint explains to her sister Marie again, a few days after her offering. It is not a question of offering oneself to God's justice, but to His merciful Love: «Then, you see, one has nothing to fear because, from this Love, one can only expect Mercy» (Mss II, 60). Concerning martyrdom in the strict sense, Thérèse holds herself back, it seems to us, only from the experience of a foreign superior force and final death. See also CSG, 2nd ed., 1954, pp. 219-223 and GABRIEL DE SAINTE-MARIE-MADELEINE, «L'atto di offerta all'amore misericordioso in rapporto alla sofferenza,» *Rivista di Vita Spirituale*, 4 (1950), pp. 284-302.

[20] In fact, from now on she will carry her act always on her heart. One sees on the photocopy how much it was used.

Thérèse's longings is laid out with greater clarity: the substitution of God's holiness for her own and for her essential insufficiency — in other words, union with God, brought about by God, so radical and effective that Thérèse will live this perfect love which she had not yet attained and for which she begs.

How will this be realized? The two descriptions, the one more symbolic from the narration of the discovery of the «little way» and the other a little more conceptual from the Act of Oblation, suggest the same dispositions in the actors. On the one hand, there is God Who brings about this union: He invites, He carries, He fills mercifully, He raises to holiness (the narration); He Himself is Thérèse's holiness, her justice, and He consumes her with love to the point of making her die (the Act). On the other hand, Thérèse recognizes her nothingness straightforwardly and she surrenders herself with a loving confidence to the merciful Almighty[21]: she «comes» to God's maternal love like a child (the narration), she offers herself with the greatest receptiveness to the workings of God Who mercifully will make her perfect (the Act). There is a dialogue therefore between the confidence which is eager for consummation and the mercy which fills to the brim. If one considers the dialectical play on the part of man alone, the interaction is between an active confidence and a more passive receptiveness. If one considers it on the part of God, it is a combination (according to Thérèse's own expression, of course, and always keeping in mind that it is God Who brings about in us both the will and the operation itself, Ph 2:13) of the perception of our confidence and the response of giving.

A remark is in order here. In the presence of a fundamental convergence — which does not, however, exclude a difference of accentuation — the difference of formulation is very instructive. The Act of Offering does not use the symbol of the child nor that of the father (mother), and instead of lifting (arms, elevator), it

[21] Thérèse puts the same conditions to Marie of the Trinity before this latter one pronounces the Act: «The only preparation that God asks of you? Well! it is to humbly recognize your unworthiness. Ah! since He gives you this grace, abandon yourself to Him without fear» (Mss II, 60). Sister Geneviève summarizes the matter very well: «In her mind [it was a question of] abandoning herself with total confidence to the infinite Mercy of God» (CSG, p. 90).

speaks rather of condescension on God's part. But it is sufficient to observe the context to realize how unessential this difference is. On the conceptual plane, the two descriptions are revealed as synonymous. However, it is interesting to note that Thérèse, while consciously living her «little way,» does not yet give to the symbols of the child and its father the much more extended exclusive rights that she will give them in 1897.

A brief digression on their utilization in 1895 confirms this. It is true, and perhaps characteristic, that one encounters on this date for the first time in the Thérésian corpus the *explicit and paired* mention of the words «father» and «child» to indicate relationship with God,[22] but this combination is made only rarely: God is the Father who shows the future to His children (A 21 r, 102), Thérèse is the child who looks at her Father's treasures as her own (A 66 v, 161), and if, in 1893, it was still Jesus who tossed aside the stones from the path of His «spouse» (LT 149, 826), now it is the «Father» who does this for His «child» (A 39 r, 132). Thérèse also compares herself to the child who is pleasing to its parents, even when it sleeps (A 75 v, 197). As we see it, with the explanation of mercy, the idea of the father is made more explicit, and with the dazzling awareness of being mercifully favored, the assimilation to the child intensifies. On July 20, 1895, the Saint writes: «I who am and want to remain always a child.»[23] In October, she sings: «I abandon myself and I fall asleep without fear / In your arms, O my divine Sav-

[22] It is abundantly clear that Thérèse considers herself as the child of the Heavenly Father and that the term «child» is implied when she sometimes refers to the Father, as when, in the loss of her father, she better discovers «our Father who art in Heaven!» (LT 101, 601; 127, 724): «What infinite horizons [this word] opens to our eyes!» (129, 728); see also A 75 v, 197. Let us note that this discovery is made from an emptiness; later the recourse to the Father will proceed from a sense of plenitude or in the biblical reminiscences of the Father of Jesus (LT 130, 731; 142, 794; 145, 808; 165, 860; PN 17). In the same way, when she compares Saint Cecilia to a little child who sleeps on the «heart of her God» (PN 3), the image of the father seems to be implied.

[23] LT 178, 907. See «Ask [that I may be] happy to be everywhere the littlest, the last!...» (LT 173, 896); «I wanted to become [poor] more and more each day» (LT 176, 902). In the same letter of July 20, she praises 'the great mercies of God for His poor children' (LT 178, 907).

ior.»[24] While the reality of the «little way» is beginning to blossom radiant with life, the symbolical formulation of it is still in progress. Its great success is reserved for later. Note, finally, the expression «to practice the virtues of childhood» in the month of October 1895.[25]

Let us now return to the Act. From everything which precedes, we may conclude that it is between the signposts of the «little way» that Thérèse engaged herself, on June 9-11, in a more radical way. Was there progress? By all means. If Thérèse for some time already knows God's maternal tenderness for those who approach Him as a child, now she probes this mother's heart more deeply. She discovers in it an infinite mercy, a real inclination to communicate itself, a passion to lavish its love, impulses that He can hardly resist which, once set free, pour out like a stream which has been dammed up too long. There is no doubt that where sanctification is concerned Thérèse's attention must now be fixed even more on God alone. The oblation as victim, which Thérèse will repeat «an infinite number of times» (Act), therefore ushers in a more intimate self-giving to God, a faster walking on her «way of spiritual childhood.» Let us add, finally, that henceforth the expression «Merciful Love» becomes a consecrated phrase in the vocabulary of the «little way.» One can be surprised that it only returns four times in the entire Thérésian corpus.[26] The reason for this is that God's love became in the eyes of Thérèse of Lisieux so essentially mercy — and mercy became so essentially love — that, on the plane of ideas, the formula «Merciful Love» seems to the nun a little redundant. Already the prologue of Manuscript A expressed her persuasion that God's love for us is by «its very nature» condescending, merciful. How much more is this true after June 9! It is no surprise, then, if Thérèse speaks of her oblation to Merciful Love as an of-

---

[24] *Remember*, PN 24. Thérèse had also made Marie Guérin promise, as she was about to enter Carmel, «to remain as calm as a little child in its Mother's arms» (LT 177, 907).

[25] *Remember*, PN 24, str. 9.

[26] LT 197, 998; 261, 1163; 262, 1170; and in an act of offering written for someone in the world (Pri 10). This concerns her writings. It goes without saying that Thérèse will have *spoken* of it several times.

fering of oneself very simply to «love» in the list of her days of grace at the end of Manuscript A.

Let us note again that Thérèse's opening to mercy is not merely passive. Moreover, total passivity is rare in the spiritual life. Almost always, the soul is called to be at least active enough to welcome God's work. But Thérèse's Act implies more. It is not about offering oneself once and for all; one must repeat this Offering as Thérèse so often repeated it (DE 29.7.9), if not in words, then at least by the living attitude of confidence and abandonment. We will have the opportunity to speak again of the activity contained in these virtues. It is now sufficient to quote Gabriel de Sainte-Marie-Madeleine: «This offering is not a transitory act, but an attitude that the soul assumes and feeds in a continuous way by an uninterrupted adherence, active and passive, to God's will.» And farther on: «The doors that the Act of Offering opens to the divine invasion are closed immediately when one departs voluntarily from the divine will.»[27]

As for the importance of the Act of Offering for the «way of childhood,» it has been wisely observed that it is not optional or accessory,[28] but instead it constitutes the *essential* means to progress in this way.[29] It is all too clear that here we are not speaking of a formula pronounced with the lips, but of an interior attitude that one must cultivate. If the «way of childhood» aims at receiving holiness from God, it follows logically that confidence and the concrete opening to mercy — and this is the heart of the Act — are also at the heart of the «little way» which Thérèse Martin taught with such great theological intuition.

---

[27] «L'atto di offerta,» *Vita e dottrina spirituale di S. Teresa del B.G.*, Florence, 1949, pp. 152 and 169.

[28] GABRIEL DE SAINTE-MARIE-MADELEINE, «Settimana di studio su Santa Teresa del B.G. Risultati,» *Rivista di Vita spirituale*, 2 (1948), pp. 219-220 and *L'Atto di offerta...*, pp. 176-177.

[29] M.-M. PHILIPON, *Sainte Thérèse de Lisieux...*, p. 290.

IV. MANUSCRIPT A, PAGE 32: A NEW SKETCH OF THE «WAY OF CHILDHOOD»

In one of the numerous digressions of Manuscript A, Sister Thérèse painted a restrained but useful picture of her views on perfection in 1895. The six and a half lines of interest[30] reflect faithfully, although in their own way, the main ideas of the Act of Offering and the «little way.» Here is how the Carmelite thinks about her desire for holiness which goes far back in her life but remains always present: «This desire could certainly appear audacious if one were to consider how weak and imperfect I was, and how, after seven years in the religious life, I am still weak and imperfect. I always feel, however, the same bold confidence of becoming a great Saint, because I don't count on my merits since I have *none*, but I trust in Him Who is Virtue and Holiness itself. God alone, content with my feeble efforts, will raise me to Himself and, clothing me with His infinite merits, He will make me a *Saint*.»

Even in the absence of the word «mercy» and of the double image of father-child, this passage where Thérèse uses simple and precise concepts constitutes one of the best formulations that she has given us of her «little way.» It contains a clear indication of the goal: to become holy and a great saint. Of her perception of herself: she is «weak and imperfect.» Of the means that she uses: she tries but her efforts are «weak» and insufficient; she does not have any 'merits' and therefore does not intend «to count» on them. Her assurance consists in her «bold confidence,» in her 'trust in Him Who is and gives Virtue and Holiness.' This trust, in appearance «audacious,» is legitimized by the mercy of the One Who Himself «will be content» with her weak efforts and will intervene to sanctify the «weak.» He 'will clothe her with His own merits' and — descending and rising again — «will raise her to Himself,» to holiness.[31]

---

[30] Manuscript A 32 r, 120; compare with Pri 6.

[31] Note the expression «to raise to» that Thérèse will use again in her account of the origin of the «little way» (C 3 r, 237). She likes to present sanctification as an ascension. See, for example, the «mountain of love» that she wanted to climb in 1890 (LT 110, 651).

The following comparison demonstrates the relationship of thought and even of formulation that exists between page 32 of Manuscript A and the Act.

A, p. 32	*Act of Offering*
1. «I am... weak and imperfect.»	1. «I feel my powerlessness»; Thérèse foresees her «imperfections» and «weakness.»
2. She has the «desire... to become a great Saint.»	2. «I desire to be a Saint.»
3. Her desire is great to the point of seeming «audacious.»	3. Her desires are «immense.»
4. She has the «bold confidence» of becoming holy.	4. «It is with confidence» that she asks for it.
5. She has 'no merits.'	5. She will always have «empty hands.»
6. «I don't count on my merits.»	6. She doesn't dare 'to ask the Lord to count her works, because all our justice is stained.'
7. «I hope in the One who is... Holiness itself.»	7. «I beg You, O my God! to be Yourself my *Sanctity*.»
8. She leans on the «infinite merits» of the Lord.	8. «The infinite treasures of His merits are mine.»
9. She will be «clothed» with His merits.	9. She wants «to be clothed» with His own divine justice.

The relationship between these two noteworthy texts is explained only by the common origin of the same source of inspiration. In fact, they were both written *around the same time*. Unfortunately, we are unaware of the pace of Thérèse's writing of Manuscript A and thus we do not know with certainty to what text we should grant chronological priority. This does not prevent us from concluding, after the basic identity of the two texts, that Thérèse had already conceived of her doctrine of the «little way» and (especially if page 32 is earlier) that she carried her Act within her «as the Virgin carried the *Magnificat*, long before the song sprang from her lips.»[32]

[32] S. PIAT, *À la découverte...*, p. 154.

V. THE SPRINGTIME YEAR

For Thérèse, 1895 was perhaps the most beautiful year of her life. Having just discovered the «way of childhood,» she knows all the joy of penetrating it with clear vision and impetuosity. Her race toward love picks up speed. On February 26, she spontaneously composes her poem «Living on Love» (DE 5.8.7), in which she projects all her dreams of love for Jesus and for others, both during her life and after her death, allowing us to glimpse God's life in her. To believe Thérèse of Saint Augustine on the point, Thérèse had expressed this confidence during the month of April: «I will die soon. I am not telling you that it will be in a matter of months, but in two or three years: I feel, in everything that happens in my soul, that my exile is close to its end» (PO, p. 406). This is what she had already expressed in «Living on Love.» «I sense that my exile is about to end....»[33]

But the light and the decision of June 9 outweigh everything. At the same time, they mark the beginning of a new flood of graces and experiences. «You know,» Thérèse said to Mother Agnès, «the rivers or rather the oceans of graces which flooded my soul.... Ah! since that happy day, it seems to me that *Love* penetrates and surrounds me, that at each moment this *Merciful Love* renews me, purifying my soul and leaving no trace of sin within it.»[34] Even if the hypothesis of Albert du Sacré-Coeur is justified, according to which Thérèse's sensitivity plays an intensive role at this time under the influence of the tuberculosis which is progressing, thus becoming an instrument of grace,[35] the self-confession which she makes is such that it would seem very imprudent to deny a mystical character to it.[36]

---

[33] PN 17, str. 14.

[34] A 84 v, 212. See A 31 v-32 v, 119: 'Now I am flooded with lights.' This is *perhaps* an indication that the famous text of A 32, which follows five lines farther on, was written after June 9.

[35] See *Approches...*, p. 187. However, it is not easy to have a clinical certainty about her physiological state in 1895.

[36] It doesn't enter into our intentions to examine Thérèse's life of prayer. Let us note however that it has sometimes been seen in the graces she described here what is called "transforming union." For whoever supports this thesis the subsequent trials against the faith are then purely redeeming or the fulfillment of her desire for the «martyrdom of the heart.» Other authors — and we are included in agreeing with them — differentiate this union and for them the trials against the faith also have a real purifying role.

In other places as well, Thérèse describes the secret work of Jesus in her. «I have frequently noticed that Jesus doesn't want me to lay up *provisions;* He nourishes me at every moment with a totally new food; I find it within me without my knowing how it is there.... I simply believe that it is Jesus Himself hidden in the depths of my poor little heart who is giving me the grace of acting within me and making me think of all He desires me to do at the present moment» (A 76 v, 198). And there is this other passage: «I understand and I know from experience that "The kingdom of God is within us." Jesus has no need of books or teachers to instruct souls; He, the Doctor of doctors, teaches without the noise of words.... Never have I heard Him speak, but I feel that He is within me at every moment; He is guiding and inspiring me with what I must say and do. I find, just at the moment I need them, certain lights which I had not seen until then, and it is not most frequently during my hours of prayer that these are most abundant, but rather in the midst of daily occupations...» (A 83 v, 211).

Such graces as this cannot remain without effect. Thérèse confesses to no longer being «downcast by any passing thing» (A 43 v, 139), to having a great deal of boldness (A 48 v, 148); to thinking «of God all day long.»[37] 'Abandonment alone guides her; she desires neither suffering nor death any longer, but only love; she can no longer ask for anything with fervor except the perfect accomplishment of God's will; her only work is to love' (A 83 r, 210).

Of course, Thérèse remains «weak and powerless» (see above), with an «extreme weakness» in her own eyes,[38] and she asks God «to look not at what I am, but at what I should be and would want to be, that is to say, a nun all inflamed with your love.»[39] But in her opinion, «knowing how *to draw profit from everything,* love very quickly consumes *everything* that can be displeasing to Jesus, leaving behind only a humble and profound peace in the depths

---

[37] A 79r, 203. See A 80r, 205: «I make the resolution to be thankful all through the rest of the day.»

[38] *Living on Love* (PN 17, str. 7).

[39] Prayer for Father Bellière, composed spontaneously in the month of October 1895: Pri 8.

of the heart....»[40] The divine fire burns away every trace of imperfection.[41] Thérèse became humble, very little, and poor, and it is this poverty of spirit that she teaches in her Manuscript A.[42]

How does she look at the future at the end of 1895, after the long reflection on the divine mercies strewn all throughout her life? «Now, I have no other desire except to *love* Jesus unto folly....»[43] The desire is not yet the full realization, the Carmelite still remains incomplete, but will she ever be able to doubt again? She discovered her strength forever: «What I am certain about is that God's Mercy will accompany [me] always» (A 84 v, 213)! So ends Manuscript A, as it had begun. The circle of mercy closes itself around her entire existence.

In the first months of 1896, the psychological thrust continues. A new event even reinforced it: on October 15, 1895, Thérèse was designated as spiritual support of Abbé Bellière, a future missionary priest.[44] The reverberation of this decision in the soul of the nun was most happy: «Not for years had I experienced this kind of happiness. I felt my soul was renewed; it was as if someone had struck for the first time musical strings which had been left forgotten until then.» And she tried «to redouble her fervor» (C 32 r, 278). Even the community elections of March 21, 1896, which inaugurated a new three-year term for Marie de Gonzague, disturb her only for a single instant.[45] She speaks of the period before Easter 1896 in this way: «At this time I was enjoying such a living and clear *faith* that the thought of Heaven made up all my happiness» (C 5 v, 241); «a short time before my trial against faith began, I was saying to myself: I don't really have any great exterior trials and for me to have interior ones God would have to change my way. I do not believe that He will do this, and still I cannot always live in repose as I am now» (C 31 r, 277).

---

[40] A 83 v, 210. The underlined words are borrowed from the poem *Glose sur le divin* by Saint John of the Cross.

[41] A 84 r, 212; Act; Pri 10; and the sixth stanza of *Living on Love* (PN 17).

[42] A 32 r, 120; 49 r, 149; 56 v, 163; see LT 176, 902.

[43] A 82 v, 210. Compare the explanation of her coat of arms (A 85 v, 214).

[44] Maurice Bellière was a seminarian at the time, but the French custom then was to address a seminarian as "Monsieur l'abbé."

[45] For an instant, she was «as if struck with stupor» (Mother Agnès, PA, p. 154).

Her first hemoptysis on April 3, 1896 makes her very happy. It is a sign for her: 'a sweet and distant murmur which announced the Bridegroom's arrival'(C 5 v, 240).

But the bride is not yet ready. The Spouse is going to prepare her Himself. The radiant Heaven of her soul will change soon.[46] A deep night envelops her soul, throwing a terrible anguish upon her faith in the existence of Heaven. Only death and Heaven will deliver her from it.

[46] G. MOREL notes: «When we declare that the mystical life is the normal result of the religious life, we do not mean to say that every man can have a very vivid *thetical* consciousness of this life, nor *a fortiori* express it in as brilliant a manner as John of the Cross. We call thetical consciousness the explicit consciousness that makes life ebb to the natural psyche and body of the individual. It is distinct from the non-thetical consciousness which is essentially certainty lived from union with the Absolute: this one is evidently the essential. When, to use an example, at the end of her life, Thérèse of Lisieux entered into a new abyss of darkness where her religious consciousness seemed to collapse, who could meanwhile believe that her mystical life then disappeared? It is not then by the acuteness of the explicit thetical consciousness that one must judge the mystical life of an individual, and it is to be feared that some judge the mystical by the category of consciousness, as if this category was the supreme category of human existence.» (*Le Sens de l'existence selon saint Jean de la Croix*, t. I, Aubier, 1960, p. 43, n. 78.)

CHAPTER II

The Manifesto

(September 1896)

We now come to the major document of the «way of spiritual childhood»: Manuscript B, in which Thérèse explains herself *ex professo*! But, from our point of view, what a disconcerting disproportion there is between the attention that this writing deserves and that which it has actually received! Assuredly it contains both the attraction and the resistance of a mystery. In fact, these pages which have often been ranked among the most sublime of Christian spirituality do not easily lend themselves to exegesis; their logic is hidden under a torrent of feeling, and the language of the heart is difficult to express in ideas. This is why people usually confine themselves to admiring them and quoting them[1]; they fear they won't reach their depths in an adequate way. The difficulty of the task, however, cannot excuse us from an attempt at penetrating them, while we remain humble and aware of our limitations.

The extraordinary nature of the desires that Thérèse expressed does not at all prevent Manuscript B from being the real charter of the «way of spiritual childhood.» Quite the contrary! The phrase of Thérèse who spoke of her «little doctrine,»[2] as well as

---

[1] It is what has been shrewdly observed by A. COMBES («Sainte Thérèse de Lisieux, modèle de vie contemplative,» *Ephemerides carmeliticae*, 13 [1962], p. 111, with examples). The «uneasiness» that he notices in the interpreters of the passage where Thérèse narrates the discovery of her role in the heart of the Church extends throughout Manuscript B.

[2] For Marie of the Sacred Heart who asked for Manuscript B, «little doctrine» and «little spiritual way» are synonymous (compare PO, p. 237 and PA, p. 246).

internal criticism of what she wrote prove this. And this is what justifies the length of the explanation which we offer here.[3]

I. SITUATION

1. The night and its rays of light

Let us first of all situate Manuscript B. At what moment does it come on Thérèse's spiritual journey? Shortly after Easter 1896 (April 5) and maybe on Easter Sunday itself,[4] «the thickest darkness» invades her. She enters into a «dark tunnel»; fog surrounds her, envelops her, penetrates her soul, and hides the comforting image of the land of light, Heaven. The thought of Heaven, up until then so sweet, becomes «a cause of struggle and torment.» It seems to her that the darkness is borrowing a voice to speak to her of «the night of nothingness» which will follow death. This is Thérèse's impressive description, although it is only a weak «sketch» of the terrible reality, of this «wall which reaches right up to the Heavens»[5] and which will collapse only with death.

---

[3] If A. COMBES could say (*ibid.*, n. 72) that a whole dissertation would be necessary to thoroughly examine the Thérésian page indicated by him, how much more a commentary on the whole of Manuscript B has need of a lengthy development! This one seems much more necessary since an analysis of the whole has rarely been done. FRANÇOIS DE L'IMMACULÉE («La Charte de la spiritualité thérésienne» VT, 1961, April, pp. 3-12) is more or less limited to making a beautiful summary, while the preoccupation of ROBERTO DI S. TERESA DEL B.G. («Il martirio d'amore,» *Vita e dottrina...*, pp. 181-220) deals mainly with love.

[4] C 5 v, 241 speaks of «Paschal time.» B 2 v, 222 said: «Since... the radiant feast of Easter.»

[5] See C 5 v-7 v, 241-244. «Thérèse of Lisieux experienced terrible doubts against the faith, before dying.... Nothing remained of her faith but the highest degree of abandonment: her desire to believe sustained her little faith. Thus this girl became a saint, worthy of occupying a great place among the heroes mentioned by Hebrews 11. In the midst of the great crisis of faith that her contemporaries, the intelligentsia and workers of Europe had to go through, she endured eighteen months of this suffering with them in extreme abandonment of love. How much life found its birth therein.» That is how the *New Dutch Catechism for Adults* puts it (*De nieuwe katechismus. Gelooofsverkondiging voor volwassenen*, Brand-Malmberg-Romen, 1966, p. 346). «Thérèse of Lisieux thinks and lives in the plural: she understands that the history of the individual is not only her own history but the history of the world. The night of the individual is her own night and that of the world.» G. MOREL, *Le Sens de l'existence selon saint Jean de la Croix*, t. II, Aubier, 1960, p. 345.

Sometimes, the storm gives way to a ray of light, as in the mysterious dream that the Carmelite is going to narrate. It comforted her so much that, after four months, her memory had lost none of its freshness and its charm (B 2 v, 223) — unlike the other 'very small rays of the sun' that vanish after an instant, making her darkness even more dense (C 7 v, 244).

Against this dark background, one measures more accurately the heroic character of her love. And also the mercy of the Lord. Thérèse dared to write this unprecedented sentence: «Never have I felt before this how sweet and merciful the Lord really is, for He did not send me this trial until the moment I was capable of bearing it; a little earlier I truly believe it would have plunged me into a state of discouragement» (*ibid.*). Henceforth, she became very little and very convinced of God's love: in the trial, she will not be shaken and her progress will not slacken. How we admire the way which prepared her for this new and incessant suffering![6]

A reflection is in order here. Manuscript B radiates joy and spiritual enthusiasm and yet, Thérèse's heart is habitually assailed by a distressing storm. It appears likely, then, that Manuscript B borrows its vivacity and heartiness in part from the intensity of the moment of the actual writing[7]; Thérèse *re-lives* the most beautiful times of the preceding months.

2. *Dates*

Can we date the insights concerning her place «in the heart of the Church» which Manuscript B describes? We must certainly situate them after May 10, the day of the mysterious dream which was their «prelude» (B 2 v, 224). Would they be the fruit of her annual retreat of September, as has been suggested?[8] There is no way to be sure.

---

[6] This is not her only trial. Her health declines. Daily life brings other sufferings, for example when it is a question of a departure to the missions of Mother Agnès, and later of Sister Geneviève and Sister Marie of the Trinity (C 9 v-10 v, 246 f.).

[7] Her poems present an analogous case: «I sing simply what I WANT TO BELIEVE» (C 7 v, 244).

[8] For example, A. COMBES, *Introduction…*, p. 101 and Mss II, 62.

As for the dates of the writing of Manuscript B, we must keep the following facts in mind. On September 13, in a letter to Thérèse, Marie expresses her desire to hear «again» 'the secrets that the Lord confides in her': she thus alludes to one or several previous conversations.[9] In her response, Thérèse clearly mentions this letter (B 1 r, 219); however, in the second part of the Manuscript, which was written *before* the first (as we shall see) and dated *September 8*, Thérèse explained 'her dream and her little doctrine as Marie had asked her for it' (B 1 v, 220 f.). She therefore wrote this second part, not following her sister's letter of September 13, but following a previous conversation. In our judgment, Thérèse did *not* back-date this second part,[10] but things happened as follows: conversations between the sisters (no one knows when); Marie's request to write her dream and little doctrine; Thérèse did this on «September 8» (B 2 r, 222), «today, the sixth anniversary» of her profession (B 2 v, 224); perhaps this letter remains incomplete; whatever the case may be, Thérèse delays in handing it over; on the 13th Marie renews her plea; then Thérèse writes the *first* part of the letter: we are going to explain how.

In any event, the absence of other writings of Thérèse during these days allows us not to attach too much importance to the chronological problem of Manuscript B.

3. *Structuring*

While reading this small masterpiece, we see the enthusiasm with which Thérèse composed it. Her heart overflows into it. Sometimes her account seems to be whirling around, and two or three thoughts fight with one another to assert themselves.[11] Even for one

---

[9] For Marie's letter, see LC 169, CG II, 991. As for the conversations, one keeps at the Carmel of Lisieux a note of Mother Agnès according to which «many times» Marie had asked Thérèse «by word of mouth to write out her little doctrine» (see LC 169, note a).

[10] This is what A. COMBES suggested, *Introduction...*, p. 102 and Mss I, 46. By this literary stratagem, the Saint would have liked to evoke the atmosphere of the anniversary of her profession.

[11] More than elsewhere the discriminating demand of P. PLOUMEN is present here: «What is the association of thoughts during Thérèse's narration? It seems to me that this could be a very useful examination for the knowledge of her psychology and

who is unaware of the subtleties of the art of graphology, Thérèse's handwriting gives evidence of her interior emotion.[12] Many times she retouches what she has written. Often she questions, exclaims, multiplies exclamation points, underlines, showers suspension points, addresses herself directly to Christ. She re-lives her graces in an undeniable interiority. This is why Manuscript B will remain as much a document of human sensitivity as a testimony of the mystical life. And Thérèse roundly confesses her powerlessness to express what she feels.[13]

However, she has the explicit intention of communicating a «little doctrine,» of teaching, and of writing something that resembles a synthesis, however little there is of the theoretical and systematic in her teaching. It is this synthesis that we would like to search out in these sometimes chaotic pages.

Here, the little account of the composition of Manuscript B can help us. We are able to distinguish in it two parts: let us call them for practical reasons B1 and B2. However — and this is extremely important: B1 (page 1 r and v), which is like an introduction to B2 (page 2 r-5 v), was written *after* B2. Thérèse declares this openly at the end of B1: «You asked me.... I did this in these following pages,» of which she already knows that they are «very poorly expressed» and seemingly 'exaggerated.'[14] The first lines of B2 have in fact all the characteristics of a beginning: initials, date, and dedication.

Here is how the composition was actually put together. Thérèse takes two sheets of stationery ruled in small squares, folds them in two, and begins to write B2: in this way she fills two sheets, folded four times, making eight pages. After this — and after hav-

---

her supernatural life.» See «De manuscripten van de kleine Theresia en haar spiritualiteit,» *Bijdragen*, 18 (1957), p. 166.

[12] Typical example: big, expanded, expressive writing, when she narrates in a «delirious joy» the discovery of her vocation in the Church. Normal and more sedate writing when she speaks of her «calm and serene peace» that followed. See 3 v.

[13] B 1 r, 219. She doesn't do anything but «try to stammer some words» (*ibid.*). «After having written pages upon pages, I would find that I had not yet begun.... There are so many different horizons, so many nuances of infinite variety» (B 1 v, 221). In what she says, «there is no exaggeration,» on the contrary, her reflections are «very poorly expressed!» (*ibid.*).

[14] B 1 v, 221. Mss I, 46, n. 3, affirm the same thing.

ing received Marie's letter of September 13 — she takes a third sheet, folds it on top of B2 to create a cover, and writes B1 to the point where it meets B2. This explains why the writing is condensed at the end of B1 and why the last half-sheet, that is page 6, remains entirely blank.

From the methodological point of view, one thing is clear: in order to follow the progress of Thérèse's thought faithfully, one must read B2 first. As for B1, it is not exclusively an introduction, but perhaps also a clarification and a synthesis.

The history of Manuscript B is not yet finished. When Thérèse delivers it to Marie, the latter understands it poorly and asks for further elucidation. This is why, in her letter of September 17, Thérèse will make a new effort at synthesis and clarification.

Here therefore is the order in which we shall examine the documents: B2, B1, and the letter of September 17, which contains the «little doctrine» of the «way of childhood» and which we shall try to set in order and interpret. The ideal for the reader would be to have the text of Manuscript B before him.

II. THE DREAM OF MAY 10, 1896

Just as Thérèse announced it, B2 deals with two topics; the first is the dream of May 10, 1896, in which she sees Venerable Anne of Jesus, a companion of Teresa of Avila.[15] What message did Thérèse gather from this dream? It is fourfold: 1. The promise of an approaching death; 2. Encouragement in her night of the faith: «*I believed*, I *felt* that there is *a Heaven*»; 3. An assurance, through the words and especially the deeds of the Venerable Anne, of the love that the Blessed in Heaven have for her: «[I felt] that this *Heaven* is peopled with souls who cherish me, who consider me their child,» and this impression remained with her all the more because she was, up until then, 'absolutely indifferent' towards (Venerable Mother) Anne of Jesus. Indirectly this experience strengthens her conviction of God's merciful love in her regard: «Who could ex-

[15] See the description of this dream, B 2 v, 222. How we beg to be spared having to indicate each and every reference of our numerous quotations.

press,» she tells Jesus when she comes to the narration of the dream, «the tenderness and sweetness with which You are guiding my *little soul*!»; 4. An assurance concerning the path that she is following. In fact, Thérèse asks Anne: «Tell me further if God is not asking something more of me than my poor little actions and desires. Is He content with me?» Anne answers: «God asks no other thing from you. He is content, very content!»

Let us notice in this question, which psychologists will remember was asked in a *dream*, the old objective («to please» the Lord, that is to say, to go along with His plan completely), as well as the sober design of Thérésian littleness: poor, little actions — and, for the rest, desires. What joy to hear this conduct approved!

Thus, the transition from the dream to the «little doctrine» is well prepared! Did Thérèse make this close connection deliberately? In any case, her account is an excellent preface. And chronologically, the dream was «the prelude to even greater graces» (B 2 v, 223) which Thérèse is preparing to narrate.

But before going on, let us stop for a moment at an expression already quoted and underlined by Thérèse: *little soul*. Before, when these words were presented in the Thérésian corpus,[16] they were never accompanied by this mysterious language which is Thérèse's underlining. And this is not a case of an exception, because the seven times that the formula reappears in Manuscript B, it is always underlined. The reason for it is that, in the mind of this simple nun, these words took on a value, they became a concept. This can be deduced more clearly from the end of B2 where «*little souls*» form a special category. As anyone can see, the process of formulation of the «way of childhood» is in full swing.

The theme of her own littleness is a constant in Manuscript B, not only in the doctrine, but also in the formulation. Here is how Thérèse designates herself: *little soul, child, little child* (several times), *powerless and weak child, little bird, little creature, littlest of creatures, littlest of hearts, littlest of all souls, a poor little being, an imperfect soul like no other, the most weak and little soul that one can find*. The epithets *little, weak, imperfect* keep returning. Thérèse will sign herself

[16] For example A 46v, 144; 67v, 182; 83v, 211. Soon after Manuscript B, sometimes Thérèse will underline, sometimes she won't.

as «the *very little,*» thus evoking a memory already old and always fresh. All this terminology has an obvious significance: littleness is the heart of Thérèse's life.

III. «THE LITTLE DOCTRINE»

It is not without apprehension that we come to the analysis of the second theme of B2, the «little doctrine,» 'the secrets that Jesus alone taught' (B 5 v, 232). Nearly every sentence opens a rich perspective. However, a large part of this wealth will remain hidden from us.

It seems impossible to uncover an entirely logical order from this impetuous outpouring of the heart. The «little bird» to which Thérèse compares herself, pecking seeds on the left and right, jumping forward and returning back, escapes easily through the mesh of the net of logical structure! But since it is certain that she intended to communicate a «little doctrine,» her account must contain a development of progressive thought. As for the main sections, the following outline, to be used with flexibility, is suggested:

1. The torment of incompatible desires.
2. Pacification in love.
3. The «little way» toward love:
    a. indication and justification,
    b. love and its works,
    c. more detailed description of the «way of childhood,»
    d. Thérésian synthesis.

Sometimes we will be obliged to introduce a thought which goes beyond this general plan, but so long as the context permits it, that is perfectly fitting.

1. The torment of incompatible desires

The impetuosity of the desires which Thérèse describes (B 2v - 3v, 223-224) is not a surprising phenomenon. Had she not undergone the invasion of Merciful Love, penetrating her and renewing her at every moment? Had she not 'redoubled' her fervor (C 32 r, 278) once she was given a future missionary as a brother? Her trial against the faith takes away from her «everything that could have been a natural satisfaction in [her] desire for Heaven» (C 7 v, 244); but, for all that, it does not break the fundamental tendency of this love which she does not stop singing about in her Poems, from the month of March to August of 1896.

Should we perhaps relate her ardent apostolic desires to the date of May 30, 1896, when a second «spiritual brother» was assigned to her? Whatever the case may be, at the time when she will make a great discovery concerning her vocation in the Church, her desires torment her. In her opinion, it would be 'unreasonable for her to wish to express her desires and longings which reach even unto infinity' (B 2 v, 224). Here is how the Carmelite describes them during the course of Manuscript B: the desire for all the most heroic works, follies, desires greater than the universe, immense desires which equal the immense longings of great souls and eagles. More concretely, in addition to her Carmelite titles (spouse of Jesus and mother of souls), she lists the following desires: to be a warrior (crusader, soldier, to give her life for the Church), priest, missionary, martyr, prophet, doctor, and apostle.

The last three vocations that Thérèse mentions in one stroke (and underlines!) are probably inspired by 1 Cor 12:28, a verse which she read at the time of finding an answer to her problem. This inclines us to believe that we are looking at a subsequent explanation of her desires. Several desires detailed here probably belong to the editing work, however spontaneous it was, indeed thanks to this spontaneity. Moreover, Thérèse declares expressly that she is recalling her desires «today» (*ibid.*), while projecting them backwards.

She could not suppress these desires because they spring from an interior «need» which she must seek to «relieve,» and which makes her desire a «cure» in the way a sick person needs and desires one. Their deepest source, however, is the love of Jesus: «for You» resounds throughout this narration like a refrain.

Why are these desires, more so than violence would be, «a real martyrdom,» without Thérèse being able to abandon herself to this kind of torment? It is because of the strong tension existing between her love and the experience of her own limitations. There is within her the life of a love for God which, according to the description of several mystics, bursts into ardent desires, those which are also apostolic.[17] Thérèse experiences this clearly and, besides, on the plane of principles, she knows that «*Love* is proved by works» (B 4 v, 228). On the other hand, there are limits: not only those imposed by her cloistered life itself and for which she has not yet found a definitive solution,[18] but also those that are intrinsic to her interior possibilities (she is «weak,» «little,» «powerless») and to her desires. Indeed, they are so strong that they would like to escape human laws of time and space, which circumscribe our ability to be present. The moving description of all these very disparate vocations, which open one by one before her in a range of irreconcilable ambitions, gives evidence that this universality of her desires exceeds the possibilities of a single human being.

It is clear that this experience does not conflict with her old persuasion about the non-necessity of «striking works,» so lively for example in 1893, nor with the already inaugurated movement of the «little way.» Rather, we must remember that in the spiritual life there are no positions that, once conquered, remain firm forever. They must constantly be re-conquered, reinstated always

---

[17] This makes us think, for example, about Teresa of Avila. Living in her first reformed monastery of San José, her desires to do good for souls are so great that even in spite of her ardent prayers, she has the impression of having «bound hands.» (See *Le Livre des Fondations*, first chapter; see also for example, *Pensées sur l'amour de Dieu*, chap. VII). Before her, Saint Bernard of Clairvaux had written: «It is proper to true and pure contemplation that sometimes it fills the soul, which it has inflamed with divine fire, with so much zeal and desire to win for God other souls that love Him similarly, that it very gladly interrupts contemplation for preaching [*ut otium contemplationis pro studio praedicationis libentissime intermittat*]. Her desires granted, she returns with much more fervor to contemplation, which she is conscious of having interrupted with profit. When she has again tasted contemplation, she returns valiantly to the conquest with her usual alacrity» (*In Cant. Canticorum*, 57, 9. PL 183, 1054).

[18] It would be a little disconcerting, however, to speak of a «crisis of vocation.» Thérèse greatly loved her contemplative life which had led her to such high summits. But it is true that she greatly appreciated apostolic works inspired by charity (she had, for example, a real and holy desire for priesthood) and she experiences pain at not being able to become an apostle, 'to do the works, to preach the Gospel' (*ibid.*). After the discovery of the role of love in the Church and consequently her own role, she can say with all her heart: «it doesn't matter» (*ibid.*). On a deeper level, contemplation and action then interlace.

from a more elevated point of view.[19] In 1896, Thérèse's love increased a great deal, and so did her own rules with a new vigor. She is then called to answer to herself about the non-necessity of «striking works,» either by the old incentives or by new realizations if the first are no longer sufficient. (Let us note that this work is done much more by intuition and conviction than by clear and learned reasoning.) Confidence in her «little way» and in her additional role in matters of perfect love is not thereby decreased. But it is not a question, to use Thérèse's language, of getting settled in the elevator once and for all! We must return to it continually, to renew — «an infinite number of times» (Act) — this interior movement. For the fervent Carmelite, as the ideal of holiness became more sublime and more infinite, she had to penetrate further into her «little way,» a penetration which love itself, and its constant practice, had made natural. It is not astonishing that Thérèse will now resort once more to her «little way» in order to attain the ideal of rediscovered love, which we must describe.

There is the embarrassment, then, of this twenty-three year old woman, who is powerless to accomplish, as she would like, the 'actions of all the saints, reported in the book of life.' Twice, she clearly posed this question to herself: «How can I join these contrasts? How can I realize the desires of my poor *little soul*?» (B 3 r, 224). «What is Your answer [Jesus] to all my follies?... Is there a soul more *little*, more powerless than mine!» (*ibid.*). To whoever does not love as Thérèse loves, an easy solution presents itself: curb these foolish desires, for they are illusory. But the flames of her love already rise too high for her to be able to extinguish them. There is only one true answer: to change the impossible into reality.

[19] F. ROUSTANG has observed that spiritual progress must not be conceived as the spatial course of a journey. It is necessary to always keep in mind, as far as one can, the *totality* of the spiritual life. Spiritual growth, he continues, is comparable rather to an ascension, discovering horizons ever more vast, making the harmony of things appear with ever greater evidence (See *Une initiation à la vie spirituelle*, Paris, 1963, pp. 189-190.)

2. Pacification in love

One day (the date is undetermined), the martyrdom of desires reached its paroxysm. With the explicit intention of «looking for some kind of answer,» Thérèse opens the New Testament to 1 Cor 12 and 13 during her meditation.[20] 1 Cor 12 explains how there is, in the (mystical) body of Christ, a plurality of ministries and charisms; every member has his own task and «the eye cannot be the hand *at one and the same time,*» says Thérèse. This is a «clear» answer, but one which, at bottom, does not meet the needs of this Carmelite, who is anxious to be all things at the same time, to be each member. It «did not fulfill my desires and it gave me no peace.» However, the last verse of Chapter 12 invites her to push her research further: «*Strive after the* MOST PERFECT GIFTS, *and I am going to show you a yet more excellent way.*» What could this way be — this way which is capable of surpassing everything that Thérèse desires?

«And the apostle explains how all *the most* PERFECT *gifts* are nothing without LOVE.... That *Charity is the* EXCELLENT WAY that leads most surely to God.» Finally, Thérèse finds «rest»! She had to engage in a long search and an original exegesis — well guided, it should be noted, by her supernatural instinct — which surpassed to some degree the *immediate* conclusions of Saint Paul's text. Developing the biblical image, Thérèse places in the Mystical Body, which is the Church, a heart 'burning with love.' However, exactly as the physical heart is essential for human life, so Thérèse sees in love[21] the supernatural principle of life in the Church. A first conclusion follows: «I understood that *Love alone* made the Church's members act, that if *Love* ever became extinct, Apostles would no longer preach the Gospel and Martyrs would refuse to shed their blood....» There is only a single step to clear in order to arrive at the second deduction: «I understood that LOVE COMPRISED ALL VOCATIONS, THAT LOVE WAS EVERYTHING, THAT IT EMBRACED ALL TIMES AND PLACES.... IN A WORD, THAT IT WAS ETERNAL!....» And she who wanted to be at the same time

---

[20] See B 3 v, 225. These chapters «fell under (her) eyes.» Perhaps she opened her New Testament at random?

[21] This passage from the physical heart to the love that it symbolizes is characteristic!

each member both always and everywhere, draws the practical and definitive conclusion: «My *vocation*, at last I have found it.... MY VOCATION IS LOVE!.... In the Heart of the Church, my Mother, I shall be *Love*... thus I shall be everything.» At that very moment, a great peace comes over her.[22]

The love which Thérèse aspires to here, and which is the theological virtue of charity,[23] is love as an ideal. It is not simply the continuation of her present way of loving, but it is the quest for an even greater love — a love that is always more fruitful and that ever more fully realizes her dream of being «everything.» The love which she seeks is infinite, for it is communion with divine life itself, and it is limited only by our receptive capacities. But to the degree that God will enable her to possess it Thérèse wants to pursue it. The love to which she aspires is love as full as possible, «perfect love» (Act), love of the highest sanctity.

Further on, she will return to the apostolic fruitfulness of love. From now on, her inability to work no longer matters to her, because she «*loves* in the place of her brothers while they do the fighting» (B 4 r, 228). Her little acts of fervent love will acquire, through the merits of Christ, «an infinite value» for the struggling and suffering Church.[24]

---

[22] Thérèse first writes that her conclusion sprang «in the excess of [her] delirious joy,» but soon she corrects herself: «Why speak of a delirious joy? No, this expression is not exact, for it is rather calm and serene peace....» The difference is obvious. Again we see a sign that shows that Thérèse re-lives her experiences psychologically at the time of writing.

[23] To say that this love «is the Holy Spirit in person» (A. COMBES, *Thérèse de Lisieux modèle de vie contemplative...*, pp. 114-115; see also *Contemplation et apostolat*, p. 215) or that it is «the Holy Spirit Himself» (S. PIAT, *À la découverte...*, p. 237), is at the least equivocal. It is indeed charity, the theological virtue (in the sense of 1 Cor 13) that Thérèse deals with here. This theological love, it is true, «has been poured into our hearts *by* the Holy Spirit Who was given to us» (Rm 5:5). See also Ch. JOURNET, «L'Eglise telle que la pense et la vit sainte Thérèse de Lisieux,» *Carmel* (France), 1957, pp. 17-20 and especially P. DESCOUVEMENT, «Sainte Thérèse de Lisieux dans le coeur de l'Église,» *Spiritus*, 21, (1964), pp. 393-394.

[24] B 4 v, 228. She expresses some analogous reflections in *Strewing Flowers* of June 28, 1896 (PN 34) and more also in a note to Marie of Saint Joseph (LT 194, 989).

3. The «Little Way» toward Love

a) *Indication and Justification*. The «little doctrine,» if perhaps it contained in Thérèse's mind the ideal and the way at one and the same time, starts out as *a way* at this precise moment of Manuscript B. After the description of her vocation to a love which has no limits, Manuscript B immediately passes on to an explanation of the way which leads to it by this extremely important sentence: «O luminous Beacon of love [finally perceived], I know how to reach You, I have found the secret of possessing Your flame» (B 3 v, 226). «To reach»: it is indeed a question of the idea of the way. Thérèse will walk by her «little way,» which is itself already old, toward the old ideal of love, rediscovered at a higher and more apostolic level. Manuscript B first *indicates* it, then further *justifies* it (B 4 r, 227).

What is this «secret» which permits her to possess the flames of love? Here it is: «I am only a child, powerless and weak, and yet it is my very weakness that gives me the boldness of offering myself as *Victim of Your Love, O Jesus*!» An offering, then, or better, an offer, a hope, a demand, a sacrifice of oneself as a victim to Jesus, Who is Merciful Love (as Thérèse will immediately explain), motivated by her own weakness (seen in the light of divine mercy). All this is indeed a «boldness,» a very great confidence founded on God alone. How could we not recognize, in different vesture, the fundamental identity of thought in the account of the discovery of the «way of childhood» with the Act of Offering in June of 1895?

Several times again during the course of B2 that same fundamental thought returns. We do well to cite some of these allusions here. «Even because of my weakness..., You desire, today, to grant [my] *desires* that are *greater* than the universe» (B 3 v, 226). «My own *folly* is to trust that Your Love will accept me as a victim [... it is to beg] to obtain the favor of flying towards the Sun of Love with *the Divine Eagle's own wings*!» (B 5v, 231). There is the same underlying principle, when Thérèse declares herself 'happy to be weak and little' (B 5 r, 230). B1 and the letter of September 17 will formulate an identical way, while further specifying it.

If Sister Thérèse knows that this old and new ambition — to

rise by the way that she described — contains, as do all her other desires, something «audacious,» «daring,» 'foolish,' she truly does not believe that it is a matter of an irrational leap into the unknown. She knows the One Who guarantees her bold project.

By a recourse to the new economy of salvation which Christ has established, Thérèse has justified her conduct very strongly. Let us listen to her explanation of it: «In times past [in the Old Testament, whose introduction is a little one-sided here] victims, pure and spotless, were the only ones accepted by the Strong and Powerful God. To satisfy Divine *Justice*, perfect victims were necessary, but the *law of Love* has succeeded to the law of fear, and *Love* has chosen me as a holocaust, me, a weak and imperfect creature.... Is not this choice worthy of *Love*?... Yes, in order that Love be fully satisfied, it is necessary that It lower Itself, and that It lower Itself to nothingness and transform this nothingness into *fire*.»

The law of love, therefore, replaces the law of fear[25]; the God of condescending love instead of the God of justice; riches from one's own nothingness, if one entrusts oneself and lets oneself «be chosen as a holocaust» by divine mercy. This reminds us of the prologue of Manuscript A and the morning of June 9, 1895. In two ways Thérèse will return to this same fundamental reasoning. First she addresses herself in 'a bold prayer' to the angels and saints, recalling 'her misery and feebleness,' but appealing to their 'noble, generous, and understanding hearts.' She begs the Blessed 'to adopt her as their child and to obtain for her their twofold love.'[26] She reasons then in an inverse manner, passing from her title of a child to the kindness of parents who 'in order to please their children, do foolish things, even going to the extent of becoming weak for them.' Thérèse's desire of love, 'child of the Church, rich Spouse

[25] In her letter of July 12, 1896 to Léonie, a letter totally filled with the spirit of «spiritual childhood,» Thérèse had laid the same foundation. We shall have the opportunity to quote this beautiful passage again (LT 191, 965).

[26] See some exegeses of this expression «twofold love,» in Mss II, 64-65. See also G. LEFEBVRE, «Le Double Amour» in his book *La Foi dans les oeuvres*, Desclée De Brouwer, 1962, pp. 146-167, and especially p. 154 (for the author, it means the love of God and Neighbor). Whatever the case may be, Thérèse considers here a very great love, greater than that which she currently possesses.

of Christ'[27] is therefore legitimate. Her way of confidence, while bold in appearance, is actually justified.

b) *Love and its works*. But let us not think that the young Carmelite spends her days dreaming of an ideal love. As far as she is able, she is already achieving it. She constantly adds stories to the building by means of confidence, and she immediately arranges the already constructed floors. She transforms into works all that her «little way» continually obtains for her in the way of love. For Thérèse understood very well the dialectic of love and its deeds: «*Love* is proved by works» (B 4 r, 228) and «love is repaid by love alone» (*ibid.*).

Manuscript B therefore contains this program of generosity which one must fully translate into action: «This is how my life will be consumed.... I have no other means of proving my love for You other than that of strewing flowers; that is, not allowing one little sacrifice to escape, not one look, one word, profiting by all the smallest things and doing them through love.... I desire to suffer for love and even to rejoice through love; and in this way I shall strew flowers before Your throne. I shall not come upon one of them without *unpetalling* it for You.... While I am strewing my flowers, I shall sing, (for could one cry while doing such a joyous action?); I shall sing even when I must gather my flowers in the midst of thorns, and the longer and sharper the thorns, the sweeter will be my song» (B 4 v, 228). There we have the charter of these «little things,» to use this ambiguous term, of these 'nothings without any value.' The characteristics are as follows: all is done for and «through love» and Thérésian activity does not exceed the strengths of a weak creature; there is nothing outwardly striking in it; but there is great continuity in faithfulness; one makes the most of everything («none... all»); this activity is not interrupted by suffering, but very much the opposite is true; it is a happy heart that

[27] In 1895, Thérèse wrote: «Really, I was far too brazen!... I was acting toward [God] like a *child* who believes everything is permitted and looks upon the treasures of its Father as its own» (A 66 v, 181). Now, she says: «My bold desires... My excuse is that I am *a child*... of parents [who]... possess immense treasures...» (B 4 r, 227). In 1897, she will write: «For a long time You [God] permitted me to be bold with You. Like the father of the prodigal son speaking to his older son, You have said to me: "EVERYTHING *that is mine is yours*"» (C 34 v, 282). Beautiful is the line that continues, as is the way that she presents it!

Thérèse offers. Such is her work of love: she has no other means, «astounding works are forbidden to her,» and «she is too little to do great things.» But what a burst of heroism animates this program, even if Thérèse is the last to claim the title of heroine![28] She will still confess her little infidelities, but the whole of her day proves how scrupulously she executed the project which she set for herself.

Remembering a word from her master, John of the Cross, the disciple now wonders if «pure love» truly resides in her heart. This question has the great merit of pointing out that, even if her present love is great and fervent, it extends itself even more in a large area of expectation, confidence, and a desire for a greater love. It is true, this child's confidence, inspired by love and founded on Merciful Love, is already all loving. And this is why 'her immense audacious desires, her dreams, her follies, and her aspirations toward the most elevated regions of Love,' are full of 'sweetness, joy, delights, and bitter-sweetness.' But, finally, this confidence remains confidence, and desire. This is what Thérèse summarizes so well in these meaningful sentences: «Jesus, if the *desire of loving You* is so delightful, what will it be to possess and enjoy this Love?… How can a soul as imperfect as mine aspire to the possession of the plenitude of *Love*?» (B 4 v, 229). «The plenitude of love,» «pure love,»

---

[28] One can apply here what M. VAN DER MEERSCH said, in his romanticized biography on Thérèse (*La Petite Sainte Thérèse*, Paris, 1947, pp. 128-129), concerning her acts of charity: «All of this seems as nothing. The writer, while noting these details, feels her total powerlessness to make others imagine the greatness of these little things. Let's really consider it, however. Let's try to understand. Let's see how far this simple decision to be Christian in everything can lead, this decision to accomplish every gesture as a Christian, unto the humblest, unto the most trivial, of our daily life. If we don't understand it, let's try to live it for one day, a single day.… Let's try to live it for twenty-four hours, and we will be shocked to see that there is within our reach a new world to explore, an astonishing descent to lower regions, to the depth of the hells of selfishness and pride that we carry within ourselves, all teeming with monsters. It is something of a gigantic upset to bring about in everything that we thought we knew about humanity and our own heart. An immense battle to engage, in the unknown, in the wonderful sphere of holiness.… And we will so clearly feel the necessity, in such an undertaking, to go until the end, and we will clearly understand what "until the end" means, that we will probably remain forevermore at the awful doorstep of God's Kingdom, *without daring to go farther*, desperate at having glimpsed it, and at not having the courage to venture further. However, this is the epic of Thérèse. She was truly daring.»

«perfect love» (Act): this is the goal which requires the mediation of the «little way» of confidence toward love.

c) *A more detailed description of the «way of childhood.»* In the following pages,[29] Thérèse resumes the description of her «little way» in a more concrete manner. She proceeds to describe her attitude amid powerlessness and infidelity. The parable of the «little bird» which she uses, beautiful and expressive in its initial opposition to «the eagle,» seems to somewhat burden the further development of thought. This metaphor is not capable of expressing fully the personal and well-thought-out attitude that it should symbolize, and one notes that Thérèse goes beyond it continually by attributing to the «little bird» a very human behavior! But the literary form is the last of her preoccupations; it is enough «to please»!

Thérèse has this in common with eagles, the «great souls»: she shares their «immense aspirations,» possessing their clear-sightedness and their fearlessness ('the eyes and heart' of an eagle). But she is much more powerless. To climb like them « towards the Divine Furnace of the Holy Trinity» (an allusion to the mystics?[30]), unto the «Sun of Love,» «is not within her *little* power.» She is «extreme littleness.» Her reaction? Neither sorrow, nor fright, nor desertion, even if a storm rages and it «seems she should believe in the existence of no other thing except the clouds surrounding her» (an allusion to her own dark night of faith). On the contrary, the deeper the darkness, the more «perfect» her joy becomes. «What joy for [her] to *remain* there just the same, gazing at the Invisible Light which remains hidden from her faith.» One can summarize her entire conduct in her own words: «bold surrender.» Surrender, which is at the same time gift and waiting, sacrifice and expectation. Boldness, by reason of the obstacles and in virtue of her un-

[29] See B 4 v-5 v, 228-231. Symbols of the «*weak little bird* with only a light down as covering» and of the eagle (B, *ibid.*, 229-231) could have been inspired by Saint Teresa of Avila. (See ALBERT DU SACRÉ-COEUR, *Approches...*, pp. 244-246, which cites *Vie*, chap. 13, 19 and 20.)

[30] (*Note of 1994.*) Three times, the «Eagles» are called by Thérèse her «brothers,» twice they are the image of the «Saints.» Among these «Saints,» these «Eagles her brothers whom she [the little bird] sees climb towards the Divine Furnace of the Holy Trinity,» represent undoubtedly for Thérèse, in the first place, her spiritual parents, Teresa of Avila and John of the Cross. See also the [French] critical edition of the *Autobiographical Manuscripts*, pp. 308-309, 314.

shakable faith: she «knows that beyond the clouds her bright Sun still shines on and that its brightness is not eclipsed for a single instant.»

A new presentation has Thérèse always «remaining in her place [but allowing herself to be] somewhat distracted from her sole occupation»; she is a little too taken up with «the trifles of earth»; this is what she calls her «misdeeds,» her «misery,» her «infidelities.» She mentions her particular «weakness» of falling asleep during prayer. Her reaction is the same as above! Is she going «to hide away in a corner»? «To weep over her misery,» «to die of sorrow,» or to «feel desolate»? Not at all! Again she «turns toward her Beloved Sun» and «presents herself to its beneficent rays.» And if she must, «she accepts her numbness from the cold and rejoices in her suffering which she knows she deserves.» She «remains at peace,» she «begins once again her work of *love*,»[31] and she implores the help of the «eagles» who climb toward this same Sun which, for her, remains for now «the object of her desire.»

Everything is also summarized in these words of Thérèse: «daring surrender.» The boldness, the holy temerity of her abandonment, is always founded on God's mercy. Thus she explains that, instead of being distressed and hiding herself following her mistakes, she «trusts» (notice the choice of words) and «recounts in detail all her infidelities, thinking in the boldness of her full trust that she will acquire in even greater fullness the love of *Him* Who came to call not the just, but sinners» (Mt 9:13). It is precisely in the perspective of this mercy that she calls herself 'happy to be weak and little.' Otherwise, 'she would never have the audacity to appear in the presence of God.' Now, she is sure to be destined 'to become the prey of the Divine Eagle who attracts her.'

Thérésian Synthesis. Thérèse lets a hymn of thankful praise rise from her heart towards the God of mercy, Who became man and remained with us in the Eucharist (B 5 v, 231). And now as she arrives at the end of B2, her prayer becomes, in a few forceful lines, an extremely successful synthesis of the «little way.» There, to her

[31] «Work of love,» allusion to a passage of CS of Saint John of the Cross, str. 28. (See *Oeuvres*, IV, pp. 394-395.) Thérèse quoted this text more at length in the month of March 1894 (LT 157, 841).

astonishment, she stands before the «mystery» of a soul as imperfect as hers, still feeling these «immense longings» (B 4 v, 229).

All of the central ideas of the «little way» are represented here: the folly of mercy and confidence without limits; the distance from the «eagles» who do «great things,» and the confidence of being accepted as a victim and being raised by God Himself even to the point of being united in Love; in the meantime, she practices acceptance of her powerlessness and tireless faith. The passage is too beautiful for us not to quote it in its entirety:

«O Jesus! allow me in my boundless gratitude to say to You that *Your love reaches unto folly....* In the presence of this folly, how can You not desire that my heart leap towards You? How can my confidence, then, have any limits? [This is a beautiful expression of the dynamic core of her confidence.] Ah! I know that the Saints, too, have committed their *follies* for You and they have done great things because they are *eagles....*

«Jesus, I am too little to perform great actions... and my own *folly* is this: to trust that Your Love will accept me as a victim... My *folly* consists in begging the Eagles, my brothers, to obtain for me the favor of flying towards the Sun of Love with *the Divine Eagle's own wings....*[32]

«As long as You desire it, O my Beloved, Your little bird will remain without strength and without wings, still it will always stay with its gaze fixed upon You. It wants to be *fascinated* by Your divine glance. It wants to become the *prey* of Your Love.... One day I hope that You, the Adorable Eagle, will come to fetch Your little bird, and ascending with it to the Furnace of Love, You will plunge it for all eternity into the burning Abyss of this Love to which it has offered itself as victim.... [Here Thérèse draws a long dotted line; is it a confession of her powerlessness to express the depth of her soul? And she continues:]

«O Jesus! why can't I tell all *little souls* how unspeakable Your condescension is.... I feel that if, by some impossibility, You found a soul weaker and littler than mine, which is impossible, You would be pleased to grant it still greater favors, provided it abandoned

[32] The elevator, the arms of God, the wings of the Eagle: these are fundamentally the same image.

itself with a total confidence to Your infinite mercy» [B 5 v, 231-232].

At the end of B2, a final prayer asks Christ to reveal His secrets of love to a great number of «little souls.»

IV. B1 ON THE SUBJECT OF THE «WAY OF SPIRITUAL CHILDHOOD»

After B2, Thérèse writes B1, this letter of introduction, which is at the same time something of a summary and subsequent clarification of that which precedes it.[33]

«Do not believe that I am swimming in consolations,» Thérèse explains, but Jesus «teaches me in secret.»[34] He teaches her, for example, when she reads, at the end of an arid prayer, a word of the Lord to Saint Margaret-Mary, saying that in Him she will find *«the science of* LOVE.» This, for Thérèse, is the opportunity to join to it a beautiful summary of her «little doctrine.»

First the goal that she is seeking: «The science of Love, ah yes! this word resounds sweetly in the ear of my soul, and I desire only this science. *Having given all my riches for it*, I esteem it as *having given nothing* as did the bride in the sacred Canticles [see Sg 8:7].... I understand so well that it is only love which can make us pleasing to God, that this love is the only good that I ambition.»

And here is the school where one will learn this science: «Jesus deigned to show me the only road that leads to this Divine Furnace, and this road is the *surrender* of the little child who falls asleep without fear in its Father's arms....» Thérèse found again her most characteristic symbol! And what guarantees the effectiveness of the behavior which she counsels? The arguments are characteristically hers: Thérèse quotes Proverbs 9:4 and Isaiah 66:12-13, verses which had made such an impression on her at the time of discovering her «way of spiritual childhood,» to which she adds two other scrip-

33 B 1 r - v, 219-221. See *supra*, I, 3 (*Structuring*).

34 «Jesus teaches me in secret»: as for the «little doctrine,» Thérèse affirms, while concluding B2, that 'Jesus alone taught it to her' (B 5 v, 232).

tural texts on the mercy of the Lord.[35] «Similar language» awakens so many things in her soul: «Ah! if all weak and imperfect souls felt what the least of souls feels, that is, the soul of your little Thérèse, not even one of them would despair of reaching the summit of the mountain of love, since Jesus does not demand great actions from us, but simply surrender and gratitude,» thus openness to Him. This is what she explains a little farther on: 'to surrender to Him without reservations, to understand all the tenderness of His infinite Love.'

V. THE COMPLEMENTARY LETTER OF SEPTEMBER 17

What Thérèse had perhaps sensed, was verified: the recipient, Marie, had understood her letter poorly! The reading of the beautiful manuscript had not encouraged her! But we must quote her letter (see LC 170, 997) to better understand the answer that her younger sister is going to give to her. «A certain feeling of sadness came over me in view of your extraordinary desires for martyrdom. That is indeed the proof of your love. Yes, you possess love, but I myself, no! Never will you make me believe that I can attain this desired goal, for I dread all that you love.... Ah! you say that you are doing nothing, that you are a poor weak little bird, but your desires, how do you reckon them? God Himself looks upon them as works.... I would like you to tell your little Godmother, in writing, if she can love Jesus as you do.» [Marie was Thérèse's Godmother.] Thus, Marie was stuck on the «great things»; the essence of the «little doctrine» had escaped her.

Although the young mistress of novices concentrates her response on Marie's objection and request,[36] an excellent opportunity was offered to her to further explain, specify, and summarize

[35] «Mercy is granted to the little ones» (Sg 6:6). «The Lord will lead His flock in the pastures, in His arms He will gather the *little lambs* and will carry them on His bosom» (Is 40:11). The four quotations are all in Céline's Notebook. Having reached this point, let us point out that, historically, Manuscript B has not been appreciated properly, because in the editions of HA until 1914, everything that precedes, of B1, was omitted. It is also in 1914 that Manuscript B appeared for the first time as a separate chapter and that one mentioned the expression «little doctrine.»

[36] See LT 197, 998.

Manuscript B. Although materially distinct from Manuscript B, the letter of September 17 forms a whole with it.

In the first place she corrects the one-sided valuation of her desires for martyrdom: they «*are nothing*, they are not what give me the unlimited confidence that I feel in my heart. They are, to tell the truth, the spiritual riches that *render one unjust* when one rests in them with complacence and when one believes that they are *something great*.» These desires are a «*consolation*» for «weak souls like mine,» Thérèse explains, but their absence is «a grace of *privilege*»: to advance towards martyrdom without them would make her much more meritorious.

It is clear, then, that Thérèse, if she feels her desires, does not rely upon them. As for God, «I really feel that it is not this at all that pleases God in my little soul. What pleases Him *is to see me loving my littleness and my poverty, the blind hope that I have in His mercy*.... That is my only treasure»: spiritual poverty composed of humility and hope in God.

In some sentences which have become famous, the little Carmelite seeks then to impart — in a way much stronger than Marie had understood the opposite — what one needs in order «to love Jesus, to be His *victim of love*.»[37] «The weaker one is, without desires or virtues, the more suited one is to the workings of this consuming and transforming Love. [This is the echo of Manuscript B: love is fully satisfied only in lowering itself and transforming nothingness into fire; however, the more nothingness there is, the more fuel there is.] The desire alone to be a victim suffices, but we must consent to remain always poor and without strength, [but this desire and this consent make no small demand; that is why Thérèse notes:] and therein lies the difficulty, because "the truly poor in spirit, where do we find him? We must seek him from afar," said the psalmist [actually, the *Imitation* 2:11, and 3]. He does not say that we must seek him among great souls, but "from afar," that is to say, in *lowliness*, in nothingness. Ah! Let us remain then very far from all that sparkles, let us love our littleness, let us love to feel

---

[37] To be His victim of love: this is what she has just explained in Manuscript B; this is what Marie herself had considered, when she was making the *Act of Offering to Merciful Love*.

nothing, then we shall be poor in spirit and Jesus will come to look for us, and *however far* we may be, He will transform us in flames of love....»

Now, we are prepared to understand more clearly the expression «without desires or virtues,» which is probably astonishing at first. It goes without saying that a literal interpretation is to be avoided: Thérèse supposes that one desires (for example, to be a victim) and that one practices virtues (for example, hope, humility, and abandonment). Lucien-Marie de Saint-Joseph,[38] followed by Albert du Sacré-Coeur[39] and Stéphane Piat,[40] interpreted the text in the sense of a disclaimer of any sense of ownership. Although this had indeed been Thérèse's attitude, we do not believe, however, that she thought of this at the time of writing. The solution is more of a psychological order than a theological one. In fact, if one refers to the context, one will notice that Thérèse has just explained to Marie with insistence that it is not necessary «to want to feel joy, to have an attraction for suffering,» nor to envy her burning desires. Shortly after, she will counsel her to love «to feel nothing.»

---

[38] «In fact, the Saint's daring affirmation agrees with the sternest texts of *The Ascent of Mt. Carmel* on human virtues, very beautiful in appearance, but pharisaic, of which the Saint proclaims the uselessness. In a sense, the Saint was "*without desires or virtues.*" She did not lean on those that God had placed gratuitously in her hand; she was a true poor person.» («La Pauvreté spirituelle chez saint Thérèse de l'Enfant-Jésus,» *Carmel* [France], 1955, p. 187.) This explanation, dating from as early as 1947, appears as a note in the volume of the old edition (1948) of *Letters*, p. 341. PHILIPPE DE LA TRINITÉ (See «Actualités thérésiennes,» *Ephemerides carmeliticae*, 7 [1956], pp. 563-564) approves the interpretation of LUCIEN-MARIE DE SAINT-JOSEPH at least insofar as the point that interests us here is concerned; he prefers it to that of VICTOR DE LA VIERGE who writes: «It is here a question of desires to be a martyr or to accomplish great things.» (*Réalisme spirituel de Sainte Thérèse de Lisieux*, Paris, 1956, p. 109)

[39] *Approches...*, p. 271: «The Saint doesn't want to say here that it is necessary to refuse *to practice virtues*. She teaches something else entirely: that it is not necessary to believe oneself the author and owner of virtues that can be found in us; it is God who places the gift within us....»

[40] «One returns to the most radical "*nada*": the "nothing" of desires. The "nothing" even of the virtues, if one views them in the sense of treasures of which the soul would be an owner, and on which it would want to lean. (It is obviously in this sense, and not in a Quietist or Protestant interpretation, that one must understand the overly elliptical clause: "The weaker one is, without desires or virtues.") The instinct of possession, blemished with Phariseeism, places an obstacle to the invasion of love.» (*À la découverte...*, pp. 241-242.)

In our opinion, one must therefore understand: «without desires or virtues» which are *felt*, which are perceptible.[41]

Let us finish our reading. «How I would like to be able to make you understand what I feel!,» sighs the nun, and in a last effort she arrives at this very happy formula, a clear summary of the human activity in the «way of spiritual childhood»: «It is confidence and nothing but confidence that must lead us to Love....» This is the way; Thérèse says it literally and underlines it: «Since we see the *way*, let us run together.»

Do we still remember this sentence from 1890 to Marie Guérin: «My dear little Marie, as for myself, I know no other means of reaching perfection but love...»[42]? Two things were necessary to arrive at the present new understanding of her way: the prolonged experience of her powerlessness to realize the dream of love and a decisive light on the condescending love of the «Father of mercies» (2 Cor 1:3).

VI. SYNTHESIS

From Thérèse's communications to Marie in the month of September 1896, we can thus outline the «way of spiritual childhood.»

The «little way» seeks to lead Thérèse — and every «little soul» who follows her — to a high degree of union with God, to «the fullness of love.» Thérèse always understood it in this way and she newly discovered it with an amazing clarity, while identifying her vocation with love. [«In the heart of the Church, my Mother, I shall be *Love*.» (B 3 v).] However, perfect love remains always in the state of an ideal, being in fact infinite because it is participation in divine life. Toward this ideal — as toward «a beacon» — the «little way» is directed.

---

[41] It is also the exegesis of the publishers of (the old) HA: «Without desires or virtues *felt*» (HA 55, p. 310, note). Until the critical edition of 1948, the words in question were replaced by «[the more one is weak and] miserable.»

[42] LT 109, 640. According to S. PIAT (*Marie Guérin. Cousine et novice de Sainte Thérèse de l'Enfant-Jésus*, Lisieux, 1953, p. 51), this is a response that «prefigures the flashing elevations» of Manuscript B. It is true, insofar as the ideal is concerned, but not insofar as the way is concerned.

Certainly, Thérèse constantly proves the authenticity of the love that she already possesses by her works. What's more, her whole attitude of confidence breathes a filial love. But the «little way» is not revealed characteristically as a way of love, because it is thought, not precisely as an exercise of the present love, but according to the love it seeks to obtain, a future love, an ideal love. It is rightly introduced as a means of arriving at a goal not yet reached.

Thus the protagonists appear together under a special light. God, Who seeks to realize the union, is merciful love; He is condescension. Thérèse is the weak, the imperfect, the incomplete. Around these two poles is developed, on the part of Thérèse, specific virtues. Faced with her powerlessness, she recognizes it, accepts it, and humbles herself. In the face of Merciful Love, she believes. On these two foundations, the «little way» is built; they are like the two great pillars that support the bridge.

The very essence of the way, that is to say, what causes progress and what unites, could be defined on God's part as the merciful communication of Himself, the increase of His love in us. And on the part of man, it could be expressed in many ways: it is the offering (of oneself) as a victim to mercy, it is abandonment (which is donation and waiting), it is «blind hope,» and it is «confidence and nothing but confidence»!

Because man cannot rely on himself and possesses nothing that is proportionate to God, and because he must by faith make a leap into the merciful love of God, this way has an appearance of audacity, boldness, folly.

From Thérèse's vision of God spring peace, joy, security, and gratitude. By taking her position before her own powerlessness, Thérèse banishes fear, sadness, and infidelity.

Chapter III

The Message and Its Exterior Form

(1896-1897)

Twenty-four years is a very short time to plumb the depths of the Christian mystery! It is not surprising if Thérèse Martin's last year on earth still shows clear spiritual progress: for example, in the realm of fraternal charity. As for the «way of childhood,» the doctrine itself does not seem to evolve further. Any progress lies rather in the direction of its ever more intensive assimilation, of its application to the entire range of life, and of its more characteristic formulation where some symbols and typical expressions arise. In the realization of this, three factors have collaborated: Thérèse's educational role, her own interior life while she is slowly dying, and the consciousness she acquires of her posthumous mission. This is the object of the present chapter, which deals mainly with the genesis of the «way of childhood,» leaving aside for one moment the riches of her doctrine. Faithful to our method, we shall be careful to arrange the facts in their biographical context.

I. THE EDUCATOR

Marie de Gonzague, re-elected prioress on March 21, 1896, had, so to speak, left[1] the entire formation of the young nuns to Thérèse of the Child Jesus. It is since then, explains Sister

[1] See here, Appendix I, page 355.

Geneviève, that Thérèse gathers the novices every day after vespers to converse with them for a half-hour. The formation that is given during these gatherings is very concrete and of a practical order. Thérèse does it through private conversations in which she adapts her counsels to each one in particular (CSG, p. 3). However, owing to the inexperience and the discouragements of these beginners, the mistress of novices is constantly pushed to first 'practice what she preaches to others' (C 19 r, 260), then to have recourse to her own intuitions and Christian attitudes, to explain them, to illustrate them, and to establish them more firmly. The favorite theme of her instructions, common or private, is the explanation of her «little way,» this beautiful commentary on the Gospel. «In every meeting, [she] mentioned her *Little Way*» (CSG, p. 40). «She was inexhaustible when her conversations had to do with God's mercy and love» (CSG, p. 54). It was «the continual topic of our conversations» (PO, p. 467 f.). «She summarized all her instructions, moreover, in what she calls her little way of spiritual childhood and total abandonment» (PO, p. 287). Other sisters besides the novices also came gladly for Thérèse's teaching. With them also, the theme of «spiritual childhood» is stressed.[2]

To her disciples among the Sisters of the monastery, the novice mistress adds some people living in the world who became very dear to her: her sister Léonie and her two spiritual brothers.

Léonie is alone.[3] Her parents have died, and her four sisters are at Carmel. She suffers her third failure at religious life. However, she remains determined to dedicate herself to God. Sister Thérèse encourages her in her trials, her solitude, her desires, and her difficulties of character. She continues to insist upon fidelity to little acts of love and upon confidence.[4] Léonie is truly a «little soul» type: weak, but full of good will.

As a «little Moses» on the mountain, Thérèse sustains her two

---

[2] See LT 217 for example, 1047; 199, 1012; 200, 1013; 195, 990; 194, 989; 205-206, 1033-1034; 250, 1137, where Thérèse maintains a firm and suggestive tone, almost imperative, while adapting to the psychology of Marie of Saint Joseph, the melancholy nun.

[3] See the beautiful biographical sketch of S. PIAT, *Léonie Martin. Une Soeur de Sainte Thérèse à la Visitation*, Lisieux, 1966, 224 pp.

[4] See, for example, the letter of July 12, 1896 (LT 191, 965).

spiritual brothers who are fighting in the plain[5] with 'her invincible weapons of prayer and sacrifice' (C 31 v, 277). Ardently desiring their sanctification,[6] she reflects more than once in her correspondence about the «little way» that leads to it.

Her letters to Father Roulland are a mine of information on her own spiritual life. Besides her apostolic desires which she hopes to realize fully after her death, one reads for example about her high esteem for the divine will, her desire of the 'death of love,' and her reflections concerning purgatory. Admissions of her insufficiency to cooperate in the apostolate of her missionary brother are characteristic, but they are accompanied by a conviction concerning the completion that Jesus will bring about in her.[7] It is to Father Roulland that she explains, better than she has ever done it before, her thoughts on God's justice, followed by a beautiful description of her «way of childhood.»[8]

However, from the point of view of «spiritual childhood,» her letters to Father Bellière are more instructive, by reason of the very temperament of the correspondent and the tone of his letters. The two spiritual brothers in fact show marked differences. Roulland is already well-formed, intelligent, levelheaded, virile, and objective. His letters to Lisieux[9] testify to a lively gratitude with regard to this Carmelite sister, but are limited more or less to the narration of events: his departure from France, his first adventures in China, his first apostolate. Bellière is of another temperament. When Thérèse begins to occupy a place in his life, his ecclesiastical formation is sketchy. At twenty-one years of age, he does not yet possess the spiritual and psychological maturity of Roulland, who is five years older. During the two years of correspondence with

---

[5] LT 201, 1013. See P. DESTOMBES, «Sainte Thérèse de l'Enfant-Jésus et ses "frères spirituels,"» VT, 1963, pp. 25-43, 76-86, 103-114, 174-185 and 1964, pp. 21-44, 75-86 (*Note of 1994*:) Also M. VEYS, *Thérèse et la mission*, VT, 20 (1980), pp. 249-317.

[6] Bellière is called to be «not only a *good* missionary, but a saint» (LT 198, 1009); no, not «a saint by halves» (LT 247, 1132), but «a great saint» (LT 244, 1127). He is called «to the highest sanctity» (LT 220, 1058). Roulland must also become «a great saint» (LT 201, 1013).

[7] LT 189, 956 and 201, 1013.

[8] LT 226, 1092.

[9] They are published in VT, 1963, pp. 115-136.

Thérèse, he is faced with the difficulties of his military service, then with the approaching separation from his own.[10] However, these experiences, joined to the weakness that they occasion, as well as his very emotional character, give a special quality to his correspondence. Unlike Father Roulland, he pours out his heart and often returns to his miseries, his faults, and his past, in confessions which are probably tinted with exaggeration and subjectivity. Thérèse, touched by the spiritual distress of her brother and by the confidence in her that he shows, answers accordingly: she opens up to him more, and leaving aside Bellière's accusations, she explains to him the «little way» of loving confidence that is so dear to her. Loving the young seminarian very much,[11] she feels that their souls «are made to understand one another» (LT 220, 1058). We also have the guarantee that this correspondence contains the explanation of the «way of childhood,» because looking one day at the photograph of Bellière, Thérèse affirmed explicitly: «I am pointing out to him the way of love and confidence» (DE 12.8.2).

The ten letters that Thérèse addresses to him, in the period following October 21, 1896, often touch upon the theme of divine mercy, of daring repentance, of confidence towards the Father, and of the requisite conditions to enter into the «little way.» With the help of comparisons, she instills her ideas in him, thus building up to the definitive choice of a characteristic formulation. Her insistence becomes stronger and stronger. On July 26, 1897, she writes: «I learned, more so than in your other letters, that you are *forbidden* to go to Heaven by any way except that of your poor little Sister.... The way of simple and loving confidence is really made for

---

[10] He will embark for Africa on the eve of Thérèse's death (Mss II, 77). Bellière had never known his parents and, unaware of his true domestic situation until the age of ten or eleven years, he loved his aunt, who had adopted him, like a mother. «But a woman alone exercises with difficulty the influence and authority that the mother and father in a home usually share. Deficiencies often result from it in an education which loses in vigor what it attains in affection» (P. DESTOMBES, «Sainte Thérèse...», p. 175).

[11] «Truly, you will know only in Heaven how dear you are to me» (LT 220, 1058). See also LT 224, 1083 where she compares their apostolic union to that of Margaret-Mary Alacoque and Claude de la Colombière. Beginning with this letter, she addresses herself to a «dear little Brother» instead of a «Monsieur l'Abbé» («my heart refuses henceforth to call you» by any other title). Father Roulland, «my Reverend Father,» becomes «my Brother» (LT 193, 977).

you.» The esteem, too great in her opinion, that Bellière shows her is the opportunity for her to specify her position: that of a soul which is «*very little* and very imperfect,» not at all that of a «great soul.»[12]

II. IN THE «LITTLE WAY» WHICH LEADS TO LIFE

At this time, nothing affected the nun more in the understanding of her littleness and in her profound confidence in God's mercy than her own interior experiences. She continues her journey through the night of faith and physical suffering. Day by day, she dies. Or better yet, she assures Bellière: «I am not dying, I am entering into life» (LT 244, 1127).

Let us watch this young woman dream, live, and die in these last months: by her example, she shows us how to live in «spiritual childhood.»

1. *To love: the only thing to do*

More than ever, her only ideal is love. On June 9, 1897, she writes to Bellière: «At the moment of appearing before God, I understand more than ever that there is only one thing necessary, that is, to work *solely for Him* and to do nothing for self or for creatures.... I would like to tell you many things that I understand now that I am at the door of eternity» (LT 244, 1127). She endeavors to make her entire life «an act of love» (LT 224, 1083), and this is what she asks her brothers to beg from God on her behalf.[13]

With this love of God is connected, still more closely than before, the love of neighbor. And let us not believe that our contemplative considers the love of neighbor solely as a means of loving *God*, of «*loving Him and making Him loved*» as the perpetual refrain of the last months of her life repeats,[14] of giving to God, while saving souls, «proofs of our love» (LT 213, 1041). No, it is also *man*

---

[12] LT 224, 1083. See also LT 213, 1041.

[13] LT 189, 956; 201, 1013; 220, 1058.

[14] For example, LT 218, 1054; 220, 1058.

whom she loves, deeply conscious however that the love of God and that of neighbor rises from the one and only divine life with which we are in communion. In this regard, the year 1897 was of supreme interest: it was then that Thérèse received «the grace to understand what charity is» (C 11 v, 249). Manuscript C, begun in June 1897, expressed the depth of her evangelical insights and the refinement of her brotherly love, praised by a chorus of eye-witnesses. From 1897 we may also date, in all probability, the new light[15] on the verse of the Canticle of Canticles: «Draw me, we shall run» (1:3). Our contemplative has never better understood the hidden but real influence of every soul who loves on those whom she loves: attracted by God, she 'draws others along with her.'[16]

From now on, Thérèse will no longer be able to change her direction: «My soul is strengthened by Him whom I wanted to love uniquely» (C 22 r, 264); she only has to progress. Often, toward the end of her earthly life, she expresses this readiness to seek love alone[17]; she no longer needs a command: «only a look, a simple sign» are sufficient (C 9 r, 246). In her suffering, she is 'happy to better resemble Jesus in order to save souls.'[18] The roses with which she covers her crucifix (CSG, p. 120) symbolize the acceptance of the divine will: that is her joy, her repose, and her happiness. «What God prefers and chooses for me, that is what pleases me more!» (DE 4.9.7). To live or to die, it is all the same: *fiat voluntas Tua*.[19]

---

15 Thérèse seems to attach it to the fact of having two brothers and her novices (C 33 v, 280). This would therefore be after May 30, 1896. The fact that she doesn't allude to it in Manuscript B, which has such an apostolic thrust, and that the year 1897 is that of the great discoveries in fraternal charity, makes it very likely that the grace of «Draw me, we shall run» came to her in this same vital movement of 1897.

16 C 34 r, 281; 35 v-36 r-v, 283-285. See «What is a Carmelite existence? It is the offering of all one's personal being to the God of Jesus Christ, so that He consumes and uses this being for His redeeming work, according to the good pleasure of His love. One recognizes there the real identity of the love of neighbor with the love of God.» H.U. VON BALTHASAR, *Cordula ou L'Épreuve décisive*, Paris, 1968, p. 89.

17 For example C 3 v, 238 and 6 r, 242.

18 Marie of the Trinity, PA, p. 472.

19 For example C 8 r, 245; DE 21-26.5.5; 27.5.5; 9.6.3.

2. The night of the soul and body

Thérèse's abandonment grows in heroism when one considers the violent temptations against the faith[20] that she continues to undergo, day by day, hour after hour. She herself speaks of it very little to others, except to Mother Agnès.[21]

Sometimes interior torment pierces through to the outside for an instant, as in this response to Sister Geneviève: «If you only knew!... oh! I would not want you to suffer these temptations for even five minutes!,» or when she interrupts a conversation suddenly and, irrelevant to the conversation, asks: «Does Heaven really exist?... Speak to me about Heaven...» (CSG, p. 189). Some confessions, chosen from many, are sufficient to permit us to guess the greatness of the trial of this soul completely in love with God: «If I didn't have this spiritual trial, these temptations against the faith, which are impossible to understand...» (DE 21-26.5.10). «My soul feels truly exiled, Heaven is closed for me» (29.6.3). «[Heaven] is closed against me more and more!» (8.8.2). «If you knew what frightful thoughts obsess me!... It's the reasoning of the worst materialists which is imposed upon my mind.»[22] «No one can understand the darkness in which I live; my soul is plunged into the darkest night, but I am there in peace.»[23] The confessor of the community increases her sufferings by telling her that her spiritual state is very dangerous.[24] But the heroic Thérèse remains in peace. She does not lose her serenity.[25] Unceasingly, she renews her profession of faith. In June 1897, she writes: «I believe I have made more acts of faith in this past year than all through my whole life. At each new occasion of combat... I run towards my Jesus» (C 7v, 243). Jesus «has greatly increased the *spirit of faith* in my heart» (C 11 r,

[20] (*Note of 1994*). I had the opportunity to develop this point in the new edition of *Les Mains vides*, Cerf, 1988, pp. 131-143.

[21] PO, p. 152. Her own sister Marie will only know of them after her death (PA, p. 238).

[22] Mother Agnès, PA, p. 151.

[23] *Ibid.*

[24] Sister Geneviève, PO, p. 276. It is a question of Father Youf (DCL).

[25] Sister Thérèse of Saint Augustine, PO, p. 402; P. Godefroid Madelaine, PO, pp. 518 and 521. Better than all other testimony, Thérèse's correspondence and poetry attest to the poise that she maintains during her trial.

249). It is the martyrdom of the heart, of love, which had been so long desired.[26] «Everything has disappeared for me, only love remains,» she said during these trials (PO, p. 402).

If Thérèse's soul 'is in a black hole where we can no longer see anything, her body also entered in there' (DE 28.8.3). To the little dry cough that beset her since the summer of 1896 are added, before Easter 1897, very strong attacks of fever and, in July, frequent hemorrhages, accompanied by frightening suffocation. Her two lungs are attacked by tuberculosis (PA, p. 204). The treatment is quite inadequate at the time. «It is horrible what she is suffering, said the physician; you shouldn't wish to preserve her in this state» (PO, p. 178). Among the testimonies concerning her physical suffering, let us choose this excerpt from a letter of Marie of the Eucharist to her parents (August 27, 1897): «[The news on Thérèse] is always the same: she is weaker and weaker, no longer able to bear the least noise around her, not even the crumpling of paper, or a few words spoken in a whisper.»[27] But what the numerous confessions of her suffering[28] make very apparent is the influence of bodily exhaustion on her mind: physical suffering brings psychological suffering. It seems to her besides that the devil himself is involved (DE 25.8.6); sometimes she is even sure of it: «He is holding me with an iron hand to prevent me from getting the slightest relief, in order to lead me to despair: I'm suffering for you, and the devil doesn't want it!....»[29] She marvels that so few atheists take their own lives[30]... and she warns Mother Agnès not to leave any poisonous medicines close to patients who are prey to such violent pains.[31]

There is no doubt that so many sufferings make her practice to the fullest what she had understood in matters of confidence. Marie of the Angels, the former mistress of novices, had even af-

[26] See *Note of profession* of September 8, 1890 (Pri 2).

[27] See DE, p. 290. And to think that Thérèse had «extremely sensitive hearing»! (C 30 v, 276).

[28] See for example 10.8.5; 19.8.1; 23.8.1; 25.8.6; 28.8.3; 29.8.2; 31.8.3; 11.9.4; 15.9.2; 25.9.2; 29.9.11; 30.9.

[29] Sister Geneviève, PO, p. 310.

[30] Marie of the Trinity, PO, p. 472.

[31] Mother Agnès, PA, p. 204.

firmed — but it is historically incorrect — that these trials were like the streams of light that were at the origin of her «little way» (PA, p. 349). However, the exerted influence of these sufferings is incontestable: one's life experiences teach the way. When someone asked the Saint how she managed to be never discouraged, she answered: «This saying of Job: "Even if God should kill me, I will trust in Him" [Jb 13:15] has fascinated me since my childhood. But it took me a long time before I was established in this degree of abandonment. Now I am there; God has placed me there. He took me into His arms and has placed me there.»[32] The experience that she has of divine mercy is her guarantee: «God has helped me and led me by the hand from my most tender childhood; I count on Him. I am sure that He will continue to help me until the end.»[33] «Suffering can reach its extreme limits, but I'm sure that God will never abandon me» (DE 4.7.3). She reads in these trials God's desire to see how far she will push her confidence and her abandonment.[34] In a moment of great anguish, she will resort to Psalm 22:4: «I fear no evil because You are with me, Lord!» (LT 262, 1170.)

This confidence and the desire to please inspire her nearly constant cheerfulness, even if it verges on the heroic. «She must always be saying something funny. Ever since she has become convinced she is dying, she has been as merry as a lark,» writes Sister Marie of the Eucharist (Guérin) on July 9, and on the 31st: «I believe she'll die laughing because she is so happy.»[35] And the day of her death: she always has the same «smiling and angelic appearance that never leaves her» (PO, p. 416).

And yet, Thérèse feels that of herself she is not ready to die! Even though 'she has never refused anything to God since the age of three years,'[36] even though 'she has never given Him anything else besides love,'[37] even though 'she would do, in a new life, exactly as she has done,'[38] she often still confesses that she is imper-

---

[32] DE 7.7.3.

[33] Mother Agnès, PA, p. 159.

[34] DE 10.7.14 and 22.9.3.

[35] DE, p. 274 and 284. See S. PIAT, *Marie Guérin...*, pp. 82 and 89.

[36] Sister Geneviève, PO, p. 268.

[37] DE 22.7.1.

[38] NV 12.7.3.

fect.[39] This is why the total transformation of her soul is the last grace for which she hopes: «I dare to hope that "my exile will be short,"» she writes on April 25, 1897, «but this is not because I am *prepared*. I feel that I shall never be prepared if the Lord doesn't see fit to transform me Himself. He can do so in one instant; after all the graces He has granted me, I still await this one from His infinite mercy.»[40] More than all the others, perhaps, this passage shows how much Thérèse, at the end of her life, is penetrated with humility, with faith in divine mercy, and with the confidence of her «way of spiritual childhood»!

3. *The death of love*

The Lord will have to transform her, she said. When death approaches, an old desire will become very alive: to die of love.[41] Here, too, the lasting influence of Saint John of the Cross is visible. Since the beginning of her religious life, she had repeated these words of the mystical Doctor: «Tear through the veil of this sweet encounter,»[42] and «It is, then, of the greatest importance that the soul exercise herself much in Love in order that, consuming herself rapidly, she hardly stops here below and arrives promptly in seeing her God face to face.»[43] «And I have been answered,» she said on August 30 (DE 31.8.9). Often she repeated these words,[44] begging God to bring about in her this consummation of love (*ibid.*). Having the intimate persuasion that her life would be short (3.7.13), she profited from every instant to put her love into living action (PA, p. 172).

---

[39] See the following chapter.

[40] LT 224, 1083, of April 25, 1897, to Maurice Bellière.

[41] See also GABRIEL DE SAINTE-MARIE-MADELEINE, «Vita e morte d'amore,» *Rivista di Vita Spirituale*, 1 (1947), pp. 256-291.

[42] «I've always applied these words to the death of love that I desire. Love will not wear out the veil of my life; it will tear it suddenly» (DE 27.7.5).

[43] DE 27.7.5. This passage is borrowed from VF, str. 1 (*Oeuvres* V, p. 158).

[44] Marie of the Trinity, PA, p. 474. Thérèse also quotes them on a *farewell souvenir* to her sisters (LT 245, 1128) and in Pri 12.

From 1895,[45] the intensity of this desire seems to increase. Now Thérèse makes it clear that, after an intense life of love, *love itself* will make her die. This is what she expresses again in the Act of Offering, which she often repeats. The theme returns readily in her poetry.[46] On June 9, 1897, she says: «I no longer have any great desires except that of loving to the point of dying of love» (C 7 v, 244). During her last illness, she rereads the passages of Saint John of the Cross on the death of love.[47] But if she first believed that the death of love would happen, as Saint John of the Cross describes it, «in wonderful transports and delightful assaults,»[48] the bitter sufferings of her body and soul make her ideas about the death of love evolve[49]: «Our Lord died on the Cross in agony, and yet this was the most beautiful death of love that was ever seen! To die of love is not to die in transports.... I tell you honestly, it seems to me that this is what I am experiencing» (DE 4.7.2). And on August 15: «I shall have to say that joy and transports are *at the bottom of my soul only*.... It wouldn't be so encouraging to souls if they didn't believe I suffered very much» (DE 15.8.1). But it is always love which must cause her death, the illness being too slow an agent (LT 242, 1120), and the fear of death too insufficient a purifier (PA, p. 331). But there is nothing in this death of love that can't be imitated by the «little souls.» There is no exterior sign of happiness or of transport; there is nothing which appears extraordinary.[50] On the last day, she will say: «My littlest desires have been fulfilled... then, the greatest one, to die of love, should be...» (DE 30.9, French criti-

[45] For example in *Living on Love*, of February 25, 1895, composed spontaneously, she writes: «To die of love is a truly sweet martyrdom and that is the one I wish to suffer. / O Cherubim! Tune your lyre, / For I sense my exile is about to end... / Flame of Love, consume me unceasingly, / Life of an instant, your burden is so heavy to me! / *Divine Jesus, make my dream come true*: / *To die of love*!» (PN 17) One will refer usefully to what we said on the literary style of Thérèse in the Introduction.

[46] For example, PN 18, str. 52; 24, str. 26; 31, str. 6.

[47] See Mss II, 57-58. Thérèse marked certain passages of the first stanza of the VF with small crosses (pp. 152, 157, 158).

[48] This is what Sister Geneviève also assures (CSG, 2nd ed., 1954, p. 224).

[49] Sister Geneviève suggests the same thing in a written note (that of CSG, 2nd ed., pp. 219-225, but more extensive): see GABRIEL DE SAINTE-MARIE-MADELEINE, «L'atto di offerta... ,» pp. 289-290.

[50] DE 4.6.1; 15.8.1; 14.6.1; 14.7.4.

cal edition). But, she had said, «the death of love that I wish is that of Jesus on the Cross.»[51] And she will have it![52] But first she will experience Gethsemane and Calvary. Until September 30, 1897… until 7:20 in the evening…. The heroic courage of this young woman of twenty-four years, her body devoured by tuberculosis, her mind overwhelmed by her most holy desires, is explained only by the last words that she sighs to the Crucified: «I love You» (DE 30.9). Her «little way» has truly led to its destination!

III. THE MISSION

Toward the end of her life, Thérèse clearly realizes that she has a special mission to accomplish in the Church. In the history of the «way of spiritual childhood,» this realization remains a landmark — not in the actual *discovery* of the «little way,» but in its formulation and presentation. In 1897, she clearly manifests her desire to do good on earth after her death.[53] In the face of her oncoming death, she expresses herself in formal promises, which are sometimes very strong.[54]

It is very important to understand that, at the center of this mission, at the very core of this message, is the revelation of the «little way»: «I feel that my mission is about to begin: my mission of making God loved as I love Him, of giving my little way to

---

[51] HA 98, chap. XII, p. 250.

[52] And if one must believe the witnesses, her death had something of the death «in transports» described by Saint John of the Cross. However, the first description of HA (that of 1898, which remained thereafter the same) is more sober than that of NV. It is not a question of head movements as if someone wounded her internally, nor is the word «ecstasy» to be found.

[53] «This sentence which became famous "I want to spend my Heaven doing good on earth," I remember that she addressed it to me, literally, repeatedly, while she was still in the world» (P. Pichon, PO, p. 384). However, it seems that with regard to this testimony, we are dealing with a phenomenon of attribution. From the historical and psychological points of view, this dating of Father Pichon (1887 or previous years) appears insupportable. See DCL, «Le Père Pichon et la Famille Martin jusqu'à la mort de Sainte Thérèse,» VT, 7 (1967), p. 65, n. 28.

[54] See LT 244, 1127; 253, 1139; 254, 1141; 255, 1145; 258, 1151; 259, 1159; 261, 1163; DE 9.6.1; 25.6.1; 6.7.1; 8.7.14; 13.7.2; 13.7.17; 17.7; 2.8.5; DE II, 345; CSG, p. 149, 225, 231, 237.

souls.»[55] According to the *Novissima Verba*, Thérèse returned to this theme: «We told her that she was very fortunate to be the one to show souls a way of love and confidence. She answered: "What does it matter whether it is I or someone else who reveals this way to souls, as long as the way is pointed out; the instrument is unimportant.» Even if it seems as though the authenticity of this text cannot stand the test of textual criticism,[56] it nevertheless fits in well with the line of thought already expressed by the preceding text which is certainly authentic. Moreover, according to the testimony of Sister Geneviève, the Saint returned to this topic «many times.»[57]

Did Thérèse know that her «little way» had led her to great holiness, a canonizable holiness?

Sometimes she denies being a saint, but at those times she is considering the great actions of the saints.[58] Elsewhere, while confessing that she was imperfect to the end of her life, she calls herself a «very little saint,» distinct, it is true, from the «great saints.»[59] Another time she tells her sisters, some days before her death: «You know well that you are taking care of a little saint.»[60] She allows them to gather her tears — as she herself had gathered the last tear of Mother Geneviève, the «Saint» (A 78 v, 202 f.) — 'knowing well that she was to preserve the linen like a venerated souvenir.' She herself collects the clippings of her nails and invites Mother Agnès

---

[55] DE 17.7 to July 17. Thus literally already in HA 98, p. 241. PO, p. 195 repeats it.

[56] DE 21.7.5. In Mother Agnès' *question*, it's always a matter, in the later versions, of the same reality, even if the formula is different («a way of love and confidence»: *ibid.*; «path of love and confidence»: CV and PO, p. 196; «way of confidence»: DE 21.7.5; «way of childhood»: HA 23, p. 269 f.). It is more important to note that, in the previous versions, it is not a question, at least explicitly, of revealing a way, but «procuring God's glory» (HA 99, p. 274; HA 07, p. 265). The oldest edition (HA 98, p. 220) doesn't even mention this contribution to God's glory. The same obscurity is found in Thérèse's *response*. DE and PO agree. But HA, since 1899, only speaks of «to serve» instead of «to show a way» and «to establish the reign of God» instead of «so long as it is shown.» In HA 98, she answers only: «God has need of no one.» Is this a new, not entirely illegitimate, infiltration of the idea of the «little way»?

[57] PO, p. 287.

[58] «They told her: You are a saint! — No, I'm not a saint; I've never performed the actions of a saint. I'm a very little soul upon whom God has bestowed graces,» DE 9.8.4 (also in PO, p. 206 and HA 98, p. 228).

[59] Thus at least PO, p. 201. DE 4.8.2 has: «I don't believe I'm a great saint,» but omits (?): «I believe I'm a very little saint.»

[60] Mother Agnès, PO, p. 176.

to keep them.[61] She also asks them to preserve the rose-petals which had touched her crucifix: «They will help you to perform favors later on; don't lose one of them.»[62] Do all these, along with her other presentiments, indicate that she glimpsed her future canonization? We do not know. Nothing proves it in an absolute way.

Concerning her mission, however, no doubt is possible: «I think God has been pleased to place things in me which will do good to me and to others.»[63] And showing a beautiful ear of corn: «This ear of corn is the image of my soul; God has entrusted me with graces for myself and for many others.»[64]

This conviction inspires an attitude that is a consequence of it. Henceforth, in the hope of reaching others, Thérèse expressly seeks to communicate herself, to complete herself, to better express herself, to define her thought more clearly. This work is done in two ways: by explaining her doctrine and by presenting herself — very humbly — as its prototype. This aim, combined with a certain natural inclination, the circumstances of her illness, and the fact that she is obliged to answer to very personal questions, explains why Thérèse quite often speaks of herself. Henceforth, she considers herself as a work of God and as His instrument. She possesses the holy freedom (the audacity, she would say) of God's children. In herself she discovers only an immense mercy. The ear of corn which displays its riches brings to mind Him «who made it grow» (1 Cor 3:6).

The clarification of her «little doctrine» comes to an end. When she writes Manuscript C, containing among other things the narration of the discovery of her «way of childhood,» Mother Agnès makes her «glimpse that this manuscript could be of service to the edification of many, and that its publication would be a means which God would use to realize her desire to do good long after her death, and she accepts this thought very simply.» She gives to her 'little mother who alone knows all the secret places of her soul'

---

[61] Mother Agnès, PA, p. 199. See also Sister Geneviève, PA, p. 313; Marie of the Trinity, PA, p. 494.

[62] Thus DE 14.9.1 and PO, p. 215.

[63] DE 4.8.2 and PO, p. 201.

[64] DE 4.8.3 and HA since 1898 (p. 242).

the permission 'to either add or delete,' as it will seem appropriate to her. She knows that these pages constitute «a very important work,» that they «will do much good to souls. They will understand God's gentleness much better.» She suggests certain additions and points out the places where her thought is expressed better. In what spirit are all these preparations made? «Any glory that I shall have from this will be a gratuitous gift from God and will not belong to me.» «It is God alone whom we must credit, because there is nothing to credit in my little nothingness.» Thus she directs and issues her message to the world.[65]

Always in the light of her prophetic vocation, and almost completely unable any longer to write, Thérèse lavishes her spiritual counsels, especially upon Mother Agnès, who records several of them. She is the object of the sincere admiration of her entourage, although the sisters do not grasp in depth the extent of her sanctity nor her role in the Church. «When one has known such a beautiful soul,» wrote Marie of the Eucharist on July 10, «one would be held very accountable not to walk in her footsteps» (PO, p. 690). They want therefore to know her better, they ask questions about her life, her person, and her doctrine: «They plague me with questions,» notes the Saint; «it reminds me of Joan of Arc before her judges. It seems to me that I am answering with the same sincerity» (DE 20.7.6). While urging a great deal of care lest the publication of her autobiography be hindered (DE 1.8.2), she is sure that her message comes from God and will be spread: «[even if they threw my notebooks into the fire], I would not feel the least pain from it, nor the least doubt about my mission. I would simply think that God will grant my desires by another means.»[66]

---

[65] See for all these facts FRANÇOIS DE SAINTE-MARIE, «La Pensée de Thérèse sur la publication,» Mss I, 64-70 and J. LONCHAMPT in the general Introduction of the [French] *Autobiographical Manuscripts*, pp. 18-24.

[66] Mother Agnès, PA, p. 203. Also PO, p. 248 and 176, where the meaning is identical.

IV. THE DEFINITIVE PRESENTATION

Under the influence of the factors we have pointed out, the fundamental ideas of the «way of spiritual childhood» take a definitive and characteristic external form during the years 1896-1897. It is this that we now want to analyze briefly. As for conversations with the young nuns, one does not always know how to date them, but one is right in supposing that their most characteristic formulas belong, much like in Thérèse's *Letters*, to the last period of her life. Besides, this problem is of secondary importance.

1. The Symbols

The Father. One day during her last illness, Thérèse accidentally uses the word "Papa" when she had meant to say «God.» Everybody laughs, but she seems rather touched and says, «Oh! yes, He is indeed my "Papa" and it is a sweet consolation for my heart to call Him by this name» (CSG, p. 110). Happy with her discovery, she repeats more than once «with perfect candor» the formula: «Papa the Good God.»[67] This demonstrates how much she liked to represent God as a father. In the month of September 1896, she characterizes her «little way» as the surrender of a little child in its father's arms (B 1 r, 220). The comparison of God to a father returns again.[68] And several times she uses this term in scriptural recollections.[69] «Heaven for me,» she sang, «is... calling Him [God] my Father and being His child.»[70] However, the image of the father is much less frequent than is sometimes thought. The explanation for this is that, for Thérèse, it is her spouse Jesus Who often occupies this place, possessing all the qualities of a father. We will come back to this later.

Since 1895, it is true, Thérèse already considers God's love for mankind as mercy by definition; it is interesting to note however that the word «mercy-merciful» knows a new success in 1897. In the letters alone, it is used about twenty times.

---

[67] Marie of the Sacred Heart, PA, p. 231. See 5.6.4, for example.

[68] For example, LT 258, 1151; CSG, p. 59, 109; PN 36.

[69] A dozen times in C. Also LT 226, 1092; 258, 1151; 261, 1163, in her poetry.

The child. One would never finish counting all the occasions where Thérèse compares herself to a child. Let us listen instead to the meaningful words of Marie of the Trinity: «She never wearied of speaking about the confidence, the abandonment, the simplicity, the integrity, and the humility of the little child and always proposed it to me as a model» (PO, p. 467). These are the qualities Thérèse draws attention to in the child. On the other hand, she especially removes from her concept of the child fear, maliciousness, the desire to shine. On July 12, 1896, she points out in what direction her concrete search is going: «I am putting forth all my efforts to be a very little child» (LT 191, 965). Several of her definitions of holiness or of her spiritual way concentrate on the same symbol, reminiscent of the great truths of the Gospel. The frequent use of the word «little,» with or without a substantive, as well as the posthumous formula «spiritual childhood,» owe their origins in large part to the same inspiration. The regular use of this symbol, and especially the title «very little» that Thérèse appropriated to herself are most often a distant echo of the scriptural texts encountered just as she discovered her «little way.» In the month of June 1897, she tells of this great event.

The symbol «child» does not necessarily evoke that of «father» or of «mother.» Sometimes Thérèse compares herself to a child without identifying herself with Him. This is often the case when she stands before Jesus: Jesus is *like* a father, but at bottom He is her Spouse; Thérèse is *like* a child, but at bottom she considers herself the humble and very confident spouse of Jesus. It is important to keep this dimension of her spirituality in mind: it can avoid partial misunderstandings.

At other times, too, the word «child» is explicitly used in the biblical sense of belonging to God's family: we are the children, the sons of God, without reference to age.[71]

The arms, to carry, the staircase, the elevator. The help and love of God for us are expressed well by this other symbol that Thérèse came across just as her «little way» was about to be born: God 'carries her [in His arms]' (C 3 r, 238). The words that she associates

[70] *Heaven for me* of June 7, 1896 (PN 32).

[71] For example, C 25 r, 268.

with the expressions «the arms of God» or «to be carried» eloquently suggest Thérèse's faith in God's merciful help: to surrender herself, abandonment, to believe, to sleep, to place herself, to throw herself, child, filial confidence; and on God's part: heart, embracing, tenderness, father or mother.[72]

The symbol of *arms which carry* evokes, by contrast, that of the staircase where one is left to one's own strength,[73] and which she sometimes contrasts with the symbol of the elevator,[74] as in her account of the discovery of the «little way.»

2. A Way

When Thérèse received the decisive illumination on divine mercy, she probably understood intuitively that she had found her way toward holiness, a way that was distinct on several points from that of the saints (C 2 v, 237). Later, she will call it her «little way.» She herself considered it as «the only path» toward love (B 1 r, 220); it is *her* «way» (LT 197, 998). More and more, her spirituality appears to her as something very precise: «My way is...» (LT 226, 1092). This is not the way of all: there are, indeed, 'many mansions in the house of our Heavenly Father' (and therefore several ways which lead there[75]). As for her, she follows «the way that [Jesus] is tracing out for me» (LT 247, 1132), «*my way*» (*ibid.*), which is a «delightful way» (LT 258, 1151). And she does not doubt the goodness of the way that she teaches. She said to Marie of the Trinity: «If upon arriving in Heaven I learn that I misled you in error, I will obtain from God the permission to immediately come to warn you of it. In the meantime, believe that my way is sure» (PO, p. 454). She even dares 'to forbid Father Bellière to follow any other way than hers' (LT 261, 1163).

The teaching of a personal way supposes a group of disciples,

[72] See LT 190, 958; 191, 965; 206, 1034; 226, 1092; 258, 1151; 261, 1163; 263, 1173; PN 31; 32; 52. In order to indicate the *celestial* intimacy, Thérèse also uses these symbols often: C 34 v, 282; LT 211, 1038; 212, 1039; PN 33; 54; 18; DE 15.9.2; A 41 v, 135.

[73] PA, p. 159.

[74] C 3 r, 237 and LT 258, 1151.

[75] LT 226, 1092; 247, 1132; DE 1.8.6.

whatever their number. The «little souls,» as she will call them, the «children,» the «little ones.» They are distinguished from the «saints,» the «great saints,» the «great souls» and the «great spirits.» They have their negative criteria: for example, they do not perform «miracles,» do not have «ecstasies,» and do not practice «astonishing mortifications.» They avoid what is «great,» [outwardly] «extraordinary,» «dazzling.» They have their own patrons. But we will speak of all this again.

3. *Attempts at definition*

As she expressed herself, Thérèse sketched out a series of definitions of her way toward holiness. Or better yet, *descriptions*, for in fact, these are approaches, broad insinuations which do not pretend to be complete. A true definition will come only from her teaching taken in its totality.

Let us review some of these indications: «As for me, I find perfection very easy to practice because I have understood that it is a matter of *taking hold of Jesus by His Heart*» (LT 191, 965). «My way is all confidence and love... perfection seems simple to me; I see that it is sufficient to recognize one's nothingness and to abandon oneself as a child in God's arms» (LT 226, 1092). «Yes it suffices to humble oneself, to bear with one's imperfections with gentleness: this is true sanctity» (LT 243, 1121). She walks in «the way of simple and loving confidence» (LT 261, 1163).

Conversations during her final months offer three other examples. «It's the way of confidence and total abandonment. I want to teach [souls] the little means which have so perfectly succeeded with me, to tell them there is only one thing to do here on earth: to cast at Jesus the flowers of little sacrifices, to take Him by caresses! This is the way I've taken Him....»[76]

In the *Novissima Verba* (DE II 3.8.5a), one finds the beautiful and famous definition again: «Holiness is not in such or such a practice; it consists in a disposition of the heart that makes us humble and little in the arms of God, conscious of our weakness,

[76] HA 98, chap. XII (6.8.7), DE II, 259. Later one added to the beginning: «It is the way of spiritual childhood» (for example, DE II 17.7.2). See here part I, first chapter.

and confident even unto audacity in the goodness of the Father.» But this beautiful text, certainly Thérésian in its inspiration, is missing in all other versions before the *Novissima Verba* was printed (in 1926) and it is therefore not bold to doubt its textual authenticity.

On another occasion, they asked her what «remaining a child» meant (or having «the spirit of childhood» as HA 98 expresses it). We know of two sets of answers. We will follow here the first set (that of the first editions of HA), citing in parenthesis the important additions from the second set.[77] «To remain little is to recognize our nothingness, to expect everything from God (as a little child expects everything from its father; it is to be not too distressed by its faults).[78] *Finally, it is to be worried about nothing, and not to be set on earning our living*. Even among the poor, as long as the child is very little, they give him what is necessary; but as soon as he grows up, his father no longer wants to feed him and says: "Work now! You can take care of yourself." Very well, it was so as not to hear this that I never wanted to grow up, feeling that I was incapable of earning *my living, the eternal life of Heaven*! (I have always remained little, therefore, having no other occupation but that of gathering flowers, the flowers of love and sacrifice, and of offering them to God in order to please Him. To be little is also to not attribute to oneself the virtues that one practices, believing oneself capable of anything, but to recognize that God places this treasure of virtue in the hands of His little child, to be used when necessary; but it remains always God's treasure. Finally, it is not to become discouraged over one's faults, for little children fall often, but they are too little to hurt themselves very much.).»

---

[77] For the first set, see HA 98, chap. XII (6.8.7), DE II, 259. For the second, PO, p. 204 or DE 6.8.8.

[78] This last clause was omitted but recovered in PO.

Fourth Part

THE STRUCTURE

We have patiently followed the history of an idea, in its preparation in the midst of life, in its birth, in its growth, to the point where it brought forth the most mature fruits. It was impossible, however, to limit ourselves exclusively to its genesis: often the description of its genesis involved explanations concerning the very nature of the «little way.» Let us recall, for example, the Act of Offering to Merciful Love *and* Manuscript B.

In the following pages, partially based on facts already recorded, we shall endeavor to reconstitute the Thérésian way «of spiritual childhood» in all its fullness, to establish the hierarchy of its components, and to arrive at a complete picture of it; but first we need to probe into that which, in the end, constitutes its central core.

Regarding this last point, however, let us point out that the Norman Saint herself illustrated her rich «little way» in several ways. Sometimes she placed the emphasis on humility or littleness, sometimes on love and «little things.» Occasionally, she reduced everything to poverty of spirit; often, she summed it up in the example of the child. Weakness, nothingness, simplicity, abandonment, hope, confidence, and faith in God's merciful love: all these terms echo in the course of her teaching. But it is sufficient to observe this vocabulary for only a moment to realize that it implies rather diverse realities. It suffices, for example, to juxtapose «love» and «hope» in order to sense the delicate nuances that a good exegesis of her thought should evoke. In Thérèse of Lisieux's thought, where do we find the center of her «little doctrine»? For our part, we don't hesitate to answer: in confidence. Obviously, this does not imply that the other elements are eliminated from the «little way.» On the contrary: it is these which, revolving around this core, make a single whole with it. At the proper time, we shall describe where they fit in.

As we have said, Thérèse herself and many of her disciples have presented the «little way» and its essence differently. Rightfully so. In real life, virtues interlace. In practicing one, we are led to practice others. The dynamism of life is hardly interested in the distinctions made on the static, theoretical plane. However, we must now pause here to establish them in this vital complex of the doctrine of «spiritual childhood,» because, in a sense, they govern life.

In the following chapters, we shall show, in a way that is especially psychological, why confidence constitutes the propelling force of the «little way.» Let us first analyze Thérèse's perception of herself and her perception of God. The theme of confidence will then lead us to an examination of her works, and then to the work of confidence itself. Finally, we shall stop at the conclusions which the Carmelite draws as for the lifestyle that will characterize her search for holiness. Thus, we shall come at length to a final picture.

Chapter I

The Incomplete One

It would be superfluous, to say the least, to demonstrate the will to love in Thérèse Martin. For her, perfection is the total accomplishment of the divine will (A 2 v, 72), love in its perfection (the *Act*), love in its purity, love in its fullness (B 4 v, 229). To the degree that she possesses this love, she shares in the holiness of God. To the degree that this love escapes her still, holiness remains an ideal, a possibility. However, it is in search of this ideal that she conceives her way. In order to understand it, we must therefore examine how Thérèse sees herself relative to perfection. This perception of herself results in a deep feeling of incompleteness in the Carmelite of Lisieux.

I. The Meaning of a Confession

To read the depositions at the time of the process of beatification, the term «incomplete» seems hardly defensible. The most authoritative witnesses in the process assure us that, to their knowledge, Thérèse never committed the least fault or voluntary sin.[1]

[1] See Mother Agnès: «Never any voluntary fault» (PA, p. 163), not «one venial fault deliberately» (PA, p. 149), no *observable* progress in her religious life (PO, p. 150); Marie of the Sacred Heart: never saw «the slightest fault» (PA, p. 231); Marie of the Angels, her mistress of novices: «Never committed the smallest voluntary oversight» (PA, p. 348); Marie of the Trinity: never found an imperfection in her (PO, p. 452), never «the smallest imperfection» (PO, p. 464); Sister Geneviève: never «the smallest voluntary mistake» (PA, p. 261; see also PO, p. 280 and 293). However, her confessors are more reserved: Father Domin, her confessor before she entered the convent: «No fully deliberate fault» (PA, p. 395); Father Godefroid Madelaine: «I believe I can say… never a deliberate venial sin» (PA, p. 560).

What she says about herself is not less surprising: «Since the age of three years, I have never refused God anything.»[2] On the other hand, she did not stop confessing her weakness and her imperfection. How do we resolve this paradox?

1. Judgment from the outside and judgment from the inside

Thérèse's extraordinary fidelity to grace is beyond question, but there is room nevertheless to offer some reflections on the assertions that we have quoted.

On the one hand, the witnesses speak from their own knowledge: what they had either *seen* or *heard*. However it is clear that in large part an entire area escapes their observation and it is the sole decisive one: namely, the motives, the feelings, the interior docility. Moreover, there is a large gap between what is involuntary and what is fully deliberate. During her whole life, Thérèse was able to avoid refusing grace *deliberately* — and it is in this sense that we interpret her own words that we have quoted[3] — but it is not at all certain that she had the privilege of which the Council of Trent speaks: that of not having committed any faults that were semi-deliberate or slightly culpable.[4] Even at the end of her life, Thérèse confesses faults, as we shall see; she says that she has been preserved by God from *mortal* sin, but does not extend this grace to cover *all* sin.[5] As for «positive imperfection,» in the technical sense of an omission of a greater good, which ordinarily one would not at the time classify as sinful, Thérèse would have been, in our opin-

[2] Sister Geneviève, PO, p. 306.

[3] «Since the age of three years, I have never refused God anything» (Sister Geneviève, PO, p. 306). We are unaware of the precise context in which Thérèse pronounced these words. With D.M. DE PETTER («Theresiana,» *Tijdschrifr voor Geestelijk Leven*, 14 [1958], pp. 60- 63), we interpret them «as having dealt with an entirely conscious and voluntary refusal.»

[4] In the Decree on Justification, the Council of Trent declares that one is not able, «through the whole of a lifetime, to avoid all sin, even venial sin, except by God's special privilege, as the Church affirms of the Blessed Virgin» (D 833). «Time and again we commit mistakes, all of us without exception» (Jm 3:2). And Thérèse: «No human life is exempt from faults, only the Immaculate Virgin presents herself absolutely pure before the Divine Majesty» (LT 226, 1092 of May 9, 1897). This text is strong.

[5] See C 36 v, 285; A 70 r, 187; DE 20.7.1.

ion, a decided defender of the theological view which sees in it a guilty refusal; in her view, every voluntary omission of total adherence to the invitation of the Beloved offends Him a little, and is an indelicacy.[6]

Essentially what we mean to say is that Thérèse judged herself differently than she was judged by others. 'God alone knows the depth of human hearts,' she once remarked (C 19 v, 261), and we can apply this to the feeling that she had of her weakness. Sometimes, she notices the disproportion between the praises of others and her own feeling: «I've been told so much that I have courage, and this is so far from the truth, that I have said to myself: well, then, you mustn't make a liar out of *everybody*!»[7] There is a striking example of the powerlessness of a judgment based on observable facts alone: outward behavior reveals and hides, all at the same time, interior dispositions. To say it with Thérèse's own words: one can «be mistaken in taking for virtue what is nothing but imperfection» (C 13 r - v, 251).

2. *Dimensions of conscience*

Let us set aside the judgment of others and let us consider Thérèse's own conscience. It was extremely sensitive. The least fault had in her a great and even emotional moral resonance. As a child — and one will remember how much one's conduct as a child is revealing of the temperament of that same individual later on — she would have spent the whole night crying if she had not been

---

[6] The idea of «never refusing anything» is so intense in her, that it denotes a very pronounced psychological attitude, where each refusal must appear like an infidelity. It is normal that she extends to her relation with God what she believed to be established at the inter-human level: incomprehension and forgetfulness are the greatest sorrow (LT 108, 629; 149, 826). She is heard to say that «Jesus cries» when Marie Guérin is going to give up Holy Communion (LT 92, 567). Everything that lessens love seems to her a fault: «It always causes God some sadness to quibble a little over what Mother Prioress says» (PA, p. 192). At the end of her life, she tells how Saint Stanislas Kostka «cried bitterly» for having resisted the grace of his vocation: it is a classic example of a «positive imperfection» (see RP 8). Why would Thérèse note this fact except that she sincerely admired this scrupulous conscience which was like an echo of her own?

[7] DE 21-26.5.6. See «How can [the physician] say that I'm patient! But, it's not true!...» (DE 20.9.1).

very good during the day (A 18 v, 98). She feels the need to confess (A 5 v, 77; 7 r, 79); every confession is a feast (A 17 r, 95). The thought of having caused pain, even involuntarily, troubles her deeply (A 15 r, 92; 16 r, 94; 44 v, 141). She cannot bear that Céline remains upset with her (A 24 r - v, 107). At school, she sheds tears of sorrow when the mistress speaks of venial sin[8] and someone says — perhaps with a certain exaggeration — that at the base of her childish sadness, there was almost always the fear of having acted badly.[9]

This delicate conscience, it is true, will degenerate into the sickness of scruples but, once she regained her balance, she kept it for the rest of her life. She will preserve the keen sense of the pain that forgetfulness, ingratitude, and incomprehension cause.[10] In the last months of her life she will again ask for the pardon of a small fault from ten years before.[11] And preparing herself for confession before receiving the sacrament of the sick, she will remember having felt «a too natural pleasure» while using some eau de Cologne.[12]

As the Carmelite approaches perfection, her sensitivity in view of good and evil is developed more and more. We shall soon speak of how, according to her, love hollows out an ever-increasing distance between the soul and God which only the divine mercy can fill. John of the Cross has described the night into which the approach of God plunges the human spirit. It is this same phenomenon that inspired Teresa of Avila and other saints with impressive affirmations of their sinfulness. Thérèse will not escape this law of holiness, as we shall see: in 1897, the year of her "completion," the glimpses of her nothingness are the deepest. Will she not have, one morning, a lively sense of being «a great sinner»[13]?

---

[8] See *La Petite Thérèse à l'abbaye...*, p. 25.

[9] Mother Saint Francis de Sales, PO, p. 547.

[10] A 7v-8r, 80; 38 r - v, 130 s.; 68 r - v, 184; 70 v, 187; LT 108, 629; 122, 708; 149, 826.

[11] See *La Petite Thérèse à l'abbaye...*, p. 40.

[12] DE 8.7.2. According to CSG, pp. 185-186, it would be the only confession that Thérèse would have had to make before her death. But this is probably a subjective interpretation of facts narrated in 8.7.2.

[13] DE 12.8.3. «Union with God is for Saints the measure with which they size up their sins.... Their self-accusation must therefore not be assessed as the sign of a strict and unhealthy sense [*verkrampft*] of their sinfulness, but as the expression of a conscience purified by God's proximity.» Thus does M. SCHMAUS, who cites Thérèse of Lisieux as an example, express himself (*Katholische Dogmatik*, III, 2, Munich, 1956, 5th ed., p. 120).

In this paradox, perfection and nothingness are poised. The consciousness of her nothingness inspires in the Saint a great humility, docility, and reverence: and those who notice these virtues in her infer her perfection from it. For the observer, Thérèse can be a saint: in her own eyes, she is incomplete. And she conceives and constructs her way toward God, the «little way,» according to this personal experience: in rising from «nothingness.»

Besides, two lines intersect each other continually in the life of the nun of Lisieux: the line of duty and that of desire. According to the first, Thérèse is admired and admirable; some imperfections, real to her own eyes but imperceptible to others in the last years of her life, still elude her heroic generosity. According to the other line, an infinite area continues to hide from her power. So Thérèse Martin is twice the incomplete one. The «little way» that she conceives will have for its goal to achieve the unachievable.

In Carmel, Thérèse kept in her possession a picture of Jesus crucified which, one Sunday in 1887, had struck her so much (A 46 v, 144). She glued it onto a piece of paper on which she wrote some texts of the Gospel, arranged in the form of a dialogue. At the top, she copied the words of Jesus: «I thirst… Give me to drink» (Jn 19:28 and 4:7). Below, she formulated this response, which summarizes a whole world of conviction and deep desire: «Lord, Thou knowest well that I love Thee… but have pity on me, for I am only a sinner!» (Jn 21:15 and Lk 18:13).

II. PREMATURE HOLINESS?

The reflections that we have just made will help us to make a better judgment of an important thesis of Hans Urs von Balthasar:[14] Thérèse's conscience was for a long time clouded by her sinfulness. Two psychological moments would have contributed to this.

First, the vision of the Blessed Virgin and the miraculous cure. Soon the entourage of the child Thérèse has knowledge of it; they admire her, they expect a great deal from her. The child, aware of

---

[14] See *Therese von Lisieux*… One finds a perfect summary of this work in F. WULF, «Noch einmal Theresia von Lisieux,» *Geist und Leben*, 24 (1951), pp. 462-467.

the state of things, undergoes an «imperceptible change [*Verbiegung*]» (p. 83). «Henceforth she is the child miraculously healed, she is the one who saw the Virgin; she is thereby separated from others, she is placed — not entirely without fault on her part — on a pedestal,» and she must «learn to play the role of the little miraculous one» (p. 85). «Without wanting it, ... she must by her life, by her very existence, prove that the apparition was authentic.» It is only in the beginning of her last illness that she will be freed from this «mask» (p. 86).

The second circumstance is even more serious: Father Pichon declares to her that she never committed a mortal sin. And von Balthasar implies that the confessor said simply «sin,» all sin, which the humble Thérèse would have concealed while writing her life. No sooner is this hypothesis set forth when it becomes practically a thesis — it will weigh upon the theologian's entire book — and, by it, Thérèse is declared free from sin in her conscience. She will henceforth speak only of «imperfection,» and she is withdrawn from the communion of sinners, separated from them, «definitively banished in the isolation of sanctity» (p. 90).

These two factors, «her being set apart as a someone miraculously healed and her impeccability [*Sündenlosigkeit*]» (p. 91), would have created certain gaps in her charismatic message: «All the faults that Thérèse recalls date from her early youth. Later she no longer failed. She was not able to do so; it was not permitted to her. And thus some central mysteries remain closed for her theology: the mystery of the sin that we carry, solidarity in this sin, the mystery of the compatibility of love with the consciousness of sin, and overall the mystery of the sacrament of repentance» (p. 92).

This interpretation of von Balthasar,[15] whose poor perspective was encouraged by the old unauthentic text of HA,[16] persists

---

[15] (*Note of 1994.*) At a distance of twenty-five years, we add two important remarks which are linked with one another. See Appendix IV, page 367.

[16] As for the vision and the cure, Thérèse will experience «a spiritual anguish» lasting more than four years. She looks at herself with «a deep horror,» believing that she had lied (see here page 55). In matters of subconscious psychological influences, it would be better here to speak of an increase of the consciousness of sin than of a canonization that proves nothing. As for the declaration of Father Pichon, it indeed concerns mortal sin (A 70 r, 187; also DE 4.7.4 and PO, p. 157). The authentic text

in his conception of the «little way.» Thérèse was engaged in a «long detour of great holiness,» before arriving at her « little way» ... and yet! (pp. 94-96). This «little way» is not that of the confidence of a soul who feels incomplete, but the confidence of love,[17] obedient to a double rhythm of destruction (*Abbau*) and construction (*Aufbau*). The necessity of being a child does not derive from her state of imperfection, but it is only depicted as the preoccupation with loving purely (p. 234). First Thérèse sets out to «destroy,» and this is characteristic of the strong soul, but in reality she had little to destroy: she is rather grounded. The «construction» is not a waiting, but an activity consisting in «a progressive letting go» (p. 245): in this sense, powerlessness is not seen as a starting point, but as a fact that is willed. According to the Swiss theologian, sinners are excluded from the «little way.» By her premature canonization, Thérèse is expelled from their communion. They killed in her the consciousness of sin (pp. 90, 312-313) and her «little way» feels the effects of it: «It is a way of perfection, a way for souls who have magnanimously decided to love, essentially to no longer do anything but love. And the faults which she considers... are the faults "that don't offend God"» (p. 256). «Rather than ascribing to Thérèse's "little way" a beginning which is too low, a facility which is too great, one could object to a starting point which is too high, which presupposes too many things» (p. 270). Finally, on the occasion of a light during the recitation of the *Confiteor* (DE 12.8.3), «finally, finally, a month before her death, she feels that she is a sinner!» (p. 322). But then, let us notice that the «little way» has already been constructed for a long time.[18]

With respect to this analysis of von Balthasar, we would like to offer some reflections. Thérèse always felt imperfect. If it is true

---

quotes these words of Pichon, initially omitted: «if He [God] had abandoned you, instead of being a little angel, you would have become a little demon.» It is to these words that Thérèse exclaims: «Ah, I had no difficulty in believing it; I felt how weak and imperfect I was...» (A 70 r, 188.)

[17] For example, pp. 211, 225, 231, 243, 270.

[18] One could say with B. HONINGS («Therese von Lisieux als Lebenstheologe,» *Ephemerides carmeliticae*, 7 [1956], pp. 285-303), that von Balthasar, making Thérèse too Ignatian, makes her too little Carmelite. Indeed, the spirituality of «receiving» remains too much in the shadows.

that she feels a certain reticence in confessing herself a sinner — which I don't think she has been to any serious degree — it still remains that she conceives her way in the perspective of a distance to cover, of a gap to narrow. Not only is there the matter of powerlessness, but there is still the question of real faults (perceived at that time by the eye of a saint), which separate her from perfect love, from holiness. Her «way» is radically that of the incomplete one. And no one is excluded from it! Thérèse is too taken up with the infinite divine mercy to believe that human misery, as great as it is, remains at the doorstep of the «little way» toward God. We shall again have an opportunity to explain that preservation from mortal sin is not the basis of her confidence (C 36 v, 285) and that the presence of «all possible crimes» (DE 11.7.6) would not hinder it, because it is founded on Him Who came to call «sinners» (B 5 r, 230). It is true that, in order to enter upon the «little way,» one must divest oneself of the state of aversion to God: von Balthasar emphasizes this. But this conversion does not necessarily *precede* the «little way.» From the first moment, it is accessible; the motives that sustain it can sustain the conversion itself and can engage the person who is still a sinner.

Moreover, the concept of «sinner» is not limited to mortal sin. All those who commit venial faults, to whatever degree they are voluntary, are sinners. Thérèse could no longer avoid entering into this vast forest of human misery. And the one who von Balthasar believes was piously convinced of her preservation from *all* sin easily found matter to confess each week in the sacrament of penance.[19]

Von Balthasar has excessively reserved the «little way» for those who are perfect, and he rather confines himself to its final stage. But in order to reach this ardent love, confidence is the way. And it will necessarily remain the essential factor, because for Thérèse, love is an infinite ideal, and the soul, as near as it may come to it, remains infinitely incomplete and can have confidence only in God for its completion. From this perspective, it is also from love

[19] It is B. HONINGS (p. 302) who raised this problem of the confession. Twice, the author points out von Balthasar's personal meddling in Father Pichon's declaration, extending it to *all* sin.

that the «little way» is born. Von Balthasar, who has so much at heart to illustrate the prophetic message of Thérèse for modern man, runs the risk of restricting it. The «little way» remains open to all as long as they can say, with Thérèse, the prayer that Jesus taught us: «Forgive us our sins.»

If now we play for a moment the role of «the devil's advocate» to emphasize Thérèse's weakness, even at the end of her life, one will understand the reason for it: it is that the «little doctrine» is born of a situation involving an interior powerlessness as one of its two sources.

III. «WEAK AND IMPERFECT»

1. The present weakness

It is no longer necessary to restate here the details which have already been covered, now that we wish to paint Thérèse's weakness soberly in its two-fold manifestation of powerlessness and faults. It is sufficient to evoke the memory of her hypersensitive childhood, her unsuccessful contacts at school, her crisis of scruples, and her other spiritual pains. As a result of these experiences, Thérèse will forever be aware of her own fragility. Having entered Carmel, the experience of her weakness does not decrease in her arid prayers and her sufferings. Her encounter with Father Prou is a beneficent balm, but not an intervention that removes the roots of her powerlessness. Toward the end of the year 1894, Thérèse will henceforth welcome her «little way» as the only possible way to achieve holiness. In her subsequent writings, the idea of her weakness is a constant.

Sometimes this humble nun makes us witnesses to her struggles and her little defeats, while it is not always possible to determine where, in her confessions, pure humility ends and where there is any amount of real guilt, perceptible to her alone. There is, for example, this instant of curiosity while thumbing a fashion magazine — a poor wayfarer into her Carmel! — (PA, p. 242); or, curiosity concerning a letter, the lack of mortification regarding which Thérèse will then punish herself (PA, p. 296). Or again it is an 'interior whisper' on the occasion of the 'great struggle' when she must repair an oil lamp at a difficult hour (CSG, p. 133). It is the peace that sometimes is missing in her when someone disturbs her (CSG, p. 236). It is the movements of nature against this or that tiresome sister (LT 230, 1100; DE 29.7.3; CSG, p. 25). It is her tears, when they find fault with her concerning the length of a Pious Recreation which they interrupt (CSG, p. 19), or when she breaks a window in the refectory (CSG, p. 201), or during the course of her illness on the occasion of certain circumstances involving a drink called *"lait maternisé."* [Milk did not agree with Therese, but since she could not retain anything else at the time, the doctor ordered a kind of condensed milk — this *"lait maternisé."* When the bottles were brought to the Infirmary, she began to cry bitterly] (CSG, p. 223). Certainly, her imperfect health lessens the seriousness of these little faults too, but, on the other hand, increases the occasions of weakness. «How little it takes to lose one's patience!» sighs Thérèse (DE 3.8.4). And as far as food is concerned, she notices something she had never noticed before: «slight preferences for certain foods» (CSG, p. 167). The «sad sentiments of nature» that she finds fault with in her novices, she 'feels them in her own heart' (C 19 r, 260). She knows by experience these moments of psychological uneasiness after an infidelity (CSG, p. 61). What displeases her in others: forgetfulness, involuntary carelessness, weariness — and let us add, lack of common sense[20] — she experiences in herself (CSG, p. 138). The divine office, for example, which was 'her happiness and her martyrdom at the same time,' is in that respect a privileged domain (DE 6.8.6). Or does it cede its place of honor to the recitation of the rosary, which «is more difficult for her than wearing an instrument of penance» (C 25 v, 269)?

The closer Thérèse comes to death, the more her confessions multiply. Let us refer to the last year of her life alone. There she is, still 'at the bottom of the ladder of perfection' (LT 202, 1021). She

---

[20] Here we have the wherewithal to feed the humble feeling that Thérèse has of herself. She was, indeed, little practiced in the physical labors of daily life. At Les Buissonnets, she was apparently exempt from all household work (A 44 v, 141). At the abbey, she had only to wash two or three plates for one to notice her clumsiness (*La Petite Thérèse...*, p. 33). In 1897, Thérèse will again speak of her «inability» and of her lack of «knowledge of the things of earth» (C 10 v. 247 f.), in spite of her immense devotion.

is «very imperfect» (LT 213, 1041), «a poor little nothing, nothing at all» (C 2 r, 236). She is far from having the love that the saints have (LT 225, 1090), of being what she sings about in her Poems (LT 220, 1058). She does not always practice what she knows (C 17 r, 257), she has her «interior and exterior faults» (C 26 v, 270), and although she no longer has to struggle to practice charity, she 'still happens to make mistakes' (C 13 v, 252) and 'lets little sacrifices escape' (C 31 r, 276). They judge her imperfect and she feels that she is (DE 2.8.6). And when she has been unjustly blamed, she thinks: «How easily I might have committed the fault of which I was accused» (CSG, p. 20).

2. *Incurable weakness*

Such is the confession of Thérèse concerning her own weakness as she faced death. How much it had to have been truer still toward the end of the year 1894, when she conceived her «way of spiritual childhood.» But suppose that our Carmelite lived a few decades more, would she have been freed of imperfection?

In listening to her, one must say no, because her long personal experience as well as the penetration of God's greatness inspire in her a deep conviction: «All our justice is stained» (Pri 6) and «no human life is exempt from faults» (LT 226, 1092). When she considers the saints, she feels «that even they were subject to many weaknesses» (CSG, p. 34). They were «weak and mortal like us, they committed the same faults, and sustained the same combats» (LT 263, 1173). The «most holy souls will be perfect only in Heaven» (C 28 r, 272), and it is indeed «spiritual imperfections» of which Thérèse speaks here.

Imperfection is, for this Carmelite, a world where the humble person will never have finished making discoveries. On the contrary, as she progresses, she more clearly sees what she is not. This slow clearing up of her own misery, Thérèse Martin keenly observed in one of the most profound and most human passages that the Saint had written: «When I think of the time of my novitiate I see how imperfect I was.... I made so much fuss over such little things that it makes me laugh now. Ah! How good the Lord is in having matured my soul, and in having given it wings.... Later on, no doubt, the time in which I am now [it is three months before her death!] will appear filled with imperfections, but now I am no longer astonished at anything. I am not disturbed at seeing that I am *weakness* itself. On the contrary, it is in my weakness that I glory, and I expect each day to discover new imperfections in myself» (C 15 r, 254). If she then speaks gladly of her «nothingness,»[21] it is because she has probed the possibilities of her «extreme weakness» (PN 17). It seems to us that Sister Geneviève understood her sister well, when she said: «This very strong soul was so distrustful of herself that she easily believed herself capable of committing the greatest sins» (CSG, p. 25). We shall have the opportunity again to quote some similar words. One will object that Thérèse, out of concern for humility, accentuates her weakness here. But one will not forget that humility is truth. And precisely by this truth (saints understand it better than we do), there is deepened in Thérèse the conviction of being incomplete. Another source nourishes her conviction as well.

IV. THE INFINITENESS OF LOVE

Now, we must study one of the most beautiful themes of Thérèse's spirituality, where she showed herself as magnanimous as anyone could be. We want to speak of her conception of the ideal of love. Some important consequences for the doctrine of the «way of spiritual childhood» result from it.

1. The possibilities of the heart

«To give ALL,» to love «Jesus alone,» «with all her power to love,» with a «jealous» love, «with passion,» how much these vehement desires of love which we noticed at the beginning of her religious life[22] have increased with the years! Later on, she will often have tears in her eyes while speaking of her desires of love (PO,

---

[21] For example B 3 v, 227; C 2 r, 236; DE 6.8.8; 8.8.1; 13.8; LT 226, 1092; 243, 1121; 261, 1163.

[22] See here pp. 61-63 and 92 f.

p. 277). She would like to be «magnetized» by Jesus, she said (PA, p. 474). Must we recall the graces of the month of June 1895 which cast light on the theme: «how much Jesus desires to be loved,» or the impetuous thrust of Manuscript B, or her ultimate desire for a death of love?

Let us emphasize here that to her desire of completeness was added very soon the dimension of the *infinite*. Wanting to give all is condemned to never giving all, because in giving all, one wants to give more. 'God cannot set a limit on Thérèse's sanctity: His limit is that there is no limit!' (LT 83, 541). The divine Beggar of love says 'thank you' «by always asking more and more in proportion to the gifts He receives» (LT 172, 894).

On the day of her profession, Thérèse binds herself to Him, knowing that she will never again belong to herself. She asks for «infinite love without any limits other than Yourself... love which is no longer I but You» (*Note of profession*). She will love «to infinity» (LT 127, 724), in «plenitude» (B 4 v, 229), «unto folly»: this last expression is like a leitmotiv of her entire life.[23] The thought that such a love, infinite and inexhaustible as God Himself, is never completely realizable, does not frighten her. Another thought sustains her: «nothing seems impossible to the soul who loves.»[24] She forgets that she is delivering her own verdict: her realizations will always be incomplete.

Beside this dimension of the infinite, inherent in her ideal of love, there is another dimension which the nun understood well: that of the possibilities of her own heart. As she loves, she feels that her capacity to love becomes greater, and she notices that the psychological riches of her act of love are going to increase.

Without doubt, her «sensitive and affectionate» heart (A 38 r, 130) was well prepared for that. The little philosopher had been nourished with strong convictions: «What do all created beauties mean to me? I would be unhappy possessing them, my heart would

[23] See for example, LT 93, 575; 96, 587; A 39r, 132; 82 v, 210. The word «folly» is used ten times in Manuscript B!

[24] LT 251, 1138. It is probably in allusion to *Im* 3, 5, 4, that she had already quoted in 1888: «Love can do all things; and *the most difficult things don't appear difficult to it*» (LT 65, 467) and in 1895 (A 53 v, 158, in 1888). All her religious life has therefore been based on this principle.

be so empty!... It is incredible how big my heart appears to me when I consider all earth's treasures, since all of them together could not satisfy it; but when I consider Jesus, how little it appears to me!... I would so much like to love Him!...» (LT 74, 499). Her heart is, like that of Marie Guérin, an «*immense void*» (LT 93, 575); it will never be satisfied on earth (LT 56, 445). The «miserable affection» of creatures cannot fill it (A 84 r, 212). Thérèse never met a heart «capable» of understanding hers (A 38 r, 130): «There is only one Being who can understand the profundity of this word: Love!... It is only our Jesus» (LT 109, 640).

However, in loving God and neighbor, Thérèse has the happy experience of seeing her big heart enlarge and become enriched: «The more we advance in life, the more we love Jesus» (LT 132, 740); «When the human heart gives itself to God, it loses nothing of its natural tenderness; in fact, this tenderness grows while becoming more pure and more divine» (C 9 r, 245 f.). «Love is nourished only by sacrifices, and the more a soul refuses natural satisfactions, the stronger and more disinterested becomes her tenderness» (C 21 v, 263). In 1897, she notes with happiness that her heart had enlarged, «that it can give... incomparably more tenderness than if it had concentrated upon one egotistical and unfruitful love» (C 22r, 264). Often she expresses to those who are dear to her this development of tenderness in their regard.[25] And it is her love for Jesus that causes it (LT 133, 743), as it is her love for Jesus that benefits from it.

«I do not know how far this will go» (LT 177, 907). What she writes here to her aunt, she could just as well have written to Jesus! Our religion, she said, renders hearts «capable of loving, of loving with a love that is almost infinite» (LT 166, 865). Already in 1887, she had noted this mysterious psychological progress that she describes in 1895: «The more I gave Him [Jesus] to *drink*, the more the thirst of my poor little soul increased, and it was this ardent thirst He was giving me as the most delightful drink of His love.»[26]

---

[25] LT 58, 451; 70, 482; 125, 715; 133, 743; 177, 907.

[26] A 46 v, 144 f. Compare this with this verse from the month of October 1895 (PN 24, str. 25): «The more I feel myself burning with your divine flames / The more I thirst to give you souls.»

Every satisfaction causes a new thirst. Thus her heart discovers its own possibilities: it will always be able to surpass itself. Never will it have loved its last love. Thérèse knows where the true measures are: «How great a soul must be to contain a God!»[27] And she would like to reach the furthest limit: «I want my [heart] to give Jesus everything possible» (C 10 r, 247). As burning as her heart is, she already said on May 31, 1896, that her love was not at its end yet: «Your Love is my only martyrdom; / The more I feel it burning within me, / The more my soul desires You» (PN 31).

2. Two unequal loves

The desires of Thérèse of Lisieux do not have anything to do with a thirst to assert oneself (in truth, that is what kills love!) or to be a performer on the spiritual plane. Her love is completely *response* and it is along this line that we shall find the deepest cause of its impetus toward the infinite without limits: the Carmelite would like to love God *even* as God loves us. But that is devoting oneself to failure: God loves us infinitely, Thérèse will therefore remain always short of the love she dreamed of; the realization of her program will necessarily remain incomplete.

The law of the love-response is an old one with her. To prove this, it would be sufficient to verify when her efforts to quench the thirst of Jesus began. She soon quotes (Lk 12:48): «*Much will be demanded from those to whom He [Jesus] has given much*» (LT 83, 541). But it is Jesus alone who knows to what extent the gift of His love for us goes, and, consequently, unto what love we are invited: «Jesus' love for Céline can be understood only by Jesus!... Jesus has done foolish things for Céline.... Let Céline do *foolish things* for Jesus...» (LT 85, 546).

However, it is possible that the law of inequality between the two loves only manifested itself in all its happy cruelty in 1894. (And one could, in this case, compare this realization to the last period that precedes the discovery of the «little way,» when Thérèse

[27] LT 165, 860. Compare with: «We are greater than the whole universe. One day, we *ourselves* shall have a divine existence...» (LT 83, 541).

vigorously assesses her incompleteness and seeks a new way. But let us note that we do not have the facts to reach a conclusion that is certain.) In any event, it is then that we find this thought clearly stated for the first time. If, in 1893 again, Jesus and Thérèse were an ocean of love each for the other (LT 142, 794), in 1894, the two oceans are revealed in very different measures: «We shall never be able to carry out the follies He carried out for us, and our actions will never merit this name, for they are only very rational acts and far below what our love would like to...» (LT 169, 881). In the beginning of 1896, she says while explaining her «coat of arms»: «In order to respond to Jesus' love she would like to do for Him what He has done for her [but] she is only a weak *reed*» (A 85 v, 214). In the evening of her life, she will make this moving declaration about the true dimensions of the two loves: «Your love has gone before me since my childhood, it has grown with me, and now it is an abyss whose depths I cannot fathom. Love attracts love, and, my Jesus, my love leaps towards Yours; it would like to fill the abyss which attracts it, but alas! it is not even like a drop of dew lost in the ocean!.... For me to love You as You love me, I would have to borrow Your own love, and then only would I be at rest» (C 35 r, 282). But, she will not find this rest on earth.[28]

So, other desires matured in the meantime: that of concentrating all her love in one moment of extreme intensity in order to die the *death of love* and that of *Heaven* where one will possess *perfect* love: «There, where I shall love Jesus without reserve» (LT 79, 514), where is found «the reality above all thought» (PA, p. 157), where she will sing another — a «NEW» — canticle of love (C 16 r, 256), where she will love «more and more... without limit and without law» (PN 33). When Thérèse will spontaneously describe her «little way» toward perfect love, she will establish the goal of it as Heaven (B 5 v, 231; C 3 r, 238). Two and a half months before her death, some days after the intimate outpouring of Manuscript C on the abyss of love, she will formally declare: «What attracts me to the homeland of Heaven is the Lord's call, the hope of lov-

[28] At the beginning of stanza 38 of CS (*Oeuvres*, V), Saint John of the Cross insists on the fact that the soul, eager to love God as she is loved by Him, remains necessarily unsatisfied during this life. Thérèse was certainly familiar with these pages.

ing Him finally as I have so much desired to love Him» (LT 254, 1141). It is at the same time the confession of the incompleteness of a great saint.

V. HUMILITY: THE ESSENTIAL CONDITION OF THE «WAY OF SPIRITUAL CHILDHOOD»

In 1890, during her retreat for her Profession, Thérèse had a premonition: «… provided that one day I reach the summit of the mountain of Love; but I believe that this will not be here below» (LT 112, 658). Life had to give her a reason. Powerlessness which is great in her eyes, and trifling faults convince her that she does not yet possess the perfect love that she seeks. Besides, how will she ever reach this summit? Her ideal is without limits, it rises up as she approaches it.[29] She is two times the incomplete one. Not that she hasn't loved a great deal, but «even if I had accomplished all the works of Saint Paul, I would still believe myself to be a *useless servant*, I would find that I had empty hands» (DE 23.6). In view of God's infinite love for us, all our works are as nothing. The gap remains just as large and deep. There remains for Thérèse only the hope that God Himself will fill it.

But, obviously, before one can hope for completion from God, one must accept being incomplete. One must understand one's situation, one's «empty hands,» one's «nothingness.» This is humility.[30] However, the energy that pushes onward in the «little way» cannot rest there. Humility accepts the incompleteness, and the «way of spiritual childhood» endeavors to bring about the completion. But it is without difficulty that one sees the true value of humility in the whole of the «little doctrine.» It is a foundation, a point of departure, a *sine qua non* condition. «In order to walk in the Little

---

[29] See: «It frequently happens that, during mountain climbs, the true summit is discovered only once one has scaled successive and ever higher slopes which at each thrust one had been tempted to take for the culminating point. That is a bit what happens in the great spiritual adventure [of Thérèse].» ALBERT DU SACRÉ-COEUR, *Approches…*, p. 151.

[30] We use humility here in the strict sense of the word. In a large and improper sense, one sometimes includes in it all the human activity of «spiritual childhood.»

Way,» said Thérèse, «one must be humble, poor in spirit, and simple.»[31] «To enjoy these treasures [the merciful love of Jesus], one must humble oneself, recognize one's nothingness» (LT 261, 1163). In the private instructions that she gave to each of her novices, she was always returning to the virtue of humility (CSG, p. 21). She exhorted Marie of the Trinity continually «to become more and more humble and little» (PO, p. 488). As for herself, she knows very well «on which side to run.» «I don't hasten to the first place, but to the last; instead of advancing like the Pharisee, I repeat, filled with confidence, the humble prayer of the Publican.»[32] Sometimes she summarizes sanctification as humility: «Let us line up humbly among the imperfect, let us esteem ourselves as *little souls* whom God must sustain at each moment. When He sees us very much convinced of our nothingness, He extends His Hand to us; if we still wish to attempt doing something *great*, even under the pretext of zeal, Good Jesus leaves us all alone. *"But, as soon as I said: 'My foot has stumbled,' your mercy, Lord, strengthened me"* [Ps 93]. Yes, it suffices to humble oneself, to peacefully bear with one's imperfections: that is real sanctity.»[33]

Thérèse is humble because she is in the truth. Under the light of God she sees herself as she is, in her true proportions. «It seems to me,» she said, «...that humility is truth. I do not know whether I am humble, but I do know that I see the truth in all things.»[34] «There is always present to my mind the remembrance of what I

---

[31] Sister Geneviève, PA, p. 291.

[32] C 36 v, 285. Sister Geneviève said somewhere that Thérèse's «natural tendency» was humility, and that she did not have to make «a lot of effort to acquire it,» but she means by that rather simplicity and integrity (PA, p. 306). Thérésian humility is not apathy and it isn't acquired without effort. The Saint had felt «this sadness one experiences when one is made to feel inferior or less privileged than others» (CSG, p. 209).

[33] LT 243, 1121, of June 7, 1897. Mother Agnès, Sister Geneviève and Marie of the Trinity seem to also reduce «spiritual childhood» to humility (see PA, p. 165; CSG, pp. 18 and 41; PA, p. 488 respectively). But the preoccupation to establish the ultimate motive of the «little way» seems strange to them. They have, moreover, neutralized these particular accentuations (see PA, p. 150; CSG, pp. 18 and 63; PA, p. 474 f. respectively).

[34] CSG, p. 21. She repeats this definition of humility in her Pious Recreation on Saint Stanislas Kostka (see RP 8). It is likely that it is borrowed from Teresa of Avila: humility is «to walk in truth [*andar en verdad*]» (VI *Demeures*, chap. 10).

am» (C 26 v, 270). «I am really only what God thinks I am» (CSG, p. 202). And the very day of her death, she summarizes her attitude in a supreme testimony: «Yes, it seems to me I never sought anything but the truth.... Yes, I have understood humility of heart» (DE 30.9).

And what about all that is good in her? It comes from pure divine mercy: «the gifts which God showered upon me ... drew me to Him» (A 81 v, 207). Humility, truth, magnanimity, and mercy go hand in hand with Thérèse: «I am *too little* to have any vanity now, I am also *too little* to compose beautiful sentences in order to make you believe that I have a lot of humility. I prefer to agree very simply that the Almighty has done great things in the soul of His divine Mother's child, and the greatest thing is to have shown her her *littleness*, her impotence.»[35] Why this last sentence? Because the recognition of her nothingness opened to her the door toward many other graces, not the least of which was that of the «little way.» 'As loaded with abundant gifts as was the ear of corn' to which she compares herself, she no longer knows how to divert her glance from their real Source: «Yes, it seems to me that I am humble.... God shows me truth; I feel so much that everything comes from Him!» (DE 4.8.3).

Thus, Thérèse of Lisieux lived her «little way» which, before serving others, was considered in terms of her own personal poverty. To see this, humility was necessary. But it was a humility completed by the vision of the God of mercy!

---

[35] C 4 r - v, 239. See: «As for me, I have lights only to see my little nothingness, but this does me more good than all the lights on the faith» (DE 13.8). Thérèse was very convinced of her littleness. This is possibly the reason why she never quotes Mt 18:3: «Unless you become like little children, you won't be able to enter into the kingdom of Heaven.» Thérèse doesn't have «to return» (or «to become,» as they translated then): she *is* little (see A. COMBES, *Introduction...*, pp. 279-280, 295, 308). However, this is conjecture, and it is not necessary to insist too much on the point, for one always has to *grow* toward this ideal. Thérèse herself had understood this while discovering her «little way»: «I had to remain little, and become this more and more» (C 3 r, 238). Littleness, childhood, these are for her dynamic notions. Childhood is *before* us. According to Mother Agnès, Thérèse loved to meditate on Mt 18:3 (PA, p. 165).

Chapter II

The Merciful

The incomplete love to which the young Carmelite sees herself condemned has but a single possibility of escape: the hope in a Being who can perfect her. Left to her powers alone, she cannot succeed, so she returns to God. But the centrifugal force which moves her away from herself is united with the centripetal force of the divine Center. Thrust away from herself, she is attracted by God and her flight picks up speed.

In other words, God, from Whom Thérèse invokes help, is the Father of mercies. It is in this way that she discovers Him: He is good like a mother. Since the nature of His love is to lower itself, God, Who is love, is henceforth *mercy* for the little one. Thérèse acquires this conviction in light of Revelation and in light of her own vital experience. To deepen Thérèse's conception of divine mercy, and thus to understand her confidence better, we shall consider it first as experience and then as belief. It goes without saying that these two aspects are not completely separable: it is because Thérèse believes in divine mercy that she knows how to discern it in life and it is because she has experienced it that she believes in it more strongly.

I. THE EXPERIENCE

1. *«Totally gratuitous gifts»*

Through the events of her life, the Carmelite sees the golden thread of the goodness of the Lord. To write about her life is to write a book about the «mercies of the Lord» (A 2 r, 71). To take up her pen again to do a second autobiographical essay is simply «to finish» singing of these mercies (C 1 r, 235).

The prologue of Manuscript A condenses all of God's work in Thérèse into a suggestive formula: it is about the «totally gratuitous gifts of Jesus; [Thérèse] knows that nothing in herself was capable of attracting His divine glances and that His mercy alone brought about everything that is good in her» (A 3 v, 74). But let us not return to what we have already explained.

However, let us pause for a moment at a particular event: the «day of grace» of her «conversion» (A 85 v, 215) of Christmas 1886, the «miracle» of «mercy.»[1] The importance of this experience is evident from the mere fact that Thérèse places it as an historical landmark of her life (it is the beginning of the «third period» of her life); but it is an important event still more because of the way in which she arrives at it. For one can see in Manuscript A a real convergence toward the «Christmas grace.» If this literary setting is not deliberate and is only a reflection of the facts, it thereby becomes even more significant! Whatever the case may be, after having told of «the complete change from her happy nature» (A 13 r, 89) caused by her mother's death, Thérèse illustrates it by a large number of details. In the pages that precede «the grace,» we hear a sharp complaint against her puerile hypersensitivity. Everything cries out for the «miracle.» It will occur, and Thérèse will remain so lastingly impressed by it that she seems to amuse herself, at a distance of years, in disclosing her defeats from days gone by, in order to highlight further God's victory in her. One can deduce from this what the intensity and the influence of this fundamental experience were. It is a tangible proof of divine goodness which can and wants to accomplish the work in which her good will was unsuccessfully engaged for ten years. Christmas 1886 is at the foundation of all Thérèse's spirituality: in spite of a profound helplessness, she continues her poor efforts, because the Merciful One comes to the aid of the good will that labors on. Her hope in Him will turn out to be legitimate.

---

[1] See here pp. 58-61.

2. The twofold preservation

There are in life some events which one does not grasp as real graces at the time they are actually taking place. This was the case with Thérèse. Certain experiences of her youth have little by little merged into a realization that makes a clear appearance in the autobiography of 1895: she recognizes how the fundamental grace of her choice for Jesus is due to divine solicitude alone.

For Thérèse, the choice of God is embodied in a religious life, vowed solely to the love of God, and assuming in this love all other love of people and of things. In this perspective, human friendship and earthly joy for a long time held threats of a lesser love,[2] of chances of sin, and, as she will say, even of perdition. That she knew how to avoid them is the work of Mercy. How many times Thérèse, who watches with a saint's eye, will have thanked her Lord for it! Let us examine more closely her reasons for gratitude.

Thérèse confesses that the world «had its charms for her and her heart would have allowed itself to be easily dazzled.»[3] Friendships (even later at the monastery, A 70 v, 188) would have 'easily won over her sensitive and affectionate heart': «With a heart such as mine, I would have allowed myself to be taken and my wings to be clipped.»[4] At that time, she would have, like her friends from Alençon, 'allied the joys of this earth too much with the service of God.' She would have fallen into «great evils,» especially the evil of a divided love, because: «How can a heart given over to the affection of creatures be intimately united with God?... I feel this is not possible. Without having drunk from the poisoned cup of a too

---

[2] It is above all in light of Jesus' love that one must interpret certain judgments on the world and on friendship. See here pp. 89-91.

[3] See, for the following details, A 32 v, 120, and 38 r-v-39 r, 130 f., unless there is another indication.

[4] See «With a nature such as mine... I would have become very bad and perhaps would have even been lost» (A 8 v, 81). When Father Pichon tells her that she could have become a little demon, «she had no difficulty in believing it» (A 70 r, 188). See also LT 147, 813 of 1893: «Perhaps were I in her place [notably that of Céline's maid], I would be even less good than she is, and perhaps, too, she would already have been a great saint if she had received half the graces God has granted to me.» And in 1894 (LT 167, 870, on Marie of the Trinity): «In her place, I would have been *lost* forever a long time ago in the vast forest of the world!»

ardent love of creatures, I *feel* that I cannot be mistaken; ... perhaps I would have allowed myself to be burned entirely by the *misleading light*.»

But everything worked out differently for her. It was a «great grace» to have not remained in Alençon. She knew the world 'just enough to despise it and to separate herself from it.' Friendships had given her 'bitterness' instead of understanding. She was not led astray by paths strewn with the flowers of praise (A 40 r, 133).

What was the divine intention in all this? «Jesus knew I was too feeble to be exposed to temptation» (A 38 v, 131). God sent her suffering 'in order for her to be offered earlier to Jesus' (A 12 r, 87). If He called her so quickly to Carmel, it is because she was *weak* (LT 57, 448; A 44 r, 140), it is by pure «condescension» (LT 224, 1083), it is by a mystery of predilection (A 2 r, 71). In short, that her heart had been raised to God from the dawn of reason is cause to sing with gratitude the mercies of the Lord (A 40 r, 134).

In a very beautiful page (A 38 v-39 r, 131 f.), the Saint thoroughly considered the ultimate consequences — the negative which were possible, and the positive which are real — of the past threats and the decisive graces of her youth. She summarizes in this passage all the human weakness and divine mercy that had joined together in the saving choice that Jesus made of her. One also measures in this the degree of her spiritual poverty and her openness to God. «I have no merit at all, then, in not having given myself up to the love of creatures, since I was preserved from it only through God's great mercy!... I know that without Him, I could have fallen as low as Saint (Mary) Magdalene, and the profound words of Our Lord to Simon resound with a great sweetness in my soul... I know that: *"he to whom less is forgiven, LOVES less,"* but I also know that Jesus *has forgiven me more* than (*St. Mary*) *Magdalene*, since He forgave me in *advance*[5] by preventing me from falling. Ah! how I wish I could explain what I feel!....» And Thérèse gives «an example which will express [her] thought at least a little»: a young man stumbles on a stone and breaks a limb; his father, a physician, takes

[5] Jesus has forgiven her in advance: she had already expressed this thought in a letter of July 23, 1891 (LT 130, 731), but, there, without concluding that, then, *all* has been forgiven her.

care of him with love until his complete recovery; the son will love him and will be grateful to him. (This is the image of the sinner after being forgiven.) But in Thérèse's case, another supposition is necessary: the father hastens, with a «tender foresight,» to remove the stone without being seen by anyone. The son, not knowing anything, will love him less than if he had been cured by him; «but if he should come to learn of the danger from which he has just escaped, *will he not love his father more?*» And the personal application follows: «I am this child, the object of the *foreseeing love* of a Father who has not sent His Word to save the *just*, but *sinners*. He wants me to *love* Him because He has *forgiven* me, not much, but ALL. He has not expected me to *love Him much* like Saint Magdalene, but He has willed that I KNOW how He has loved me with a love of *unspeakable foresight*, in order that now I may love Him unto *folly*!»

Thérèse had scrutinized all the potentialities of her misery: she is Mary Magdalene, if not in fact, then at least in right.[6] She is preserved, but the depth of her being continues to be thirsty for Redemption: for her, too, the Savior of sinners came. This is the true mover of her love: mercy, which is greater for her than for sinners because it is an *obliging* mercy. If he loves more to whom more is forgiven, then Thérèse to whom God has forgiven «all» while even preventing falls, can surpass the Magdalene in love. The little Carmelite has unmasked a great fallacy: «I have heard it said that one cannot meet a pure soul who loves more than a repentant soul; ah! how I would wish to give the lie to this statement!»

Experience of mercy? These lines written in the evening of her life summarize it: «O my Jesus, it is perhaps an illusion, but it seems to me that You cannot fill a soul with more love than the love with which You have filled mine; ... here on earth, I cannot conceive a greater immensity of love than the one which it has pleased You to give me freely, *without any merit on my part*» (C 35 r, 282 f.).

---

[6] A. COMBES notes very well on this subject: «Innocent... of sin, she has the sense [of it], more and better than sinners do» (*En retraite avec Sainte Thérèse de Lisieux*, Paris, 1952, p. 63).

II. A CONVICTION OF FAITH

We have just pointed out the interdependence of experience and faith in Thérèse's conception of divine mercy. The passage about the Magdalene permitted us to skim the surface of the second element. We must now complete the picture, in describing the elements of Thérèse's «science of faith.» In fact, she possesses a small theology of divine mercy — the fruit of her regular reading of Sacred Scripture, of her simple and loving reflection, and of the gifts of the Spirit which this Saint knew how to welcome with a great purity of soul and which gave her a co-natural wisdom. «I am not at all jealous of your beloved disciple; I know your secrets, for I am your spouse... ,» she could sing, not without good reason.[7] Six times at least she will make reference to Jesus' words, according to which the Father reveals to the little ones — to the *littlest*, according to Thérèse's translation — that which He hides from the wise and the prudent.[8] But if she quotes these words, it is only to exalt the Mercy of which she was the object.

1. *«Through infinite Mercy»*

Let us first quote a formal declaration which dates from 1895, the «year of Mercy.» «I understand, however, that all souls cannot be the same, that it is necessary there be different types in order to honor each of God's perfections in a particular way. To me He has granted His *infinite Mercy*, and *through it* I contemplate and adore the other Divine perfections!... All of these perfections appear to be resplendent with *love*» (A 83 v, 211). There, in just a few words, is her perspective: all of God's work towards us is mercy, or — what is henceforth identical for Thérèse, as the text demonstrates it once more — is Love.

The two biblical texts which Thérèse will never be able to forget are fundamental in this conviction: «Whoever is a little one, let him come to me» (Pr 9:4), and «As one whom a mother caresses, so will I comfort you; you shall be carried at the breasts and upon

[7] PN 24, str. 20, of October 1, 1895.

the knees they will caress you» (Is 66:13-12). But our Carmelite, who voraciously read the New Testament (especially the Gospels) and the Old Testament as far as she had the opportunity to do so (especially the Psalms), will quote in her writings many other scriptural passages about mercy. There is a good chance that these belong to her favorite texts.

Among the Psalms, 22 (23) and 102 (103) seem to be her favorites. Psalm 22 («The Lord is my Shepherd») is quoted at least three times.[9] Through it, Thérèse summarizes her own life (in the prologue of Manuscript A) or her «little doctrine» (in a lost letter to Father Pichon). As for Psalm 102, quoted at least four times,[10] here are the passages she picks out: «The Lord is filled with gentleness and compassion: He is slow to punish and abundant in mercy [v. 8]. As far as the east is from the west, so far has He removed our iniquities from us. As a *father* has compassion on his *children*, so the Lord has compassion on us.[11] For He knows our frailty. He remembers that we are only dust [vv. 12-14].» The image of the father brings to mind another quotation, from Isaiah 49:15: «Can a mother forget her child? Well! Even if a mother were to forget her child, I myself will never forget you» (LT 191, 965). And the image of the child reminds us of quotations from Manuscript B: «... to him that is little, mercy will be shown»[12] and «The Lord shall gather together the little lambs with his arm and shall take them up in his bosom.»[13]

---

8 Mt 11:25. See A 49 r, 149; 71 r, 189; C 4 r, 239; LT 127, 724; 190, 958; 247, 1132.

9 A 3 r, 73.

10 A 3 r - v, 73; 76 r, 197; LT 226, 1092; CSG p. 43 (reproduction of an autograph).

11 Thérèse herself wrote the words in italics (see CSG, p. 43); the meaning of this gesture is obvious. Let's note again that the version that she used translated well "*timentibus se*" of the Vulgate at the end of verse 12, by «those who fear Him» (DCL). But «to fear» a father is an impossible thing for Thérèse and she changes it therefore into «us» (LT 226, 1092 and CSG, p. 43). Again, this is one of the thousand details that reveals the interior world of Thérèse Martin.

12 Sg 6:6. See B 1 v, 220.

13 Is 40:11. See *ibid*.

2. Divine fatherhood

We have already drawn the reader's attention to the great place that the fatherhood of God occupies in Thérèse's life, especially in the last years. The *Our Father* became the nourishment of her soul (C 25 v, 269). Her sisters caught her meditating on the *Our Father* one day, with tears in her eyes: «It is so sweet to call God *our Father,*» she explained.[14]

Without any doubt, one must interpret in part her notion of God as our Father through her happy childhood experience of her own earthly father. But this does not mean that this notion is the end of a progressive transposition or a successive sublimation.[15] *Above any other factor*, it is the discovery of the «little way» that illuminated for Thérèse the idea of God as our Father and it is only thereafter that it has been completed by the old images of her earthly father, images which, in their turn, have enriched the notion of the celestial Father.

What type of father was M. Martin, then, in the eyes of his daughter who, in her boundless reverence, could have enlarged his moral qualities further? How perfect he is, how loving! Here are

---

[14] See HA 07 (the oldest version of this text), p. 225. See here Part III, chap. I, p. 157 f. and chap. III, p. 209 f. J.F. SIX summarizes well: Thérèse of Lisieux, one of «these prophets for our time... truly knew how to reveal the Father to us.» See the Introduction of *Au coeur même de l'Église*, Desclée De Brouwer, 1966, p. 9.

[15] It is in this sense, we believe, that C. BEAUVALET interprets («Le Thème de l'enfance chez Sainte Thérèse de Lisieux,» ED, 29 [1953], pp. 67-80). Thérèse passes through to spiritual childhood, «without there being any break, simply by successive sublimations.» There is only «transposition.» This one took place under the influence of the illness of M. Martin, when Thérèse develops her spirituality of the Holy Face, thus comparing M. Martin with God. Thérèse passes «from one father to the other» (pp. 73-75). But, in our opinion, «the psychological substratum» is too decisive here. This doesn't mean that the example of M. Martin didn't bring Thérèse to God. «When I think of you, dear little father,» she writes in 1888, «I naturally think of God, for it seems to me that it is impossible to see anyone more holy than you on the earth» (LT 58, 451). But as this text said, it is God the Holy One, the Perfect One, not the Father as such, whom she approaches here. Already in 1931, F. FLORAND («La "Petite Voie" de Sainte Thérèse de l'Enfant-Jésus,» *La vie spirituelle*, 13 [1931], t. 29, pp. 161-179) saw this as a «psychological preliminary» of the discovery of the «little way.» «In the deep recesses of her unconscious mind, Thérèse *had not accepted her mother's death* and, as though blind, she was still looking for her arms.... And it is in this way, we think, that is insinuated, in the natural order, the inspiration of the "little way".... It is certain that the initial idea of our "little doctor" had been to *copy the ways of little children* with regard to their parents.» Our response to these interpretations proceeds from what we have already said.

the praises that we glean in the Carmelite's writings: M. Martin is incomparable, not of this earth, covered with merits and crowns, admirable, of a perfect fidelity, more worthy of Heaven than of earth, an image of the saints, the elect of God, the heroic Patriarch, the new Abraham, the beautiful old man with the venerable, beautiful and dignified look, with a handsome face, a Heavenly, simple, and honest expression, the most handsome and most distinguished gentleman, endowed with an artistic soul, with a greatness of soul, holy, so tested and so holy, without equal, the wisest man in France, of a patriarchal simplicity, of an entirely natural distinction, in short: 'everything in him causes admiration.' Evidently, this paternal goodness crowns everything: in fact, Thérèse praises his usual gentleness, the sweetest nature that exists, his forbearance, his condescension, and his tenderness. It is impossible for Thérèse to express «all the tenderness» and the «thousand little actions» of love from her father towards her «that crowd into [her] memory.»[16] Since her mother's death, «Our Papa's very *affectionate* heart seemed to be enriched now with a truly maternal love!....»[17]

3. *The «paternal» goodness of... Jesus*

Nevertheless, it would not be very consistent with the truth to think that our nun always refers to the first Person of the Most Holy Trinity when she alludes to the paternal traits in God. She will never cease being very Christocentric. This does not mean that, since 1895, the Father no longer enters into her loving piety, but oftentimes, in exalting God's paternal goodness, Thérèse considers Jesus, the Son, the God-made-Man. Often the texts do not permit us to determine which divine Person she is thinking of con-

[16] A 14 v, 91. Céline (PA, p. 257) and Léonie (PO, p. 342: PA, pp. 378, 380) testified to the special affection of M. Martin for his youngest daughter.

[17] A 13 v, 89. With this experience, Thérèse will have no difficulty in passing from a representation of God as a mother (for example in Is 66:12-13) to his representation as a father. See also these verses from a poem: «O You who knew how to create the mother's heart, / I find in You the tenderest of Fathers! / My only Love, Jesus, Eternal Word, / For me, your heart is more than maternal!» (PN 36).

(*Note of 1994.*) Drawn from the poem «*Jesus Alone,*» these verses on the very «maternal» heart of *Jesus*, «the tenderest of fathers,» illustrate well what we are going to explain in the following pages.

cretely — if she is even thinking about a determined Person! But at other times, not only does the identification of «God» with «Jesus» impose itself clearly,[18] but even when it is a question of goodness, of mercy, or of paternal condescension, Thérèse almost always refers to Jesus: the case is verified, for example, in the narration of the discovery even of the «little way.» The God of Isaiah who is «like a mother» is Jesus.[19]

Thérèse's devotion had therefore undergone an evolution. First, «God» for her is above all Jesus, seen as a Spouse. In the spirituality of «spiritual childhood,» «God» remains Jesus, but without His ceasing to be a Spouse, He is clothed with paternal attributes, and He becomes *like* a father.[20]

---

[18] Among so many examples, let us take one from each of the *Autobiographical Manuscripts*: A 84 r, 212; B 3 v, 226; C 34 v, 282.

[19] C 3 r, 238. See also the example of note 17. In B 5 v, 231, the Eagle that carries on high is still Jesus. In the letter of September 17, 1896, it is also Jesus who returns to look for Thérèse (LT 197, 998). Again: the mercy of God is that of Jesus (LT 230, 1100). The Mercy that attracts her so much is that of Jesus' Heart. In this fire of love, she casts her faults with an entirely *filial* confidence (LT 247, 1132). Stronger still: the *mother* (LT 191, 965) or the *father* (LT 258, 1151), relative to which Thérèse describes the different attitudes of the child, is the image of *Jesus*!

[20] Thérèse's devotion is therefore more predominantly Christocentric than Trinitarian. If special devotion to the first Person as such is revealed less present in Thérèse than one believes it sometimes, her devotion to the third Person seems to be even more absent, although not entirely. Let us make it very clear that we are not speaking of intensity, but of *customary* attention, of *psychological structure* in devotion. One finds however a beautiful Trinitarian prayer: Thérèse asks that the «merciful Father» will give to her, in Jesus' Name (and in the name of Mary and the saints), the Spirit of love (LT 220, 1058). Other Trinitarian references, especially in her Poetry and Prayers, are no longer missing, but it is Jesus who dominates for the most part. In her *Act of Offering to Merciful Love,* Thérèse addresses herself twice to the «Blessed Trinity.» But that is, probably, but a reminiscence of the day, the liturgical feast of the Holy Trinity. Indeed, the light of June 9, 1895 doesn't deal with the intra-Trinitarian life nor does it invite one explicitly to associate in a more intimate way to the Trinitarian mystery. It concerns a work typically *ad extra,* common to the three Persons: the communication of divine mercy to mankind. Moreover, as much in the *Act* as in Manuscript A (84 r, 212), Thérèse's attention is displaced without difficulty from the «Trinity» or from «God» to Jesus. Later, the expression «merciful Love» applies to Jesus (see HA 55, p. 264; LT 261, 1163; one can doubt about LT 197, 998 and 262, 1170).

(*Note of 1994.*) It is interesting to compare with the much more Trinitarian devotion of Blessed Elizabeth of the Trinity (Dijon, 1880-1906), though she too is very Christo-*centric*. On this point, Elizabeth marvelously completes Thérèse, her elder and her sister of Carmel, to whom she is so similar in her distraught love of Christ. See our study «Thérèse de Lisieux et Élisabeth de Dijon,» in *Carmel*, 1981 (new series, double number 22-23, *Cahier du centenaire*), pp. 89-125.

Moreover, this psychological crossover is prepared and made naturally. 1. Already the Carmelite has made the comparison of the Servant of Yahweh with M. Martin: henceforth Jesus of the Holy Face is tied closely to the image of her own suffering father and she can project without difficulty the paternal features of the latter onto the person of Jesus. 2. What is more, at the very moment of making her great discovery of «spiritual childhood,» she had come across the comparison of Jesus to a mother (father) and she identified herself with a child in relationship to Him. 3. Furthermore, Thérèse always remained young both in age and in her psychology: Jesus, the Strong, the Powerful, the Great, her «elder» by many years; without difficulty she can attribute to Him the qualities of a father. 4. Finally, she has been touched deeply by Jesus' paternal actions which she had discovered in the Gospel: His invitation to children, His blessing of them, His exhortation to become like them.[21] The Carmelite possessed several pictures of these evangelical scenes and identified herself with a child such as the one seated on the knees of Jesus (DE 5.7.3; picture reproduced in DLTH, p. 224).

4. *The Humanity of Christ*

The digression that we have just made on the paternal face of Jesus brings us to the manifestation of divine mercy in the humanity of Christ. The God-Man is for Thérèse the acme of divine condescension: Jesus is mercy incarnate.

In her Christmas poems, she sings with tenderness of Our Lord's Incarnation. This was accomplished «for love of us.»[22] On a holy picture, representing His birth, she had copied this small dialogue of Saint Bernard: «Jesus, what has made You so Little? — Love!»[23]

The last picture that Thérèse will paint represents the Host with the Child Jesus in the manger. Thérèse will add to it this mes-

[21] See CSG, p. 42: she had copied these passages. She will make allusion to it in her poem on the Holy Innocents, see PN 44, str. 9.

[22] For example A 44 v, 141; LT 201, 1013.

[23] LT 162, 852; cf. CSG, p. 46.

sage for Father Bellière: «I cannot fear a God who has made Himself so little for me… I love Him! … because He is only love and mercy» (DLTH, p. 251). She quotes Saint Paul: «He was rich and made Himself poor,»[24] «He humbled Himself taking the form and nature of a slave.»[25] One day she will tell Mother Agnès: «For our human nature which needs so much to understand what it loves, the thought that God is only a spirit would make us dizzy. Oh! how He did well to make Himself Man!»[26]

As much as the Incarnation, the Passion and Death of Jesus also speak to her of love. The very first sermon that she understood as a child dealt with the suffering Christ and, she says, it «*touched me deeply*» (A 17 v, 96). At Carmel, her devotion towards the Holy Face of the suffering Christ is known.[27] The Holy Face is a mirror in which one sees «how He loves us.»[28] The contemplative has a special love for the songs of Isaiah about the Servant of Yahweh, Who was burdened with 'our offenses, pierced with wounds for our iniquities, broken for our crimes.'[29] She quotes the letter to the Galatians: «He loved me and He gave Himself up for me»[30]; she quotes Jesus Himself: «Greater love than this no man has than that he lay down his life for his friends.»[31] In her eyes, Jesus' death is «the most beautiful death of love that one has ever seen!»[32] Let us

---

[24] 2 Cor 8:9. See LT 109, 640.

[25] Ph 2:7. See LT 201, 1013.

[26] PA, p. 151 f. See PO, p. 157: «How fortunate that God made Himself man, so that we can love Him: O! how He did well; without it, we would not dare.»

[27] See here p. 111 f.

[28] LT 87, 552. But this mirror is veiled, because Jesus' eyes are lowered: «It is better thus,» Thérèse observes, «because otherwise, what would have become of us? We could not have seen His divine glance, without dying of love» (PO, p. 158).

[29] She has quoted these words for a long time (LT 108, 629) and elsewhere she refers to it again often.

[30] Gal 2:20. See LT 184, 935.

[31] Jn 15:13. See C 12 r, 250; LT 226, 1092; PN 31.

[32] DE 4.7.2. That Thérèse had said, in the month of May 1897 also, that Jesus died «to appease the Father's justice» (*Why I love you, O Mary*, PN 54, str. 23) doesn't affect in any way her fundamental conviction that Jesus dies through love for the Father and mankind. See PHILIPPE DE LA TRINITÉ, «Le Thomisme de Sainte Thérèse de l'Enfant-Jésus en matière de Rédemption,» VT, 1962, October pp. 1-8. The author affirms: «The spirituality of Saint Thérèse of the Child Jesus is in the line of the dogmatic theology of Saint Thomas Aquinas» (ID., *La Rédemption par le Sang*, Paris, 1959, p. 117).

summarize with her: «The only crime with which Jesus was reproached by Herod was that of being *foolish*... and I think like him!... He *was foolish*, our Beloved, to come to earth in search of sinners in order to make them His friends, His intimates, His *equals*, He, who was perfectly happy with the two adorable Persons of the Trinity!» (LT 169, 881).

The word «sinners» is used and Thérèse counted herself among them. Jesus' merciful actions in their regard touch her personally and move her. Innumerable times she will have meditated on them, and this stands out in her writings. Twice, she quotes His words in which she also finds personal comfort: «I came not to call the just, but sinners.»[33] And these other words: «People who are in good health do not need a doctor; sick people do.»[34] She recalls that «in Heaven there will be more joy over one sinner who does penance than over ninety-nine just who have no need of repentance.»[35] And echoing the passage on the lost sheep, we read in a letter to Céline: «Do not fear, for the poorer you are, the more Jesus will love you. He will go far, very far in search of you, if at times you wander off a little.»[36] «The perfumes of Jesus' life» which indicate to her 'on which side she must run,' while even 'all the sins that can be committed' could not keep her from Him, relate to: the Publican, filled with confidence and humble prayer[37]; the prodigal child who returns to the father and who is beloved 'by God'[38]; Mary Magdalene.[39] Magdalene is one of her favorite saints: the «profound words» of Jesus on the forgiveness of her sins «resound with a great sweetness» in Thérèse's soul[40]; her «loving audacity» seduces the Heart of Jesus... and of Thérèse,[41] so much that she does not hesitate to identify the Magdalene with Mary, the sister of Martha, who

---

33 Mt 9:13. See A 39 r, 132; B 5 r, 230.

34 Mt 9:12. See a prayer of July 16, 1895 (Pri 7).

35 Lk 15:7. See A 46 r, 144.

36 LT 211, 1038. See Mt 18:12-14.

37 Lk 8:9-14. See C 36 v, 285.

38 Lk 15:1 l-32. See C, *ibid*.

39 See Lk 7:36-50. For Thérèse, the woman of which Luke speaks here is Magdalene.

40 A 38 v, 131; she quotes, besides, Jesus' own words: LT 130, 731; 224, 1083; RP 4; and in a prayer of July 16, 1895 (Pri 7).

41 C 36 v, 285; LT 247, 1132 (written twenty days before C 36 v).

for that reason is the object of an even greater mercy: «total sinner» that she had been, she reaches «the highest summits of contemplation»[42]; her example of lover is often mentioned.[43] Thérèse also recalls Jesus' acquital of the adulterous woman.[44] As we see it, the good news that Jesus announces to sinners delighted her. In the month of May 1897, she told Sister Geneviève (Céline): «See what Saint John the Evangelist wrote: 'My little children, I tell you this to keep you from sin. But if anyone should sin, we have an advocate Who is Jesus.'» And she appeared very moved.[45]

She also likes to recall that Jesus is «meek and humble of heart»[46] and His comparison of the hen and her chicks moves her to tears.[47] But above all the Eucharist speaks to her of Jesus' 'love unto folly' (B 5 v, 231); the «Jesus of the EUCHARIST» is «the *Merciful God*»! (LT 234, 1110).

Jesus loves us in spite of the «infinite distance» (C 12 r, 249) which separates us. What is the grandeur of this merciful Love? Jesus gave the response and Thérèse cherished it deeply: «O my Father, You love those whom You have given Me with the love with which You have *loved Me Myself*.»[48]

III. FAITH IN MERCY: FOUNDATION OF THE «LITTLE WAY»

To fathom even a little the depth of Thérèse's faith[49] in Merciful Love, it is necessary to analyze God's merciful presence in the

---

42 See LT 247, 1132; LT 169, 881. All this is very apparent in *Jesus at Bethany* (RP 4).

43 A 67 v; 183; 60 v, 171; B 3 r-v, 225; C 36 r, 284; LT 169, 881; 247, 1132.

44 Jn 8:1-11. See LT 230, 1100.

45 Jn 2:1. CSG, p. 223. L. LOCHET writes: «[Thérèse] embodies marvelously in her life this entire Christian attitude of confidence in the Love that the first epistle of Saint John described to us. She understood in the Gospel God's secret» (*Fils de Dieu*, Paris, 1963, p. 40).

46 Mt 12:29. She listens to it «with delight» (DE 15.5.3).

47 Mt 23:37. See 7.6.1. ["How often have I yearned to gather your children (O Jerusalem), as a mother bird gathers her young under her wings, but you refused me."]

48 Jn 17:23-24. CSG, p. 44 and C 35 r, 282.

49 We use here the term «faith» in the narrow sense of acceptance by the intelligence of a revealed truth, containing the idea of an initial submission of will. It is in this

life of Thérèse, as an experience that intimately penetrates her entire existence and as a knowledge of God which is attached to the essence of the God-Man Himself. Thus, Thérèse dares in her weakness to approach God and to present herself to Him in order to be filled with His benevolence. Just as the acceptance of one's own nothingness is a condition required to be able to renounce oneself, in the same way faith in mercy is required to be able to open oneself positively and trustingly to another in whom one recognizes the power and the will to help us. Humility and faith in Merciful Love are the two conditions of being able to engage oneself in the «little way.» They are, so to speak, its foundation.

After all that has been said, it would be superfluous to want to prove again that Thérèse truly possessed this faith: without it, she could never have penetrated into the mystery of Jesus the Merciful, or recognized His presence in her life. Let us limit ourselves to gathering some manifestations of this faith. For Thérèse, God's condescension is «incomprehensible» (A 72 v, 192), «unspeakable» (B 5 v, 232); His (merciful) Love an «ocean without shores» (C 34 r, 281) and in her own regard: «an abyss whose depths I cannot fathom» (C 35 r, 282). 'Jesus is so fatigued,' she thought, 'with always having to take the initiative and to attend to others' (A 75 v, 197); 'He gives His greatest treasures to us for nothing.'[50]

---

sense that one can speak here of a «basis.» If one grants to the expression «to believe in the [merciful] love of God» a richer meaning, implying also the engagement of the will, one can no longer speak of a «basis» or of a «condition,» but of the very *essence* of the «little way.» Let us mention that the Carmelite never uses in her writings, as far as we know, the entire expression «faith [to believe] in divine mercy» or another similar one in the line of faith in the strict sense. She immediately looks at God's mercy with the eyes of *confidence*. While including this faith, she passes over the act of intelligence at the very onset in order to move toward God with all her will: it is an impulse of the heart, her entire being. Her choice of words which express her «faith» in merciful Love indicates this: she «throws herself,» «offers herself» (A 84 r, 212), «abandons herself» (B 5 v, 232), «hopes blindly» (LT 197, 998), «entrusts herself,» she has «confidence.»

[50] PA, p. 335. Bursting into sobs one day, she says that she wanted to die, seeing that God Who is so good was not loved enough (PO, p. 478). Let us note again that the current expression «the good God» has for her a very literal meaning. She shows it by underscoring: «the *good* God is too *good* to...» (C 33 v, 280); «the *good* God is *good* to me» (LT 178, 907). He is the «God of Goodness» (LT 189, 956) «much better than you believe» (LT 191, 965), she writes to Léonie.

She would have liked to have become an apostle of mercy in a 'shelter for unfortunates' (PO, p. 467), and she often repeated this very little phrase which summarizes this chapter: «Everything is grace.»[51]

Before being formulated, before having been proposed to others, the «little way» was thought by Thérèse in the precise perspective of her encounter with the God of mercy, toward the end of the year 1894, and following the experience of her entire life. This is why it was necessary to insist on Thérèse's vision of God. It is there that «spiritual childhood» begins and never ends.

---

[51] Sister Geneviève, PA, p. 293. (See, for example, DE 5.6.4). See LT 201, 1013, from November 1,1896: «More than ever, I understand that the smallest events of our life are conducted by God.» As we know, it is with this sentence: «Everything is grace» that G. BERNANOS ends his *Journal d'un curé de campagne*. Bernanos greatly loved Thérèse of Lisieux and NV was one of his bedside books. H.U. VON BALTHASAR even affirmed: «Saint Thérèse is especially present in the work of Bernanos» (*Le Chrétien Bernanos*, Éd. du Seuil, 1956, p. 289). See also Sister RAYMOND-MARIE, «Bernanos et l'Esprit d'enfance,» *Carmel*, 1959, pp. 292-317; G. GAUCHER, «Bernanos et Sainte Thérèse de l'Enfant-Jésus,» *Revue des lettres modernes*, 1 (1960), pp. 3-44; P. BLANCHARD, «Georges Bernanos et l'Esprit d'enfance,» VT, 1964, pp. 69-74.

CHAPTER III

The Confidence that Produces a Result

Thérèse apparently doomed herself to failure: the more she loves, the more she sees herself far from the goal, as we have already seen. Only the hope that God Himself will make up for what is lacking in her love remains to her. And God seems to encourage her in this hope by the manner in which He reveals Himself to her. In this chapter we shall demonstrate how much the incompleteness of Thérèse and the divine attraction converge in confidence, which is the core of the «little doctrine.»

I. CONFIDENCE: THE CORE OF THE «WAY OF SPIRITUAL CHILDHOOD»

1. Incompleteness and helpful hope

As we have already said: the constant experience of her weakness and faults (minimal it is true, but real for Thérèse) and the infinitude of her ideal of love leads to the keen sense of her own incompleteness. It is unavoidable. Already toward the end of the year 1895, Thérèse had expressed it in one of the psychologically and theologically richest sentences in all her writings: «The more one advances in this way [of perfection], the more one sees the goal is still far off, and now I am simply resigned to seeing myself always imperfect and in this I find my joy…» (A 74 r, 195).

«To resign» herself to it, truly? Yes, as far as a perfection that, objectively, would no longer be capable of growth is concerned. For God alone is infinitely perfect. But as for progress toward that degree of personal perfection that God has established for each of us according to His wise providence, Thérèse does not give up. She 'does everything that is in her power,' and if she must confess herself after all is said and done as a 'useless servant,' 'she hopes nevertheless that the Good God will give her, through His grace, all that she desires' (CSG, p. 57). So, according to the vital experience that she expresses shortly before her death, 'she has never been able to do anything all alone' (DE 11.8.3) and therefore she does not lean on her «strength which is only weakness» (LT 247, 1132). She leans, rather, «on the strength of Him Who, on the Cross, has overcome the powers of hell.»[1] If it is necessary for God to transform her so that she is prepared to die, Thérèse *awaits* this transformation from Him (LT 224, 1083)! Now she is putting into practice what she expressed in 1890: «It is only our Jesus who knows how to return infinitely more than we give Him…» (LT 109, 640.) She hopes, then, that Jesus will give her this love which she is incapable of acquiring by her powers alone, and this hope spontaneously takes the form of a prayer which is touching in its beauty: «If we had the love of all hearts, this love would be Yours… Ah well! give us this love.»[2] Or:

> Ah! give me a thousand hearts to love You!
> But that is still too little, Jesus, Beauty Supreme.
> Give me your divine Heart Itself to love You.[3]

And especially:

> It's your love, Jesus, that I crave.
> It's your love that has to transform me.
> Place in my heart your consuming flame,
> And I'll be able to bless You and love You.
> Yes, I'll be able to love You and bless You
> As they do in Heaven.

---

[1] This is a quotation from Théophane Vénard, which Thérèse makes her own in the month of June 1897, see LT 245, 1128.

[2] *Consecration to the Holy Face*, from August 6, 1896 (Pri 12).

[3] *Remember*, of October 21, 1895 (PN 24, str. 31).

I'll love You with that very love
With which You have loved me, Jesus, Eternal Word.[4]

2. *Condescension and confidence*

Thérèse is therefore led by her very incompleteness to hope that God will make up for her deficiency. But because she addresses herself to a God of mercy, this hope becomes *confidence,* a virtue which implies faith not only in the strength of the other, but also in His fidelity and in His benevolence, and which thus contains, with a greater certainty of being granted what she asks, a more pronounced nuance of familiarity. In her last years, when Thérèse used the words *«espérer- espoir-espérance»* [various forms of the word "hope"], it is important to understand the qualities implied by them.

As for her vision of divine mercy, it does not need to be emphasized again. Let us rather see how a great confidence springs from this vision. Evidently, Thérèse is not bound to the two words mercy-confidence. Although they express her intention marvelously, she uses other, equivalent ones. It is rather rare that she associates the two words in the same context[5]; many times however, she uses one of the two, using for the other a synonymous expression. Thus, one finds for mercy: love, heart, goodness, tenderness, folly, condescension, to humble oneself, father, mother, arms, to carry, etc. And for confidence: hope, trust, to hope, to wait, abandonment, to abandon oneself, audacity, to sleep (on the heart or in the arms of someone), folly, love, to be (or to become) a child, little, to throw oneself, or simply the refusal of a contrary action or prayer, etc. This overview of her lexicon, while neglecting the nuances, allows us to discern the general direction of Thérèse's confidence.

Personal incompleteness and divine mercy both push her

---

[4] *How I Want to Love,* 1896 (PN 41). On a more philosophical plane, the phenomenology of friendship also illuminates the human powerlessness to give oneself *completely* to the other. One always wants to give more. Thus each true love implies a more or less pronounced dimension of waiting and of infinite desire that the Infinite alone can fill. See L. VAN DER KERKEN, *Menselijke liefde en vriendschap. Een filosofisch essay over de persoonlijke menselijke verhoudingen*, Anvers, 1962, pp. 120-122.

[5] A 46 r, 144; B 5 v, 232; LT 226, 1092; 247, 1132; 261, 1163.

towards confidence. But if we now wonder to which of the two stimuli must we attribute the priority, we have to say without any hesitation: mercy. For imperfection alone cannot be a source of confidence to her. What is not cannot be a *raison d'être*. My incompleteness can be the basis of my confidence only insofar as the recourse toward another that it provokes in me is supported by another movement in me, a movement justified by the positive and attractive qualities of the one upon whom I count for my completion. It is in this sense that Thérèse's words must be interpreted when she says that her nothingness causes her joy. The observation of her nothingness brings her to confidence in Him who loves to lower Himself toward misery that entrusts itself. And even if she is delighted to have the opportunity to progress in *humility*, she is especially delighted that, becoming more humble, her confidence will be more pure and strong. This is what is verified in the last years of her life, at least, because on this point also she must have developed. When, in 1890, she 'rejoiced with Saint Paul in her infirmities,' it was because her weakness brought her to love Jesus more generously and more exclusively.[6] When, in 1897, she 'glories in her weakness' (C 15 v, 254), it is especially because of divine mercy that finds in her a greater prey, a prey that through confidence gladly yields to the loving undertakings of God.

Thus Thérèse draws her confidence from divine condescension as its deepest source. «Close to this Heart, we learn courage, and especially *confidence*» (LT 200, 1013). This is her surety: «The Lord is the Rock to which I am raised. He teaches my hands to fight, and my fingers to make war. He is my protector, and I hope in Him!»[7] The rock: sure, unshakable, of one piece, a symbol of fidelity. And Thérèse takes her stand upon it.

In the face of death, the interplay between incompleteness and confidence in divine mercy seems to increase further. «I can depend on nothing, on no good works of my own in order to have confidence.... But this poverty was a real light for me. I was thinking that never in my life would I be able to pay my debts to the good God; but this was real riches, real strength for me, if I wanted to

---

[6] 2 Cor 12:5; see LT 109, 640. See here pp. 108-109.

[7] Ps 143:1-2. Thérèse quotes these verses, C 8 v, 245.

take it in this way. Then I made this prayer: O my God, I beg You, pay the debt that I have acquired with regard to the souls in Purgatory, but do it as God, so that it be infinitely better than if I had [fulfilled my obligations] myself [that is, if she had said her Offices for the Dead]. And then I remembered with great consolation these words of the canticle of Saint John of the Cross: *'Pay all debts'*! I had always applied this to Love. I felt that this grace can't be expressed in words.... It's far too delightful! We experience such great peace when we're totally poor, when we depend on no one except the good God.»[8] And more or less at the same time: «I felt [during the recitation of the *Confiteor*], like the publican, I felt I was a great sinner. I found God to be so merciful! ... How extraordinary it is to have experienced that at the *Confiteor*! I believe that it's because of my present disposition: I feel so miserable! My confidence is not lessened, on the contrary; and the word "miserable" is not exact, because I am rich with all the divine treasures: but it's exactly because of this that I humble myself even more.»[9]

3. *The central place of confidence*

The central place of confidence in the «little doctrine» also follows from its different descriptions and definitions, although the formulation sometimes uses terms like «abandonment» and even «love» and others too, but ones that are revealed in their context as being more or less synonymous with «confidence.» We shall return to their nuances.

Let us look first at the *ex professo* explanation of the «little way,» Manuscript B: 'The boldness of offering oneself as victim of God's condescending [merciful] Love' (B 3 v, 226), 'the folly to trust that (God's) Love will accept her (as a victim)' (B 5 v, 231 f.), 'the abandonment with total confidence to infinite Mercy' (*ibid.*), 'the surrender of the little child without fear in its Father's arms' (B 1 v, 220), 'the blind hope that she has in His Mercy' (LT 197, 998).

---

[8] DE 6.8.4 or PO, p. 203. The quotation of John of the Cross is borrowed from the second stanza of VF.

[9] DE 12.8.3 and PO, p. 207.

Thérèse is going to summarize everything in this very stark formula: «It is confidence and nothing but confidence that must lead us to Love» (*ibid.*). In her correspondence, she insists on the same meaning. She writes to Leonie that perfection consists in «*taking hold of Jesus by His Heart,*» for «us who are living under the law of love, [in order to] profit by the loving advances that our Spouse is making to us» (LT 191, 965). To Father Roulland: in order to reach perfection, «it is sufficient to recognize one's nothingness and to abandon oneself as a child in God's arms»; «my way is all confidence and love» (LT 226, 1092). To Father Bellière: before «the abysses of love and mercy of the *Heart of Jesus,*» one must act with a «loving audacity,» «with an entirely filial confidence» (LT 247, 1132); to reach the treasures of Jesus' merciful Love, one must follow «the way of simple and loving confidence» (LT 261, 1163).

Let us consult her oral teaching now. To her sister Marie: «As imperfect as we are, Jesus will transform us into flames of love, provided we hope for all from His goodness» (PA, p. 234). To her novices: her apostolate was «a constant preaching of confidence in God»[10] and «it is confidence in God that she insisted upon most in her conferences of the Novitiate»[11]; to be a little child is to be humble and «to expect everything from (the good) God» (DE 6.8.8). And when they finally ask her: What is the «little way»?, she answers: «It is the way of confidence and total abandonment.»[12]

In the final analysis, confidence bridges the gap between reality and the ideal. Or better: God is invited by Thérèse's confidence to intervene. But this bridge is never definitive. When God fills the gap a little, the drama is revived: the more Thérèse loves, the more she *wants* to love. The goal seems to move away as she approaches it. Confidence must make a new bridge every time. Thérèse understands perfectly well the two perfections: that of God, which can always be communicated further without ever being exhausted; and that of a human being which consists, according to her mas-

[10] Mother Agnès, PA, p. 161. See: «Confidence in God had become like the special seal of her soul» (PO, p. 155).

[11] Father Godefroid Madelaine, PA, p. 559. For this witness, the «little way» is confidence which he identifies with abandonment (*ibid.*).

[12] HA 98, chap. XII; DE II 17.7.2.

terly definition, «in being what [God] wills us to be» (A 2 v, 72). It is as if Thérèse believes, as long as she lives, that she has not yet reached that perfection. (Besides, how could she be sure of it....) It would seem, from the Carmelite's existential perspective, that God always wants us to be more than we actually are. Thus, our own present love can never be the road which unites to the ultimate love, to the ideal of perfection which Thérèse dreams of. Yes, it is love indeed which must reach its ideal of perfection, but the Saint is condemned to always beg God for it. She will remain the Saint of love *and* confidence. The «little way» is the last way of perfection she thought of on earth and the last one she could have thought of. And because it is thought of relative to the *ideal*, «spiritual childhood» is, in the end, a way of confidence.

This confidence — as we have already said and as we heard Thérèse say — is very loving. One is truly before a Father, before a love filled with mercy. Before Him, all fear must vanish. «I am far from being on the way of fear» (A 80 v, 205), writes Thérèse; «ever since I have been given the grace to understand the love of the Heart of Jesus, I admit that it has expelled all fear from my heart» (LT, 247, 1132). We shall return to this.[13]

II. DESIRE AS A PLEDGE

Thérèse's doctrine on confidence presents another psychological foundation, and it is a rather curious phenomenon: *the desire itself is the sign of a future realization.*

From where does this thought come? One could answer that Thérèse did nothing more than formulate an experience here. In fact, she likes to repeat that all her desires have been fulfilled: «The good God showed me the same mercy that He showed to King Solomon. He has not willed that I have one single desire which is not filled, not only my desires for perfection, but also those whose vanity I have *understood* without having experienced it» (A 81 r,

[13] This way which excludes fear accords well with Thérèse's natural inclination: «My nature was such that fear made me recoil; with *love* not only did I advance, I actually *flew*... » (A 80 v, 206).

206 f.). He alone «could fulfill my immense desires» (A 82 v, 209). And hours before her death: «Even my littlest desires have been fulfilled.»[14] She recognizes there on the part of God an «immensity of love» for her (DE 16.7.2). It is undoubtedly the same intuition that makes her perceive in the desires not granted — because they indeed exist![15] — a greater love, and therefore a better fulfillment.

But this answer does not explain everything. We must resort to an authority. It will be the Gospel, then, in which Thérèse believes blindly. Here is a passage which alludes to Mt 7:8 and Jn 16:23, and evokes so many other formal assurances that Thérèse could have come across in her scriptural meditations: «Through beautiful parables, and often without even using this means which was so well known to the people, [Jesus] teaches us that it is enough to knock and the door will be opened, to seek in order to find, and to hold out one's hand humbly to receive what is asked for.... He also says that everything we ask *His Father* in His Name, He will grant.»[16] Texts such as these inspired in her this assurance: «one has only to ask for it» (PA, p. 181).

However, her theology of desire does not stop there! Not only does God *grant* the desire, but it is He Himself who *inspires* it. It is quite likely that she had found this conviction in Saint John of the Cross — this conviction which will have such an important role in the construction of her «little doctrine.» Sister Geneviève testifies that Thérèse made these words of the mystical Doctor her own: «The more God wishes to bestow on us, the more He makes us desire.»[17] In her *Act of Offering*, Thérèse expressly quotes this text

---

[14] DE 30.9: French critical edition, p. 391. See also A 71 r, 190; C 22 v, 264; 33 v, 280; DE 31.8.9. Even sureness as for the future life: «All my hopes will be realized... Yes, the Lord will do for us marvels that will infinitely surpass our *immense desires*!» (LT 230, 1100 of May 28, 1897).

[15] That God tests her and makes her wait before answering her, as was the case with her entrance into Carmel, doesn't have any importance. When God doesn't answer her (see 11.8.5: «I often pray to the saints without receiving any answers»; 25.8.7 and 22.9.3), Thérèse loves more. The paradox of desires not granted and the affirmation of always being heard finds its solution in the conviction already manifested in a letter of 1888: God doesn't grant us our petitions, because He loves us too much; giving us of the best, suffering, He treats us as His chosen friends (LT 67, 477).

[16] C 35 v, 283. In her *Act of Offering to Merciful Love*, Thérèse bases her demand on this same verse of Saint John. From these words of Jesus, she concludes radically: «I am certain, then, that you will grant my desires!»

with Jn 16:23. Several times again she repeats it: it is God who makes her desire.[18] Both the desire and its realization are therefore pure gifts from God: «He is the One Who makes us desire and Who grants our desires...» (LT 201, 1013).

A last feature finishes the outline of Thérèse's thought: it is *impossible* that the desire, inspired by God, is not realized. This is another formulation of what we find in Saint John of the Cross. This idea, which appears for the first time in her writings in 1891,[19] greatly helped her in the search for and the conception of her «little way.» One finds it at the time of her more sensitive moments. First, at the time when she noticed that she was still far from holiness, without knowing how to remedy it: however, a solution had to exist, *because* «God cannot inspire unrealizable desires» (C 2 v, 237). Less than one year later, the same conviction is latent in her *Offering to Merciful Love*: feeling in her heart «immense desires,» it is «with confidence» that she invites God to take possession of her. In the month of September 1896, she offers the same argument to Marie, who fears being unable to follow the program of Manuscript B: «God would not give you the desire to be *possessed* by Him, by His *merciful Love*, if He were not reserving this favor for you; or rather He has already given it to you, since you have given yourself to *Him*, since you *desire* to be consumed by *Him*, and since God never gives desires that He cannot realize...» (LT 197, 998).

Before illustrating Thérèse's thought on the productive power of confidence, it is important to notice two things.

1. The one who conceives the desires has an extremely well developed *feeling* about divine things,[20] which makes her very in-

---

[17] CSG, p. 58. This thought of Saint John of the Cross is found in the Saint's letter to Mother Eléonore (*Oeuvres*, I, p. 335). It is found almost verbatim in the Saint's maxim (*ibid.*, p. 391).

[18] For example, A 71 r, 190; 31 v, 277; LT 253, 1139; DE 13.7.15 and 18.7.1.

[19] LT 129, 728. Another time, she draws her assurance of her desires being granted from the fact that God, inspiring these desires, cannot desire *useless* sufferings (A 84 v, 213). See also: «God would not have given me this desire to do good on earth after my death, if He didn't will to realize it; He would rather have given me the desire to rest in Him» (DE 18.7.1).

[20] JOHN WU said in his opuscule *The Science of Love. A Study on the Teaching of Thérèse of Lisieux* (Dublin, 1941, p. 31): «Her soul was like an extremely sensitive film that records even the slightest movements of grace.»

sightful in discerning God's will. She senses that she is living in an atmosphere of great truth. It will therefore be rather difficult for her to imagine desires which are not likely to be fulfilled, for God illuminates her and assists her internally in her choice. Back in 1894, she wrote: «"We do not know how to ask for anything as we ought, but the Spirit pleads within us with groanings that cannot be expressed in speech" (Saint Paul). We have, then, only to surrender our soul, to *abandon* it to our great God.»[21] Saint John of the Cross emphasized this 'secret elimination' in the domain of desires conceived by saints: if the requested thing is not according to God's will, they do not have the strength to desire it intensely.[22] Moreover, does not Thérèse's confession at the end of the year 1895 go in the same direction? «I can no longer ask for anything with fervor except the perfect accomplishment of God's will» (A 83 v, 210). Thus, she chooses her desires instinctively. Practically speaking, she no longer has anything but holy desires, which will be surely granted if the soul asks insistently for them.

2. And there is this second factor: He Who answers finds Himself before a very pure soul, desiring only His will. Such a soul possesses a great power of love over God. Thérèse betrays her own secret when she says that God showed her «once again how pleased He is to grant the desires of souls who love Him alone» (LT 189, 956). She follows a way «of total confidence,» and we are going to see how very great, according to her, this virtue's power of supplication is.

III. THE PRODUCTIVE POWER OF CONFIDENCE

Is the solution which Thérèse proposes to her powerlessness and which consists in confidence in God a good one? Does the

---

[21] LT 165, 860. The quotation is Rm 8:26.

[22] See *The Ascent of Mount Carmel*, Book III, 2. We shall return to this. Concerning this «elimination» in our desires and our prayers, see E. SCHILLEBEECKX, *God en mens* (*Theologische peilingen*, II), Bilthoven, 1965, 2 ed., pp. 180-181, that cites Thérèse of Lisieux as an example. See also Saint Teresa of Avila, speaking of Saint Joseph: «When my petition is somewhat awry, he sets it right for the greatest good of my soul» (*Vie*, chap. VI, trans. Grégoire, Paris, 1949, p. 59).

«little way» lead to the goal? Let us analyze her thought on this point, still reserving the more theological analysis for Chapter V.

1. *The example of Saint Thérèse of Lisieux*

More than all other arguments, the example of the Saint herself is illuminating. She who conceived the way has demonstrated its effectiveness by her life. Her heroic fidelity to the least signs of the divine will and her very great fraternal charity have demonstrated that God had indeed realized her hope and that He had led her to the summits of sanctity. The Church has confirmed it. Thérèse herself recognized the «great things» that the Lord had done in her (C 22 r, 264; LT 224, 1083) and that 'the breath of the Spirit, which goes where it wills' had filled her with grace.[23]

2. *The power of confident prayer*

Besides the supreme argument of her example, there is the *conviction* of this prophetic soul. We could summarize it in this maxim of her master John of the Cross — a great authority for her! — whom the Saint loved very much and often repeated: «One obtains from God as much as one hopes for.»[24] «Really keep your confidence,» she said to Marie of the Trinity, when the latter was passing through great difficulties concerning her vocation. «It is impossible that God will not respond to it, because He always measures His gifts according to our confidence» (PA, p. 472 f.). The

---

[23] Mother Agnès, PO, p. 208.

[24] See Sister Geneviève, PA, p. 271, and Sister Marie of the Trinity, PO, p. 453 and PA, p. 472. This sentence was part of a maxim of the mystical Doctor which we fully reproduce: «God is so pleased with the hope of a soul that is unceasingly turned toward Him, without ever lowering its eyes to another object, that one can say in truth of this soul: it obtains as much as it hopes for» (*Oeuvres*, I, 391). This sentence returns literally and in the same context in *The Ascent of Mount Carmel*, Book III, chap. 6, and in a poem: «The hope of Heaven obtains as much as it hopes» (I, French edition, pp. 486-487). See also *The Dark Night*, Book II, chap. 21 and VF, str. 2, n 31 (V.) and *The Ascent of Mount Carmel*, Book III, chap. 2 (n 10). We should notice that the quoted maxim is immediately followed by this one: «The more God wants to give us, the more He increases our desires,» another favorite text of Thérèse. In reading these maxims on hope, one is struck by their parallelism with the reflections of Thérèse.

young sister will persevere; Thérèse will perhaps then have been reminded of what she had written in 1891 to Céline, probably without meaning it in the same deep way: «Confidence works miracles» (LT 129, 728). The same conviction sustains her prayer, this «invincible» weapon (C 24 v, 267) which 'lifts the world' (C 36 v, 284). «She employed a holy audacity. She told me that it was necessary in our prayers to imitate the foolish who don't know where to stop in their requests,»[25] or «the beggars who, on the strength of their importunity, can obtain what they desire» (LT 99, 596). «It is impossible,» Thérèse will say toward the end of her life, «that all my great desires, about which I've so frequently spoken to the good God, will not be completely answered» (DE 16.7.2). In the same way, humility attracts God's gifts.[26] And concerning Mother Geneviève: «Ah! Surely, God does not disappoint a trust so filled with humility» (A 78 v, 202).

It goes without saying that she leans entirely on the condescension of Him who does not allow Himself to be «outdone in generosity» (LT 226, 1092), and whose faithful assistance appears to her a «delightful promise.»[27] To Marie of the Trinity she explained that «it was to misunderstand God's infinite goodness to restrict her desires and her expectations. My infinite desires are my riches, and for me Jesus' word will be realized: "to those who have, more will be given and they shall have in abundance"» (PA, p. 472). She said «that it was not necessary to fear desiring too much, or asking too much of God: "Here on earth, there are people who know how to ingratiate themselves into everyone's affection. They know how to obtain all they desire.... So when we importune God

[25] Sister Geneviève, PA, p. 278. See also Marie of the Angels: Thérèse had «an unlimited confidence in prayer and said often that God... could not refuse anything to a fervent prayer» (PA, p. 351). She often thought that she herself owed 'perhaps all the graces that she had received to the prayers of a little unknown soul' (DE 15.7.5).

[26] For example, LT 243, 1121; 261, 1163; PN 54; RP 7; 6.

[27] LT 191, 965. Thérèse seems to be aware of having very well scrutinized divine condescension; the following fact testifies to it. One of her sisters said to her one day: «You have shown us the way of love and confidence in a delightful and entirely new manner. The venerable Mother Marie de Sales Chappuis had good reason to say: "that she saw in God *loves that are still hidden*"; that which has been discovered by you is certainly one of these hitherto unknown loves...» and Thérèse's only response was a beautiful smile (French edition of DE 25.9.1).

for something He had not intended to give us, He is so powerful and so rich that it is a matter of honor for Him not to refuse us, and He gives..."» (CSG, p. 54). Mother Agnès attests that Thérèse was struck by a word of Our Lord to Saint Mechtilde which recalls the maxim of Saint John of the Cross: «I tell it to you in truth, it is a great pleasure for Me that people expect great things from Me. However great is their faith or their presumption, as much and more still I will remunerate them beyond their merits. It is indeed impossible that people don't receive what they believe and hope for from My power[28] and My mercy» (FA, p. 617). One can understand why Thérèse was 'delighted' (CSG, p. 38) by this passage from the Book of Sirach (11:21-22): «Trust in God and stay in your place, for it is easy for the Lord in an instant to make the poor man rich. The blessing of God hastens to reward the just, and in a swift hour His blessing bears fruit.»

3. *Divine magnificence*

Marie of the Trinity is once more the happy confidante of Thérèse when she speaks directly of the effects of her «little way.» «One is happy to feel weak and miserable because the more one recognizes it humbly, expecting everything gratuitously from God without any merit on our part, the more God lowers Himself toward us to fill us with His gifts magnificently» (PA, p. 488). And

---

[28] *Divine omnipotence*, the sister of divine mercy, is so obvious for Thérèse that she never thought much about clarifying it. One nevertheless encounters it in her writings. Thus, for example, at the time of her difficulties in entering Carmel: «Fortunately, as far as God is concerned, these obstacles don't exist» (LT 27, 288). Thérèse «wasn't surprised by God's marvels, finding that His power is always at the service of His infinite love for us» (Mother Agnès, PA, p. 162). She repeated Jesus' word: «God can raise up children to Abraham from these very stones» (Mt 3:9. See Sister Geneviève, PO, p. 289). She knew that God could transform her «in an instant» (see the *Act of Offering* and LT 224, 1083) and that it is not necessary «to measure divine power according to our own narrow minds» (C 4 r, 239): «The One whom I love is not at a loss as to the means He uses,» she wrote (C 31 r, 277). She liked to say that her Spouse is *rich*! (for example: A 29 v, 115; B 4 r, 227; LT 65, 467; 125, 715; 131, 739). It is true, no one can govern God: «He is free, and no one is to ask Him why He gives His graces to one soul rather than another» (LT 57, 448). But as for Thérèse... 'He doesn't make divisions': «He can give without any measure everything I ask Him...» (C 33 v, 280).

Thérèse compares her young novice to a little child who does not even succeed in climbing the first step of the staircase: «Agree to be this little child. By the practice of all virtues, always lift your little foot to climb the staircase of holiness. You won't even manage to mount the first step, but the good God only asks for good intention. Soon overcome by your useless efforts, He will come down Himself, and taking you in His arms, will carry you away forever in His kingdom» (*ibid.*). Elsewhere, she compared God to a giant who gives to the little child with only one arm what this little one is incapable of catching by itself (CSG, p. 231).

Thus, the «little way» leads «great saints» to holiness! As her personal commentary on the workers of the eleventh hour — a Gospel passage that «delighted» her — the «little» Saint said: «See, if we place all our confidence in God, and constantly put forth our best efforts, while hoping for everything from His Mercy and not from our miserable works: we too shall receive the reward of the greatest saints.»[29] It is even possible that littleness attracts God's attention more than 'the actions and the admirable writings of the saints' (CSG, p. 209). «I somehow feel,» she also said, «that these special places [those for which the mother of Zebedee's sons had asked], refused to the great saints and martyrs, are reserved for little children…» (CSG, p. 53). 'What the great saints won by their works, Thérèse will obtain by a stratagem of love' (CSG, p. 47).

4. Nature and grace

We will return to the value of confidence, but it would be hardly excusable not to draw attention to a very important point of Thérésian doctrine: it is not essential to *observe* spiritual progress. Here, Thérèse shows her astonishing psychological penetration. She knew so well that someone can be a greater friend of God than one could presume based on appearances. Had her own childhood experience of a troubled psyche been a lasting lesson for her? Thérèse knew perfectly well how to distinguish between «chronic moral infirmities» and «spiritual imperfections» (C 28 r, 272), thus

[29] Sister Geneviève, PA, p. 310.

the sister 'with the faculty of displeasing her in everything and in her *very disagreeable* ways, words, and character' could be «a holy religious who must be *very pleasing* to God» (C 13 v-14 r, 252). «On the Last Day, you will perhaps be astonished,» she told Geneviève, «to see your Sisters delivered from all their faults and imperfections and appear to you as great saints» (CSG, p. 139). She affirmed furthermore that «very often, what appears as negligence to our eyes, is heroic in God's eyes. A sister who has a migraine or who suffers spiritually, does more, while accomplishing half of her task, than another one, healthy of body and mind, who does it in its entirety» (PO, p. 284). «It is a great trial to see everything on the *black* side,» she wrote to Sister Martha, «but this does not depend on you completely. Do what you *can*» (LT 241, 1117). And concerning Sister Aimée of Jesus: «The peel is rough, but I assure you that the fruit is excellent. The good God doesn't judge as we judge one another based on appearances.»[30]

To every human being who endures his or her weakness and who, like Marie of the Trinity, would like to have more energy to practice virtue, Thérèse answers: «And if the good God wants you weak and helpless like a child… do you believe that you will have less merit?… Agree to stumble at every step therefore, even to fall, to carry your cross weakly, to love your helplessness. Your soul will draw more profit from it than if, carried by grace, you would accomplish with enthusiasm heroic actions that would fill your soul with personal satisfaction and pride.»[31] And who knows if after so many years of good will and confidence we won't experience a «grace of Christmas» as Thérèse did: «But,» she notes — and it is an important remark — «I had to buy, so to speak, this inestimable grace through my desires» (A 43 v, 139).

This has brought us to the problem of works on the way of holiness, and then, to the investigation of the work of confidence itself.

[30] See her *Obituary Circular*, p. 5.

[31] PO, p. 468.

Chapter IV

Poverty and Works

After the reading of the previous pages, two questions present themselves. The first: Didn't Thérèse of Lisieux stress confidence too much to the detriment of works? The second: *how* does confidence bring about spiritual progress? The answer will occupy the two chapters that follow. One could believe, in fact, that the Carmelite retains from the New Testament above all «faith without works» in a too literal interpretation of the epistle to the Romans (3-4), without keeping in mind the exhortations to works given by the same Saint Paul or the affirmation by Saint James (2:17) according to whom «faith without works is dead» — an affirmation which itself is easily subject to one-sided interpretations.

I. Way of Confidence and Love

Thérèse of Lisieux seems to present a very beautiful balance of work and confidence: one loves as much as one can, and proves it by works, but in one's impotence or insufficiency, one trusts in the One Who is infinitely Merciful. The «little way» is conceived first, it is true, as a way of loving confidence, in spite of the deficiency of works, of perfect love, of holiness. But until the fixed point where one rises toward God by confidence alone, «spiritual childhood» is also the way of love. While laying emphasis on confidence, it does not exclude love.[1] It is from this basis of love, even imper-

1 All her life testifies to this, and it is the climate in which her confidence is immersed; we don't have to return to that. Let us notice only that, alongside the loving nature

fect love, that one aspires to perfect love through confidence in mercy. And in the measure that confidence is revealed effective, thanks to God, and increases love, this one must, according to a very solid Thérésian principle, blossom through works in a life of love. Moreover, confidence itself is, in a certain sense, a work of love, as we will explain. On the other hand, true confidence leads to love and its works: I can only have confidence in someone whom I already love initially, having recognized his or her kindness toward me, and if I am not inclined to maintain my love, I feel it languish and with it my faith in the other, and, as a consequence, the basis of my confidence.

If, then, Thérèse can seem sometimes to underestimate works, we must understand this in the context of her whole thought: we must distinguish to whom she speaks and what category of works she considers, we must recognize the dimensions in which a saint sees herself before God, and we must respect her loving will to give all glory to infinite Mercy.

Before studying in detail the coexistence of confidence and works, we would like to emphasize the relevance of Thérèse's response in two areas.

The first is the threat of a certain «mystique of weakness» where the overly easy acceptance of sin and imperfection relies on a confidence which is not pure enough. Karl Rahner pointed out the danger of this after the Second World War and his words have not lost any of their relevance.[2]

The second area is ecumenical. Hans Urs von Balthasar has emphasized very well the similarities. «One has to be blind not to see that the Thérésian doctrine of the "little way" often sees eye to eye with the fundamental theses of the Reformation, and also that it contains in a remarkable way the audacious and sure answer of the Church to Protestant spirituality. The rejection of the Old Testament mentality of justification by works [*Werkgesinnung*]; the demolition of all one's own perfection to make room for the per-

---

of confidence, Thérèse sometimes emphasizes expressly the role of love in her «little way»: «My way is all confidence and love» (LT 226, 1092), «the abandonment and the love of a child who knows that his Father loves him» (LT 258, 1151), «the life of confidence and love» (*ibid.*), etc.

[2] *Gefahren im heutigen Katholizimus*, Einsiedeln, 1950, pp. 31-48.

fection of God in mankind; transcendence in the structure of the act of faith whose center resides in God, whose supernatural plan asks from man an orientation toward God which is ever more intense; the existential plenitude of the act of faith, which, beyond the intellectual acceptance of the content of the faith, implies an act of total and personal fidelity towards the divine and personal truth; finally, the benevolence [*Unwichtignehmen*] towards one's own faults, yes, the joy that they cause, in the sense of a *felix culpa*: these are like so many lines of union between Thérèse and the Reformers.»[3] In these respects, Thérèse's «little way» «can be taken as a Catholic answer to the requests and demands of Luther.»[4]

II. THE PARADOX

1. *Holiness without works*

On the one hand, the humble and sincere nun confesses herself to be poor in works. Preparing for her First Communion, she had made the resolution to make an effort to have, at the end of her life, «a lot of good works to present to the good God.»[5] And how does the balance sheet look? To take her word for it, like a complete failure. She will appear before God with «empty hands» (the *Act*). She will have only her «desires» to present (LT 218, 1054). «If I had been intent on storing up merit for myself, how terribly disheartened I would be at present» (CSG, p. 64). «I can depend on nothing, on no good works of my own in order to have confidence» (DE 6.8.4). And if God must reward her according to her

---

[3] *Therese von Lisieux…*, p. 256.

[4] *Ibid.*, p. 82. See: «Did not the daughter of Saint Teresa of Avila, who prayed with so much fervor for those whom the Reform had separated from Rome, in this way have a providential role which she probably didn't suspect, and prepared the way to contacts with our separated brothers by dispelling excesses and hardenings that could legitimately upset them and by putting in a better light the price that we grant to the religious values that are to them rightfully and particularly dear» (G. LEFEBVRE, *La Foi dans les oeuvres*, Desclée De Brouwer, 1962, p. 11). See also B. MILLER, «L'Évangile vécu chez Sainte Thérèse de Lisieux,» *Bible et vie chrétienne*, 25, 1959, pp. 76-86; and UNE MONIALE BÉNÉDICTINE, «Sainte Thérèse de l'Enfant-Jésus et l'OEcuménisme,» VT, 1965, pp. 117-137.

[5] Mss 11, 22.

works (Mt 16:27), «He will be very much embarrassed in my case, because I haven't any works.» What then? There is only one solution: «I have confidence that He will reward me according to His own works» (DE 15.5.1).

But, the way Thérèse sees it, works are not necessary, because God seems to be able to sanctify us without them. «He has no need of our works» (B 1 v, 220). «For a long time she understood that God needs no one.» She likes to repeat this.[6] He «has no need of our beautiful thoughts and our dazzling works» (LT 141, 783). He «has no need of books or teachers» (A 83 v, 211). Often He is satisfied with our good will.[7] He «looks more upon the intention than upon the greatness of the act» (C 28 v, 273). The desire can make up for the deficiency of the work, and even surpass it in value.[8] Thérèse finds strong support in Saint Paul: «God will have mercy on whom He will have mercy, and He will show pity to whomever He will show pity. So then there is question not of him who wills nor of him who runs, but of God showing mercy.»[9] Other passages delighted her as well, ones which she kept in her breviary: «Blessed are those to whom God reputes justice without works, for to those who work, the reward is not regarded as a grace, but as their due.... It is, then, *gratuitously* that those who do not work are justified by grace in virtue of the redemption of which Christ Jesus is the author.»[10]

---

[6] C 3 v, 238; A 53 r, 157; LT 221, 1069; CSG, p. 205.

[7] C 8 v, 245; 10 v, 248; 25 v, 269; LT 152, 832. The purification of the will is found in this good will (LT 167, 870).

[8] See CSG, p. 66. Compare CSG, p. 72: «You will do as much good as I and even more, by your *desire* to accomplish such good and by lovingly exercising yourself in the practice of the most hidden virtue.» And this word of Our Lord to Saint Gertrude which Thérèse comments on: «He who possesses this *good will* might derive more profit from such a desire than other souls gain from the performance of good works» (CSG, p. 23).

[9] Rm 9:15-16. See A 2 r, 71 and also LT 224, 1083, where she quotes verse 16.

[10] See CSG, p. 42. This is a fusion of Rm 4:6 with 3:24.

2. *The necessity of works*

Furthermore, Thérèse has some unshakable principles: 'God needs our love,'[11] «love is repaid by love alone»[12] and this love demonstrates its authenticity by works: «*Love* is proved by works» (B 4 r, 228).

The exceptional heart of Thérèse has already discovered this law under the impulse of her own psychology. As a child, she endeavors to show her tenderness for her father and mother «in a thousand ways» (A 4 v, 75). Later, wanting to love Jesus passionately, she feels the need of «giving Him a thousand proofs of her love» (A 47 v, 146). The experience continues. She writes, in 1897: «It is in loving Him that I understood that my love was not to be expressed only in words, for: *It is not those who say: 'Lord, Lord!' who will enter the kingdom of Heaven, but those who do the will of God.*»[13] She likes to quote Jesus' words: «If anyone loves me, he will keep my word.»[14] Otherwise, she thinks, one will settle for «beautiful thoughts [that] are nothing without good works» (C 19 v, 260).

Commenting on a verse from the Book of Sirach, «Mercy shall make a place for every man according to the merit of his works,» the Saint, who confesses herself to be without works and preaches a way of confidence, pointed out the need «to run» (and not «to rest,» she adds) in her «little way.» «We must do everything in our power to give without counting and to deny ourselves constantly. In a word, we must prove our love by all the good works of which we are capable.»[15] «You often ask me for the means of arriving at pure love,» she told Sister Geneviève; «it is to forget self entirely and never to seek your own gratification in anything» (CSG, p. 144). And to her sister Marie, who wants to know if one can hope to go straight to Heaven when one offers oneself to Merciful Love, she answers: «Yes, but one must also practice charity towards one's

---

[11] B 1 v, 220: «He is thirsty for our love» (*ibid.*). He has a «need» of souls who are willing to open themselves to His merciful Love (A 84 r, 212).

[12] A 85 v, 214; B 4 r, 227; LT 85, 546.

[13] Mt 7:21. See C 11 v, 249.

[14] Jn 14:23. See LT 142, 794; 165, 860 and *Living on Love*, PN 17.

[15] CSG, p. 57 or PO, p. 289. The verse from the Book of Sirach is 16:12 (or 15 according to the Vulgate, which is the basis of this translation).

neighbor» (PA, p. 239). She constantly teaches her novices about personal cooperation, through acts of generosity (CSG, p. 56). We do not have to press the point further that she herself gives a heroic example of practicing what she preaches. Sister Martha of Jesus is even 'desperate' in the face of this example (PO, p. 431).

Finally, let us listen to this formal declaration, made to Marie of the Trinity. «I had the opportunity to hear from her mouth an important explanation on what she called "her Little Way" of love and confidence. I had made her aware of my intention to teach this spiritual doctrine to my parents and friends. "Oh!" she said to me, "pay very close attention while I am explaining it to you, because our 'Little Way' poorly understood could be taken for Quietism or Illuminism." She then explained to me these false doctrines, unknown to me. I remember that she mentioned Mme. Guyon as heretical. "Don't believe," she said to me, "that to follow the way of love is to follow a way of rest, all of sweetness and consolations! Ah! it is very much the opposite! To offer oneself as Victim to Love is to surrender oneself without reserve to the divine good pleasure; it is to expect to share with Jesus His humiliations and His chalice of bitterness."»[16]

III. THE SOLUTION

1. Love, the true measure

In order to solve the paradox of the necessity and the non-necessity of works, a first step consists in determining the role of love. According to Thérèse, however, a work is good, not because it is lofty, but in the measure that it is a proof of love; therein lies its real greatness. Teresa of Avila had already taught this to her in 1888: «*Jesus doesn't look so much at the grandeur of actions or even at their difficulty as at the love which goes to make up these actions*» (LT 65, 467). The light became brighter toward 1893: «I understood that without *love*, all works are nothing, even the most dazzling, such as raising the dead to life and converting peoples...» (A 81 v, 207).

[16] PA, p. 480.

If Sister Thérèse later wants to be sent to a mission Carmel [to a Carmel founded in Hanoi], she does not consider the usefulness of her services over there, «but I would suffer and I would love. This is what counts» (DE 15.5.6): «My one purpose, then, would be to accomplish the will of God» (C 10 v, 248).

On what must have been the only occasion when Thérèse became a technician — it was to disassemble a «kaleidoscope»! — she discovered a «great mystery»: «So long as our actions, even the smallest, come from the source of love (from "love's kaleidoscope"), the Blessed Trinity... imparts to them a marvelous brightness and beauty. Yes, so long as love is in our heart and we do not withdraw from its center, *all is well*.... The good God... finds everything quite beautiful, even our miserable straws of effort and our most insignificant actions; but, for this, one must not withdraw from the little center» (CSG, p. 76). Sister Geneviève, to whom Thérèse explains this, will receive, on the vigil of the Saint's death, this word of farewell: «It is love alone that counts» (NV 29.9.6).

The *relativity* of «great works» follows from this at once. «The smallest and most hidden work, when inspired by love, is often of greater value than the most outstanding achievements. It is not on their face value that God judges our deeds, even when they bear the stamp of apparent holiness, but only on the measure of love we put into them» (CSG, p. 74). An act of love, a little sacrifice, is worth more than «thinking beautiful and holy things, writing the lives of saints, or composing other spiritual works»[17] if in these actions love is missing. One of the consequences of this primacy of love is that a long life is not necessarily more meritorious than a short one.[18]

Besides, it is precisely love that also confers the value upon «great works.» If Thérèse's contemplative vocation as well as her providential mission incline her more to humble and hidden ac-

---

[17] CSG, p. 141.

[18] DE 27.5.7. As early as 1890 at least, Thérèse already glimpses the decisive importance of love: «It seems to me that love can make up for a long life. Jesus does not look at time since there is no longer any time in Heaven. He must look only at love» (LT 114, 662); «it seems to me that God has no need of years to carry out His work of love in a soul; a ray from His Heart can in one instant make His flower bloom for eternity...» (LT 124, 713).

tion, she is far from reproving actions which are great and exterior. She esteems, encourages, and sustains by her sacrifice the labor of priests and missionaries.

«God has need of no one,» however «He wills to be helped» (A 53 v, 157). Some are called to «great works» (LT 141, 783) and for them faithfulness to this call embodies and expresses their love: 'In following the inspiration of the Holy Spirit, they are pleasing to God' (C 2 v, 237). Have we not noted, in Manuscript B, how Thérèse herself felt inwardly inclined toward «dazzling actions,» toward apostolic and grandiose works? These great dreams necessarily remained at the stage of desire, but who does not understand what their value would have been if Thérèse had been able to put into practice these inspirations of a passionate love![19] It is no tragedy for her, however, that they cannot be realized in action: she will nevertheless be the love that «alone» makes the members of the Mystical Body act (B 3 v, 226), and she will express it heroically in «little things.»

2. *The dazzling... and the little*

The second step for the solution of our paradox concerns the *nature* of the works that Thérèse says are on the one hand secondary and on the other hand necessary.

In the sense of «striking» works, Thérèse is without works. Ever since her first call to holiness, she had understood that they were not necessary (A 32 r, 119) and this conviction became engraved always more deeply in her thought: the program of Manuscript B will only mention the humble «flowers» of her love, of little «nothings,» of looks, words, little sacrifices, and smiles (B 4 v, 228).

---

[19] Thérèse repeats her principles, however, also to the apostles. Her «spiritual brothers» will often hear her repeat that they are called to be missionary *saints*. What Christ blames in Martha is her «*restlessness*,» because this means she is leaning too much on her own strength and neglecting union with God, the source of all supernatural energy, the school of divine science, the lever that lifts the world (C 36 r, 284). Thérèse had on this point a precious experience in her apostolate to young Sisters: «From the moment I understood that it was impossible for me to do anything by myself, the task you imposed upon me no longer appeared difficult to me. I felt that the only thing necessary was to unite myself more and more to Jesus and that *the rest would be given to me besides*. In fact, never was my hope mistaken» (C 22 v, 264).

She possesses nothing that is remarkable in appearance, nothing which is outwardly dazzling. This is forbidden to her by her contemplative life, her arid prayer, her discreet bodily mortification,[20] and her natural talents which are, after all, not exceptional.

But she proves — and must prove — her love through little works, and, on this score, could she not pride herself on the grandiose work of a flawless interior heroism?

Without a doubt she is aware of the helping graces that God gives her. However, the consciousness of her incompleteness, caused by the loftiness of her ideal itself and the experience of her own weakness, is very great. It will lead to this conviction: «All our justice is stained in Your eyes.» And what is not perfect must not be taken into consideration: 'the Lord must not count her works'; 'she has empty hands' (the *Act*).

Furthermore, the heroic program of Manuscript B is, on the whole, a program, an orientation. The Saint herself confesses her little «infidelities» (B 5 v, 230), and this is encouraging. This is not to say that love does not try to do works that are perfect; however, it is not obliged to succeed: when one has done everything one can, one has loved well. Getting started, which is necessary, will not always be getting the task done, which is not necessary. Thus, one will remain in the end the useless servant who hopes that God will make up for what is lacking (CSG, p. 57). It follows that «the work» is not always synonymous with the «full execution»; it will often mean — and this is very specific to the «little way» — that the *effort alone*, the *attempt* is the real bearer of love, the witness to weakness, the appeal to mercy.

In light of her nothingness, Thérèse comes to a new conviction: she has no works because everything that is good in her comes from divine Mercy. «God shows me truth; I feel so much that everything comes from Him.»[21] What about her supernatural beauty? «I see only the graces I've received from God» (DE 10.8.2). The treasure of her virtue? It is placed in the hand of the little child by God (DE 6.8.8). Her patience? «You're always wrong»[22]: it comes from

---

[20] See here chap. VI.

[21] DE 4.8.3. See also DE II 9.7.1 a; DE 8.8.1; C 2 r, 236; 4 r, 239.

[22] DE 18.8.4; 22.8.2; 23.8.1.

God. Her radiant and golden soul? It is thanks to the divine Sun (DE II 25.7.6). The good that she does around her? It is the work of grace (C 22 v, 264). Her posthumous glory? It will be a gratuitous gift from God (DE 11.7.3). God nourishes her from moment to moment (A 76 r, 198; 83 v, 211). «You know well,» she tells Sister Geneviève, «how poor I am myself, but the good God *measures out* to me everything I need at each moment» (CSG, p. 72).

Let us sum up. In the «little way,» works of love are necessary, but they do not need to be astounding. They do not even need to be accomplished in every respect. There will still be a time when human strength will be incapable of reaching perfection which, in the existential perspective of Thérèse, remains always a beyond which is not yet reached and to which one will arrive thanks to divine Mercy and to this alone. Thérèse thinks, moreover, that God must assist us in our weakness in everything. But what does our poverty matter? In the final analysis, God has no need of our works, for everything comes from Him, and His merciful omnipotence is capable of sanctifying even those who are most miserable. For He «alone sanctifies works and can sanctify without works.»[23] He can accomplish all our desires suddenly. If our works are necessary, it is in the end only to prove the authenticity of our collaboration, even if this is limited to the effort and the acceptance of God's blessings.

IV. DOING, OR THE WORK OF «LITTLE THINGS»

It is with a great deal of spiritual realism that Thérèse Martin dreams of the death of love: «In order to die of love, it is necessary to live on love.»[24] What is love? «To love is to give everything, and to give oneself.»[25] «In order that [one's] love is very pure and disinterested, this love must not be shared, it must belong to Jesus

[23] These are Thérèse's words; see Geneviève, PO, p. 289.

[24] Thérèse of Saint Augustine, PO, p. 399.

[25] *Why I love you, O Mary*, of May 1897 (PN 54, str. 22).

entirely.»[26] She must prove her love then «by the greatest thing and by the littlest» (LT 164, 854). And, she explains to Sister Geneviève «that the nature of love [is] to *sacrifice everything*, to give generously, to become a spendthrift, to freely forego all hope of any fruits, to act with folly, to be prodigal to excess and never count the cost. Oh! happy recklessness! Oh! blessed intoxication of love! Love gives all with the total surrender of self besides.... Love is blind; it is a torrent that rapidly sweeps up everything in its wake!» (CSG, p. 70).

However the most characteristic activity in Thérèse's «way of spiritual childhood» looks at the «little things,» of which she allows not one to «escape.»[27] «I am a *very little soul*,» she says, «who can offer God only *very little things*» (C 31 r, 276). If she sets aside what is dazzling, because it is foreign to God's will for her, she embraces much more generously what is little, what is common to the humble. She devotes herself fervently to 'small sacrifices carried out in the shadows' (A 58 r, 167), emphasizing their value, if they are continual: «It is true that in the world there are very big and heavy crosses... Those of the religious life are daily pinpricks; the struggle takes place on an entirely different terrain: one has to fight oneself, *to destroy oneself*, and it is in so doing that true victories are won.» Is this an *easier* fight? «I have seen for myself that often it is the nuns who apparently have the strongest natures who are most easily overcome in little things; how true it is that the greatest of victories is the conquest of self...» (CSG, p. 192). No, the spirituality of the «little way» does not contain a withdrawal from heroism, but a displacement of it.[28]

---

[26] Martha of Jesus, PO, p. 426 s.

[27] «Not allowing one little sacrifice to escape, not one look, one word... profiting by all the smallest things and... doing them through love» (B 4 r-v, 228). The definition of the «little way» mentions: flowers, little means, small sacrifices, caresses (HA 98, chap. XII, DE II 17.7.2). Thérèse expresses herself otherwise as well: «little [hidden] sacrifices» DE 9.5.3; 6.7.8; DE II 239 (3.8.2 b), «my little sufferings» (DE 23.8.6), «little virtues [and] charity practiced in the shadow» and the formula which has become classic, «to please» (CSG, p. 128).

[28] On this point, opinions are sometimes expressed unfortunately. Let us quote, for example, V. SACKVILLE-WEST: «The "Little Way" is a path that parts with the great road of heroism» (*Les Deux Thérèse. Sainte Thérèse d'Avila, Sainte Thérèse de Lisieux*, London, 1944, p. 118). That is not so. It is DANIEL-ROPS who is right: «Whoever has the least experience of the moral life knows that nothing is, in fact, more diffi-

Sister Geneviève attests that her sister revealed her strength of soul in «the multiplicity of her microscopic acts of virtue» practiced «consistently and at all times» (CSG, p. 166). What this formula could suggest of meticulousness, of exaggeration, of constraint, is corrected by the words of Hans Urs von Balthasar: «The letter that Thérèse fills is not a dead, Old Testament letter. It is above all the living, spiritual letter of the Lord: the commandment of love that she fulfills veritably until the last iota.»[29] Such is the true motive of this extraordinary fidelity: love that goes to the last extreme. Nothing dull, nothing impersonal,[30] no laziness! It is remarkable that on July 21, 1895, at the very time she was completing her discovery of Merciful Love, Thérèse emphasizes the necessity of effort: «*Energy*... is a most necessary virtue; with energy one can easily reach the summit of perfection.»[31] And when her abandonment to Mercy nearly reached its apex, she notes: «Many souls say: I don't have the strength to accomplish this sacrifice. But let them exert a great effort! God never refuses that first grace that gives one the courage to act» (DE 8.8.3).

Thérèse indicated the value of these small continual sacrifices: 'signs of attention to God,' which 'touch Him extremely.'[32] Besides, she takes careful note of their psychological repercussion: «They procure in our soul the advantage of not slackening and of maintaining itself in a supernatural state.»[33] And they «prepare the

---

cult than to pass the boundaries of small daily misery, to disregard trivial daily bitterness.... Well far from being a path lined with roses, the little way is a path all filled with thorns. Between the daily and secret heroism of the life that has no other witness but God, and the one that shows itself dazzling, there is no real separation. It is a question of one and the same attitude, admirable in the little as in the big things» (*Mystiques de France*, 1958, p. 290). See also GABRIEL DE SAINTE-MARIE-MADELEINE, «L'Héroïsme de la "petite voie",» *La Petite Voie* (*Spiritualité carmélitaine*, n. 6), pp. 41-59, and D.M. DE PETTER, «De H. Theresia van Lisieux en de huidige humanistische gezindheid,» *Tijdschrift voor Geestelijk Leven*, 23 (1967), pp. 196-200.

[29] *Therese von Lisieux...*, p. 53.

[30] See: «I tell you I myself could not remain one moment in the monastery through constraint. No one could ever force me to live a life like this; I could not do it, except that it is I who desire it... » (CSG, p. 178).

[31] LT 178, 907. See: «I felt that you must have a courageous soul, and it was for this that I was happy to become your sister» (LT 247, 1132, to Father Bellière).

[32] Marie of the Trinity, PO, p. 461

[33] Marie of the Trinity, PO, p. 464.

heart» to welcome even heavier crosses, if such is the will of the good Master (LT 148, 815).

V. LETTING GO, OR THE WORK OF REFUSAL

The «way of spiritual childhood» traverses another vast field of asceticism: that of the refusal of everything that is not appropriate for the poor one who relies on God alone. Thérèse stresses this further still: 'to climb is rather to descend,' 'to acquire is rather to lose.'[34]

1. *Poverty of spirit*

«The *only good* is to love God with all one's heart and to be *poor* in spirit here on earth» (A 32 v, 121). Without this poverty, love and her program of spiritual childhood are unthinkable for Thérèse: the one who is «*very little*» is the one who does not want 'to have possessions,' who 'leans on nothing' because it is in leaning on nothing «that we are seeking only the truth» (CSG, p. 33). And Thérèse's beloved disciple, Céline, must be told that «she must keep herself in her position, and that she must never try to be a great lady, never!» (CSG, p. 231).

However, whoever is poor in spirit must strip himself of purely earthly assurances: «It does so much good to recognize that He alone is perfect, that He alone must be enough for us, when it

[34] CSG, p. 28. See: «Her lesson is a succession of paradoxes (although the formulation of these paradoxes is my own, it was inspired by the Saint's writings): to empty oneself in order to be filled, to be poor in order to become truly rich, to love, to suffer, to be humble in order to be raised up, to make oneself small in order to become great, to draw one's strength from one's weakness, to find the greatest activity in passivity, to die in order to be born, to live here on earth as in exile, to find joy in the absence of joy, to be without shelter and to give shelter to the Lord, to forget oneself in order to be remembered by God, to drink more in order to be always more thirsty — and the true thirst possesses the wherewithal to quench itself — to love those whom one cannot love in order to discover real love, to work with all one's strengths but to despise one's work, to give all while knowing that one is giving nothing, to choose nothing while knowing that one is choosing all, to bind oneself to the Unique One in order to embrace the entire universe» (J. WU, *Humanisme chinois, spiritualité chrétienne*, Casterman, 1965, pp. 123-124).

pleases Him to take away the branch supporting the little bird!» (LT 250, 1137). It is not in vain, then, that Thérèse meditated on the Gospel where she found in the example of Jesus, «meek and humble of heart,» everything that she had to do (DE 15.5.3), and that she had read Saint John of the Cross: indeed, she insisted «that her little way of humility and love was none other than that of Saint John of the Cross: the *nothing* of us, the *all* of God.»[35] The nothing! One must strip oneself, Thérèse teaches, of «what sparkles» and of the feeling (LT 197, 998) and the desire for spiritual «lights» (C 19 v, 260), because those who are very little have no beautiful thoughts (CSG, p. 229), and «do not need to understand» (CSG, p. 236).

We must renounce even the desire *to not fall*. «Where is the soul who does not desire to possess virtue! This longing is common to us all! But how very few there are in the spiritual life who are willing to stumble and fall, to be weak, to be happy when they see themselves prostrate on the ground or when others find them like this» (CSG, p. 24). «You constantly hope that you have finally reached the end; then you are surprised when you stumble and fall. The truth is that you must always be expecting to fall.»[36] «We must consent to remain always poor and without strength,» she wrote in the supplement to Manuscript B, the great document of spiritual poverty (LT 197, 998). Then, we will hope with a purer confidence: «Let us never be distressed over our powerlessness, but rather apply ourselves solely to the practice of love» (CSG, p. 71). The humble in spirit are not worried or preoccupied with the future; they remain in peace, losing neither joy nor courage, living from minute to minute.[37]

This involves renunciation also of *success*, of the desire to see results. «The goal of all our undertakings should not be so much a task perfectly completed but the accomplishment of the will of

---

[35] Thus Marie of the Trinity. See Mss II, 58.

[36] CSG, p. 33. In spite of all our efforts, God sometimes leaves us in our weakness. This absence of *felt* virtue — the nuance is from Thérèse herself — is advantageous if it brings us to humility (see CSG, pp. 190 and 24). She even dared to tell Sister Geneviève: «You should be happy when you stumble and fall. I would go even further and say that if in your fault there is no offense against God, you should really stumble intentionally in order to humble yourself» (PA, p. 291).

[37] On this subject, see here chap. VI.

God» (CSG, p. 173). «Offer to God the sacrifice of never gathering the fruits of your virtue; that is to say, if He wills that throughout your entire life you should feel a repugnance to suffering and humiliation, if He permits all the flowers of your holy desires and good will to fall to the ground without producing any fruit, offer this up.»[38] When death approaches, Thérèse is clearer than ever: «I try to be no longer occupied with myself in anything and I abandon myself to what Jesus sees fit to do in my soul» (LT 247, 1132). She 'plays at the bank of Love, does not concern herself with these "financial" matters, and simply returns later to see if she is rich or poor' (CSG, p. 77). In summary, Thérèse forbids herself to keep count.[39] According to her, she would like to renounce even merit! And that requires a special explanation.

2. *Without «merits»*

As for merit, we notice in Thérèse of Lisieux a remarkable theological phenomenon. She had a defective idea of merit. Her environment must have taught her that merit is, so to speak, a claim which all good action gives us upon God, and with which one can purchase rewards and graces. It creates a real *right* to a reward. One can also transfer it to others. To this conception is easily joined a certain feeling of self-sufficiency, independence, equality: one is in a business relationship, or in court. However, Thérèse succeeded on her own in rejecting this notion — without coming to a new

---

[38] But one will have beautiful fruits at the time of death, Thérèse adds (CSG, p. 38). See also LT 109, 640. Even abandonment as far as success in the apostolate is concerned: one must sow, without looking to see if the seed bears fruit, Jesus tells her: «Give, give always, without being concerned about the result» (DE 15.5.5). See also C 28 v, 273.

[39] *Living on Love* (PN 17, str. 5). See G. MARCEL: «We must add, however, that the assurance in question here [the light that springs from hope] would not know how to be presumptuous, it maintains a clear and simple character; it is certain that it is very closely connected to what has been called the spirit of childhood, and thereby is opposed absolutely to any wisdom, be it undeceived or calculating, which is founded on a certain ensemble of stock experiences. It is in this sense that hope is fearless, that it is fearlessness itself, laying oneself open inevitably besides to jesting, even to the sarcasms of all those who lay the foundation of invariably discouraging forecasts on carefully inventoried precedents» («Structure de l'espérance,» *Dieu vivant*, 19 [1951], p. 77).

formulation of it — wanting to depend completely and solely on divine Mercy alone. Without knowing it, she arrives at the healthy and very profound theological intuition that God's condescension remains entirely central: «God's goodness to us is so great that it wants His gift to us to be our merit.»[40]

Let us listen now to Thérèse, the novice. What are merits? Her sister Marie taught her that they are «eternal riches[41] that one can so easily amass each day» (A 33 r, 121 f.). They are «treasures for Heaven» that one can «accumulate» (more easily than money), the «diamonds» that one «gathers» («with a RAKE»!). Thérèse went off at this good news with her «heart filled with joy, filled with good resolutions.»[42] One feels one can see a reflection of these statements persisting throughout her first years at Carmel: she desires to have «a very beautiful crown» (LT 43 B, 400); «in spite of her smallness [she] *wishes* to form beautiful Eternities,» «the obscure *grain of sand*» wants to become «brilliant and bright» in Heaven (LT 54, 440); «let us hurry to fashion our crown, let us stretch forth our hand to seize the palm.»[43]

When in 1893 she understands that «it is Jesus who is doing all in me» (LT 142, 794), it seems that her change of perspective in the area of abandonment opens her mind to a new attitude toward merit. She no longer loves in order «to weave [her] crown, to gain merits, [but] in order to please Jesus» (LT 143, 800). She plays at the 'bank of love' — «or rather, He plays for her» — without desiring to know «how much the bank is returning to her,» and she does not count up her acts.[44] The shift of attention shines clearly through this definition: «Merit does not consist in doing or in giving much, but rather in receiving, in loving much» (LT 142, 794).

After the subsequent discovery of divine Mercy, the reaction

---

[40] Chap. XVI of the *Decree on Justification* of the Council of Trent (D 810).

[41] (*Note of 1994.*) In *Les Mains vides* (Cerf, new edition of 1988, pp. 78- 82), I have highlighted the *economic* language of Thérèse, daughter of two tradespeople.

[42] LT 91, 563. See also LT 65, 467, where she invites Céline to «gather our treasures.»

[43] LT 94, 577. The Heavenly reward («the palm,» «the glory») attracts her: LT 81, 529; 82, 536. This in no way prevents Thérèse from nourishing her desire to love Jesus alone. But most often the context concretely demonstrates that she then excludes *herself* or *earthly* gifts (for example, consolation).

[44] LT 142, 794.

— one would almost say the aversion — of Thérèse to the old conception shows through more clearly. In her *Act of Oblation to Love,* she affirms: «I do not want to lay up merits for Heaven, I want to work for Your *Love alone*»; she will die with «empty hands» and the Lord is invited to not 'count her works': He alone will be her justice and her sanctity. Not only does she confess herself to be without merits and therefore leans on nothing,[45] but while knowing that the faithful Rewarder is by His goodness 'obliged... to reward our love and our sacrifice,' she does not want «Him to have to go to this trouble.»[46] And when she encounters Psalm 118:12 while saying the Office, in the translation of the Vulgate: *Inclinavi cor meum ad faciendas justificationes tuas in aeternum propter retributionem* ["I have set my heart to act justly because of retribution"], she always pronounces it «reluctantly» and «hastens to say: O my Jesus, You know well that it is not for the reward that I serve You, but solely because I love You, and in order to save souls.»[47]

Because, according to her, «to obtain graces» is «selfishness,» «love of self.»[48] Yes, she wants «to acquire merits» (DE 18.8.3), but for others.[49] She does nothing to keep herself from purgatory.[50] «If I were to live to eighty, I would still be as poor as I am now!» (DE

---

[45] *Act*; A 32 r, 120; LT 189, 956. See what we have just said on «the absence of works» with Thérèse.

[46] DE 9.5.3. Because Thérèse believes firmly that God rewards «according to interior merit» (DE 8.8.4; and A 56 r, 163). From there sprang her persuasion of the apostolic fruitfulness of her entire contemplative life (see LT 218, 1054).

[47] Marie of the Trinity, PA, p. 474. It is interesting to note that Thérèse, quoting words of Saint John of the Cross: «Love is repaid by love alone» (LT 85, 546; A 85 v, 214; B 4 r, 227) and «Pay all debts» (DE 6.8.4), shifts the perspectives: with John, it is God who pays for the debt, with Thérèse, it is the soul.

[48] Mother Agnès, PA, p. 172.

[49] See, for example, DE 4.6.1; 12.7.3; 13.7.17 ; 30.7.3; 18.8.3. But it is also by Jesus' mediation that her actions obtain value: B 4 v, 228 and LT 194, 989; 189, 956. Thérèse had even made «the heroic Act» by which one delivers into Mary's hands all one's merits, so that she may apply them at her will (Sister Geneviève, PA, p. 286). Theologically, this act has little consistency, because merit, in so far as it is tied to a personal act and consists in an increase of grace, is inalienable. One can «earn» for others only in the way of satisfaction and supplication. But Thérèse probably took the transfer of her merits, of her own «gains,» in a very literal sense! It is Mercy that will be her only gain.

[50] For example, LT 221, 1069; DE 4.6.1; 30.7.3.

12.7.3). 'A child works to please her parents, not to earn a name for herself or to become a saint.'[51]

For Thérèse, merits are possessions, or rights. They seem to lessen her poverty and therefore her total dependence on God. Her faith in divine Mercy would become less pure by giving thought to merits, her confidence less blind, her love less disinterested. She wants to free herself of merits in a saintly manner. She cannot admit, consequently, that the graces she has received have been given her because of her own merits.[52] «I know that of myself I would not merit even to enter [purgatory]» (A 84 v, 212). She does not understand that «merits» are a free gift granted by divine Mercy in response to our love, consisting in a growth of our friendship with God, thus preparing a greater glory for us, that is to say a fuller participation in divine life. Accordingly she thought up imaginary situations which are quite unreal (but with what a desire for a totally pure love!): «[Even if others merited more in giving less,] I would prefer to have less merit for myself in giving Him more, simply because that would be God's Holy Will for me» (CSG, p. 68), or: «If the good God were to say to me: "If you die immediately, you will obtain great glory; if you die at the age of eighty, your glory will be far less, but it will please me much more," then I would not hesitate to answer: My God, I want to die at eighty for I am not seeking my own glory, but only to please You.»[53]

What is very beautiful in this attitude and what Thérèse inserts into the program of her «way of spiritual childhood» is the flight from all desire to credit her own riches, replacing it with the desire to expect everything from God's pure goodness, including the grace to be able to prove her love by works. Is this not spiritual poverty without a single false note? It is the antithesis of the

[51] CSG, p. 53. As characteristic of the three phases that Thérèse passed through in her conception of merit, here are three confessions. In 1889: «Let us hurry to fashion our crown» (LT 94, 577). In 1893: «it is not for the purpose of weaving my crown» (LT 143, 800). And finally the third phase, the Thérésian one: «I haven't yet made my crown, but it's God who has made it!» (DE II 9.7.1 a, of 1897).

[52] A 38 v, 131; 44 r, 140; C 35 v, 283.

[53] Marie of the Sacred Heart, PA, p. 236.

Pharisaism fought by Saint Paul.[54] Thérèse 'will not earn her own living.' She expects it from the Father. This is why she 'doesn't want to grow up' (DE 6.8.8). It is her radical refusal! And her greatest 'merit'! Once more, her supernatural instinct, which led her to «spiritual childhood,» has guided her well.

VI. LETTING BE, OR ABANDONMENT TO THE WORK OF GOD

We come to the third aspect of Thérésian asceticism: openness to God's activity in us. This is not total passivity, but rather an intense, conscious, and willed attitude which mobilizes many spiritual forces.

Thérèse's fundamental openness concerns the infusion of divine Love. It comes to her in the great light of June 9, 1895; one must accept God's infinite Love, 'to throw oneself into it, to let oneself be flooded and consumed' by it (A 84 v, 212); Manuscript B will say «to surrender to Him without reservation» (B 1 v, 221). But since Thérèse is not thinking of an invasion into the human psyche by way of so-called mystical phenomena, the art of opening oneself comes down to a daily, loving, personal cooperation under its different aspects: in suffering, abandonment, and especially confidence.

1. Suffering

The realist of Lisieux warns us: «to abandon oneself to love [is] to surrender oneself to suffering.»[55] This is an important aspect

---

[54] It was an appropriate idea of A. GELIN to finish his book on the *Anawim* by a reference to Thérèse of Lisieux (*Les pauvres que Dieu aime*, Paris, 1967, p. 145; English translation available: *The Poor of Yahweh*). The author adds, in connection with this spiritual poverty: «It is undoubtedly the essential message which the young saint of Lisieux was commissioned to convey to our time that is eager for authorities.» Ch. DU BOS had already said: «In this regard, the word of Saint Paul (Ph 2:10) was fulfilled in our days by the holiness of Saint Thérèse of the Child Jesus, a holiness of which the way itself consists in the refusal of all "purchasing," the refusal to ever *anticipate*» (*Journal*, t. IX, Paris, 1961, p. 63). See P. BLANCHARD, «Charles Du Bos et Sainte Thérèse de l'Enfant-Jésus,» VT, 1962, July, pp. 31-33.

[55] Mother Agnès, PO, p. 159.

of her «way of spiritual childhood» and she recommends that her sisters make it «known to souls [that she had] suffered very much here below» (DE 31.7.13). Otherwise, she thought, those who would be inspired by her example could be discouraged (DE 15.8.1). She even defined her «way» as «suffering united to love» (LT 258, 1151).

If, from 1895 on, she no longer loves suffering except as God's concrete will for her (A 83 r, 210), the cross nevertheless is always awaited as «pure and unmixed suffering» (C 10 v, 248); it remains 'the only thing desirable' (LT 253, 1139). It is her «joy» (C 7 r, 243), her «passion» (LT 253, 1139), her «happiness» (LT 258, 1151), «the most precious of treasures» (C 10 v, 248), her «Heaven here below» (LT 254, 1141).

But the suffering of the «little way» is something that is not *sought*.[56] One welcomes it with love when it comes, but one remains in pure abandonment as far as its duration, intensity or choice is concerned. «I don't ask for anything; that would mean leaving my way of abandonment,» says Thérèse.[57] «I would never want to ask God for greater sufferings. If He increases them, I will bear them with joy because they will be coming to me from Him. But if I were to ask for sufferings, these would be mine, and I would have to bear them alone.»[58] Thanks to this attitude, God «is obliged to give me courage» (DE 26.8.2). And, needless to say, Thérèse received this courage in abundance. At the climax of her suffering, she will say: «A little victim of love cannot find frightful what her Spouse sends her through love» (25.9.3). And four hours before her death: «No, I am not sorry for delivering myself up to Love; on the contrary!» (30.9) She had no regrets… even if the Son of Man had not exempted her from passing through the way of suffering which He Himself had followed.

---

[56] Thérèse of Lisieux thus departs from her Mother, Teresa of Avila, who holds that one may ask for suffering. Do we have here two positions that reflect two temperaments? Whatever the case may be, the distance is less great than one would believe it at first, because *Mother* adds that in this case God will give us courage (see *The Way of Perfection*, chap. 32). Both of them exclude depending on their own strengths therefore. One thinks of Saint Augustine: «Give, Lord, what you command, and command what you will» (*Confessions*, Book X, chap. XIX, XXXI, XXXVII).

[57] HA 98, chap. XII, DE 9.6.1.

[58] PO, p. 207, or, in part, DE 11.8.3.

2. *Abandonment*

But Thérèse is not content with simply welcoming the grace of suffering. She *embraces* the full extent of God's work in her. We have spoken often of this desire of conformity that governs her life, especially during the last years. Then, the term «abandonment» returns very frequently.

What is «abandonment — to abandon oneself»[59]? A survey of all Thérèse's writings reveals its fundamental meaning.[60] Although she never describes abandonment with precision, she so often connects it to God's will[61] that one can see it, in a first definition, as the pursuit of conformity of the human will with the divine will, putting the stress however on the divine initiative to which one desires to adhere faithfully. This effort is neither forced nor servile, but free and *loving*.[62] However, is all conformity considered to be abandonment? Using a distinction made by Saint Francis de Sales between "*intended* will" and the "will of God's *good pleasure*" (depending on whether it is already clearly manifested to us or not), M. Viller calls the first conformity «obedience,» reserving for the second the name «abandonment,» provided that it is generous. Thus abandonment differs from resignation or acquiescence.[63]

---

[59] On the evolution that Thérèse underwent in terms of abandonment, see here, pp. 76-77.

[60] In French, the word «abandonment-to abandon» can also mean: *disengagement*, *simplicity* («to speak with abandonment,» A 3 v, 731); *dereliction*, *desertion*, for example by God (A 64 v, 177; 69 v, 186; 70 v, 188; 75 v, 197; 79 v, 204; C 16 v, 256; LT 27, 288; 32, 332; 36, 353; 89, 556; 129, 728; 165, 860; 171, 888; DE 27.7.15; 23.8.1; 30.9); *surrender* (of life): PN 3; (of one's coat): C 16 v, 256; (of a work): PN 36, str. 5; (of desires): LT 247, 1132 or even *to confide* (the *Act*). We set aside these meanings of the word «abandonment-to abandon» because they are foreign to our goal.

[61] For example, at the end of 1895, she summarizes her interior life in these words: «Now abandonment alone guides me; I have no other compass!... I can no longer ask for anything with fervor except the perfect accomplishment of God's will in my soul» (A 83 r, 210).

[62] Thérèse must necessarily distinguish it from *resignation*. This one 'is still distinct from God's will. There is in it the same difference as exists between union and unity: In union, we are still two, in unity we are only one' (LT 65, 467. She mentions Mme Swetchine).

[63] See art. «Abandon,» *Dictionnaire de spiritualité*, I, col. 3-4.

Is abandonment for Thérèse pure passivity? Not at all! Let us distinguish first between the *act* of abandonment and its ongoing *state*.

In the first stage of abandonment, activity is more manifest: conforming himself to God's will, a person disengages himself from his own will, through love. He experiences an inner movement of detachment from himself and of blind self-giving to God. Thérèse herself sometimes matches the term abandonment with formulas which emphasize the activity of the will, as for instance at the end of Manuscript A: «How I want to apply myself to doing the will of God always with the greatest self-surrender!» (A 84 v, 213). Elsewhere, she assimilates it practically to «surrendering oneself» (LT 142, 794; 165, 860). In the second stage of abandonment, the ongoing *state*, human activity is more hidden, although it is real. The soul is then in an *attitude* (a sustaining and a continuation of the act). Its activity consists in holding fast to the decision that has been taken, so that the abandonment is a complete offering, a continuing oblation. Very often this attitude crystallizes in new acts through which it is nourished and formed anew: one finds an example of this in Thérèse's last illness.

Are abandonment and confidence the same thing? In a first meaning of the latter word — that is to say the relative certainty which the other person causes me to have — confidence is no more than a basis, although a necessary one, of abandonment. How am I going to abandon myself to God and surrender to His will, if I am not sure of His love?[64] In a second meaning — the «theological hope all filled with love»[65] — confidence does not seem at first to differ from abandonment except by reason of the object: normally, confidence makes it more explicit, while abandonment views its object more in general, a trust in God's will whatever it is. A greater passivity in the attitude of abandonment also results from this;

[64] Monsignor GAY notes judiciously that one first abandons oneself to God who is good, and not to His particular wills, which are perhaps difficult (*De la vie et des vertus chrétiennes considérées dans l'état religieux*, Paris-Poitiers, 1888, 11th ed., t. III, pp. 174-175).

[65] So MARIE-EUGÈNE DE L'ENFANT-JÉSUS (*Je veux voir Dieu*, Tarascon, 1956, 3 ed., p. 837). He adds: «Abandonment is confidence which no longer expresses itself solely through distinct acts, but which has created a spiritual attitude.»

confidence, on the other hand, shows itself to be more *dynamic*. However, confidence can perhaps also be considered as a *state*, in which case it is very close to abandonment.

In any case, as far as the confidence of *Thérèse of Lisieux* is concerned — such a loving, universal, and lasting confidence — it is hard to distinguish it from abandonment. It is as if the two were considered as two stages of a same outpouring of the heart: abandonment is only the face of confidence in its time of *waiting*, which precedes the realization of the desire — this, at least if it is a question of hope (for example in the case of Thérèse's sanctification or God's help which she anticipates). When abandonment concerns conformity with the divine will, it clearly is closer to love than to hope.

Actually, Thérèse seems often to use the two words as synonyms.[66] The same abandonment («audacious,» «bold,» «fearless») which is described in Manuscript B is still called confidence and, when Thérèse wants to emphasize for her hesitant sister the dynamic nature of her attitude, she calls it «confidence and nothing but confidence.»[67] Elsewhere, the Carmelite defines her way, sometimes as abandonment, sometimes as confidence.[68] These notions of hers are so very practical, so existential, that the nuances tend to overlap in concrete reality. Their content is revealed as a perpetual and coordinated movement of faith, hope, and charity. We shall now explain this.

[66] For example, A 61 v, 173: she admires in Saint Cecilia «her *abandonment*, her limitless *confidence*.»

[67] Compare B 5 r, 230; 5 v, 231 f.; LT 197, 998.

[68] See chap. III of this part, p. 269. Her way goes «with the abandonment and the love of a child who know that his Father loves him and would be unable to leave him in the hour of danger» (LT 258, 1151).

Chapter V

The Work of Confidence: Doctrinal Outline

We have just said that the authentic way «of spiritual childhood» does not excuse us from an assiduous asceticism, made up of generosity in various acts of renunciation which are not dazzling or conspicuous, and of openness to God's work in us. However, Thérèse's engagement does not stop there, because that would then make it lack the fundamental and most characteristic activity required by the Saint of Lisieux: the work of confidence, which is the object of our present reflections.

We would now like to analyze confidence, not so much as an attitude, but above all as an action, and to articulate its complex content toward which several virtues converge. This examination will lead to a judgment on its theological value (when it is a question of supernatural confidence) and on the processes by which it increases charity, because according to Thérèse it is confidence which must lead us to love. One should not expect a complete study here; we only establish some necessary beacons to shed more light on this fundamental theme.

I. ANALYSIS OF THE ACT OF CONFIDENCE

«I have confidence in you.» A rich psychological ensemble lies hidden behind these sober words. In order to explore it, one must first be aware of a few things: on the one hand, of the person who pronounces these words and the intensity of her faith in others, and on the other hand, of the kindliness and possibilities of others, and finally of the need which causes this appeal to be voiced. These conditions make us see at once the infinite variety of circumstances to which confidence is susceptible. If we now want to analyze its action,[1] we shall limit ourselves from this point on to thinking of it in connection with *Thérèse's* confidence, after 1894, and in connection with *God*, the God of mercy.

1. The emptiness to fill

«I have confidence in you.» The interpersonal character of my act becomes clear here, with the greatest evidence: I am in the presence of another. However, at the origin there is first 'something' in myself, namely, the experience of a certain «emptiness» that confidence is called to fill. Without it, I would tell the other simply «I praise you» or «I love you.» Confidence in others is therefore never solely *because*..., but always *that*..., although this need does not necessarily have to be formulated, or detailed, or even conceived clearly. By this need which secretly resounds in my words, confidence is linked closely to hope. If it surpasses it, which will be explained, it nevertheless contains all that there is to be in hope, adding its own values to it.

Let us analyze the object of my confidence. First of all this object presents itself to my eyes as something good, because it will fill an emptiness, substituting a presence for an absence. It therefore does not leave me indifferent. On the contrary, if I desire it, it is because it matters to me, and so confidence manifests itself as a *movement toward a good*. But the emptiness still exists and the good is *yet to come*: it therefore imposes a *waiting* for a time and it enjoins perseverance. This good also seems to me *possible* to attain; otherwise I would not set out in search of it lest I fall into despair. Moreover, the realization of my goal appears to me more or less *difficult*, otherwise I would simply «desire»[2] it.

---

[1] The studies that have helped us here are: G. MARCEL, «Esquisse d'une phénoménologie et d'une métaphysique de l'espérance,» in his book *Homo Viator. Prolégomènes à une métaphysique de l'espérance*, Aubier, 1944, pp. 39-91; J. HERMANS, «Het hopen. Een analyse van de houding,» *Bijdragen*, 21 (1960), pp. 117-143; R. KWANT, «Hoop en vertrouwen,» *Kultuurleven*, 23 (1956), pp. 95-99.

[2] *Hope* is the movement toward a future and possible good, but more or less difficult to attain: it constitutes «a mixture of promise and threat» (J. KIJM, «Het verwachten,»

It is precisely in the last two aspects of the good which one seeks that confidence begins to detach itself from hope. When I say «I have confidence that...,» I express by this that my goal appears to me less difficult to attain, and consequently more possible than if I say «I hope that....» In fact, confidence implies *greater certainty*[3] of a happy outcome, because of the resources that I discover in myself or by reason of the help that I anticipate from another.[4]

2. *Interpersonal relationship*

At this point, the interpersonal relationship which I establish, if I have confidence in another, comes into play. «I have confidence in you»: two people and two worlds oppose one another.

Oppose one another? No. For reasons which are at least subjectively valid, I look for in the other and I find in him a *support*. I believe with a certain fervor that he will help me. Confidence in another always supposes, therefore, an act of *faith* in his goodness, his power, his sensitivity, his fidelity — an act that is facilitated by the experience that I already have had of his help.

My confidence is in some way an anticipation of the goodwill of others. The other is no longer entirely other, already he enters into me by this something that I drew from him and transfused into me: we communicate, we *commune*, and we do this in a more perfect manner as my confidence becomes more legitimate and the goodwill of the other more real.

Consequently, confidence supposes a certain degree of *familiarity*, of «confidentiality»: scrutinizing in the other the ability and the will to help me, I approach him; having confidence, I come to confide in him: my confidence is always a *gift of self*, I put myself a

---

Streven, 21 [1953-1954], p. 110). *Desire*, on the other hand, makes abstraction of this difficulty. The *expectation*, in the psychological sense, can also refer to an evil as well as a good and its object is less future: already it announces itself, it is in the air.

[3] It is this faith in her own power or in the help of others that, strictly speaking, is called confidence: I hope *with* confidence... But, by a passage from cause to effect, the entire thrust that follows this apprehension is also called confidence. This confidence is therefore «a corroborated hope.» See ST. THOMAS, *Summa Theologica*, 2.2, 129, 6 and 1.2, 40, 2.

[4] Faithful to our plan, we will only interest ourselves in confidence in others. Thérésian confidence belongs to this kind.

little in my friend's hands. Thus, confidence is accompanied by *humility*: if I did not recognize my need and often my incapacity to remedy it alone, I could not resign myself and take refuge in the other.

For these reasons, confidence cannot be characterized as a love that is no more than «interested» love. It is true that through confidence I am seeking to obtain a good for myself, and on that score I am interested in my own welfare. But at the same time I am sounding out the other in himself, and so I am not only opening a door to «disinterested» love, but in a way I have already passed through it. Could I have confidence in someone whom I do not in the first place love? As my confidence grows stronger and more pure, my attention to the other for himself, for *his* sake, will gain ground. It is even possible that I shall give up manifesting my need. The one in whom I have confidence will himself think of discovering it and will offer me his hand in the way that is most appropriate. The help of others will seem to me a *grace*, an exercise of pure generosity. Confidence, therefore, predisposes me to *gratitude*.

We should again mention the fluctuating use of the terms «hope» and «confidence.» To consult the concrete situations in which one commonly uses them, one needs to distinguish them. But nuances are not so different that they do not often allow us to pass from one to the other. This is especially the case with our relationship with *God*, the Almighty One Who loves us and Who generally is loved by us: we are then on the terrain of friendship where hope blossoms into confidence. The holy books of the Old Testament did not even know the exact equivalent of our word «hope»: in the presence of God, hope was mingled with confidence.[5] And does Thérèse of Lisieux not pass easily from «confidence» to «hope» and vice versa[6]? While examining the theological value of confidence, we shall not recoil from an alternating usage of the two words, without forgetting the nuances that assert themselves from the start.

---

[5] See J. VAN DER PLOEG, «L'Espérance dans l'Ancien Testament,» *Revue biblique*, 61 (1954), p. 494.

[6] For example, B 5 v, 231; LT 197, 998.

II. THE THEOLOGICAL CONTENT AND DYNAMIC NATURE OF CONFIDENCE

The previous analysis brings us to the theological content of confidence, which will reveal its dynamic character at the same time.[7]

Let us first correct a false way of looking at the theological virtues. One would be wrong to present them as three «degrees» of an order which does not vary: faith would be the first, hope would follow faith and would contain a greater perfection, and charity would follow hope and would be the most perfect of the three. To descend from charity to hope would be to regress. In this way of seeing them, the three degrees would be well defined and would in no way mingle one with the other. Each virtue would be a plant that would push neither its roots nor its offshoots into the domain of the neighboring plant.

We thus arrive at realities that are static and frozen. But, if the theological virtues are clearly separated on the theoretical plane, they very often intersect on the existential plane.

1. *Interaction of faith and confidence*

To have confidence in God presupposes first of all a belief in Him: to believe in His veracity, to believe also in His power, to believe in His fidelity to promises made, in essence always «to believe in the love that God has for us» (1 Jn 4:16), all the more so when, in difficulties, one is inclined to feel far from Him. Charles Péguy said it well: «The faith that I like best, said God, is hope.»[8] The more one penetrates further into God's love by faith, the more one feels moved to abandon oneself blindly to Him.

This is to say that *faith* not only precedes, but also *invites* and *leads* to confidence, and more deeply if it is lit up by charity. How can one know God's condescension and not feel a first impulse

---

[7] One finds beautiful studies on this subject in Ph. DELHAYE and J. BOULANGÉ, *Espérance et vie chrétienne*, Desclée, 1958, 317 pp., and in Ch.-A. BERNARD, *Théologie de l'espérance selon Saint Thomas d'Aquin*, Paris, 1961, 175 pp., among others. Lastly, we borrow the translation of texts from Saint Thomas.

[8] *Le Porche du mystère de la deuxième vertu*, Gallimard, 1954, 81 ed., p. 16.

towards Him, in order to love Him in return and also to receive from Him the perfection of our being? We think again of Charles Péguy: «It is necessary to have confidence in God, my child, for He had confidence in us. He showed us this confidence by giving us and entrusting to us His only Son.»[9] Let us return to Saint Thérèse and let us recall this single fragment from Manuscript B: in the Eucharist, the mystery of our faith, she recognizes a «folly» of divine love for us and her reaction follows at once: «How can my confidence have any limits?» (B 5 v, 231).

If faith leads to confidence, confidence increases faith. The familiarity that it implies with the One in Whom one trusts, pushes the truths that faith accepts about Him towards a more intimate area of our consciousness. For example, it is clear that confidence helped Thérèse to overcome without «discouragement» (C 7 v, 244) the long crisis of faith through which she passed toward the end of her life. It is there that one discovers the undeniable influence of love. But this love is still in part the fruit of confidence. It is this relationship that will presently hold our attention.

2. *Hope and charity*

Taking up a felicitous formula of Saint Ambrose who sees between hope and charity «a sacred circuit,»[10] Saint Thomas affirms: «According to Ambrose's words, charity and hope, as in a sacred circle, influence each other reciprocally: when someone has been introduced to charity by hope, his hope becomes more perfect, his fear more chaste, and his faith more firm. And this is why when he says that hope springs from charity, he does not speak of the first birth of hope, but of its second influence: once infused in us, charity makes us hope and believe more perfectly.»[11]

Let us first of all observe the first movement: from hope to charity.

---

[9] *Ibid.*, pp. 129-130. «God shows confidence in us.» This is essentially an anthropomorphism.

[10] *Expositio evangelii secundum Lucam* (PL 15, 1865): *Et rursus in se sancto quodam circuitu refunduntur.*

[11] *Quaestio disp. de spe*, a. 1., ad. 1.

The difference between hope and charity consists in that, through hope, I love God Whom I hope to fully possess in Heaven and from Whom I expect help in order to reach this possession, as a good that is mine and for me, whereas by charity I love God as a good — the supreme Good — *in Himself and for Himself*. Both of these are centered on God, but hope loves with an «interested» love, a «love of concupiscence» as the expression puts it, and charity loves Him with a so-called «disinterested» love, a «love of benevolence» which one also calls a «love of friendship.»

Let us now specify how hope can «lead to charity.» Spontaneously, admiration will join itself to the consideration of divine goodness as our help and our goal. Hope will also keep company with gratitude. It is touching to see that our desire for God is not a «one-way street,» but that our «interested» love corresponds to a reciprocal love: He Himself greatly desires our happiness and our future glory, which are at the same time His own glorification. The door opens to the love of God in itself, to «disinterested» love, the love of friendship: aided by grace, we pass through the door. Besides, it is possible, especially in certain phases of our spiritual and psychological rhythm, that the thought of future reward exercises a favorable influence on our observance of the divine commandments.[12] Ph. Delhaye and J. Boulangé, to whom the previous reflections are indebted,[13] refer to an experience of daily life: it is normal that we hope that the people with whom we associate because of advantages eventually become good friends. It goes without saying that God's love will increase more intensely in the measure that theological hope will be more developed. Gabriel Marcel has remarked: «Hope is a life and, I will add, a radiant life, not at all a life withdrawn into itself.»[14] He who hopes, gives of himself.

3. *Thérésian confidence and charity*

What a beautiful example of this communion of hope and charity we find in Saint Thérèse of Lisieux! Truly we are in the pres-

[12] We can mention here the example of Thérèse in the first years of her religious life.

[13] See pp. 175-183 of their work: *Espérance et vie chrétienne*, Desclée, 1958.

[14] «Structure de l'espérance,» *Dieu vivant*, 19 (1951), p. 79.

ence here of a hope that is perfect, animated by a love that is extremely fervent. All do not imitate her so perfectly in the «little way.» Would such a thing be possible? Let us raise some specific grounds which make her hope a mine of charity.

First of all, Thérèse's hope aims only at *God alone*. Without doubt, she aspires to more perfectly possess Him, and one could conclude from this that her love is «interested.» But what is the deepest motive of her longing toward a fuller possession? Solely to love Him more! There is not in Thérèse, as the years pass, any will to seek her own glory, her own happiness, her own rest, or «merits» in the sense in which she understood them. While knowing that the possession of God brings these benefits,[15] her hope joins with the fundamental desire of her entire life: to please Jesus, always to please Him more. She wants only to execute the program of her profession: «Love that is no longer me but You.»[16] This hope is therefore very chaste, tending solely toward perfect love, and already resplendent with the love of friendship which it anticipates to a superior degree. Thérèse hopes, not to make God «mine,» but to make herself all «His.» True possession resides for her in this alienation from herself. «I hope for You from You for Your sake.»

In her eyes this hope is like an offering. She knows that God has need of nothing. The way she sees it, the only «need» God feels is to give Himself. We should remember the origins of her *Offering to Merciful Love*: Jesus *desires* to be loved, His love has *need* of victims, He must *hold back* the waves of His infinite tenderness, He is a fire that sets souls aflame and consumes them (A 84 v, 212). His love is not *satisfied* unless it lowers itself to nothingness to transform this nothingness (B 3 v, 227), in other words, unless it obeys its *own* nature (A 2 v-3 r, 72). For her part, Thérèse hopes blindly, abandons herself, surrenders herself, puts up no resistance, and allows herself to be flooded by His love. Her hope is considered only as an oblation of herself to God so that He may give full vent to His conquering Mercy. It is also «to please Him,» this pleasure of permitting Him to be Himself: supreme goodness.

---

15 We recall the sentence of Saint John of the Cross who inscribed on the drawing of Mount Carmel: «All goods were given to me when I no longer sought them through self-love.» Thérèse liked these words which she quotes (C 28 v, 272).

16 Pri 2.

What *praise* this Thérésian hope is! To hope is to confess her own nothingness and to expect everything from God, from a God of goodness. To hope is to say: «You are good, You are powerful, You are great and Your greatness does not separate You from Your creatures. You are perfectly faithful; no one comes to You in vain.» Hope is humility that adores, admires, gives thanks, and praises. For Thérèse, to have confidence is to say «You»; it is to pray. 'The *faith* that He likes best' becomes a *call* to Him Who loves best.

The loving nature of her hope impels Thérèse to give it the general name of *confidence* and to see herself before God as a child before her *father*. Ch.-A. Bernard has brought out beautifully how charity, while perfecting hope, grants to it «a new modality.» Hope «will reach its perfection in the measure in which it will rise with greater ease and constantly toward its formal object; in other words, when it rises to God by the confidence that is born of love.» The assurance that confidence gives «is only the reverberation in the soul of its impulse toward God-Help.» That is to say it is love that in the first place begets it. A further perfection awaits confidence when it becomes *filial*. Then, it became familiarity.[17] It is on this level that Thérésian confidence takes its stand and it is there that the «little way» would like to carry us all: to a confidence shining with love.

4. *«One obtains from God as much as one hopes to receive from Him»*

Saint John of the Cross, as well, examined the importance of charity which hope can contain and, consequently, the influence that it exercises on God. According to the Spanish mystic, perfect hope unites a soul to God, because it leaves what it possesses and seeks in God what it does not yet possess; hope is a renunciation and a union with the Other. Let us listen to this great Doctor of the sixteenth century: «In the measure that the memory becomes dispossessed of things, in that measure it will have hope, and the more hope it has, the greater will be its union with God; for in relation to God, the more a soul hopes the more it attains. And when, pre-

[17] See Ch.-A. BERNARD, *Théologie…*, pp. 120-123.

cisely, it is more dispossessed of things, it hopes more; and when it has reached perfect dispossession, it will remain with the perfect possession of God in divine union.»[18] Perfect hope looks at God alone, and there is so much love in this look that the Friend does not know how to resist: «The ordinary task of hope in the soul [is] to raise the eyes to look only at God.... [Because she gazes only at God and looks at nothing else, and is not content save with Him alone, she] is so pleasing to the Friend that it is true to say the soul obtains from God all that she hopes to receive from Him.... Without this green livery of hope in God alone, it would not behoove a person to go out toward this goal of love, because he would obtain nothing, since what moves and conquers is unrelenting hope.»[19] It is a question here of the hope of a soul who has secretly been moved by God in its desires and who has for his goal only the possession of God, relying on Him alone, in a great poverty of spirit. This supposes a great charity and it is by this charity, contained in hope and increased by its practice, that hope has so much influence over God.

But already we are closing the «sacred circuit» leading from charity to hope. Is this to say that the charity by which I love God for Himself can give rise to God's love *for me*? Does charity not thus degrade itself? No. It rises to a hope that emanates from it and surpasses it. This is the most beautiful aspect of hope, and of Thérèse's hope especially, which we wish now to describe.

5. *From charity to hope*

Without delaying over an analysis of charity or discussions on interested and disinterested love, let us borrow the findings of a good interpreter of Saint Thomas. «To love someone is to desire good for him. It is therefore to desire for him some good that is lacking to him. And on the other hand to love someone is to desire to possess him and to unite oneself to him. "Benevolence [says Saint Thomas] is not enough for friendship but a reciprocal affection is

[18] *The Ascent of Mount Carmel*, Book 3, chap. 7.

[19] *The Dark Night*, Book 2, chap. 21.

necessary, for the friend is friend for a friend; such a reciprocal benevolence is based on a communication." If, then, I love God, and if God loves me, the desire to possess Him is born in me.»[20] This desire for a more perfect communication is inherent in the dynamism of the love of friendship itself. Consequently, «perfect love... does not exclude love of self at all. From the love of self, when communication of the divine good is yet *to come,* springs hope, and this so much more strongly and purely that this love proceeds from a more lively charity: one can give up interest in everything when one loves, except from being united to the beloved.... In the measure where this necessary communication with charity is not yet perfect, it is "in hope," and not to hope is to deprive charity of its foundation.»[21] A completely disinterested love is therefore inconceivable in this life. The authentic love of friendship cannot keep from hoping that the friend will communicate himself further. Let us ask Saint John of the Cross again if he pushes his doctrine of «nothingness» up to this point. The soul inflamed with love, he teaches, experiences fervent desires to possess the Beloved; the separation is painful to her. «In spite of all her conformity to the will of her Beloved, [she] cannot cease longing for the wages and salary of her love, for which she serves Him. Otherwise, her love would not be true, because the payment for love is actually nothing else — neither can a soul desire anything else — than more love, until the perfection of love is reached. Because love... is repaid by love alone.» But Saint John warns that the soul that loves does not await the end of her *labor*, but «rather the end of her work. Her work is to love, and of this work, love, she awaits the end, which is the perfection and completeness of it.»[22]

Let us return to Thérèse now. Is her hope different? It is a hope produced by love. Let us consult the charter of the «little way,» Manuscript B: Thérèse loves Jesus with an ardent love; her love

---

[20] Ch.-A. BERNARD, p. 114. The quotation from Saint Thomas is taken from the *Summa Theologica*, 2. 2, 23, 1.

[21] J.-H. NICOLAS, art. «Espérance,» *Dictionnaire de spiritualité*, VI, col. 1222-1223. W. LUIJPEN calls hope precisely «the consciousness of the direction» of love (*Existentiële fenomenologie*, Utrecht-Anvers, 1959, p. 333).

[22] CS, str. 9 (*Oeuvres*, IV, pp. 179-180).

causes desires of a greater love; she hopes that Jesus will give her this new, perfect love.

As we see it, this hope surpasses the charity from which it springs: it is both charity and hope at the same time. In this hope, there is all the activity of charity which is *forma virtutum*, the soul of the supernatural virtue of the justified person, but it is an intensified activity, which gives to charity the new face of hope.[23] However, this hope remains still short of the hoped-for love, the more perfect love to which it aspires. But it facilitates it and will obtain it! Thus charity would like to go from charity to charity by the way that passes from hope to hope. To hope as Thérèse did is not to regress. «The more man rises to God by confidence, the more he becomes perfect.»[24] Péguy had seen clearly: «Little hope advances between its two big sisters and they don't just take care of her, [...rather] it is she in the middle who brings along her big sisters.»[25]

Thus ends the «sacred circuit» which goes from hope to charity and from charity to hope. Or better, a new circuit already attaches itself to it. Like the links of a long chain.

III. PERSEVERANCE IN CONFIDENCE

Up to this point, we have considered the individual act of confidence. But this act must necessarily be renewed. Indeed, hope aims toward a future good and it must be prolonged until it reaches it. It is with reason that Saint Paul invites us to «the constancy of hope.»[26] «Hope is a long patience.»[27]

The work of confidence should continue endlessly. One will not immediately see the results of it, as Thérèse warns us. But it is in this repetition that confidence and also charity are practiced: in

---

[23] See 1 Cor 13:7: «Charity hopes.»

[24] Ch.-A. BERNARD, p. 124. See this thought of Saint Thomas which one can apply wonderfully to the case of Thérèse of Lisieux: «By the growth of charity, hope becomes more perfect, because, for our friends, we hope to the maximum» (*Summa Theologica*, 2.2, 17, 8).

[25] *Le Porche*, pp. 27-28.

[26] 1 Th 1:3 and Rm 8:25.

[27] Ph. DELHAYE and J. BOULANGÉ, p. 253.

a sense, one already lives the hoped-for charity in entrusting oneself. If one does not obtain from God what one hopes for from Him, it is that one did not hope sufficiently. By perseverance, our confidence is called to be purified, to be intensified unto obtaining, unto being what it hopes for.

Here is the road that the fulfillment of our desires often follows: by confidence, accompanied by effort as by its testimony, the image of the desired object is inscribed so deeply in our consciousness, and we anticipate the desired object so intensely in advance, that our psychology ends up adjusting to the laws and requirements of the glimpsed ideal and thus receives the wherewithal to attain it. The response of grace thus already merges with the question itself, although without exhausting itself, without imposing limits on the free action of the Spirit.... Once a degree of love has been reached, the order of love will inspire the desire of a more perfect love: confidence is invited to a new perseverance.

In the «way of spiritual childhood,» one must imitate Thérèse: the more she loved, the more she hoped with confidence. It is the first and last work of this life. Just as her charity proved itself by an untiring fidelity, and her faith, in the crisis through which it passed, was proved by constant acts of faith (C 7 v, 243), so her very characteristic attitude of confidence must have bloomed innumerable times in this prayer of love and praise: «I have confidence in You, I hope for You from You for Your sake!»

CHAPTER VI

Thérèse's Deductions

After analyzing the components which make up Thérèse's «little way,» we should now have a look at certain beneficial results which flow from it. First, the additional virtues which are part of this way; second, some of its practical forms; and third, the effect it had on Thérèse's attitude toward human guilt.

I. «THIS HAPPY LIFE»

On July 18, 1897, in a letter to Father Bellière, Thérèse describes her way as «delightful.» «This happy life» is the phrase she uses to summarize the emotional effect it has on her relationship with the Lord. She discovered a «method» of being happy, an «art of living,» only through what she calls «the practice of familiarity with Jesus.»[1]

1. Joy

A first psychological result of her entire life of holiness is *joy*, *happiness*, or *peace*, three words which often intermingle in the last years of her life.

[1] LT 258, 1151. First of all, some of Thérèse's assertions could suggest a natural optimism, and even, on occasion, a certain opportunism which makes of necessity a virtue. Thus: «I always see the good side of things. There are some who set about giving themselves the most trouble. For me, it's just the opposite. If I have nothing but pure suffering... I make *this* my joy!» (DE 27.5.6). Or: «I always manage... to preserve interior peace» (18.4.1). But such grounds could never have given to Thérésian joy the consistency that it had. And many other testimonies show how it is necessary to interpret the quoted texts.

What is the source of this joy? It is the awareness that God loves us with a maternal love. One has to open oneself to this love by «doing God's will.» Thérèse often ascribes her happiness to doing the will of God.[2] «The only happiness on earth is to apply oneself in always finding delightful the lot that Jesus is giving us» (LT 257, 1148). She refuses to choose for herself, therefore; she lets God choose for her.[3] So she is always right: «When He seems to mislead me, I pay Him all sorts of compliments and He doesn't know what to do with me» (DE 6.7.3).

The will of God for Thérèse will often be synonymous with «suffering,» which is another source of joy.[4] The days when she has greater trials are called 'her Sundays and her feast days' (CSG, p. 199). She declares herself to be ready for everything (DE 25.8.8), and invites the Lord to never «put Himself out» on her account (DE 10.6). «Since we are on earth to suffer, the more we suffer, the happier we are!... Oh! how poorly we know how to arrange our little affairs on earth!»[5] Is this not the portion that she chose deliberately? For a Carmelite, joy «sought and tasted in works and sufferings is a very sweet reality, a foretaste of the happiness of Heaven» (LT 221, 1069). And she even goes to the point of wondering how she will be able to be happy in Heaven without suffering.[6]

In recalling Thérèse's story, we notice that she evolved a great deal in her appreciation of suffering. As a young child, she obviously did not like it and did not believe it necessary in order to arrive at holiness (A 32 r, 120). At the age of nine, she understands

---

[2] For example: LT 176, 902; 255, 1145; 258, 1151; DE 10.6; 15.6.2; 6.7.3; 14.7.9; DE II 10.8.4; DE 29.8.2; 30.8.2; 5.9.2; PN 24, str. 32; PN 45. Thérèse indicates still other sources of her happiness, that are the concrete forms of God's will. Thus: her presence at Carmel (A 53 v, 158; 65 v, 179; 69 r, 186; 77r, 199; LT 106, 620), obedience (C 11r, 248), poverty (A 74 r-v, 194 f.; CSG, pp. 162-164), her 'ignorance of created things' (38 r, 130; 81 r, 207), renunciation of herself (A 50 v, 152; C 22 r, 264; 31 r, 276; DE 18.7.9; 3.8.1; DE II 3.8.2 b; CSG, pp. 130, 135, 171; PO, p. 452 f.), the love of God (A 45 v, 143; B 4 v, 228 f.; C 16 r, 255; PN 45). «When we really love, we rejoice in the happiness of our Beloved,» she told Marie of the Trinity (PO, p. 459).

[3] For example: DE 27.5.4; 4.9.7; 14.9.3; 29.9.11. See CSG, p. 228: «we desire to become like *little children*.... Well, little children do not know what is best for them, they think everything is good. Let us imitate them.»

[4] For example: LT 226, 1092; DE 19.5; DE II 21-26.5.6; DE 27.5.6; 25.7.1.

[5] Marie of the Sacred Heart, PO, p. 248.

[6] LT 254, 1141; 258, 1151.

the necessity of it (A 10 r, 84). But she suffers «without *loving* suffering» until the age of eleven and a half: then, suffering becomes the object of a «real love» and of a «great desire» (A 36 r, 127). Reflecting on this grace, she will confess later: «I had a perpetual desire to suffer. I wasn't thinking, however, of making suffering my joy. This is a grace that was given to me only later on» (DE 31.7.13). When does joy appear, then? It seems to be the fruit of a slow maturation, historically difficult to lay hold of. At Carmel, Thérèse often speaks of the privilege of suffering and her letters of 1889 sometimes make mention of her joy.[7] But after all, this seems to be a wise joy, a joy of conviction: «The one who says *peace* is not saying *joy*, or at least, *felt joy*; to suffer in peace, it is enough to will all that Jesus wills» (LT 87, 552). We must wait, it seems, until the last years of her life to see joy caused by suffering fill her entire existence; it then seems to win even the emotional area. «I have suffered very much since I was on earth, but, if in my childhood I suffered with sadness, it is no longer in this way that I now suffer; it is with joy and peace. I am truly happy to suffer» (C 4 v, 240). «I am as one risen… I have come to the point where I cannot suffer any longer, because all suffering is sweet to me» (DE 29.5). And the height of the trial which has taken away from her «all my joy» is also the height of her joy (C 7 r, 243).

It is not suffering *in itself* and *for itself* which is the object of joy for Thérèse. She is not a masochist. Let us listen to her, during the course of her last sickness: «I didn't expect to suffer like this; I'm suffering like a little child. I would never want to ask God for greater sufferings. If He increases them, I will bear them with pleasure and with joy because they will be coming from Him. But I'm too little to have the strength all by myself. If I were to ask for sufferings, these would be my own, and I would have to bear them alone, and I've never been able to do anything alone» (DE 11.8.3). Thérèse does not therefore ask for nor does she seek on her own the sufferings which come to her. If she says that she loves this suffering and finds in it her joy, it is because she accepts it as the concrete and existential situation in which she seeks and loves Jesus, the object of her joy. What is important is not to suffer; it is

[7] For example LT 78, 511; 85, 546.

rather to love Jesus here and now, even in painful situations. Thérèse never explained so clearly as she did at the end of Manuscript A that it is the concrete will of God which attracts her and fascinates her: «And now I have no other desire except to *love* Jesus unto folly.... I no longer desire suffering nor death, and still I love them both; but it is *love* alone that attracts me.... Now, abandonment alone guides me. I have no other compass! I can no longer ask for anything with fervor except the perfect accomplishment of God's will in my soul without any creature being able to set obstacles in the way» (A 82 v - 83 r).

When suffering comes, Thérèse remembers that Jesus Himself is there also and that she can live through the difficult situation with Him. The presence of suffering becomes for the generous Thérèse even a challenge. She experiences a reawakening of fervor which makes her consider the difficult situation like a high point where she can love intensely, more intensely. Desirous of «martyrdom» — that of the «heart» and of the «body» (Pri 2), that of «Love» (Pri 6) — Thérèse, who feels in herself «the vocation of warrior and martyr» (B 2 v, 224), knows that she can now «crimson the battle area with the blood of (her) heart» (Pri 18). Desirous of «resembling» Jesus (Pri 11), Thérèse desires to imitate Jesus in His unconditional fidelity to the Father and in His redeeming attitude; she desires, with suffering or without suffering, «to quench» the «thirst of love» of Jesus, through saving «souls» with Him (Pri 12).

Thérèse does not recoil before any situation. It is this which makes her appreciate and love suffering, not for itself, but for the opportunities of love which suffering contains and which Thérèse wants generously to exploit. Let us remember Manuscript B, written one year before her death. Already sick and sure to die, plunged in her trial of faith, Thérèse suffers, but more than ever her desires for «martyrdom» are at their zenith (cf. B 3 r, 225). «The longer and sharper the thorns,» the more she will sing (B 4 v, 228), because in the heart of the Church, she wants to «be Love» (B 3 v, 226). Therein lies the secret of her joy, even in the midst of suffering. The total self-giving of her love gives her the joy of being for Jesus an «unpetalled rose» (PN 51). The mystery of Thérèse's joy....

But the most typical Thérésian joy is that which is born of the encounter between her littleness and mercy. This is why she speaks of «the true joy that she experiences in her heart, seeing herself as she really is in God's eyes: a poor little nothing, nothing at all...» (C 2 r, 236). We have preserved several memories of a Thérèse radiant with joy after someone had reproached or humiliated her.[8] But more still than when she is judged imperfect, her joy is «especially when I feel I actually am. This joy is sweeter than all praise, which only bores me» (DE 2.8.6). It's not that she does not say «alas!» in seeing herself 'still at the same place as she was formerly,' but she notes it «with a great peace, and without any sadness. It is so good to feel that one is weak and little!»[9] So she knows how to «always find a way of being happy and of profiting from her miseries» (A 80 r, 205). One day, after a number of failures she confides to Sister Geneviève: «It fills me with joy to have been imperfect; today God has granted me great graces; it has been a profitable day indeed» (CSG, p. 25).

If Thérèse radiates joy around her (C 28 r-v, 272 f.) and brings cheerfulness and vivacity to common recreation, the Sisters really feel that this exterior brightness springs from an interior joy.[10] Her smile had already become legendary. But they probably all do not understand that this smile is most often produced by «the habit of always welcoming suffering eagerly» (CSG, p. 215), or because she feels thorns: «And the longer and sharper the thorns, the sweeter will be my song» (B 4 v, 2 28).

2. *Liberty*

Bound with all her heart to God's purpose, Thérèse feels more and more free: 'not doing her own will, she does it nevertheless'

---

[8] See PO, pp. 145 f., 403, 433, 467; PA, pp. 243, 417. Sometimes Thérèse answers: «You are very right, I am still much more imperfect than you believe» (PO, p. 467). Concerning an event of this sort, she writes: «It is more than a pleasure, it is a delightful banquet which fills my soul with joy» (C 27 r, 271).

[9] DE 5.7.1. See CSG, p. 27: «[If someone] judges you to be without virtue, and if deep in your heart you agree with her, that would indeed be a cause for true abiding joy!» For the connection between humility and joy, see also CSG, pp. 28-30.

[10] Mother Agnès, PO, p. 166. In her last illness, we find her happy, cheerful, in peace (DE 5.7.2; 6.9.2; CSG, pp. 215-216, etc.). Yes, she appears more cheerful because of the suffering itself (CSG, p. 215; PO, p. 175).

from a more elevated point of view (CSG, p. 178). This liberty, this fruit of love, this reflection of her spiritual poverty (intensified by the filial atmosphere of her relationship with God), is surrounded by the most generous attentions.

This «child of God» declares that she is then free from herself: «For a long time I have not belonged to myself since I delivered myself totally to Jesus» (C 10 v, 248). She travels light, she runs (C 16 r, 255), she has wings (C 15 r, 254). Human praise will not make her withdraw into herself: «All creatures can bow towards her, admire her, and shower their praises upon her; I don't know why this is, but none of this could add one single drop of false joy.»[11] She is no longer attached to the «inspirations of the mind and heart» (C 19 r, 260): «All that He has given me, Jesus can take back!»[12] She does not worry that the Lord gives more beautiful things to others (DE 14.7.5). Health or death: «These things don't even skim the surface of my soul and they don't upset the peace within it.»[13] Succession of joy and sadness: «These changes only touch the surface of my soul» (DE 10.7.13). She is free from tribulation,[14] worry,[15] disappointment,[16] trouble,[17] fear.[18] While still on earth, she is in Heaven already: «I really don't see what more I'll have after my death that I don't already possess in this life.... I shall

[11] C 2 r, 236. See Mother Agnès, PA, p. 159: «It doesn't penetrate into the interior, it is a nothing that slides easily away, like water that cannot mix with oil.» Jesus can also «make me appear better than I am,» she says, «this is none of my affair [since He is free to act as He likes]» (C 2 r, 237).

[12] *Why I love You, O Mary* (PN 54, str. 16).

[13] Thérèse of Saint Augustine, PO, p. 400.

[14] It is the moment to notice that we don't want to exclude the physical or psychical oppressions that sometimes assail the young exhausted patient. Her attitudes of joy, peace, etc., withdraw then necessarily into a more interior area.

[15] C 10r, 247; LT 224, 1083; DE 4.6.1; 15.6.1; 30.6.1; 23.8.8; 25.8.1; 28.8.3; 29.8.2; etc. The fact that this peace is sometimes protected as a matter of life or death — proceeds from this confession of Thérèse: «The slightest infidelity» (for example of voluntary pride) would beget «frightful troubles» (DE 7.8.4). To avoid this misfortune, she knows a «very easy» means: humble prayer (DE 7.8.4).

[16] C 10 v, 248; DE 9.6.3; 10.6.

[17] DE 27.5.5.

[18] It is sufficient to recall that she is living under the law of love, not under that of fear (B 3 v, 226; LT 191, 965; 247, 1132). She doesn't climb «the rough *stairway* of fear» (LT 258, 1151), «a fear not fitting for a little child» (LT 205, 1033). See also B 1 r, 220; LT 191, 965; 226, 1092; 258, 1151.

see the good God, it is true! but as far as being in His presence, I am totally there here on earth» (DE 15.5.7). She is this just person for whom «ALL is well» (C 2 v, 237), this child for whom «everything is grace» (DE 5.6.4). She very much loves the verse that Saint John of the Cross wrote at the summit of Mount Carmel: «Here, there is no longer any path, because there is no law for the just man» (CSG, p. 105). If there is a law still, it is the supreme law of love and the search for it. Other than that, she has no more worry:

No, nothing worries me,
Nothing can trouble me.
Higher than the lark
My soul knows how to fly![19]

Yes, 'her soul flies' to Heaven, but without being preoccupied: «Since I am putting forth all my efforts to be a very little child, I have no preparations to make. Jesus Himself will have to pay the expenses of the journey and the cost of entering Heaven!»[20]

3. *Courage*

It has been said of Thérèse that she was «impervious to discouragement.»[21] But it is again an effect of her confidence in God. Thus, she does not get discouraged in the face of her imperfection and her faults,[22] which is, moreover, a characteristic of «little children.»[23] She counts on the Heavenly Father: «God gives me courage in proportion to my sufferings. I feel that at this moment I couldn't endure any more suffering, but I'm not afraid, since, if it

---

[19] *Abandonment,* of May 1897 (PN 52, str. 16). This poem summarizes very well what we have just said about her liberty.

[20] LT 191, 965; see also LT 197, 998 («He wills to give us His Heaven gratuitously») and DE 9.6.5.

[21] Thérèse of Saint Augustine, PA, p. 331. At the beginning of her religious life, she sometimes admits to being without courage (LT 65, 467; 75, 501; 82, 536; 89, 556). Later, this changes and one of her slogans becomes: «If I fall to the ground, I will surely be found» (CSG, p. 152).

[22] C 31 r, 276; LT 202, 1021; DE 3.7.2; DE 20.7.1, etc.

[23] DE 6.8.8. See 18.8.5 on the devil: «With the very little, he cannot do anything....»

increases, He will increase my courage at the same time.»[24] Truly, she is not deceiving herself! She knows that real courage does not consist in momentary fervor in which beautiful dreams are conceived. No, it consists in being willing to accept suffering «in anguish of soul and, at the same time, with a natural desire to turn away from it, as Our Lord experienced His own suffering in the Garden of Olives.»[25]

Since courage depends on Jesus, one need not be anxious about tomorrow: «We shouldn't be thinking of sufferings that can take place in the future. This shows a lack of confidence, it's like meddling in the work of creation» (DE 23.7.3). No, we must live «now» (DE 20.5.1), «just for today» (PN 5), «to think of nothing but the present moment» (DE 23.8.3), to suffer «one instant at a time» (DE 19.8.10), «from minute to minute» (DE 26.8.3), because «from one moment to the next, we can put up with very much» (DE 14.6). According to Thérèse, the way of the poor in spirit demands that we «live day to day, without laying up any spiritual provisions,» without «seeking signs» (CSG, p. 34). To think about the future is «childishness,» says the Saint of «spiritual childhood» (LT 167, 870). And in order to overcome difficulties, she counsels wisely «to pass under» them, that is to say «not to consider them at very close range, not to reason too much about them» (CSG, pp. 49-50), but to run towards Jesus.[26]

4. *Gratitude*

Knowing that everything comes to her from God, Sister Thérèse, who shows herself to be so thankful in her letters, often lets a hymn of gratitude towards divine Mercy spring from her heart.[27] «When I think of all the graces God has given me,» she said,

---

[24] DE 15.8.6. See also 25.8.2; 26.8.2; 29.9.11; PO, p. 400.

[25] CSG, p. 191. «I don't pity the saints who suffer; united to God, they have the strength to support their sufferings and even find sweetness in them. But for those who are not saints, this is something else; oh! how I pity them!» (*Obituary Circular* of Sister Marie-Philomène of Jesus, p. 4).

[26] C 7 r, 243. See «When I don't understand the turn of events, I keep on smiling. I even turn to Our Lord and say 'thank you'; I always appear happy before the good God» (CSG, p. 98).

[27] For example: A 40 r, 134; 43 r, 139; 70 r, 188; 84 v, 213; B 1 r, 219; 5 v, 231; LT 201, 1013; 230, 1100; etc.

«I restrain myself so as not to shed tears of gratitude continually» (DE 12.8.3). But let us be brief. We would be wrong to insist too much on her many words of gratitude. For in friendship, this gift of oneself is the best and most real answer to the gift received! Whatever the case may be, Thérèse's response was very magnanimous, even if it was clothed in humble forms.

II. HOLINESS AND ITS EXTERNAL MANIFESTATIONS

1. *At the very heart of the notion of holiness*

Father Godefrey Madelaine was right when he said: Thérèse Martin was a very «magnanimous» soul (PO, p. 522). The dream of her youth to become 'a great Saint' (A 32 v, 120) never disappeared. Her «little way» will bring new means, but will not alter the goal. It is perhaps on the very day that she narrates her discovery in Manuscript C that she exhorts Marie of the Trinity to «be a great saint, while remaining *little* and becoming more so each day.»[28]

But ever since her first call to holiness, she was oriented toward a way in which «striking works» are not necessary (A 32 r, 119). She will always understand their relativity, as we have emphasized. When she defines or describes holiness, she therefore does not attach it to this or that exterior form. She aims at the fundamental elements: love,[29] the perfect accomplishment of the divine will,[30] abandonment,[31] God's mercy,[32] confidence,[33] humility,[34]

---

[28] LT 242, 1120, of June 6, 1897. Addressing herself to others, she also encourages them to dream of great perfection: for example: LT 198, 1009; 201, 1013; 211, 1038; 220, 1058; 244, 1127; 247, 1132; 257, 1148.

[29] For example: LT 109, 640; 224, 1083; 244, 1127; Manuscript B and the *Act*.

[30] For example: A 2 v, 72, LT 142, 794.

[31] For example: LT 201, 1013.

[32] For example: LT 224, 1083; Manuscript B; the *Act*; C 3 r, 238; DE 4.8.2; LT 243, 1121.

[33] For example: C 3 r, 238; DE 4.8.2; Manuscript B; LT 191, 965, 197, 998; 226, 1092; A 32r, 120.

[34] For example: A 32 r, 120; C 3 r, 237; DE 4.8.2; LT 82, 536; 224, 1083; 226, 1092; 243, 1121.

suffering,[35] and renunciation.[36] The essence of holiness resides in the beauty inside a person and not in any exterior glory,[37] nor in striking works,[38] lights, or experiences.[39] Already, through the terminology alone, the outside face of Thérésian holiness is shown: she almost always calls it «little,» opposing it vigorously but without contempt to the «great saints,» «great souls,» «great spirits,» the «lilies and roses,» «Fathers of the desert,» «martyrs of penance,» «eagles,» «beautiful toys,» «magnificent flowers.»[40] Thérèse said, with respect to her autobiography: «There will be something in it for all tastes, except for those in extraordinary ways» (DE 9.8.2). What, then, is this «extraordinary» that she excludes from her way? She gives us some examples: to want to die after Communion (PO, p. 469), to desire a celestial vision (FA, p. 303), to want to see a sign of her happiness after her death (DE 4.6.1), to desire that her body be found intact after her death (PA, p. 311). Let us study more closely Thérèse's life of prayer (in a broad sense) and her ascetic life: two important domains for a contemplative and a novice mistress.

2. *Flight from the extraordinary in her life of prayer*

We do not know whether Thérèse, recognizing the non-necessity of «striking works» since 1882, had applied her principle immediately to extraordinary mystical phenomena. At Carmel, she endures God's silence with love. She had already declared in 1890: «I have no desire to go to Lourdes to have ecstasies. I prefer the monotony of sacrifice!» (LT 106, 620). She does not want to invite Geneviève to aim for the «*seraphic* sanctity» of Teresa of Avila (LT 107, 621). The more than three years of martyrdom caused by her father's illness are worth more to her than «all the ecstasies and revelations of the saints» (A 73 r, 193). She admires the holiness of

---

[35] For example: A 10 r, 84; 32 r, 120; LT 89, 556; 184, 935; 244, 1127.

[36] For example: A 10 r, 84; 33 r, 121; LT 257, 1148.

[37] CSG, pp. 205-208.

[38] A 32 r, 120.

[39] A 78 r, 201; C 19 r-v, 260; LT 89, 556.

[40] For example: A 2 v-3 r, 72 f.; B 5 v, 231; C 2 v-3 r, 237; LT 176, 902; 226, 1092; 247, 1132; DE 16.7.6; CSG, pp. 23, 46, 48, 53, 175; PO, p. 403.

Mother Geneviève, «seeing the high degree to which Jesus was living within her and making her act and speak,» without her needing revelations (A 78 r, 201 f.). The constant aridity of her prayer does not distress her at all; on the contrary, it is a joy.[41]

What, then, is the character of her prayer? «I do not have the courage to force myself to search out *beautiful* prayers in books. There are so many of them it really gives me a headache!... and each prayer is more *beautiful* than the others. I cannot recite them all and not knowing which to choose, I do like children who do not know how to read, I say very simply to God what I wish to say, without making up beautiful phrases, and He always understands me. For me, *prayer* is an aspiration of the heart, it is a simple glance directed to Heaven, it is a cry of gratitude and love in the midst of trial as well as joy; finally, it is something great and supernatural which expands my soul and unites me to Jesus» (C 25 r-v, 268). «I simply tell Him my pains and joys as if He did not know them...» (C 32 v, 279). «It is especially the *Gospels* which sustain me during my hours of prayer, for in them I find what is necessary for my poor little soul» (A 83 v, 211). «At times, when I am reading certain spiritual treatises in which perfection is shown through a thousand obstacles, surrounded by a crowd of illusions, my poor little mind quickly tires; I close the learned book that is breaking my head and drying up my heart and I take up Holy Scripture. Then all seems luminous to me; a single word uncovers for my soul infinite horizons and perfection seems easy to me.»[42] «For simple souls there must be no complicated ways» (C 33 v, 280). In her frequent aridity she uses a book, especially Sacred Scripture, or a vocal prayer.[43] The structure of Thérésian prayer is very simple.

---

[41] A 75 v, 197; B 5 r, 229.

[42] LT 226, 1092.

[43] See A 73 v, 194; 83 r-v, 210 f.; B 1 r, 219; C 25 v, 269; LT 193, 977. It can be interesting to note, in regard to simplicity in the life of prayer, that Thérèse didn't believe it contrary to the rather numerous vocal prayers. Let us recall however that we are considering a nun in the contemplative life. Here is a list of vocal prayers that Thérèse recited *every day*. Sister Geneviève informs us of it. Apart from the Divine Office and common prayers: the Rosary (PA, p. 267); a *Memorare* (*ibid.*); the prayer «O Saint Joseph, father and protector of virgins» (*ibid.*); the prayer «O good and very sweet Jesus» (PA, p. 287); «the six *Our Fathers* and *Aves* of the scapular of the Immaculate Conception» (*ibid.*); another practice of devotion rich in indulgences (*ibid.*). In addition, the Way of the Cross, several times per week (PA, p. 264).

The refusal to desire extraordinary mystical phenomena is clear from her own statements. Concerning prayer: «Extraordinary graces never tempted me» (PO, p. 175); concerning visions: «I never desired extraordinary graces for myself, this is not my little way» (PA, p. 303). She said, following Saint John of the Cross, that to desire extraordinary graces is a venial sin (CSG, p. 204). All this takes root in a larger principle of the «little way»: to live on faith. «It is in the spirit of my *little way* not to desire to see anything» (DE 4.6.1). She prefers faith to «seeing and understanding everything» (DE 11.8.5), to seeing God or the saints on earth (DE 4.6.1; 11.9.7), to visions (DE 5.8.4), or to lights on the faith (DE 13.8). «It is so sweet,» she said, «to serve God in the night of trial; we have only this life to practice our faith» (CSG, p. 197). Pushed by the same love of the life of faith, she reacts against all exaggeration of the marvelous in the life of Mary, Joseph, and Jesus in Nazareth.[44]

3. *Flight from the extraordinary in corporal mortification*

Thérèse also understood that exaggeration in the area of bodily penance can easily lead to the exaltation of oneself, a danger which she knew how to avoid. And for such a «little soul,» she foresaw that, in the house of our Heavenly Father, her dwelling place would not be that of those who practice «astonishing mortifications» (LT 247, 1132), those who are «martyrs of penance» (CSG, p. 48).

However, Thérèse underwent an evolution in this domain. If before her entrance she turned away from mortification by means of penitential instruments (CSG, p. 186), practicing only these 'nothings that break her will' (A 68 v), at Carmel her taste changed. «The love of mortification,» that is to say, «bodily penances,» was given to her then, but the superiors did not allow her to perform any.[45] Nevertheless, she profited from opportunities. During her novitiate she would eat her food unflavored and at times would choose those

[44] See DE 20.8.11; 23.8.9.

[45] A 74 v, 195. See also Mother Agnès (PO, p. 168) and the mistress of novices (PA, p. 357) who adds that Thérèse asked, repeatedly, for permission to multiply penances.

dishes which were even repugnant to her.[46] Besides this, she was very faithful — and with great generosity! — to the three disciplines of the rule each week and to the wearing of penitential instruments which she also used three times per week for hours at a time, at least after a certain time in religious life.[47]

Two things changed her original appreciation of harsh penances: first, the disproportion that she noted in some nuns between the love of great austerity and their progress in holiness[48]; and then, her own experience. Having worn a small cross with iron tips for too long a time, she cut herself and needed to be taken care of. Thérèse believed that this is a sign from the Lord: «You can see for yourself that extraordinary penances are not for me; God knows very well that I desire them, but He never willed the realization of this desire, otherwise, I would not have been sick for such a little thing. What is that next to the mortifications of the saints? Besides I would have found too much joy in it, and natural satisfactions are very capable of mingling with the most austere penance. We must be aware of this. Believe me, my Mother, never set out along this way, this is not the way of very little souls like ours.»[49] Mother Agnès liked to emphasize that this light was very important. However, let us note that it came late, after Easter 1896, and that at this time the Saint had already asked for permission several times to wear penitential instruments (DCL).

If Thérèse avoids excessive corporal mortifications after a time, she was certainly always very mortified with regard to her body, inspired by the love of Jesus which profits from the least opportunities. Thus, she never leaned back in her chair while sitting, did not cross her feet, always stood straight, and did not sit down haphazardly (PO, p. 295). She ate everything served in the refectory, did not mix foods, and advised others to end their meal with something distasteful (PO, p. 464). She drank a loathsome

---

[46] See Mother Agnès, PA, p. 184.

[47] CSG, p. 186 and DCL. See here p. 101, footnote n. 60.

[48] CSG, p. 186 and *La Fondation du Carmel de Lisieux et sa Fondatrice la Révérende Mère Geneviève de Sainte-Thérèse*, Paris-Bar-le-Duc, 1912, pp. 56-57.

[49] Mother Agnès, PO, p. 168 s.; HA 07, p. 230 had added: «Nor for the little souls who will follow the same way of childhood.»

remedy slowly (HA 99, p. 261). Already suffering in her throat (and therefore very sensitive to moisture and dust), she never excused herself from the laundry, the dishes, or sweeping (PA, p. 190). She wore without complaining the habits which did not fit her very well (DE 15.5.4; 5.8.1). She volunteered for all the unpleasant tasks, especially for the laundry where, in the summer, she remained at the wash-house, and in the winter, washed in cold water (PA, p. 354). In the winter, she did not want to warm up in the kitchen, her hands were sometimes swollen and covered with chilblains (PA, p. 416), and she covered them rarely and exposed them intentionally to the cold weather (PO, p. 296). She taught others never to avoid, except by obedience, the smallest practice of mortification, not to stoop when it was cold: even not to shiver (PO, p. 464 f.) or to rub their hands together or close their sleeves![50] The cold weather was her most afflicting penance in her unheated monastery, she confessed: «I've suffered from the cold so much that I believe it's not possible to endure more of it» («to the point of dying from it,» PA, p. 241), but she asked for nothing (PO, p. 464 f.). «She never complained about anything,» summarized Mother Agnès (PO, p. 168).

The prioress adds however: «I saw her apply herself to mortification with more simplicity and moderation as she approached the end of her exile» (PA, p. 184). «She would have believed she had sinned against temperance in not enjoying the charms of nature, of music, etc., when she was attracted to these by a thought of love and gratitude towards God. She told me that, love being the only goal, the action into which we put more love, even though it were in itself indifferent, must be preferred to another one, perhaps better in itself, but in which we put less love» (*ibid.*).

What is to be concluded from all this concerning Thérèse's bodily mortification? 1. It is at the service of love: all bodily mortifications (without love) are nothing when placed in the balance with charity (CSG, p. 187); 2. It is inspired by the concrete requirements of love (for example the love of neighbor, duty, the Rule) in all the providentially «offered» opportunities, which thereby become crosses that are truly «sought»; 3. It is practiced without constraint, so that the mind remains free (DE 1.8.6). As for instruments

[50] PA, p. 295.

of penance, Thérèse insists: «We must be very restrained in these practices, for often nature is involved in this matter more than anything else» (DE 3.8.5).

4. Examples

In order to illustrate her thought, the young Carmelite offers some examples to us. Thus, she often praises Saint Cecilia because of her fearless abandonment (DE 30.6.1). She also speaks to us of Mother Geneviève with whom she lived: the «*Saint*, not one that was inimitable, but a Saint who was made holy by the practice of the hidden and ordinary virtues.»[51] More still she loves Blessed Théophane Vénard: he is simplicity itself, he leads an ordinary life, he is always cheerful, he loves his family and the Mother of God very much, and in his difficulties he practices a loving abandonment.[52] Sometimes she mentions other examples too, but in a *negative* sense: Saint Simon Stylites, the «admirable» (DE II, 30.6.1) or Blessed Suso, whose «frightful» penances she had read.[53]

But the greatest example of the «little way» is the Virgin Mary. Thérèse obligingly applies herself to describing her. For a long time she had wanted «to express, in a poem, everything that she thought about the Blessed Virgin» (CSG, p. 122). The last time that she cel-

---

[51] A 78 r, 201. Often she gives her the title of saint (A 69 v, 186; 78 r, 201; 78 v, 202; 79 r, 203; LT 130, 731; 134, 747). Thérèse is rather generous with this title: her father is a saint (A 50 v, 152; 76 v, 199); the mistress of novices is «*really a saint*» (A 70 v, 188), the Sister with the talent of displeasing her in everything is «a religious saint» (C 13 v, 252), M. and Mme. Guérin are saints (LT 178, 907), their daughter and her husband are also (*ibid.*), their other daughter isn't one yet, but will become one easily (*ibid.*), M. David, although he converted on his deathbed (LT 59, 453), is one too (LT 60, 455).

[52] DE 27.5.10; 21-26.5.1; HA 98, chap. XII, see DE 17.8.5 and 21- 26.5.1; Mother Agnès, PO, p. 166; Sister Geneviève, PO, p. 291. Thérèse had read his biography which had «interested me and touched me more than I could express» (LT 221, 1069); she borrowed his thoughts, because their souls «resemble each other» (LT 245). To Blessed Vénard, she sometimes contrasts Saint Aloysius Gonzaga, who was less cheerful (PO, p. 166) and had a more extraordinary life, at least, she adds, according to his biographer (DE 21-26.5.1). See also P. DESTOMBES, «Une amitié céleste. Sainte Thérèse de l'Enfant-Jésus et le bienheureux Théophane Vénard,» *Carmel* (France), 1961, pp. 6-24.

[53] DE 3.8.5. One must read the narration that the Rhenish mystic made in his autobiography (chap. 17-20) of his mortifications, to better understand what Saint Thérèse wants to avoid.

ebrated the month of May on earth, she will succeed in doing it. «Why I love You, O Mary,» and «Why the thought of your supreme greatness / could not bring fear to my soul,» she wonders. She responds: because «I am your child» and because «I see you [in the Gospels] human and suffering like me.» Indeed, Christ's glorious Mother appears to Thérèse as the prototype of the «very little»: Mary is the «little handmaid,» the humble one. «It's not impossible to follow in your footsteps… the narrow road to Heaven,» says Thérèse. «You made it visible, while always practicing the humblest virtues. Near you, Mary, I like to stay little.… You teach me… *to glory in Jesus, my Savior.*» Then follows the description of Mary's vicissitudes on earth: Thérèse especially emphasizes the ordinary life setting which invites us all to believe, to have confidence, and to abandon ourselves. Thus Mary is the example for little ones, and this is the main reason why Thérèse admires her so much. One stanza summarizes the entire poem:

> *Mother full of grace, I know that in Nazareth*
> *You live in poverty, wanting nothing more;*
> No rapture, miracle, or ecstasy
> Embellish your life, O Queen of the elect!…
> *The number of little ones on earth is truly great,*
> *They can raise their eyes to you without trembling;*
> *It's by the* ordinary way, *incomparable Mother,*
> *That You like to walk to guide them to Heaven.*[54]

Speaking of the Holy Family, she makes the same points: «a life that was very ordinary» (DE 20.8.14), «everything in their life was done just as in our own» (*ibid.*). «They show the Blessed Virgin to us as unapproachable, but they should present her as imitable, bringing out the hidden virtues she practiced and saying that she lived by faith, just as we do.»[55]

---

[54] *Why I love you, O Mary* (PN 54, str. 17).

[55] DE 21.8.3; see also DE II 11.7.4; DE 20.8.11; 21.8.3. More than once people have pointed out the line that joins the «poor of Yahweh,» Mary, and Thérèse: see A. GÉLIN, *Les pauvres que Dieu aime*, pp. 144- 145; R. LAURENTIN, *Court Traité de théologie mariale*, 1959, 4 ed., p. 22; E. SCHILLEBEECKX, *Marie, Mère de la Rédemption*, Paris, 1966, 2 ed., p. 37 f.

Thérèse illustrates her «way of childhood» in another way as well: in referring to the example of the child itself! She did this often. But notice that she almost always uses the word «child» in its positive sense. Thérèse knows well that there exist poorly raised, spoiled, and ungrateful children,[56] but she does not seem to think of them spontaneously. At worst, and only *exceptionally*, she speaks of a sulky, mischievous, and disobedient child[57]; she also negatively observes the lack of personality or the childishness in some children.[58] But this is nothing in comparison with all the good that she sees in children. Just as she projected the idea of fatherhood through her own experience of an «incomparable» father, she looks at the image of a child only through her own experience as a very good and well-behaved child. To analyze this image would take us afield. Let us be content to point out the strong points of children, such as: littleness, poverty, humility, love, affability, simplicity, honesty, confidence, and abandonment.

5. *The criterion*

There still remains one last question, perhaps the most delicate one. What criterion does Thérèse use when she excludes this or that element from her «way of spiritual childhood»? What does she mean by «extraordinary»?

First of all, let us remember the original core which oriented her entire search for perfection: in order to become holy, one must be very little, and become so more each day. However, it is clear that the essential part of holiness — the life of grace, the growth of virtues[59] — cannot be considered as foreign to the «little way,» although Thérèse demands that we must never take pride in the gifts received from God nor think of them as if they were our own. She

---

[56] As a girl, she liked to observe children: see A 52 v, 156 f.; PO, p. 347, 365; PA, p. 479 f.; *La Petite Thérèse à l'abbaye…*, p. 20.

[57] LT 191, 965; 258, 1151, in the comparison of the two children after their mistake.

[58] A 43 v, 139; 44 v, 141; LT 201, 1013; 206, 1034.

[59] Sometimes, depending on the context in which they are found, the same words indicate what she either wants or what she doesn't consider suitable to her «little way» (for example, «sublime virtues», A 76 r, 198 and LT 176, 902; «striking works», PN 24, str. 19 and A 32 r, 119; «follies» of love, LT 225, 1090 and B 5 v, 231).

also does not exclude mystical graces, even those which are very intense, as long as they are communicated according to God's ordinary means of acting.[60] She herself was certainly familiar with these graces, which anyway are only a blossoming of baptismal grace,[61] but «she usually kept silent on the favors that she received»[62] and was not inclined to analyze their nature and their degree. She therefore speaks very little of them and never in a technical sense, and her mystical life thus remains very mysterious, so much so that the depositions of the witnesses sometimes raise problems of a critical order and we may question whether they are *objectively* trustworthy. She also notices how Jesus nourishes her and illuminates her internally at each moment (A 76 r, 198; 83 v, 211).

It is not so easy to discern what Thérèse looks upon as unsuitable for a «little soul» because she only gave some general indications of this. We can, all the same, say that such a soul avoids

---

[60] Thus we exclude those that are communicated by way of the external senses (exterior visions, words, etc.) or formed in the imagination (imaginary visions) or communicated directly to the understanding (intellectual visions, revelations, interior words). Let us add those that appear externally (raptures, ecstasies). See MARIE-EUGÈNE DE L'ENFANT-JÉSUS, *Je veux voir Dieu*, Tarascon, 1956, 3 ed., pp. 706-708.

[61] See A 35 r, 125 (First Communion); 36 r, 126 f. (Second Communion and others); 47 v-48 r, 146 f. (the time of the conversations at the Belvédère); DE 11.7.2 (an entire week during her novitiate; see also HA 98, chap. XII — DE II 11.7.6 — of slightly different formulation); Mother Agnès, PO, p. 174 f. and PA, p. 198 («in the garden several times, at the hour of great silence in the evening, I felt in such great contemplation and my heart was so united to God, I formed with so much ardor and yet so effortlessly, such longings of love, that it really seems to me that these graces were the "flights of the spirit," as Saint Teresa calls them»), but DE 11.7.2 said in a more accentuated way: she «told me that she understood then by experience what a flight of the spirit was»; her experience during the Way of the Cross, on the Friday after her *Offering to Merciful Love* (HA 98, chap. XII — DE II 7.7.4.; DE 7.7.2; PO, p. 175 and PA, p. 198 say it all: «Wounded suddenly with such an ardent fire that I thought I would die»); A 84 r, 212 (months after her offering: love penetrates her, surrounds her, renews her, purifies her); CSG, p. 167 («very often, it is in the refectory that the sweetest aspirations of love come to me. Sometimes, I am forced to stop.»).

The silence which Thérèse generally observed concerning "mystical phenomena" is to be noted carefully. Most of the testimonies noted above come from others. She associated mysticism not with extraordinary phenomena, but with loving Jesus, in the growing consciousness of being loved by Him. «To love Jesus and to make Him loved» (LT 218, 1054; LT 220, 1058) was the *raison d'être* of her life. God is in everybody's present moment all the time, irrespective of how one may feel and experience one's relationship with Him.

[62] Thérèse of Saint Augustine, PA, p. 339

everything that threatens the ideal of littleness; so she thinks first about exterior things which are not essential to holiness and which ordinarily stir up — especially in the way of thinking and the environment which were current in her time — the admiration of others: for example, penitential feats, ecstasies, visions and revelations, miracles and, in general, the whole range of the marvelous[63] that one finds in certain hagiographers. What is specific to the «way of childhood» are «the ordinary means» according to an expression of Sister Geneviève (CSG, p. 48). The marvelous, however, even if it had only been «the exception»[64] in Thérèse's life, was not completely absent from it. One could object that these events took place in good part before the discovery of the «little way,»[65] but the

---

[63] Let us note that her profession was made «not in the midst of thunder and lightning, that is to say, in extraordinary graces» (A 76v, 199).

[64] Mother Agnès, PA, p. 197. «Very rare,» says Sister Geneviève (CSG, pp. 40 and 48).

[65] Thérèse mentions a «truly extraordinary *vision*» in her childhood concerning her father, of which she is sure that it comes from God (A 20 r - v, 100 f.), while she assures us that her dream of little devils has «nothing extraordinary» about it (A 10 v-11 r, 85). One knows of the vision of the Virgin Mary and the miraculous cure. We are not here making a serious examination of their supernatural authenticity. It is sufficient for us to note that Thérèse herself recognizes them as such. On her «ecstasy» while dying, see here p. 219, footnote n. 50. Sometimes she asks for a sign from Heaven (A 46 r, 144; 80 r, 205; 82 v, 209) and obtains it too, but not by any extraordinary way. As for her dreams, she «attaches no importance to them» (A 79 r, 203). However, some of them leave a great impression on her: about the little devils (A 10 v-11 r, 85), of Mother Geneviève who leaves her heart to Thérèse (A 79 r, 203), of Sister Fébronie in purgatory who asks for prayers (Mss II, 61) and particularly (in 1896) the one about Venerable Anne of Jesus (B 2 r - v, 222 f.).

Two words on a difficult passage from the *Act*: «I ask You to come and take possession of my soul. Ah! I cannot receive Holy Communion as often as I desire, but, Lord, are You not *All-Powerful*?.... Remain in me as in a tabernacle and never separate Yourself from Your little victim....» Is this a matter of a very extraordinary demand for the continual real Eucharistic Presence in her? We don't see any warrant for interpreting her words in such a manner. Thérèse asks for more intense and more complete union of the Lord with His little «victim» of holocaust, and that made her think about eucharistic union, about the continual Presence of Christ in the Eucharist. But this doesn't mean, in our opinion, that she asks for «the miraculous preservation of the Eucharistic species in her,» as A. BARRIOS MONEO thought (see «El problema de la conservación de las especies sacramentales en Santa Teresa de Lisieux,» *Revista de Espiritualidad*, 16 [1978], pp. 337- 382): he maintains that Thérèse not only asked for this grace, but obtained it.... The rather sparse and vague testimonies of the Processes of Beatification (Mother Agnès and Sister Marie of the Trinity) don't seem convincing to us. Moreover, Marie of the Trinity herself declared: «She never explained to me the manner of this presence, and I don't believe that she herself was ever preoccupied to search for what the mode of pres-

marvelous predictions and the charismatic consciousness of the last months undoubtedly remain as facts which cannot be denied.[66]

This leads us to another criterion, the most fundamental: *the interior attitude*. The one who does not receive anything nor ever does anything extraordinary or striking, but nevertheless desires it, is not in the «way of spiritual childhood.» On the other hand, the one who leads a life of holiness which is outwardly extraordinary, but does not glorify herself nor desire it, is in the same spirit of the «way of childhood.»

Is it enough to have the right spirit? No, one must also live a life that is generally *imitable*, like that of Thérèse of Lisieux: «Little souls must not be able to envy me in anything.»[67] «The extraordinary» will therefore be at least very rare.... But «in our Father's house, there are many mansions»... and Thérèse is convinced that it is through obedience to the Spirit that 'all is well' and pleasing to God (C 2 v, 237). One does not always choose one's own path.

But much more important than the absence of the extraordinary is true love of «the ordinary,» and it is especially this that Thérèse emphasized: love which manifests itself faithfully and generously in actions «within reach of all» (CSG, p. 40), humility, spiritual poverty, and confidence in divine Mercy alone.

III. HUMAN CULPABILITY AND DIVINE CLEMENCY

Thérèse of Lisieux's characteristic conceptions are also reflected where sin and imperfections are concerned. She understood human culpability until her death: she herself was imperfect, her novices struggled with it, and the fate of her brothers, the sinners, constantly preoccupied her.

---

ence was» (PA, p. 469 f.). See also B. JIMÉNEZ DUQUE («Literatura Teresiana,» *Revista de Espiritualidad*, 17 [1958], p. 603) who is opposed to the findings of Barrios Moneo. As for the demand — or better 'the hope,' which is more discreet — of Thérèse, expressed also in her *Act*, to receive the stigmata, let us note that she doesn't expect the realization of it except in Heaven, where the course of faith ends.

[66] The expression «total absence of charisms» of M.-M. PHILIPON (*Sainte Thérèse de Lisieux...*, p. 275) is unfortunate. As for predictions, H. PETITOT (*Sainte Thérèse de Lisieux...*, pp. 113 and 117) calls us to consider, alongside the supernatural light which is incontestable, «the part of genius.»

[67] Geneviève, PA, p. 311. See also PA, pp. 169, 311 and DE 15.7.1.

1. The Justice of Mercy

It is difficult to specify the precise time when Thérèse withdrew from the current opinion that tended to identify justice with severity. Her offering of the month of June 1895, born as we know in some way from contact with the idea of divine justice, must have contributed heavily to making her think about the coexistence of justice and mercy in God. Some months later, she writes in the very beautiful page where she explains that she sees all of God's attributes through mercy: «Then all [His perfections] appear to be resplendent *with love*; even His Justice (and perhaps this even more so than the others) seems to me clothed in *love*.[68]... What a sweet joy it is to think that God is *Just*, that is to say, that He takes into account our weakness, that He is perfectly aware of the fragility of our nature. What should I fear then? Ah! Must not the infinitely just God, Who deigned to pardon all the faults of the prodigal child with so much kindness, be just also towards me who "am with Him always"?» (A 83 v-84 r, 211-212).

Before dying, she returns to this theme and explains herself quasi-officially. «I know,» she writes to Father Rouilland, «that one must be very pure to appear before the God of all Holiness, but I also know that the Lord is infinitely just; and it is this justice, which frightens so many souls, that is the cause of my joy and confidence. To be just is not only to exercise severity in order to punish the guilty; it is also to recognize right intentions and to reward virtue. I expect as much from God's justice as from His mercy. It is because He is just that *"He is filled with gentleness and compassion, slow to punish, and abundant in mercy. For He knows our frailty. He remembers that we are only dust. As a father has tenderness for his children, so the Lord has compassion on us!"*»[69]

Justice is no longer for Thérèse the justice which requires *perfect* victims, but that of the New Covenant of love which turns its

[68] See S. THOMAS, *Summa Theologica*, I, q. 21, a. 4: «The work of divine justice presupposes the work of mercy and is based on it.... And so in all God's work appears mercy as for its first root.» See also Ch.-A. BERNARD, *Théologie de l'espérance selon Saint Thomas d'Aquin*, Paris, 1961, pp. 137-138.

[69] LT 226, 1092, of May 9, 1897. According to [French] DE II, 80 f., this passage constitutes the supplement to Manuscript A and it contains 'all the thought of Thérèse well explained.' The quotation is Ps 102, 8.14.13.

gaze upon the weak and imperfect creature (B 3 v, 227). She will still speak of severe justice, but only to emphasize that she does not feel called to it herself.[70] She does not follow a way of fear which leads to «strict» justice, but rather a way of confidence which leads to the experience of love (LT 197, 998). Her «Judge» will even carry her in His arms (CSG, p. 59).

2. *Confident repentance*

Convinced of the law of mercy, Thérèse no longer hesitates to determine her attitude where her own faults are concerned. To make up for them she lays hold of love. It is there that she finds a «rich mine» of justification (C 15 v, 254), «the chief plenary indulgence» (HA 55, p. 233), much more effective than corporal penances (CSG, p. 187). But if in these references to love it is a question of fraternal charity, Thérèse also applies them, of course, to the love of God, to whom one entrusts oneself in order to be purified. «As for me,» she said, «the only thing that will purify me is the fire of Divine Love» (CSG, p. 224), «a loving glance toward Jesus and the recognition of one's own misery is full reparation» (CSG, p. 137).

This loving glance is characterized in her by confidence in divine goodness. In order to explain herself, she uses the comparison of two little brothers who have disobeyed their father. One hides himself in fear and trembling and runs away. Thérèse thinks he will not be spared from punishment. The other throws himself into his father's arms, expresses his regret to him, assures him of his love, and promises to do better; he asks him «to punish him by a kiss.» The father will not resist this «filial confidence.» He presses the little fellow to his heart with tenderness, and forgets all about his fault and his punishment. Thérèse calls this taking hold of God «by His Heart.» He knows very well that the little boy will commit these same mistakes again, but when he comes back again, he will not punish him but will again forgive him.[71] Faults «sadden»

---

[70] See, for example, LT 230, 1100.

[71] See LT 191, 965; 258, 1151; CSG, p. 59. Thérèse was moved to tears when Marie of the Trinity asked one day for her forgiveness, and she said: «What must happen in the Heart of the good God when someone returns to Him?…» (PO, p. 463). As for

God, but she adds «it seems to me that it is *only* when those who are His own, unaware of their continual indelicacies, make a habit of them and do not ask His forgiveness.... [But] as for those who *love* Him and who come, after each indelicacy, to ask His pardon by throwing themselves into His arms, Jesus is thrilled with joy,» like the father of the prodigal child.[72]

When she adopts this attitude, Thérèse has her patrons: Saint Augustine and Saint Magdalene. She loves their repentance, but she especially loves «the loving audacity» of (Mary) Magdalene[73]: «I feel that *her heart* has understood the abysses of love and mercy of the *Heart of Jesus*, and, sinner though she is, this Heart of love was not only disposed to pardon her, but also to lavish on her the blessings of His divine intimacy.» Thérèse knows the way toward the Heart of God which undoes every fault — and how effectively He does it! «Ever since I have been given the grace to understand the love of the Heart of Jesus, I admit that it has expelled all fear from my heart! The remembrance of my faults humbles me, and persuades me never to depend on my strength which is only weakness; but more still this remembrance speaks to me of mercy and love.[74] When we cast our faults with an entirely filial confidence into the devouring fire of Love, how would these not be consumed beyond return?» (LT 247, 1132). The love of God is a fire. Thérèse

taking Him «by His Heart,» Thérèse also has other expressions of the same 'wisdom' of the child and she emphasizes the effectiveness of it. These are her «arrangements» (C 3 v, 238), «to draw profit from everything» (A 83 r, 210), her «stratagem of love» (C 1 v, 235), «to cover with caresses» (PN 45, str. 4). Remaining humble, she has the right of doing «stupid things» (DE 7.8.4). 'Through *her way*, she will do more work' (LT 247, 1132).

[72] LT 261, 1163. To fall «as a child» is not serious (DE II 7.8.2). And «children fall often, but they are too little to hurt themselves very much» (DE 6.8.8). See here pp. 123-125 on the encounter with Father Prou. Thérèse's conviction, then confirmed and according to which there are faults which don't cause pain to God, helped the nun in her reflections.

[73] LT 247, 1132; C 36 v, 285.

[74] Elsewhere she emphasizes the same effects of her faults: gratitude, love, deepening of God's mercy, joy, stronger hope (LT 230, 1100), humility (DE 7.8.4). Forgiveness has stronger effects for her than reproach (A 80 v, 206)! But sometimes she feels *sadness* after an infidelity: then she offers this feeling of sadness to God as a trial that He sends her through *love* (DE 3.7.2; CSG, p. 61). And the sadness passes very quickly (DE 2.9.6).

casts her faults into it with a complete confidence. She feels renewed and purified of all trace of sin.[75]

And what if it is a question of more serious sins? If one has the same confidence, she answers — but this supposes many things — one will obtain the same results. In the last lines of her autobiography, she repeats again that she would never abandon this attitude: «Yes, I feel it; even if I had on my conscience all the sins that can be committed, I would go, my heart broken with sorrow, and throw myself into Jesus' arms.» It is because of God's abundant mercy alone and not «because God, in His *anticipating* Mercy, has preserved my soul from mortal sin that I go to Him with confidence and love» (C 36 v, 285). She reveals her conviction again to Mother Agnès, showing how much she believes in the great effectiveness of a great confidence: «Really tell them, Mother, that, if I had committed all possible crimes, I would always have the same confidence; I feel that this whole multitude of offenses would be like a drop of water thrown into a fiery furnace.» She insists that they insert into her narration the story of the public sinner who, after a single night of loving repentance, died and entered Heaven: «Souls will understand immediately, and this example will encourage them... it's such a striking example of what I'm trying to say. However these things cannot be expressed in words...» (DE 11.7.6). To Marie of the Trinity, she explains herself again even more forcefully: «If the greatest sinner on earth, repenting his offenses at the time of death, dies in an act of love, immediately, without calculating on the one hand the numerous graces which this poor wretch abused or on the other hand all his crimes, [God] counts only his last prayer and receives him without delay into the arms of His Mercy» (PO, p. 454). According to Thérèse, he will therefore not even experience purgatory.[76]

---

75 Such is her experience after her *Act of Offering*, A 84 r-v, 212 f. See also PN 17, str. 6 and HA 55, p. 264.

76 In 1888 already, she wrote of M. David who converted only on his deathbed: «With dispositions as perfect as this, one can go straight to Heaven» (LT 60, 455).

3. Thérèse and purgatory

In 1895, «the year of Mercy,» the Saint of Lisieux confided: «I cannot fear purgatory.[77] ... [I know] that the Fire of Love is more sanctifying than the fire of purgatory. I know that Jesus cannot desire useless sufferings for us, and that He would not inspire the longings I feel unless He wanted to grant them.»[78] She explained many times that 'God who is all gentleness, would moderate to excess the temporal punishment due to sin, because of our love.' And she went further: to those who are humble and abandon themselves to God with love, He will respond to their confidence and will inspire in them at the hour of their death an act of perfect contrition which will take away all indebtedness. Consequently, they will not go to purgatory.[79] Thérèse certainly included in her theological hope the desire for immediate entrance into Heaven. Purgatory, she said, is «the least of my worries.»[80]

But let us emphasize that this desire is caused by the spirituality of spiritual childhood. That is its true climate. With regard to purgatory, she insists on littleness. «Little children are not damned!» (DE 10.7.1). There is more: they will not even be judged, but saved immediately (DE 25.9.1). She loved this verse from the Book of Wisdom: «To him that is little, mercy is granted.»[81] But to this humility is clearly joined confidence: this is what clearly appears in her conversations. One day, Sister Marie-Philomène of Jesus tells Thérèse: «I fear purgatory.» The Saint answers: «My Sister Marie-Philomène, you are not confident enough, you have too much fear of the good God. I assure you that He is grieved by it.

[77] See PHILIPPE DE LA TRINITÉ, *La Doctrine de Sainte Thérèse de l'Enfant-Jésus*, Paris, 1950, 48 pp.

[78] A 84 v, 213. See also *To the Sacred Heart of Jesus* of June 1895 (PN 23, str. 8: «I choose for my purgatory/Your burning love»).

[79] CSG, p. 61. In Thérèse's writings, one encounters the same idea twice: 'On leaving this life, my exiled soul/ Would like to make an act of pure love,/ And then, flying away to Heaven, its Homeland / Enter straightaway into your Heart' (PN 23). And nineteen months later: God will give to missionaries, by the intercession of the Virgin Mary, «the grace of making an act of perfect love» that will make them enter Heaven (LT 226, 1092).

[80] Marie of the Angels, PA, p. 351 f.

[81] Sg 6:6. See CSG, p. 52 and Mother Agnès, PA, p. 169.

Don't fear purgatory because of the pain that souls suffer there, but desire not to go there, in order to please God who imposes this atonement with so much regret. From the moment you seek to be pleasing to Him in everything, if you have the unshakable confidence that He is purifying you at every instant in His love and allows in you no trace of sin, be very sure that you won't go to purgatory.» And to Sister Fébronie: «You desire God's justice, so you will have God's justice. The soul receives precisely what it expects from God.» Later, after a dream about the same religious, Thérèse will say: «She is in purgatory, undoubtedly for not having counted enough on the mercy of God.»[82] Toward the end of her life, she heard nuns speaking of purgatory; here is her reaction preserved in a letter of Marie of the Eucharist to M. Guérin: «Oh! How you grieve me! You do a great injury to God in believing you're going to go to purgatory. When we love, we can't go there» (8/7/1897. Cf. DE, p. 683, and PO, p. 495).

So Thérèse's thought on human guilt is that love and confidence remit everything, even purgatory. Certainly, this very great confidence which she possessed, and consequently its productive power, is still for many only an ideal. Thérèse did not arrive at this point in a single day; she had to traverse a long «little way.» But as those who follow her penetrate into her way, they open themselves up to the «abysses» of divine mercy (LT 247, 1132).

[82] See Mss II, 61.

Conclusion

Called to evangelical perfection, the Christian tries to love God with «all his heart» and his neighbor as himself. In this quest, he sees how dynamic his vocation is. Discovering his state of imperfection better, together with the possibilities which the God of condescension nevertheless opens up for him, he understands the distance that separates him from perfect love and which will always separate him from it — a distance which demands to be bridged. But at the same time all this is seen in the warm light of God's infinite mercy. From this a tension develops between today and tomorrow, between reality and design, which has for its name *hope,* and which, together with *love,* is at the very heart of his existence as a believer.

Thérèse of Lisieux's desire for perfection, as it appears after some years of contemplative life, shares in the same religious phenomenon, situating itself thereby straightaway at the very heart of the Christian experience. The first task which Thérèse sees incumbent on her from then on is that of recognizing her imperfection — «my nothingness,» she said — in all its dimensions. Otherwise she is simply outside of the truth, without this real foundation necessary to assure her spiritual progress and without any chance of succeeding. The second task consists in believing in God's mercy — or simply in «Love» because, after 1895, God's love *is* mercy for Thérèse.

We say first and second, but this is only for the sake of explaining. What one distinguishes on the static plane of ideas — and this remark is applicable to everything that we say — remains, on the dynamic and existential plane, within the same unity. Humility and faith in God's mercy grow together in Thérèse, fertilizing one another, and to separate them in their vital relationship would cause a spiritual unbalance, and in truth could lead to their disintegration as far as Christian values are concerned. But, unless we accept them in a very broad and perhaps somewhat improper sense, they do not yet constitute the bridge which, resting on the two shores of the imperfect being and of the All-Perfect Being, straddles the distance. This is the work of hope. Thérèse will say it is the work of confidence, understood as a more expressive psychological whole of the climate of intimacy and certitude where the soul, for whom God is condescension and maternal love, settles. In response to the prayer of confidence on our part, God descends to meet us, progressively communicating to us His divine life, thus increasing in us the state of grace, of friendship with Him, of holiness. One will understand that the spiritual situation in which a human being entrusts himself to God is different in each person. One can love God intensely, as was the case of Thérèse. Confidence will not be less in that case — on the contrary. Perceiving his own weakness more clearly in the light of the God who illuminates him, and grasping both the height of the Christian vocation and the potentialities contained in God's infinite mercy, the person will be much more convinced of the distance which still separates him from perfect love. It is possible, however, that love will make him less sensitive to this «distance» than to his own «possibilities of further growth,» and that the «confidence» will reveal itself, as with Thérèse, more and more «loving.» In fact, her confidence is wholly filled with love and carries within it the very riches of love from which this confidence is born and which it brings to a higher level.

Although Thérèse conceived her «little way» above all in terms of a love not yet reached — and thus it is first a way of confidence in mercy — she extends this original notion to her entire search for holiness. And thus love, in its pure sense, enters into the attitude of «spiritual childhood.» Its activity — which is an essential law of her spirituality — will have a very characteristic aspect, however. It will employ, faithfully and generously, the ordinary means, the simple things of every day, all that is neither dazzling nor spectacular. It will often become abandonment to God's will. It will be in the first place effort and good will, striving for the full execution of the program of holiness of course, but accepting in poverty of spirit its own incompleteness under all its forms. And all the while it will trust only in the sanctifying mercy of God.

Thérèse called this way of «confidence that must lead us to Love» her «little way.» Why «little»? Because in her very magnanimous search for a great holiness, she preferred humble virtues and humble means. Because it is the way of the imperfect and poor in spirit. Because she constantly illustrated it by the example of the child; this is the image that she encountered at the very moment of her great discovery. Because in this way one must not «grow up» (which is not synonymous with «to grow»!) but on the contrary must learn to profit from one's misery in order to attract divine mercy. Let us add a fifth reason; one will smile at it perhaps and yet it seems important to us: because Sister Thérèse of the Child Jesus had *named* it the «little way.» Of course, this title has succeeded, but it seems to us that the same realities could be designated by another name, with other symbols and other accents.

This invites us to question ourselves on the originality of Thérèse. «It is Jesus alone who instructed me,» she said, «no book, no theologian taught me» (PA, p. 480). She found her way all alone. Is the idea of «the elevator» a true «invention » (C 2 v-3 r, 237)? It would be astonishing, and perhaps disquieting, to pretend to present a Christian way of sanctification which never existed before. Thérèse's invention is a *rediscovery* of realities often forgotten, especially at the time when the influence of Jansenism still persisted. Thérèse went directly to the essential, to the authentic. «It is the Gospel itself, the heart of the Gospel that she rediscovered, but with how much charm and freshness,» said Pius XII.[1] She acquired her great riches from this treasure, although her «little doctrine» highlights especially mercy, littleness, and loving confidence.

We use the word «especially» here. And what about the fraternal charity of which this amiable Saint was a great herald? And the mystery of the Church which she lived so admirably? Here, there is room for a comment. People have often identified her way variously as the «way of spiritual childhood» and «Thérésian spirituality.» In our opinion, the two formulas do not overlap each other. Just as the «little way» is larger than the «loving confidence» which is the core of it, in the same way «Thérésian spirituality» is larger than «spiritual childhood.» However, «spiritual childhood» is the

[1] Radio message of July 11, 1954, in *Acta apostolicae sedis*, 46 (1954), p. 405.

central light — because sanctification was the center of her life — which illuminates everything, and we see that it is reflected in Thérèse's fraternal charity and in her apostolate to the novices, based on the same fundamental principle: recourse to the Lord with confidence that *He Himself* will love and will nourish our brother by means of us (C 12 v, 250; 22 v, 265). The same light shines in her vision of Mary. Mary is for her «the most tender of Mothers» (26 v, 269), the Mother of the poor and the prototype of «spiritual childhood.» Thérèse's prayer for its part too is entirely imbued with the spirit of the «little way,» which is itself, by its continual reference to God, a marvelous school of prayer.

We have spoken of the Gospels. The expression that Pius XI used is most fortunate. He spoke of «evangelical childhood.»[2] This expression characterizes «spiritual childhood» so well. Indeed, it was to adults, rough and enterprising, that Jesus said to become again like children (see Mt 18:1-4). «Spiritual childhood» is not some kind of backward step, a regression. It is a progression, a step forward. «We must gradually grow to the point of becoming very little in the Hands of Jesus, the Creator of our holiness.»[3] The apostle of «spiritual childhood» has also become the apostle of spiritual maturity.[4] Thérèse herself was called «a baby who is an elder» (PA, p. 231). «There are two kinds of simplicity,» said Jean Guitton, «like two kinds of childhood: the simplicity of need, the childhood of one's setting out in life, which is only an image of the goal; and the simplicity of completion, the childhood that is impossible to attain, a sort of return of the mature being toward its origin.»[5] Georges Bernanos had said it before, with as much depth: «Once we have left childhood we must suffer for a very long time in order to re-

---

[2] Homily from the solemn Mass of Canonization, May 17, 1925. VICTOR DE LA VIERGE has succeeded well in revealing this formula (*Réalisme spirituel de Sainte Thérèse de Lisieux*, Paris, 1956, p. 75).

[3] R. VOILLAUME, *Lettres au Fraternités*, t. I, Paris, 1960, p. 233.

[4] See LUCIEN-MARIE DE SAINT-JOSEPH, «Sainte Thérèse de l'Enfant-Jésus ou l'enfance unie à la maturité,» *La vie spirituelle*, 85 (1951), II, pp. 304- 323, and L. BEIRNAERT, *Expérience chrétienne et psychologie*, Paris, 1964, pp. 143-154. Let us listen to the exhortation of Saint Paul: «Brothers, do not be childish in your judgment; be like children as far as evil is concerned, but in mind be mature» (1 Cor 14:20).

[5] «Le Génie de Sainte Thérèse de l'Enfant-Jésus,» VT, 1964, p. 103.

turn to it, as at the end of the night we discover another dawn.»[6] Thérèse, too, had to suffer and search for a long time before making her discovery. Then, Jesus appeared to her as He is. This is why her message is universal and eternal like that of Jesus Himself, because she refers us to Christ who shows us the Father.

«God is love» (1 Jn 4: 8). Thérèse invites us to understand «all the tenderness of His infinite Love» (B 1 v, 221). She wants to «tell all *little souls* how unspeakable [His] condescension is» (B 5 v, 232). God is for us a true *Father*, she says. To that, she only knows one response: to be His *child*.

«See what love the Father has bestowed on us in letting us be called children of God! — Yet that is what we are.... And what we shall later be has not yet come to light» (1 Jn 3:1-2). Before this mystery of love which illuminates the life of children, we can only pray, filled with deep joy and astonishment: «What is man, that You should be mindful of him?» (Ps 8:5).

---

[6] *Dialogues des carmélites*, Paris, 1961, p. 36.

Appendix I

Thérèse, Mistress of Novices

On a text from Manuscript C and its connection with Thérèse's nomination

Previously in this book[1] we quoted a passage from Manuscript C (C 22 r-v, 264 f.) which clearly displays an attitude «of spiritual childhood.» Many authors have connected this text with the designation of Thérèse, in 1893, as an aid to the novice mistress. Logically enough, they did not hesitate to situate the discovery of the «little way» *before* this date.[2]

We cannot agree on this point. In our opinion, this passage from Manuscript C deals with an experience which took place in 1896.

We believe that we are the first to defend this important chronological thesis. André Combes,[3] Stéphane Piat,[4] and François de Sainte-Marie (Mss II, 74 and the published edition of the *Autobiographical Manuscripts* of 1957, p. 284) all defend the date of 1893. To clearly explain our ideas, we shall take the matter in two stages: what was Thérèse's role with the novices after 1893 and after 1896? And to what time does the quoted text from Manuscript C relate? This is the point in question.

Elected prioress in the month of February 1893, Mother Agnès

[1] See Part I, chap. II, p. 19 f.

[2] See Part II, chap. V, n. 5.

[3] A. COMBES, *De doctrina…*, pp. 150-152.

[4] S. PIAT, *À la découverte…*, p. 132.

names Marie de Gonzague as novice mistress; but «to counterbalance the annoying influence» of the shortcomings and deficiencies of the latter, she assigns Thérèse to assist her (Mother Agnès, PO, p. 144). Marie de Gonzague herself, overwhelmed by her work, designates Thérèse «to be her aid to fill in for her when needed» (according to Geneviève, PO, p. 273), but «because of the fickleness [of Marie de Gonzague], Sister Thérèse hardly had one moment of security in this so-called position that was given to her and taken away every two weeks.... If the action of this young servant of God appeared too intense, Mother Marie de Gonzague got angry, saying that Sister Thérèse did not have the right to give us counsels and that she went beyond instructions that were given to her» and her novices had to resort to «a thousand stratagems» (*ibid.*). Mother Agnès testifies in the same way (PA, p. 148).

Whatever the facts may be, for the first fifteen months (!), Thérèse has little to do: her two companions are older than she and one of them avoids her (PO, p. 479). Marie of the Trinity then enters (June 16, 1894) and Thérèse becomes her «angel» (religious jargon to designate the sister charged with initiating a postulant to the external practices of the Order). Mother Agnès also summons Marie of the Trinity to take counsels from Thérèse [for her religious formation] (PA, p. 466). Later, Geneviève and Marie of the Eucharist, both members of Thérèse's family, will enter. The conversations and counsels will be numerous; however, Thérèse does not give any *instructions* (conferences) and does her best to avoid displeasing Marie de Gonzague. In letters of this time, when she refers to the novices, Thérèse calls herself simply their «companion» (LT 144, 803), the «*old* senior» of the novitiate (LT 180, 915), while at the same time she calls herself «the angel» of Marie of the Trinity (C 24 v, 267), expressly distinguishing herself from the «novice mistress» (LT 167, 870). It is by virtue of this that she can call Marie of the Trinity «my girl» (*ibid.*), whereas actually she already has *three* «girls,» and that she will speak of her later as «the one and only novice» in the novitiate with whom she «was occupied» (C 24 v, 267), whereas there were *four* of them at this time.

In the month of March 1896, Marie de Gonzague was elected prioress again, and she decided to combine this office with the functions and official title of novice mistress. However, she entrusts —

she, and no longer Mother Agnès! — the instruction of all the novices to Thérèse and «leaves her practically the entire direction of the novitiate.» It is only after this time that Thérèse «assembled the novices together, every day, after Vespers» in order to teach them in a way that was in no way systematic. In spiritual direction, she finishes her teaching with special counsels (CSG, pp. 2-3). Thérèse was therefore not the official «mistress» and does not think of herself as such (C 26 v, 270), but in reality that is what unofficially she was.

To what situation does the text of Manuscript C concerning her mission to novices now relate? We do not hesitate to answer: to the *second*, to her situation *since* the month of March 1896. We have four reasons for saying this, all based on the internal criticism of Manuscript C, which, as we recall, is addressed like a long letter to *Marie de Gonzague*, the new prioress.

1. Writing about her powerlessness at the time of «entering into the sanctuary of souls,» Thérèse specifies immediately that it relates to «the task that *you* [emphasis ours] imposed upon me» (C 22 v, 264). It does not relate to the measure taken by Mother Agnès in 1893, then, but in fact to that of Marie de Gonzague in 1896. Also, Thérèse assures us that, if she had in the least depended on her own strength, «I would very soon have given *you* back this office» (*ibid.*). Let us point out here that the words «that you imposed upon me» were published for the first time only in 1956, on the occasion of the facsimile edition.

2. Even if we take literally the testimony of Sister Geneviève which we have already quoted, according to which Marie de Gonzague «designates Thérèse as her aid and to fill in for her when needed,» and if we want to see a real imposition of task there, in the text of Manuscript C it is nevertheless always a question of the nomination of *1896*. In fact, Thérèse recalls this task several times. Speaking in the beginning of Manuscript C (C 3 v, 238) of this «mission,» she tells Mother Marie de Gonzague: «*You* told your child: *Feed my lambs*.» Thérèse had reacted: I am too little (just as in C 22 v, 264!). Then Mother Marie de Gonzague had «retained the little lambs [the novices] with the sheep [the professed nuns]»: that is to say, she had combined the two functions of prioress and novice mistress, which *only occurred in 1896* (she was not a prioress in

1893). But nevertheless, she «orders» Thérèse «to go often and pasture [the lambs] in the *shade*, pointing out the best and most nourishing herbs,» etc. (C 3 v, 239). It is clear, then, that the task with the novices to which Thérèse alludes in Manuscript C is that which was pointed out to her in 1896! (Let us point out again that the important words: «You retained the little lambs with the sheep» appear only in the edition of 1956). In writing Manuscript C, Thérèse will repeat no less than *six* times more that it is Mother Marie de Gonzague («you») who had imposed the task upon her (C 10 r, 247; 19 r, 260 [twice], 20 v, 2 61; 27 v, 271; 35 v, 283).

3. Let us also consider the *content* of this task: it is to give a spiritual «nourishment» to the novices (C 3 v, 239; 22 r-v, 264), «to listen to their temptations» (C 19 r, 260), and «to paint the image of Jesus in their soul» (C 20 r, 261). In fact, Thérèse describes how she exercises in their regard a true spiritual direction and corrects all their faults (C 22 v-24 v, 264-267). However, this task far surpasses the one she was given in 1893.

4. Let us add one last argument that is psychological. In 1893-1895, the touchy and jealous character of Marie de Gonzague provokes a few scenes as soon as Thérèse takes up her task a little too intensely. Marie de Gonzague will also have understood the reason behind Mother Agnès' gesture, that of giving Thérèse to her as an assistant. When Thérèse addresses Mother Gonzague in Manuscript B, it is unthinkable that, charitable as she was, Thérèse would make the least allusion to the situation of the preceding period. On the contrary, Manuscript C is a model of deference!

All these reasons convince us that the passage from Manuscript C concerning Thérèse's interior experience, on the occasion of her nomination as novice mistress, relates to 1896.

Appendix II

«Céline's Notebook»[1]

«Céline's Notebook» (see part I, chap. III) is a small handwritten anthology of the Old Testament, which Thérèse had at her disposal since September 14, 1894 and in which she had read the two scriptural texts that opened up her «little way» to her. Thereafter, she appears to often have used this source again in her *Autobiographical Manuscripts* and her Letters. The importance of this notebook was all the greater for her because the young Carmelites of Lisieux did not have permission to read a complete Bible (the Old Testament).

Here is the index of texts that it contains. The list has been drawn up according to the Jerusalem Bible by the Carmel of Lisieux, and it is with their kind authorization that we are publishing it. The Notebook indicates the books and chapters but does not contain any reference to verses. The translation that it gives is sometimes imperfect. And besides, Thérèse does not hesitate to quote freely.

Song of Songs: 1, complete except 2b and 3a; 2, complete; 3:1-6; 4, complete except 5; 5, complete except 15; 6, complete; 7, com-

[1] (*Note of 1994.*) What we call «Céline's Notebook» (see Mss I, 37; it is the «[hard-cover] notebook bound in dark imitation leather») is not to be confused with the «scriptural notebook of Thérèse,» composed for her by her sister Céline (Sister Geneviève) and of which the content, made up of other non-scriptural texts as well, vary. (See Mss 1, 37-38 [This is the «(hard-cover) notebook bound in dark canvas»] and see especially VT, n. 78 (1980), pp. 146-160; n. 79 (1980), pp. 215-240 and n. 81 (1981), pp. 60-68). The list that follows here has not been, until now, published elsewhere. This is why this Appendix has been preserved in our new edition.

plete except 1a, 2b-4, 8b, 9b, 13b; 8, complete except 5b, 10a, 11b, 12.

Ecclesiastes: 1, complete except 1; 2, complete except 12-17; 3, complete except 13, 16, 18-19, 21, and in part 22; 4, complete except 5-6, 9-16; 5, complete except 3-8, 10-13, 17-18.

Wisdom: 1, complete except 1-2, 7, 13-15; 2, complete except 24; 3:1-9, 14-15; 4:1-2, 7, 10-15, 17-19; 5, complete except 17-22; 6:6, 12-18; 7:6-14, 16, 21-30; 8:1-10, 16; 9:6, 13-18.

Proverbs: 1:17, 19; 3:5-7a, 9-12, 24b-26, 29-30, 32, 34; 4:7-8a, 10- 12, 18; 7:1-4; 8:5a, 17, 35; 9:4 a, 10; 10:3a, 9a, 12b, 19, 24b; 11:2b, 6a, 21b, 30a; 12:21a; 13:7-8a; 14:13, 23a, 31b, 32b; 15:1a, 4a, 15b, 25b, 26b, 29b, 31, 33b; 16:6a, 19, 20b, 21b, 32-33; 17:3, 5a, 12, 17; 18:7, 10, 12, 19; 19:2, 8b, 11a, 17, 21, 22a, 25a; 20:3-4, 6, 10, 18, 24, 30; 21:3, 21-23, 31; 22:6, 9a, 11-12a; 23:11-12, 16a, 25; 25:11, 13, 15, 21-22, 27; 26:2a, 12, 27; 27:18; 28:1b, 5b, 18a; 29:23b; 30:4-5,

Isaiah: 40:1-8, 10-11, 12a, 13, 15, 17-18, 22b-23, 27-31; 53, complete; 54, complete except 6 and 11-17; 55, complete; 56, complete except 8-12; 57:1-2, 12-19; 58:5-12; 59:1; 60, complete; 61:1-3, 10-11; 62, complete except 9 and 12; 63:1-3a, 5a, 8-9, 13; 64:1-5a, 10; 65:1-2, 8-10, 13-14, 15b, 17-20a, 21-25a; 66:1-2, 4-5, 9-15a, 18-21.

Tobit: 12:12-13.

Book of Sirach: 1:1, 6, 8-10, 23; 2:1-6a, 10-11, 18b; 3:2, 5, 18, 26b, 31; 4:11, 17, 28; 6:5, 18, 28-29, 37; 7:10a; 10:12a, 14-17, 24, 28; 11:2-3, 8, 12-14, 21-22, 25; 13:21-22b, 23b, 25; 14:14; 15:6, 10, 14, 16-18a; 16:14; 17:22, 28; 18:4, 6-11, 13a, 14, 16, 20, 22; 19:24, 29-30; 20:3, 8a, 11; 21:4b, 13, 15a, 17, 20, 26; 22:6, 11a, 16, 19; 23:17-27; 24:1, 10-12; 25:19; 26:15, 28b; 27:5, 25-27; 28:2, 8a, 12, 17, 24-25; 29:12, 19; 30:1a, 16b, 18, 22; 31:10, 15a, 18; 32:7, 8b, 19, 24b; 33:1, 11, 12a, 13-15; 34:10a, 16-18; 35:2b, 9-10, 17a, 19a, 23b, 24; 36:25b; 37:19; 39:13-14, 20; 40:21; 43:11, 27-28, 30, 32. And then, repetition of 32:11-13.

Ezekiel: 16:5-14; 34:12-16.

Hosea: 6:6; 9:5-6a; 10:12; 11:1-4, 8b-9; 12:10-11; 14:5-7a, 9b, 10a.

Habakkuk: 2:18; 3:2b-3, 6, 18-19.

Zephaniah: 1:14a; 3:8, 12, 14-17, 19-20.

Malachi: 1:8; 2:3; 3:10-12, 16-17, 20.

Joel: 2:10-14; 3:1-5; 4:1-2, 9-13, 16, 18-21.

Amos: 7:2-3.

Micah: 4:1, 3-7; 6:6-8; 7:11.

Zechariah: 2:8, 9, 17; 3:1-5, 9; 7:9-10; 9:17; 12:10; 13:6-7.

Appendix III

On Thérèse's Crisis of Scruples

During the course of this study we said that the «terrible sickness of scruples,» from which Thérèse suffered at the ages of twelve and thirteen, seems to have been located in the domain of chastity.[1] Nowhere do we find a direct confirmation of this assertion, but several arguments lead to this conclusion.

1. Thérèse says that «all her most simple thoughts and actions became a cause of trouble for her» (A 39 r, 132). We do not see any reason for excluding attention to her body and the biological reactions brought on by the psychological and physiological development appropriate to adolescence. In this domain, too, Thérèse would have had specific scruples.

2. A letter from Thérèse of May 30, 1889 provides us with what we may take as a most convincing argument. It is a response to a letter from her cousin, Marie Guérin. This latter was in Paris and the sight of certain statues, and the memory of them, bother her with scruples and anxiety regarding purity.[2] Thérèse answers: «You did well to write me, and I understand *everything... everything, everything, everything*!... You haven't committed the *shadow of any evil*; I know what these kinds of temptations are so well that I can assure you of this without any fear.... However, I hear you saying to me: 'Thérèse is saying this because she doesn't know how I really

[1] See here Part II, chapter I, I, 6.

[2] LC 113 in CG I, p. 565. Moreover, Marie Guérin will always remain scrupulous: see her *Obituary Circular*.

do it on purpose.' Yes, your poor little Thérèse does know; I tell you that she understands it *all*....»[3]

3. The perfect silence when it came to specifying the *object* of the scruples that we notice in Thérèse's writings and in the depositions to the Process on the part of her sister Marie and others, can be understood as reverential respect for the intimate things of chastity. Céline, «the soul» of Thérèse's soul, will have this astonishing thing to say (while speaking of chastity!): «I didn't know what her scruples as a little girl consisted of» (PO, p. 299).

4. The Saint's entourage surely did not favor frank answers on questions about the mystery of life and the problems of chastity, to say the least. Without any doubt, the Martin family is exemplary in many ways, but silence on these matters was the practice of the time. Christian education was in these days often marked by a notable exaggerated flight from the world, by the aftermaths of Jansenism, and by a fear sometimes more harmful than beneficial of everything that seemed to compromise the salvation of the soul, including sexual initiation. The Martin family had not always escaped these negative influences. Her mother — a woman worthy of being ranked among the greatest mothers of saints — who had seen her plans for religious life unravel (just as her father had), got married without being informed about conjugal relationships, the discovery of which caused her many tears. In agreement with her husband, the two lived for ten months in perfect virginity. After this, they wanted many children whom they hoped would be dedicated to the Lord.[4] All this describes the ambiance in which one might consider these problems of chastity. Also, one of the family's main virtues was «contempt of the world» (PA, p. 256). «Life, at home, was simple and patriarchal; we avoided the agitation of worldly relations there and we tended to remain alone as a family» (PO, p. 264), in the small paradise of Les Buissonnets, well surrounded by walls. The rich positive education in virtue went hand-in-hand with a sharp vigilance towards all dangers. The fa-

---

[3] LT 92, 567.

[4] See S. PIAT, *Histoire d'une famille...*, pp. 42-51 and also LT 261, 1163. Thérèse will give this beautiful testimony to her parents: «[It is toward Heaven that] all their actions and their desires were directed» (LT 226, 1092).

ther recommends that they «avoid with the greatest care what could tarnish the purity [of their] heart» (PA, p. 226). One of the central objects of the combat is vanity, in the sense of cultivating an exaggerated estimation of one's appearance; Mme. Martin «let nothing go unnoticed, particularly things touching upon vanity» (PO, p. 136). Thérèse, who was in no way deprived when it came to her appearance, was five years and eight months old when she received her first compliment, and her father gave the person a sign not to praise her (A 21 v, 103). She was nine and a half when she received «compliments for the second time» (A 26 v, 110), a fact she thought worthy of mention! When someone says in her presence that she is pretty, Pauline tells her the opposite (PA, p. 194). The only scruple that Thérèse confesses to us in her autobiography is a so-called sin of vanity: notably a feeling of joy over a pretty blue hat of which she was very fond (A 42 r, 136). In a climate like this, confusion about purity can easily grow, and so can scruples.

Regarding Thérèse's sexual initiation, let us note first that she no longer has a mother to help her on this point and, second, that a healthy source of education was missing to her: namely, the presence of brothers. (Thérèse does not seem to ever have played in the company of boys.) Sexual initiation for her was completely missing. Mother Agnès will testify that her sister discovered the «facts of life» without the help of anyone, but «without looking for [it], while observing the flowers and birds» (these are Thérèse's own statements) and all this took place after her journey to Rome and therefore after the crisis of scruples (PA, p. 190). This is what Thérèse tells us herself: before the departure for Rome, she prays to the Blessed Virgin in Paris to keep far from her everything that could tarnish her purity: she was fully aware that on a trip such as this she could easily meet with things capable of troubling her, «especially because she was still unacquainted with evil and so was apprehensive about making its discovery. She had not yet experienced that *to the pure all things are pure*, that the simple and upright soul sees evil in nothing since it resides only in impure hearts, not in inanimate objects» (like pictures and statues? — A 57 r, 165). Therefore, it is at least after her fourteenth year, that is to say after her crisis of scruples, that she acquired sufficient knowledge on this subject.

However, how could we not be inclined to think that every subject having something to do with the sexual domain and its biological and psychological implications, was for Thérèse, at the time of the crisis, a source of confusion and scruples. At thirteen years of age, she was unaware of the «facts of life» and in what sin consists, very sensitive to the requirements of Jesus' love, having suffered from a generalized sickness of scruples, having always held chastity in the highest reverence and impurity in supreme horror, having been raised in an enclosed environment, and having experienced since her tender childhood 'shame,' 'embarrassment,' and 'uneasiness' with respect to her own body?[5]

All that we have just said does not contradict certain statements of Thérèse about being exempt from *real* temptations against chastity,[6] although the texts are not always categorical.[7] In fact, Thérèse, then a religious, had been for a long time healed of her scruples. She now appears sovereignly free in spirit,[8] she understands the «mysteries of life,» and she knows therefore how to distinguish a real temptation from scruples, these «chimerical fears» (LT 92, 567). Thus we can conclude that Thérèse has probably never known real temptations against purity, thanks to a very generous fidelity and vigilance. Much more than that, she never sinned against chastity (and it is here that the greatness of the graces that God gave her on this point is revealed). But Thérèse was not spared from the confusion of scruples in this domain.

---

[5] DE 30.7.1. See also DE 8.8.4 and LT 180, 915: Thérèse «never liked things to eat.»

[6] «She confided in me, at Carmel, that she "regretted not to have suffered temptations against chastity in order to offer to God all the kinds of martyrdom"» (Sister Geneviève, PA, p. 302). «She revealed [to me] that she had never been tempted against the holy virtue» (Mother Agnès, PA, p. 190). «She confessed to me humbly that she had never been tempted against purity» (Marie of the Trinity, PA, p. 485). She said: «There is only one thing that I never experienced, and it is what they call pleasure in this matter» (Marie of the Trinity, PO, p. 466). «I can say that she had temptations against hope, but never against purity» (P. Godefroid Madelaine, PA, p. 563).

[7] Before, Mother Agnès expressed herself more carefully: «I believe that she never had any very violent struggles on this point» (PO, p. 170).

[8] «One could confide to her any temptation on this subject. One felt that she would not be disturbed by it» (Marie of the Sacred Heart, PO, p. 252). «I found her very illuminated in the counsels that she gave to the novices» (Mother Agnès, PO, p. 170). «You can without fear confide to me everything that you wish, nothing will astonish me» (Marie of the Trinity, PO, p. 466).

Moreover, she had well understood that it is not the presence or the absence of temptations that matters, but the intensity of one's love, whether under temptation or apart from it.[9] And surely the troubles that Thérèse experienced on this point, just as in other things, if they weighed down the flight of her love, they did not hinder it. On the contrary. For «we know that God makes all things work together for the good of those who love Him and those who have been called according to His decree» (Rm 8:28).

---

[9] See CSG, p. 208 and PA, p. 302.

Appendix IV

Cardinal von Balthasar's Opinion on Saint Thérèse's Sense of Sin

(See page 238, Footnote 15)

A) Hans Urs von Balthasar was aware of our critique. In a re-edition of his work (in *Schwestern im Geist, Therese von Lisieux und Elisabeth von Dijon*, Einsiedeln, 1970, p. 35), he writes: «It is only after having finished this re-edition that I had knowledge of the vast work of Conrad De Meester, O.C.D., *Dynamique de la confiance* (…). One finds in it on pages 285-289 a discussion of my book.» However, based on what we know, the author did not revise his views and, in a subsequent text, he continued to defend them. In fact, at the time of the centenary of the birth of Thérèse (1973), in a conference at Notre Dame in Paris (see *Actualité de Lisieux*, in *Thérèse of Lisieux, Conférences du Centenaire, 1873-1973*, special issue of the *Nouvelles de l'Institut catholique de Paris*, May 1973, pp. 107-123), he explains himself again on the subject of the declaration made by Thérèse's confessor, Father Pichon, saying: «However, from all of Thérèse's declarations (in particular about her love of innocent souls and the souls of sinners), it clearly comes out again that Thérèse understood this declaration as affirming that she had *never sinned*. The idea of venial sin doesn't appear anywhere in her writings. Whereas Mother Agnès, in the *Novissima Verba*, writes: 'One could believe that it is because I have been preserved from *mortal sin* that I have such great confidence…,' the «Yellow Notebook» (11.7.6), the «Green Notebooks» and the «Diocesan Process» read as follows: 'One could believe that it is because I *haven't sinned* that

I have such great confidence.' Hence, nearly insurmountable difficulties, but ultimately overcome, when the time will come to sit at the table of sinners, to confess, in the indistinct communion of saints, the common sin» (p. 119). — But von Balthasar forgot to consult another source, the oldest, most personal, most exact from the critical viewpoint, that is to say, the *Autobiographical Manuscripts* of Thérèse herself, who speaks of mortal sin: «It is not because God, in His *anticipating* mercy, has preserved my soul from mortal sin that I go to Him with confidence and love» (C 36 v, 285). This is moreover what one could read for a long time in the old revised edition of *Histoire d'une Ame* (the *Story of a Soul*) from the very first: «... preserved from mortal sin» (HA 98, p. 198).

In addition to what one reads in our work, one could still respond to von Balthasar that Thérèse, in her autobiography, speaks clearly of the «sins» that she confesses (for example, A 16 v, 94, and 41 v, 136) — venial sins, it is true, but sins — of the «traces of sin» of which Merciful Love purifies her (A 84 r, 212). At the age of twelve and thirteen, at the time of her scruples, she had even believed, erroneously, that she «had committed *great sins*» (she underlines *great sins*, LT 92 of May 30, 1989, 567). The text evoked by von Balthasar on the «innocent souls» is about the innocence of a grave sin determined, in the domain of purity, in reference to Mary Magdalene, who confesses to being a «poor sinner,» but Jesus sees «the rose of (her) ardent love» and «This crimson rose / knew how to ravish my heart / By me she is loved / More than all other flowers.» Her sister Martha, whose virginity is highlighted, argues humbly: «You prevented me from falling» (see RP 4 of July 1895). However, precisely in the same months, Thérèse explains in her autobiography that she is like Martha: the Lord «forgave me *in advance* by preventing me from falling,» whereas «without Him, I could have fallen as low as Saint Mary Magdalene,» and she confesses herself to be the «object» of the foreseeing love of the Father, who sent His Word, not for the «*just* but (for) *sinners*» (A 38 v-39 r, 131-132; these meaningful underlinings are her own). «With a nature such as my own... perhaps (I) would have even been lost» (A 8 r, 81). More soberly, while speaking of lilies, a symbol of the «purity» that she seeks, Thérèse had already expressed four years earlier that one is «forgiven more» when «Jesus has forgiven sins *in advance*» (LT 130, of July 23, 1891, 731).

If Thérèse speaks rather of her «faults» and her «imperfections,» her experience of «falling» and her «weakness,» she knew to always pray with the *Our Father*, with all her heart and innumerable times, and in her own name, «forgive us our trespasses»; and with the *Ave* to rank herself among the «poor sinners» who ask Mary to pray for them. The events of Thérèse's life that von Balthasar touches upon, and that would have been the cause of a lack of understanding (partial but long) of her mission, have been deprived of their real import, and clothed with a significance which was in a very great measure unreal.

B) Concerning the thesis of von Balthasar, we now know that we also touch upon the legacy left by Adrienne von Speyr. One knows the communion of heart and thought that united these two great spirits and the direct influence of von Speyr on von Balthasar, from whom she received a great deal. In subsequent publications, von Balthasar spoke of it, not without taking up his approach to Thérèse, an approach which owes nearly all its originality to von Speyr. In *Unser Auftrag. Bericht und Entwurf*, Einsiedeln, 1984, von Balthasar explains that, «since 1941, his books have been much influenced by the thought» of Adrienne (p. 50), who translated the old edition of *Histoire d'une Ame* into German (p. 49) in 1947; one can «never clearly separate» what belongs to von Balthasar and what comes from von Speyr (p. 81).

With regard to his book on Thérèse (French translation: *Thérèse de Lisieux, Histoire d'une mission*, Apostolat des éditions et Editions paulines, 1973), von Balthasar clearly discloses this fundamental influence: «*Therese von Lisieux, Geschichte einer Sendung* (1950) would never have been born without Adrienne's theology of mission. The intense interest of the latter in the Saint, but also her critical presentation of Thérèse's interior path (for note, refer to *Allerheiligenbuch* 1/2, pp. 64-68), her displacement of the accent from psychology to the theology of mission are the presuppositions of my presentation, which clothed what Adrienne had recognized with a rich anthology of the Saint herself» (p. 83).

In fact, when one reads, in *Das Allerheiligenbuch* (*Die Nachlasswerke*, Einsiedeln, 1977, vol. 1/2, pp. 64-88), what von Speyr set forth in her mystical perceptions of Thérèse, one recognizes without difficulty all the «presuppositions» of von Balthasar, even down to their literal wording. (And one can well suppose oral exchange during the course of the writing of the book or the proofreading by Adrienne of the manuscript and proofs; see *Unser Auftrag…*, p. 64). In order to limit ourselves to the themes treated in the present pages of our work, Adrienne von Speyr speaks of «the setting apart» (*Sonderstellung*: twice on page 65, twice on page 66, p. 82; *auf eine Seite geschoben*: p. 65), of the «slightly skewered position» (*eine leicht schiefe Stellung*, p. 64), «the false position» (p. 66) of Thérèse, following her revelation of the apparition of the Virgin (pp. 64, 65, 66, 75). Because of this, Thérèse is pushed «into a sort of position of being displayed, without wanting it» (p. 65), a position which is going to persist until «the end of her life» (p. 65). Placed on «a pedestal» (pp. 66, 67) «of future holiness» (p. 66), she finds herself «in a situation of having arrived» (p. 76), but «this is not her fault, they made her like this» (p. 82). Henceforth, for a long time, she «must play a role» (p. 82), «to demonstrate» something (p. 82), bearing «a too great consciousness of her own holiness» (p. 80). «She is regarded as a 'Saint' and so she is conscious of being a Saint» (p. 75), but «a saint of plaster» that they made her (*Gipsheilige*: p. 65, and with von Balthasar, p. 86) and it will take her a long time before losing this image (p. 65).

As for the declaration of Father Pichon, it is (in an erroneous way) interpreted by Adrienne von Speyr as if someone had told Thérèse that she had «never sinned» («she knows that she has never sinned, because the confessor told her,» p. 74), «she had committed *no* sin at all, as Thérèse says in her *Autobiography*» (the word *kein* [none at all] is underlined by von Speyr, p. 84). Thérèse is «without sin,» argues von Speyr (*sündelos*, p. 75), she is in a state of «impeccability» (*Sündelosigkeit*, p. 76), finds in herself «the lack of sin» (*Sündenmangel*, p. 76) and, if one is to believe Adrienne, «it is only unusually that Thérèse, throughout her life, spoke of her faults» (p. 66).

According to von Speyr, serious inconveniences for the mission of Thérèse result from this. Faced with the suffering Christ, «she perseveres unshaken in her attitude of consoling Him, where perhaps she could be involved in the experience of enduring it with

Him (*Miterfahrung*). In all suffering she keeps a touch of autonomy (*Selbstverwaltung*). The barrier is always found in the fact that she cannot become co-sinner (*mitsundig*)» (p. 80). Following the events of her youth, «Thérèse doesn't know the reality of *bearing with*, properly so-called (*das Mitdragen*)» (p. 82). By the fact that she was told that she had never sinned, her «mission» will suffer from it: «She was given too little room to shade the slightest nuances with the colors assigned to her» (p. 85). Consequently, Thérèse constructs her «little way» like a way of love toward the summit, while leaving those who follow her with the encouraging promises that they too will reach the summit. But, if one makes the beginning of the journey a little too easy, one won't reach there perhaps, because one will underestimate the effort of the final journey (cf. pp. 77-78). And this is the warning which is no longer entirely astonishing (in von Speyr's presentation): «For a lot of people, it would have been better if they had not known little Thérèse» (p. 78).

This would be true if there were not an elevator that rose to the summit. It would be true, if in the last analysis everything depended on our efforts alone, without recognizing the infinite Mercy so well rediscovered and praised by Thérèse. What we have just quoted and contradicted rests on another interpretation of the true history of Thérèse, after listening to its authentic sources. If our interpretation is correct, it won't fail to contain a certain warning, not at all opposed to the doctrine of Saint John of the Cross, inviting us to take up with prudence the perceptions of a visionary type of mystic, even the most authentic.

SELECTED BIBLIOGRAPHY

Primary Sources

Sainte Thérèse de L'Enfant Jésus. *Correspondance Générale,* Vol. I. Paris: Editions du Cerf-Desclée De Brouwer) 1972.

_______. *Correspondance Générale,* Vol. II. Paris: Editions du Cerf-Desclée De Brouwer, 1973.

_______. *Derniers Entretiens.* Paris: Editions du Cerf-Desclée De Brouwer, 1971.

_______. *Histoire D'une Âme; Manuscrits Autobiographiques.* Paris: Editions du Cerf-Desclée De Brouwer, 1972.

_______. *Poésies.* Paris: Editions du Cerf-Desclée De Brouwer, 1975.

_______. *Prières.* Paris: Editions du Cerf-Desclée De Brouwer, 1988.

_______. *Recréations Pieuses.* Paris: Editions du Cerf-Desclée De Brouwer, 1985.

Saint Thérèse of Lisieux. *General Correspondence,* Vol. I. Translated by John Clarke, OCD. Washington, DC: ICS Publications, 1982.

_______. *General Correspondence,* Vol. II. Translated by John Clarke, OCD. Washington, DC: ICS Publications, 1988.

_______. *Her Last Conversations.* Translated by John Clarke, OCD. Washington, DC: ICS Publications, 1977.

_______. *Story of a Soul.* Translated by John Clarke, OCD. Washington, DC: ICS Publications, 1972.

_______. *Poetry.* Translated by Donald Kinney, OCD. Washington, DC: ICS Publications, 1996.

Books

Arintero, OP, Juan G. *The Mystical Evolution in the Development and Vitality of the Church* (2 Vols.). Translated by Jordan Aumann, OP. St. Louis: B. Herder Book Co., 1949.

_______. *The Mystical Life of St. Thérèse of the Child Jesus.* Translated by José L. Morales, PhD. Salamanca: Editorial Fides, 1926.

Arminjon, Charles. *The End of the Present World and the Mysteries of the Future Life.* Translated by Martin Research Associates. Illinois: Martin Books Edition, 1968.

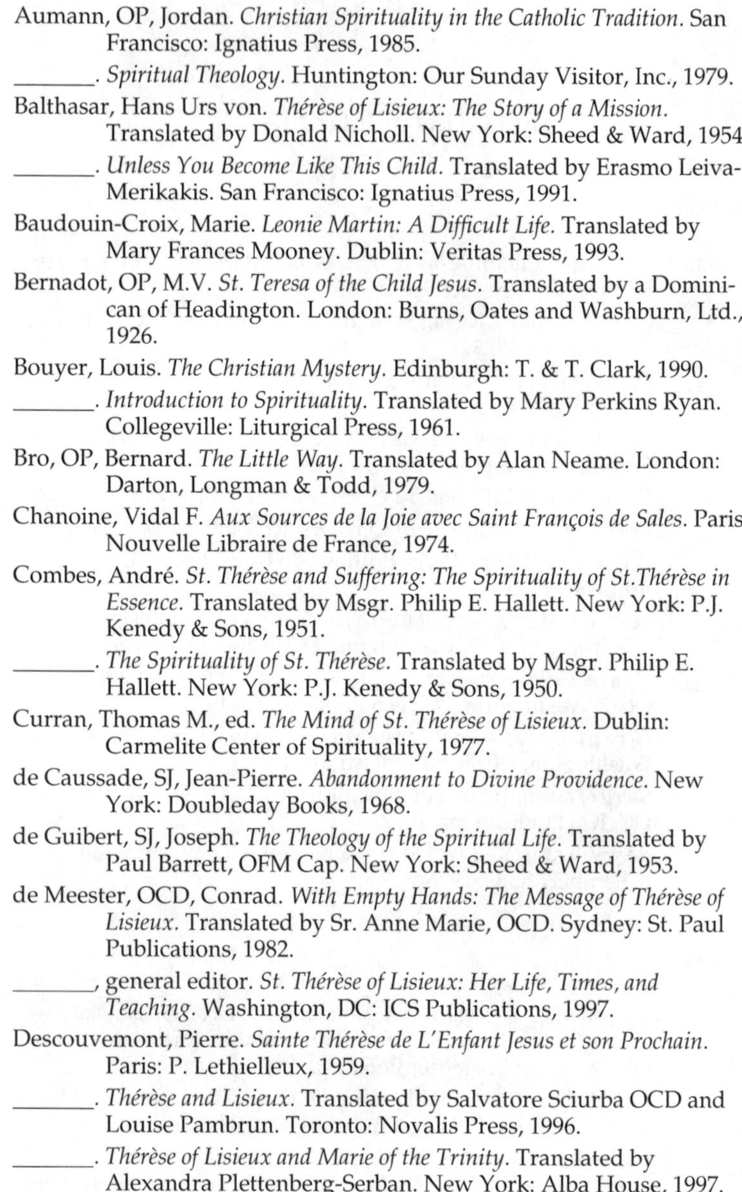

Aumann, OP, Jordan. *Christian Spirituality in the Catholic Tradition.* San Francisco: Ignatius Press, 1985.

_______. *Spiritual Theology.* Huntington: Our Sunday Visitor, Inc., 1979.

Balthasar, Hans Urs von. *Thérèse of Lisieux: The Story of a Mission.* Translated by Donald Nicholl. New York: Sheed & Ward, 1954.

_______. *Unless You Become Like This Child.* Translated by Erasmo Leiva-Merikakis. San Francisco: Ignatius Press, 1991.

Baudouin-Croix, Marie. *Leonie Martin: A Difficult Life.* Translated by Mary Frances Mooney. Dublin: Veritas Press, 1993.

Bernadot, OP, M.V. *St. Teresa of the Child Jesus.* Translated by a Dominican of Headington. London: Burns, Oates and Washburn, Ltd., 1926.

Bouyer, Louis. *The Christian Mystery.* Edinburgh: T. & T. Clark, 1990.

_______. *Introduction to Spirituality.* Translated by Mary Perkins Ryan. Collegeville: Liturgical Press, 1961.

Bro, OP, Bernard. *The Little Way.* Translated by Alan Neame. London: Darton, Longman & Todd, 1979.

Chanoine, Vidal F. *Aux Sources de la Joie avec Saint François de Sales.* Paris: Nouvelle Libraire de France, 1974.

Combes, André. *St. Thérèse and Suffering: The Spirituality of St.Thérèse in Essence.* Translated by Msgr. Philip E. Hallett. New York: P.J. Kenedy & Sons, 1951.

_______. *The Spirituality of St. Thérèse.* Translated by Msgr. Philip E. Hallett. New York: P.J. Kenedy & Sons, 1950.

Curran, Thomas M., ed. *The Mind of St. Thérèse of Lisieux.* Dublin: Carmelite Center of Spirituality, 1977.

de Caussade, SJ, Jean-Pierre. *Abandonment to Divine Providence.* New York: Doubleday Books, 1968.

de Guibert, SJ, Joseph. *The Theology of the Spiritual Life.* Translated by Paul Barrett, OFM Cap. New York: Sheed & Ward, 1953.

de Meester, OCD, Conrad. *With Empty Hands: The Message of Thérèse of Lisieux.* Translated by Sr. Anne Marie, OCD. Sydney: St. Paul Publications, 1982.

_______, general editor. *St. Thérèse of Lisieux: Her Life, Times, and Teaching.* Washington, DC: ICS Publications, 1997.

Descouvemont, Pierre. *Sainte Thérèse de L'Enfant Jesus et son Prochain.* Paris: P. Lethielleux, 1959.

_______. *Thérèse and Lisieux.* Translated by Salvatore Sciurba OCD and Louise Pambrun. Toronto: Novalis Press, 1996.

_______. *Thérèse of Lisieux and Marie of the Trinity.* Translated by Alexandra Plettenberg-Serban. New York: Alba House, 1997.

Dubay, SM, Thomas. *Fire Within*. San Francisco: Ignatius Press, 1989.

Dupré, Louis & Wiseman, OSB, Janes A., ed. *Light from Light*. Mahwah: Paulist Press, 1988.

Flannery, OP, Austin, ed. *Vatican Council II: The Conciliar and Post-Conciliar Documents*. New York: Costello Publishing Co., 1984.

Francis de Sales, St. *Introduction to the Devout Life*. Translated by John L. Reville, SJ, PhD. Philadelphia: The Peter Reilly Company, 1942.

_______. *Sermons on Our Lady*. Translated by the Nuns of the Visitation. Rockford: TAN Books & Publishers, Inc., 1985.

_______. *Treatise on the Love of God* (2 Vols.). Translated by John K. Ryan. New York: Doubleday & Co., Inc., 1963.

Garrigou-Lagrange, OP, Reginald. *The Three Ages of the Spiritual Life: Prelude to Eternal Life* (2 Vols.). Translated by Sr. M. Timothea Doyle, OP. St. Louis: B. Herder Books, 1947.

Gaucher, OCD, Guy. *The Passion of Thérèse of Lisieux*. Translated by Sr. Anne Marie Brennan, OCD. New York: Crossroad Publishing Co., 1990.

_______. *The Story of a Life*. Translated by Sr. Anne Marie Brennan, OCD. San Francisco: Harper and Row Publishers, 1987.

Gautier, Jean, ed. *Some Schools of Catholic Spirituality*. Translated by Kathryn Sullivan, RSCJ. New York: Desclee Company, 1959.

Görres, Ida F. *The Hidden Face*. Translated by Richard and Clara Winston. New York: Pantheon Books, Inc., 1959.

Guitton, Jean. *The Spiritual Genius of St. Thérèse*. Translated by a Religious of the Sacred Heart. Westminster: The Newman Press, 1958.

Hoffman, OP, Dominic M. *Living Divine Love*. New York: Alba House, 1982.

Ignatius of Loyola, St. *The Spiritual Exercises*. Translated by Louis J. Puhl, SJ. Chicago: Loyola University Press, 1951.

Jamart, OCD, François. *The Complete Spiritual Doctrine of St. Thérèse of Lisieux*. Translated by Walter Van De Putte. New York: Alba House, 1961.

John of the Cross, St. *Collected Works*. Translated by Kieran Kavanaugh, OCD and Otilio Rodriguez, OCD. Washington, DC: ICS Publications, 1979.

John Paul II. *On Catechesis in Our Time (Catechesi Tradendae)*. Boston: St. Paul Editions, 1979.

_______. *On the Meaning of Human Suffering (Salvifici Doloris)*. Boston: St. Paul Editions, 1984.

Journet, Charles. *What is Dogma?* Translated by Mark Pontifex. New York: Hawthorne Books, 1964.

LaFrance, Jean. *My Vocation is Love.* Translated by Sr. Anne Marie Brennan, OCD. New York: Alba House, 1990.

Leslie, Susan. *The Happiness of God: Holiness in Thérèse of Lisieux.* New York: Alba House, 1988.

Marie-Eugene, OCD. *I Am a Daughter of the Church: A Practical Synthesis of Carmelite Spirituality.* Translated by Sr. M. Verna Clare, CSC. Chicago: Fides Publishers, 1955.

_______. *I Want to See God: A Practical Synthesis of Carmelite Spirituality.* Translated by Sr. M. Verna Clare, CSC. Chicago: Fides Publishers, 1955.

_______. *Under the Torrent of His Love: Thérèse of Lisieux, a Spiritual Genius.* Translated by Sr. Mary Thomas Noble, OP. New York: Alba House, 1995.

_______. *Where the Spirit Breathes: Action and Prayer.* Translated by Sr. Mary Thomas Noble, OP. New York: Alba House, 1998.

Martin, Celine (Sr. Genevieve of the Holy Face). *A Memoir of My Sister, St. Thérèse.* Translated by Carmelite Nuns of New York. New York: P.J. Kenedy & Sons, 1959.

Obbard, OCD, Elizabeth Ruth. *A Retreat With Thérèse of Lisieux: Loving Our Way Into Holiness.* Cincinnati: St. Anthony Messenger Press, 1996.

O'Connor, Patricia. *In Search of Thérèse.* London: Darton, Longman & Todd, 1987.

O'Mahony, OCD, Christopher, ed. *St. Thérèse of Lisieux by Those Who Knew Her: Testimonies from the Process of Beatification.* Dublin: Veritas Publications, 1973.

Petitot, OP, Henry. *Saint Teresa of Lisieux.* Translated by the Benedictines of Stanbrook. New York: Benzinger Brothers, 1927.

Pichon, SJ, Almire. *Seeds of the Kingdom.* Translated by Lyle Terhune, TOCD. Westminster: The Newman Press, 1961.

Poulain, SJ, Augustin. *The Graces of Interior Prayer: A Treatise on Mystical Theology.* Translated by Leonora L. Yorke Smith. London: Kegan Paul, Trench, Trubner & Co., Ltd., 1912.

Redmond, Paulinus. *Louis and Zelie Martin: The Seed and the Root of the Little Flower.* London: Quiller Press, Ltd., 1995.

Regle Primitive et Constitutions des Religieuses de L'ordre de Notre Dame du Mont Carmel. Selon La Reformation de Sainte Thérèse pour les Monasteres de Son Ordre en France. Poitiers:1865.

Renault, OCD, Emmanuel. *L'Epreuve de la Foi: Le Combat de Thérèse de Lisieux.* Paris: Editions du Cerf-Desclée De Brouwer, 1974.

Royo-Marin, OP, Antonio and Aumann, OP, Jordan. *The Theology of Christian Perfection.* Translated by Jordan Aumann, OP. Dubuque: The Priory Press, 1962.

Sacred Congregation of the Clergy. *General Catechetical Directory (Directorium Catechisticum Generale).* Vatican City State: Vatican Polyglot Press, 1971.

Six, Jean-François. *Light in the Night: The Last Fifteen Months in the Life of Thérèse of Lisieux.* Translated by John Bowden. London: SCM Press, Ltd., 1996.

Sullivan, OCD, John, ed. *Carmelite Studies: Experiencing Saint Thérèse Today.* Washington, DC: ICS Publications, 1990.

Teresa of Avila, Saint. *The Collected Works* (3 Vols). Translated by Kieran Kavanaugh, OCD and Otilio Rodriguez, OCD. Washington, DC: ICS Publications, 1976.

Thomas á Kempis. *The Imitation of Christ.* Translated by Clare L. Fitzpatrick. New York: Catholic Book Publishers, 1985.

Thomas Aquinas, Saint. *Summa Theologica.* Translated by Fathers of the English Dominican Province. New York: Benzinger Brothers, 1947.

Wojtyla, Karol. *Faith According to St. John of the Cross.* Translated by Jordan Aumann, OP. San Francisco: Ignatius Press, 1981.